B. R. (Bernhard Ringrose) Wise

Industrial Freedom

A Study in Politics

B. R. (Bernhard Ringrose) Wise

Industrial Freedom
A Study in Politics

ISBN/EAN: 9783337073381

Printed in Europe, USA, Canada, Australia, Japan

Cover: Foto ©Suzi / pixelio.de

More available books at **www.hansebooks.com**

INDUSTRIAL FREEDOM:

A Study in Politics.

BY

B. R. WISE,

Sometime Attorney-General of New South Wales, and Honorary Member of the Cobden Club.

"War and Tariffs—these are the two great enemies of mankind"
— JOHN BRIGHT.

"Because right is right, to follow the right is wisdom, in the scorn of consequence."—TENNYSON.

CASSELL & COMPANY, LIMITED:
LONDON, PARIS & MELBOURNE.

1892.

To

SIR HENRY PARKES, G.C.M.G., ETC. ETC.

AN HONOURED CHIEF AND FRIEND.

PREFACE.

During the years 1880-82, a few Oxford graduates and undergraduates, who had been brought together by the influence of the late Arnold Toynbee, used to meet once a month during term time, alternately in Oxford and London, for the purpose of discussing in detail, and with complete frankness, some specified political or social question.*

One of the subjects frequently referred to at these meetings was the attitude of the working classes towards Free Trade; and it was agreed that some member of the Society should prepare a paper, under Toynbee's supervision, on the best means of fixing popular attention on the relation of political economy to fiscal questions.

The execution of this idea was allotted to the present writer, and an outline of a pamphlet was prepared and submitted to Toynbee for criticism in 1882. Toynbee in that year was engaged upon the London lectures which led to his last illness, and was, consequently, unable to carry out his plan of a conjoint work. He did, however, discuss very fully with the writer, in several conversations, the scheme of the intended work, and suggested many modifications of that which had

---

* The members of this Society, which had no name, were Arnold Toynbee; Alfred Milner, New College, Editor of Toynbee's posthumous work, "The Industrial Revolution"; P. L. Gell, Balliol College; F. C. Montague, Balliol College; E. T. Cook, New College; D. G. Ritchie, Jesus College; J. A. Hamilton, Balliol College; J. D. Rogers, Balliol College; Hon. W. Bruce, Balliol College; and B. R. Wise, Queen's College. Mr. Ritchie's essay on "Darwinism and Politics," in Swan Sonnenschein & Co.'s "Social Science Series," and Mr. Montague's book on "The Limits of Individual Liberty" (Kegan Paul & Co., 1884), both originated in these meetings.

been originally proposed. The result was that, in 1883, the manuscript of a pamphlet of about fifty pages, of which the spirit was Toynbee's, although the words were not, was submitted to the Cobden Club for publication. By a series of mischances, this manuscript, of which no copy had been kept, was lost, and the loss was not made known to the writer until after the lapse of twelve months, when it was too late to recall even the form of the argument which Toynbee had suggested. The original idea was not, however, left unexecuted. In 1885, the writer embodied something of Toynbee's opinions in a pamphlet published in Sydney under the title of "Free Trade and Wages," which is now out of print.

The present work was first intended as a new edition of this pamphlet; but as it proceeded, and the stress of controversy with Protectionists compelled attention to other aspects of the fiscal question, it gradually assumed a new and distinct form, until there is now left in it nothing of Toynbee, save some traces of his influence, and the pious feeling which acknowledges that, as the inception of the work was due to him, so its execution should be taken as a tribute to his memory. The writer's best hope is that those who knew Toynbee, and those who trace no small portion of their better selves to the influence of his luminous enthusiasm, may not think the tribute altogether unworthy.

One word more upon the scope and method of the work. Written, as it has been, at intervals during the rare and busy leisure of an active professional and public life, it cannot lay claim to either literary or scientific completeness. Its merit, if any, lies in the directly practical character of its arguments and illustrations. For seven years the writer has been engaged by the side of Sir Henry Parkes in the forefront of an active political controversy with the Protectionists of his native country, until he has gained an exceptional familiarity with the modes of thought and expression that win favour for Protection among voters. The aim of the work is to make use of this special knowledge of Protectionist arguments to put together a complete and scientific statement of the Free Trade case, from the point of view of one who is addressing himself to the voters of a Democratic country. There is thus no intention to rival or supplant other well-known text-books of Free Trade, but rather to write a work which shall be complementary both to Professor Fawcett's carefully tabulated index of arguments, and to the elaborate rhetorical presentment of the case by Mr. Henry George. If the writer has in places gone beyond this aim, or departed from his proper method, his excuse is offered in the language of a fellow-student who, defending himself by anticipation from the same charge, urges as follows:—"I cannot," he says, "think that any man with open and attentive eyes, and with confidence in his own impartiality, as based upon a rational view of life, does wrong in uttering the best reflections he can make on the way in which things are going, or the way in which he thinks they should go." *

* "Essays and Addresses," by Bernard Bosanquet, M.A. (London: Swan Sonnenschein & Co., 1889), p. vi.

SYDNEY, *February 10th*, 1891.

CONTENTS.

	PAGE
PREFACE	V

Part I.
THE REVIVAL OF PROTECTION.

CHAPTER	I. Its Nature	1
,,	II. Its Causes	7
,,	III. Its Significance	19
,,	IV. Illustrations	23

    (*a*) Great Britain . . . 23
    (*b*) The Continent of Europe . . 42
    (*c*) The United States . . 48
    (*d*) The British Colonies . . 56

Part II.
PREPARING THE ARENA.

CHAPTER	I. Definition of Free Trade . . .	73
,,	II. Division of the Arguments . . .	77
,,	III. Economics and Politics . . .	87
,,	IV. Economics and the Tariff . . .	97
,,	V. Nationalist Economics	105
,,	VI. Nationalist Economics and the Tariff	129
,,	VII. Free Trade and Laissez-faire . .	138
,,	VIII. Protection and Socialism . . .	159

Part III.
THE ECONOMIC ARGUMENT.

CHAPTER	I. Free Trade and Production . . .	165
,,	II. Protection and Production . . .	167
,,	III. Free Trade and Prices	173
,,	IV. Protection and Prices	181

		PAGE
CHAPTER V.	FREE TRADE AND WAGES	187
,, VI.	PROTECTION AND WAGES	204
,, VII.	DO HIGH PRICES MAKE HIGH WAGES?	207
,, VIII.	DOES MORE WORK MEAN MORE MONEY?	221

Part IV.

THE POLITICAL ARGUMENT.

CHAPTER I.	THE ARGUMENTS CLASSIFIED	237
,, II.	THE INFANT INDUSTRY ARGUMENT	241
,, III.	THE "DIVERSIFICATION OF INDUSTRY" ARGUMENT	259
	(a) THE ARGUMENT STATED . . 259	
	(b) THE ARGUMENT TESTED BY FACTS . 265	
	(c) THE ARGUMENT TESTED BY THEORY. 273	
	(d) THE OTHER SIDE OF THE SHIELD . 278	
,, IV.	THE HOME MARKET ARGUMENT.	286
,, V.	THE PAUPER LABOUR ARGUMENT	302
,, VI.	THE COST OF PROTECTION	323

Appendices.

APPENDIX I.	TABLES OF WAGES IN THE ENGLISH COTTON, WOOLLEN, WORSTED, AND IRON TRADES	337
,, II.	AN EXAMINATION OF J. S. MILL'S SUPPOSED APPROVAL OF PROTECTIVE TARIFFS IN A YOUNG COUNTRY	343
,, III.	COMPARISON OF THE PROGRESS OF NEW SOUTH WALES UNDER FREE TRADE WITH THAT OF VICTORIA UNDER PROTECTION.	347

INDUSTRIAL FREEDOM:
A STUDY IN POLITICS.

SUMMARY.

Part I.
THE PROTECTIONIST REVIVAL.

CHAPTER I.
ITS NATURE.
THE CHARACTERISTICS OF THE MODERN PROTECTIVE SPIRIT . . . . . . *Page* 1

MODERN Protection differs from the old form of that policy—

    (*a*) In the composition of the party who support it.
    (*b*) In its objects.

In consequence of this difference, English Free Trade arguments are not necessarily applicable to the present dispute.

CHAPTER II.
ITS CAUSES.
CAUSES WHICH HAVE AIDED THE REVIVAL OF PROTECTION. . . . . . *Page* 7

THE revival of Protection has been assisted by a misconception of the nature of Free Trade, arising from several circumstances, viz. :—

    (*a*) The mistake of Free Traders in directing their arguments principally to the effect of Free Trade upon the production of wealth, instead of to the question of its effect on wages.

(*b*) The supposition that Free Trade is hostile to the working classes.
(*c*) The supposition that Free Trade requires a general adoption of the principle of *laissez faire*.
(*d*) The supposition that Free Traders are indifferent to the evils of the competitive system.
(*e*) The growing discontent with existing social conditions.

Summary.

CHAPTER III.

ITS SIGNIFICANCE . . . . *Page* 19

1. The Protectionist revival is often exaggerated, both

    (*a*) In its extent.
    (*b*) In its significance.

2. The mere fact of Protection creates no inference against the wisdom of Free Trade. The truth is that Protection has been adopted for varying reasons of a special, local, and temporary character. There has been no general revolt against Free Trade, and no deliberate rejection of the policy.

THE REVIVAL OF RESTRICTION.
CHAPTER IV.

ILLUSTRATIONS.

SECTION I.—GREAT BRITAIN. . . *Page* 23

1. Protectionists treat the example of Great Britain in two ways: either, they admit that Free Trade is proved to be a success for her; or, they say it is a "one-sided Free Trade," and not the Free Trade that was desired.

2. The success of Free Trade in Great Britain is an incontestable historical fact.

3. Summary of investigation of the subject: Mr. Giffen's researches on the magnitude of the general advance in prosperity since Free Trade.

4. The Protectionist assertion that this increase has been caused entirely by railways and other mechanical improvements is improbable, because—

    (*a*) A sudden or (except on the hypothesis that it is due to Free Trade) an inexplicable advance in trade has taken place after every dose of Free Trade legislation.

    (*b*) The mechanical factor, when working without Free Trade, has produced a less result.

5. Examination of the statement, that England adopted Free Trade under the mistaken belief that other nations would follow her example.

6. The statement is not historically true. Conclusion: The significance of the Anti-Corn Law agitation, and the arguments by which it was supported, are in no way weakened, either by the experience of forty-five years, or by inquiries into the motives and anticipations of the Free Trade leaders.

Notes on the condition of England under Protection:—

    NOTE A.—Extract from Martineau's History of the Peace.
    NOTE B.—Extract from Paper by George W. Medley.

SECTION II.—THE CONTINENT OF EUROPE . . . *Page* 42

1. When England adopted Free Trade, the general belief in the peaceful tendencies of the age caused an over-sanguine anticipation of the universal triumph of Free Trade.

2. This anticipation was to some extent shared by Cobden.

3. Owing chiefly to the spirit of Nationalism, the period of peace came to an end.

4. Lord Sandon's Return of Tariff changes, since 1850,

shows, that until the effects of the Franco-German War were fully felt, there was a steady movement throughout Europe in the direction of Free Trade.

5. The modern revival of Protection in Europe is intimately connected with the growth of militarism, which is the chief reason why European nations have ceased to follow in the Free Trade footsteps of Great Britain.

CHAPTER IV.

ILLUSTRATIONS.

SECTION III.—THE UNITED STATES . . . . . *Page* 48

1. Difficulty of studying tariff movements in the United States.
2. The revolt of the American Colonies was largely a revolt against Protection.
3. The tariffs from 1789 to 1861.
4. Connection between tariffs and prosperity.
5. Conclusion: High tariffs have generally been the result of some morbid industrial condition. The recent growth of Protection is directly traceable to the Civil War.

CHAPTER IV.

ILLUSTRATIONS.

SECTION IV.—THE BRITISH COLONIES . . *Page* 56

1. The most deliberate repudiation of Free Trade has occurred in the British Colonies.
2. This is largely owing to the influence of Victoria,
3. Which is now decreasing, owing to a decline in the comparative importance of the colony. Protection in the other

colonies is mainly traceable to a desire to retaliate upon Victoria.

4. Protection in Canada originated partly in retaliation on the United States, and partly

5. As a revenue measure, owing to the difficulty, with such a scattered population, of devising any acceptable system of direct taxation.

6. The Revenue Question in Australia. The tendency is for the rich men to become Protectionists in order to escape direct taxation. The struggle is becoming one between the classes and the masses.

7. This was not the case in the Victorian struggle of 1866 and onward, which began as a Democratic struggle against the large land-owners. Characteristics of the struggle.

8. Summary.

NOTE.—Extract from "The Tariff on Trial," by Sir Richard Cartwright, *N. Am. Rev.*, May, 1890.

Part II.
PREPARING THE ARENA.

CHAPTER I.

DEFINITION OF FREE TRADE . . *Page* 73

1. The revival of Protection not being the result of a new economic doctrine, but of indifference to the old, it is necessary to re-state the Free Trade case.

2. Free Trade may be used in several senses; but in this controversy it bears the limited meaning of "the absence of duties of a protective character."

3. Illustrations of this from Mr. Cobden's speeches.

4. Necessity for so limiting the meaning of the term.

CHAPTER II.

DIVISION OF THE ARGUMENT . . *Page* 77

1. The issue between Protectionists and Free Traders is often obscured by neglect to observe the distinction between the political and the economic arguments, which may be adduced on either side.

2. Nature of the distinction between political and economic.

3. The political argument considered and illustrated.

4. Application to the tariff controversy. Economic arguments deal solely with the effect of a policy on the production of wealth; while the political arguments suggest other tests of its merits.

5. The economic argument ought to be considered before the political, both because most of the political arguments in favour of Protection tacitly assume an economic basis, and because the economic result of a policy is always an important, and often the only, test of its political soundness.

CHAPTER III.

ECONOMICS AND POLITICS; OR, THE VALUE OF THE ECONOMIC ARGUMENT. . . . . *Page* 87

1. The validity of any economic argument in a political discussion is sometimes denied. It is therefore necessary to consider the relation between politics and economics.

2. The nature of economic assumptions.

3. The assumption of the universality and dominance of self-interest is said to be unreal.

4. Consideration of this criticism. It is partly true; but it does not affect the validity of economic arguments when these are applied to discussions upon the best means of increasing natural productiveness.

5. Secondly, it is said "the term wealth is incapable of definition."

6. This criticism ignores the distinction between the provinces of politics and economics. Moreover, it is not quite correct. Political economy does take some account of the differences in the kinds of wealth.

7. Conclusion. Economic conclusions must be applied cautiously, and have only a limited range; but inasmuch as they concern the production of material wealth, no politician can discard them. Importance of wealth to a modern industrial community.

CHAPTER IV.

ECONOMICS AND THE TARIFF . . *Page* 97

1. Since a tariff is intended to directly affect national productiveness, the economic conclusions as to the best methods of production cannot be ignored, if the circumstances are such as to allow of economic conclusions being applied at all. Do the assumptions of political economy square with the facts of a tariff controversy?

2. The first postulate of economics as to the predominance of self-interest is not unreal in tariff discussions. A tariff is concerned directly with the production of wealth, and appeals entirely to the motive of self-interest.

3. The second postulate of economics, as to the equality of the competing units, is also sufficiently true to facts, when the matter of consideration is the production of wealth.

4. Nor does it lie in the mouths of Protectionists to evade economic conclusions by asserting that the acquisition of wealth is of little importance as compared with its right use. This may be true, but when the material advancement of a country is the thing aimed at, the degree of national productiveness is of primary importance. Besides, the political

A

arguments in favour of Protection really postulate an economic basis.

5. Summary. Full weight may be given to the objections against political economy without weakening the economic argument in favour of Free Trade.

CHAPTER V.

NATIONALIST ECONOMICS . . . *Page* 105

1. The consensus of scientific opinion against Protection has led to an attempt to frame a new system of economics.

2. It must, however, be remembered that the term "economic," as used by nationalists, no longer connotes exclusively material wealth, but includes everything which has any relation to national well-being. This leads to the result that

3. Economic investigation becomes historical and not deductive, and the tests of economic conformity alter.

4. A science of this nature cannot answer the individualist conclusions. It may justify the passing of them by, but it does not meet them on the same plane, because it does not propose to consider the effect of a tariff upon wealth production.

5. The fundamental difference between the new and the old system is that the former adopts the nation as the industrial unit instead of the individual.

6. The "science" tested by reference to its scope and method. No *scientific* results are possible from a "science" whose subject is "the comfort and happiness of a nation."

7. The "science" further tested by its practical maxims.

 (*a*) National self-dependence:—Impossible in point of fact and not theoretically desirable.

(*b*) The duty of developing the productive powers of a nation, rather than increasing its wealth.

8. Conclusion. The study has no claim to be considered a science, but is useful in its historical investigations and political suggestions.

NOTE.—On the Characteristics of Nationalist Writers.

CHAPTER VI.

NATIONALIST ECONOMICS AND THE TARIFF . . . *Page* 129

1. Further test of the so-called "science," by applying it to the tariff dispute.   Materials.
2. The argument stated.
3. It rests on two assumptions—

(*a*) That manufacturing excellence is more productive than rural skill of national intelligence and character.

(*b*) That manufacturing excellence cannot be attained without Protection.

But (*a*) is beside the mark at present, because—(i.) No country to-day is without a high degree of manufacturing skill, and (ii.) Under present conditions, country pursuits are more favourable than manufacturing to the cultivation of character and intelligence.

4. (*b*) rests on the assumption that self-interest cannot be relied upon to establish profitable manufactures. The alleged reasons for this stated and considered.

5. Conclusion: The so-called "economic" case for Protection is really a series of doubtful political propositions.

NOTE.—On Nationalists and Protection.

CHAPTER VII

FREE TRADE AND LAISSEZ FAIRE . . . . *Page* 138

1. Protection and Free Trade are almost always discussed with reference to their cognate political theories of socialism and Laissez faire.

2. Historical reasons of this: The negative character of Adam Smith's work was not at first perceived, and his doctrine of "natural liberty" was perverted to their own purposes by the opponents of all remedial legislation.

3. Laissez faire, however, is not a part of economic teaching.

4. Free Traders, who believe in Laissez faire, have a logical advantage in arguing about Protection; but no arguments which are based upon this maxim will ever convince.

5. The extension of a rule of practice justified by Free Trade within its own province to another department of human activity is neither sound in theory nor possible in practice. The maxim of Laissez faire can never be applied within the field of the distribution of wealth, both because

> (*a*) The postulate of equality of the competing units is unreal.
>
> (*b*) The political considerations would overwhelm any economic conclusions.

6. The recognition of these truths was very slow. But practical necessities gradually broke down the opposition which was founded upon "Laissez faire."

7. Conclusion: The Free Trade argument is independent of any political theory.

CHAPTER VIII.

PROTECTION AND SOCIALISM . . *Page* 159

1. The political arguments in favour of Protection are at bottom socialistic.

2. Some Free Traders (*e.g.*, Professor Sumner) consider this to be condemnatory of Protection. Many Protectionists are inconsistent enough to denounce socialism.

3. On the other hand, many Free Traders are ready to support socialistic measures under certain circumstances, viz., provided that—(i.) The end desired is on a balance of advantages and disadvantages found to be good. (ii.) That State action can achieve it. (iii.) That private enterprise cannot.

Protection fails to satisfy these three conditions of legitimate State action.

NOTE.—The limits of State interference.

Part III.

THE ECONOMIC ARGUMENT.

CHAPTER I.

FREE TRADE AND PRODUCTION . . *Page* 165

1. The material prosperity of a country must in the long run depend upon its capacity to produce wealth.

2. Free Trade increases national productiveness by applying the principle of division of employment on a large scale.

Under Free Trade, men choose their own occupations. If, then, some industries are not followed, this is a sign that they are believed to be less profitable than others.

CHAPTER II.

PROTECTION AND PRODUCTION . . *Page* 167

Protection lessens the power to produce in three ways :—

> (i.) Under Protection men are attracted by the promise of State aid from the industries they would naturally follow if left to themselves, into others from which, if left to themselves, they would hold aloof.

Protection, therefore, diminishes natural productiveness by attracting capital and labour from the more to the less profitable occupations.

This source of loss, however, will be avoided if the new industries are started with imported labour and capital.

> (ii.) A second cause of diminution in the national productiveness arising from Protection is the loss of wealth which is occasioned by the necessity of providing a fund, out of which the profits in the protected industries may be made equal to those of the national industries.
>
> (iii.) A third loss arises from the decrease in the purchasing power of the customer, arising from the increase of prices occasioned by protective duties.

CHAPTER III.

FREE TRADE AND PRICES . . *Page* 173

1. The complaint against Free Trade of causing an excessive cheapness is due to a misconception of the effect of low prices on production.

2. A low level of prices may be due to one or more of three causes, viz. : –

> (i.) To a lessened cost of production.

(ii.) To a decreased power of consumption.
(iii.) To a scarcity of gold.

The cheapness which was the chief characteristic of the recent industrial depression arose from all three causes.

3. Free Trade lowers prices by cheapening the processes of production; of this sort of cheapness there can never be too much, because every fall in prices arising from this cause only, must stimulate demand.

4. Free Trade, besides lowering prices, also steadies them :
    (*a*) By widening the area of production.
    (*b*) By widening the area of consumption.
    (*c*) By giving a more accurate knowledge of the state of markets.

5. Free Trade cannot, however, prevent commercial crises, or the disastrous falls in prices which accompany commercial crises.

CHAPTER IV.

PROTECTION AND PRICES . . *Page* 181

1. The argument of the preceding chapters rested on the unexpressed assumption that Protection raised prices.

2. Although this is sometimes denied, Protection must raise prices or else it fails to protect.

3. Protection may have been supposed not to raise prices owing to—
    (i.) The fact that prices generally have fallen all over the world.
    (ii.) That a later effect of Protection is often to reduce particular prices by encouraging an excessive internal competition.

4. The tendency of Protection to lower prices when the supply has exceeded the demand of the home market is generally checked by trusts, pools, and other forms of combination.

CHAPTER V.

FREE TRADE AND WAGES . . *Page* 187

1. Wages are the labourer's share of the product.
2. Free Trade acts on wages by improving the efficiency of labour.
3. First objection to this view—*That competition between a country of high wages and one of low wages, tends to depress the rate of the former to that of the latter.*
4. The fallacy of this lies in comparing the rate of wages with the labour-cost of production.
5. Second objection—*That Free Trade depresses wages to the profit of rent.* This can only be the case when Free Trade acts as a discouragement of industrial variety. The case of Ireland considered.
6. The objection is theoretically sound under some circumstances, but these circumstances are in practice non-existent. Free Trade does not, in fact, discourage industrial variety; nor, if it did, is Protection the best remedy.
7. Free Trade also steadies wages. Importance of this.

CHAPTER VI.

PROTECTION AND WAGES . . . *Page* 204

1. Protection affects wages by diminishing the efficiency of labour.
2. The allegations to the contrary refer to the influence of Protection in encouraging new industries. Consideration of this deferred.

CHAPTER VII.

DO HIGH PRICES MAKE HIGH WAGES? . . . . *Page* 207

1. Consideration of the Protectionist argument that employment is better than cheapness.
2. This really rests on the assumption that "high prices make high wages."

3. This assumption is unlikely to be true on *à priori* grounds.

4. It is also unsupported by evidence, and is contradicted by the records of six centuries of English industrial history, and by a comparison between wages in New South Wales and Victoria.

5. If Protection were limited to one trade, it might cause a temporary rise of wages in that trade.

6. Even if a rise occur in nominal wages, real wages may remain unaltered.

7. Protectionists, however, advocate "all-round" Protection.

8. This is impossible.

9. The argument that "high prices make high wages" is inconsistent with the argument that Protection lowers prices.

CHAPTER VIII.

DOES MORE WORK MEAN MORE MONEY? . . . *Page* 221

1. Statement of the Protectionist argument, which is really rather an allegation of fact.

Whether employment is better than cheapness is a question of evidence. Protectionists make the statement, but fail to support it by facts.

2. Discussion of the Protectionist theory of the importance "of employment." The question is not "Whether Protection causes an increase of employment in this or that trade?" but "Whether it causes an increase all round?"

Now, since the admitted object and effect of Protection is to cause something to be made in one country which, in a state of freedom, would be made in another. Protection must cause a waste of labour.

3. But labour which is wasted cannot be a source of wealth.

The question to be considered is not whether Protection gives employment, but whether the employment which it gives is more productive than that which it destroys.

Illustration from the kerosene industry of New South Wales, showing that Protection is a most costly form of outdoor relief.

4. The fallacy of the Protectionist argument lies in the assumption that the persons who are employed in protected trades would be unemployed, if there were no Protection.

This assumption, however, cannot be true, generally; since in so far as Protection causes unnecessary labour, must it diminish the labour available for productive employment.

Protection changes the nature of employment, but does not increase the total.

Illustration from Canadian trade.

5. The foregoing conclusions are conceivably open to qualifications in practice; it is, however, most questionable whether under any circumstances Protection is a good means for giving State assistance to the labour market.

Whatever employment is given by Protection must be given at the expense of others.

Protection is thus only a form of legalised plunder, and those who benefit by it are, in reality, the recipients of public charity.

Part IV.

THE POLITICAL ARGUMENT IN FAVOUR OF PROTECTION.

CHAPTER I.

THE ARGUMENTS CLASSIFIED . . *Page* 237

1. All the political arguments are reducible on analysis to one of four, viz.: —

    (*a*) The Infant Industry Argument.
    (*b*) The Variety of Industry Argument.

(c) The Home Market Argument.
(d) The Pauper Labour Argument.

2. These have had a distinct historic sequence and connection, both in America and Australia.

CHAPTER II.

THE INFANT INDUSTRY ARGUMENT . . . . . *Page* 241

1. The argument stated.
2. Its assumption is, that a time will come, when the young industry can stand alone.
3. Test of this assumption by the tariff changes of the United States, with special reference to the cotton and iron industries.
4. And by the tariff changes of Victoria.
5. These tests lead to the conclusion of fact, that the infants never grow up.
6. The assumption tested by theory: It ignores the weakness of human nature, and overlooks both the natural and the artificial inter-dependence of trades.
7. Conclusion: Protection can be established only for a time; nor can it be limited to specific industries.

CHAPTER III.

THE DIVERSIFICATION OF INDUSTRY ARGUMENT . . *Page* 259

1.— THE ARGUMENT STATED.

1. The origin of the argument is partly the sentiment of national sufficiency, and partly the economic conditions of a young country.

2. The assumptions of the argument are—(i.) That there is in fact no sufficient diversity; (ii.) That sufficient diversity cannot be obtained without Protection; (iii.) That Protection is a less evil than want of diversity.

3. Admission that diversity of industry is desirable.

4. Method of argument. What has to be proved.

II.—THE ARGUMENT TESTED BY FACTS.

5. Has any country in fact suffered from want of diversity?
6. Instance of America under the Colonial system.
7. Instance of the industrial growth of the Western States.
8. Instance of the industrial growth of Victoria.

III.—THE ARGUMENT TESTED BY THEORY.

9. It is theoretically most improbable that any country should suffer from industrial uniformity, if capital accumulates and population increases.

10. The conditions of manufacturing success are—

> (*a*) A large and concentrated population, which Free Trade is at least as likely to give as Protection.
>
> (*b*) Abundance of capital, which Free Trade is more likely to give.

IV. THE OTHER SIDE OF THE QUESTION.

11. There are certain natural limits to diversification, which cannot be passed without great risk.

12. The cost of diversification may be excessive.

13. The argument can never be used as a general defence of protective policy.

CHAPTER IV.

THE HOME MARKET ARGUMENT . . *Page* 286

1. The economic basis of the argument is the fallacy that home trade is more profitable than foreign.

2. Political supports to the argument are—

   (*a*) The dread of war, which is the only logical basis of Protection.

   (*b*) The idea that foreign trade is more precarious than home. List's views stated and examined.

   (*c*) The idea that the home market causes land to be profitably put to new uses.

   (*d*) The idea that a home market increases the number of customers. This is really an appeal to the farmer to subsidise persons to buy his products.

   (*e*) The idea first propounded by Mr. Hoyt, that the home market enables the requirements of a community for manufactured goods to be fully supplied. This ignores the danger of an over-supply.

3. The theory of the argument is opposed at every point by facts.

CHAPTER V.

THE PAUPER LABOUR ARGUMENT . . *Page* 302

1. Increasing importance of this argument.

2. What is "pauper" labour? Difficulty of getting accurate information about wages: necessity of limiting comparison to specific trades in specific places.

3. Nevertheless, for the sake of argument, it may be admitted that wages are higher in a young than an old community.

4. The argument can only apply to those industries which are exposed to foreign competition. These are chiefly handicrafts.

5. The price of goods does not depend upon the rate of wages, but upon the cost of labour.

6. Since the "cost of labour" depends upon the natural and the acquired efficiency of the labourer, and since a labourer is both more intelligent and more assisted by nature and machinery in a young than in an old country, the cost of labour is likely to be less in the former than the latter, except in the lowest and most degrading forms of handicraft, which it is undesirable to introduce into a young country.

7. The argument is also inconsistent with the theory that Protection lowers prices.

8. It is incapable of any just application, because a scale of duties would be required varying according to the rate of wages paid in every competing community.

9. Protection is generally demanded against high-waged countries.

10. But a low labour cost makes a high rate of wages.

11. Free Trade is more favourable than Protection to a low labour cost.

12. Protection hastens a fall in wages.

CHAPTER VI.

THE COST OF PROTECTION . . *Page* 323

1. The only way to completely meet Protectionist arguments is to treat the question as one of expediency; granted that Protection will do all that is claimed for it, is not the price too high?

2. Protection is an economic evil, because it is always a waste of productive power.

3. It is a political evil, because it causes inequality and corruption, and destroys the value of self-reliance.

4. It is a social evil, because it is antagonistic to progress.

5. It is a moral evil in its operation both abroad and at home.

6. Conclusion.

APPENDICES

I. Rates of wages in the cotton, woollen, worsted, and iron industries of Great Britain since 1830 . . *Page* 337

II. Examination of Mill's Defence of Protection in young countries. . . . . *Page* 343

III. Comparison between the progress of New South Wales and of Victoria , ... *Page* 347

INDUSTRIAL FREEDOM.

Part I.
THE REVIVAL OF PROTECTION.

CHAPTER I.
CHARACTERISTICS OF MODERN PROTECTION.

§ 1. ANYONE who writes a new book upon Free Trade ought, if he is not wholly graceless, to begin his work with an apology. The subject has been worn so threadbare, both by economists and politicians, that any novelty of treatment or illustration is almost impossible; while the arguments on either side of the fiscal controversy seem to possess the theological characteristic of only carrying conviction to the minds of those who are previously disposed to believe.

Nevertheless, while men continue to be exercised over tariff disputes, and while so many interests are affected by the taxation measures of Protectionists, there must always be room for a well-considered monograph upon the leading features of the controversy, especially if care be taken in compiling it to avoid the extremes of arid abstraction and partisan rhetoric.

Therefore, in this attempt to revive an old argument an effort will be made to present both sides impartially; and to present them in such a way and with so sparing a use of illustration from passing phenomena or special trades, that the application of the arguments may not be confined to particular countries or industries, but may extend over as large an area and for as long a time as the nature of the subject will permit.

First, then, let us enquire into the reasons which make a restatement of the points in controversy necessary.

By a turn of the political wheel Free Trade has gone under for a time, although its triumphant reappearance is already heralded by many signs. Still it cannot be denied that the doctrine which was thought to be dead forty years ago, and was even then spoken of as "dead and disgusting," is now full of life and vigour. That such a phenomenon, startling and disappointing as it must be to those who, only a generation past, successfully maintained the battle of industrial freedom, cannot be entirely owing to the incapacity of mankind to understand economic abstractions, nor to what Professor Sidgwick has termed "the selfish activity of the protected classes," will be readily admitted by all who recognise that every widespread popular delusion must, if it is honestly believed, contain at least a modicum of truth.

What, then, is the explanation of the survival of Protection, and how comes it that a doctrine so discredited by reason and experience is able at the present time to command the support of intelligent and honest men? To answer these questions as they should be answered, it will be necessary to pass in review and compare with each other the characteristics of Protection in its earlier and its later stage.

§ 2. A glance beneath the surface of events will soon reveal the fact, that the contest which is raging now about protective tariffs resembles that about the Corn Laws in little more than name. The old battle-cries, indeed, are still in use; but the composition of the contending forces has been changed, and the battle is being fought upon a different ground.

Broadly speaking, the old Free Trade movement was an assertion on the part of the middle classes of their rights as consumers; while the Protectionist movement of to-day is an effort on the part of the manufacturing classes to obtain privileges as producers.

This difference is illustrated by a comparison of the composition of the Anti-Corn Law League in England, and that of the Protectionist party in Australia and America. The League was in its origin a movement of the manufacturers and middle classes, which gradually attracted to itself the more intelligent among the artisans. In Australia and America, however, the purses of the manufacturers support Protection, and the working classes, who were at first inclined to follow their employers, are gradually returning to Free Trade. Nor is this the only point of contrast between the new and the old Protectionism.

In England, it was only the aristocracy of labour which became Free Traders; while the "residuum," under the leadership of Feargus O'Connor, furiously denounced the Anti-Corn Law League. In Australasia and America, on the contrary, the aristocracy of labour, as represented by the Trade Unions, is inclined to be Protectionist, while disorganised labour leans more towards Free Trade. Lastly—strangest contrast of all—the farmers and landlords, who in England were the backbone of Protection, are in Australasia and America its weakest adherents.[1]

§ 3. The reason for this change in the composition of the two parties is easily found.

[1] During the last three years there has been a tendency in New South Wales and Tasmania, on the part of land-owners of all classes, to support Protectionist candidates. But this attitude is not owing to any dislike of Free Trade, but to a belief on the part of the great land-owners that Free Trade involves direct taxation with a view to agricultural settlement; and, on the part of the small farmers, that Protection will enable them to retaliate on the neighbouring colony of Victoria. The Free Trade movement in Victoria is almost exclusively confined to farmers. Out of thirty-five agricultural associations, thirty have, up to the present date (June, 1890), declared in favour of a return to Free Trade. A Free Trade Democratic Association has now been started in Melbourne, and will soon make its influence felt in the politics of the colony.

The manufacturers and artisans of Australasia and America look upon a different side of the question of Free Trade from that which was perceived in England. It is not with them a question of obtaining cheap raw materials—these they have always to their hands—but a question of establishing new industries. They desire to create, while the Englishman desired to develop what was already created. Consequently, the classes which in England encouraged the competition of foreigners, because only foreigners could offer them the necessary raw material, wish now, in Australasia and America, to exclude the same competition, for fear it may destroy their infant industries.

§ 4. The change in the composition of the two parties has materially affected the arguments by which either policy is supported, and rendered necessary an alteration in the manner of their presentment. At the present time the feelings of unreasoning men are enlisted on the side of Protection. At the time of the Corn Laws in England it was just the reverse. Then the cry for cheap food aroused such general sympathy, that feelings made clear what the intellect might fail to grasp. But in Australasia and America similar feelings lead further on the path of error. Labour is scarce, land is cheap, capital abundant. The spectacle is consequently presented of the simultaneous existence of high wages and large profits, so that the foundation is laid for the misleading argument, that such a country cannot successfully compete against another country of low wages and small profits. This at once gives rise to the cry, that Protection is required to prevent wages and profits from sinking to the European level. Such a cry attracts the working classes, and gains the ear of the philanthropist. The Protectionist appears to be the patriot who is desirous of developing the resources of his native land, and trying to prevent a national stagnation. He is the man who would guard the well paid "native" against the competition of the ill-paid European, and who, by legislative interference, would maintain that union of high wages and large profits, which is the striking economic feature of a young country. The activity of the state in a young country is extended, so that the idea that legislation can accomplish even this result, arouses no misgiving in the minds of men who ardently desire it. Nor is it of any avail in a young country, where wages are high, to urge that Protection must increase the price of articles in daily use. An intelligent Protectionist would reply at once that he admits this fact, but that he is prepared to undergo a private inconvenience for the public benefit. He would say, as the Ballarat digger said to Sir Charles Dilke, that "he preferred to pay dearer for his jacket and moleskins, because by so doing he aided in building up in the colony such trades as the making of clothes, in which his brother and other men, physically too weak to be diggers, could gain an honest living."

It is plain that men who act under feelings like these must be approached with very different arguments from those which would appeal to working men in Europe.

§ 5. Nor are the English arguments always applicable to the circumstances of a young country, where (as has been already pointed out) labour is scarce, land is cheap, and capital abundant. The requisites of production stand to each other, in Australasia and America, in such an abnormal relation, that the abstractions of the English economists have often to be qualified before they can be taken as an explanation of facts. This is of itself a fruitful source of economic error, and offers some excuse for the popular impatience of scientific arguments. At times, indeed, the language of Free Trade arguments even gives a confirmation to the popular delusion. For example, as Professor Sidgwick has pointed out,[1] much that was urged upon the English people as an argument in favour of Free

---

[1] Address delivered before the British Association in 1886, since published under the title of "The Scope and Method of Economics."

Trade, is capable of being turned against Free Trade by those who regard the question from another standpoint. Such an argument, for instance, as that which appeared in the July number of the *Edinburgh Review* for 1841, and which has been repeated by many writers in various forms, would appeal in very different ways to a patriotic Australian and to a patriotic Englishman. "The early progress of any nation," says the Free Trade writer, "that attempts to rival England in manufactures must be slow, for it has to contend with our great capital, our traditionary skill, our almost infinite division of labour, our long-established perseverance, energy, and enterprise, our knowledge of markets, and with the habits of those who have been brought up to be our customers. . . . If these difficulties were once surmounted, this superiority—so far at least as respects the commodity in which we find ourselves undersold—would be gone for ever, in consequence of the well-known law of manufacturing industry, that—*aeteris paribus*—with every increase of the quantity produced, the relative cost of production is diminished." This argument might have come straight out of a Melbourne Protectionist newspaper instead of from the *Edinburgh Review*. For it cannot be denied (to quote the words of Professor Sidgwick again) that "a consideration of the above law, and of the *vis inertiæ* here attributed to an established superiority in manufactures and commerce, supplies an important qualification of the general argument for Free Trade. For along with the tendency of industry to go where it could be most economically carried on, we have also to recognise the tendency for it to stay and develop where it has once been planted; and the advantage of leaving this latter tendency undisturbed would naturally be less clear to the patriotic foreigner than to the patriotic Englishman. The proclamation of a free race for all, just when England had a start which she might keep up for centuries, would not seem to him a manifest realisation of eternal justice; to delay the race for a generation or two, and meanwhile apply judiciously disturbing causes, in the form of protective duties, would seem likely to secure a fairer start for other nations, and ultimately, therefore, a better organisation of the world's industry even from a cosmopolitan point of view."

§ 6. It is apparent from the considerations expressed in the preceding pages, that modern Protection requires to be met by a line of argument different from that which was in use at an earlier period. This is a truth which Free Trade writers have been slow to recognise. They have not always seen that the two most striking features of the new form of Protection, namely, the expressed intention of creating new industries, and the readiness to submit to temporary sacrifices for the purpose of securing this result, can both lay claim to be justified by the reasoning of English economists; and they have consequently fallen into the error of repeating old truths to opponents who do not deny them. The extent of this error and its results will form the subject of the following chapter.

CHAPTER II.

CAUSES WHICH HAVE AIDED THE REVIVAL OF PROTECTION.

§ 1. THE difficulty of applying the economic arguments in their old form to the circumstances of a young country has been already incidentally referred to in discussing the characteristics of the Protectionist revival. It remains to consider how other causes have assisted the progress of Protection. Among these the mistakes and omissions of the Free Trade party must take a prominent place.

§ 2. It is certain that an error has been made by many Free Trade writers in approaching the question of Protection from the wrong side, and contemplating it in a different aspect from that which is regarded by Protectionists themselves. Most of these writers deal almost exclusively with the influence of Free Trade upon the production of wealth, while the Protectionists chiefly direct their attention to the influence of a fiscal policy upon the distribution of wealth. The consequence has been that the arguments and the illustrations of Free Traders have failed to appeal, as effectively as they deserve, to the mass of Protectionist voters.

Such a mistake was natural to men reared in the midst of the old controversy, and living for the most part in Free Trade England. But in young countries, and, of late years, even in England, it is necessary to put forward the cause of Free Trade in another and more attractive light, and to consider it in its effect upon the distribution of wealth as distinguished from its effect upon production.

The reason for thus changing the point of view is the alteration which has been made during recent years in the centre of political power. In the days of Cobden and the Anti-Corn Law League, when the middle classes formed the bulk of English voters, it was most politic to dwell upon the influence of Free Trade in cheapening the price of goods; but in young countries and at the present time in England, where the electorates are controlled by working men, the voters wish to understand the influence of that policy in raising wages. Accordingly, although the old arguments remain quite true, it is desirable now, if we wish to arrest general attention, to lay them aside for a time, and bring out others which are more attractive to working men.

Unfortunately Free Traders have been slow to recognise that, under the altered circumstances of an extended suffrage, they must change the popular presentment of their views. As a rule they still deal only with the figures of production. They tell us, for example, that the trade of England has advanced by leaps and bounds; that since Free Trade was introduced, the income-tax returns are ten times what they were; that the

[Pt. I., Ch. ii., § 3.]

quantity of funded wealth is daily growing larger, and the population is increasing with an unsurpassed rapidity. They point to the table of exports, to the growing cities, to the decline of pauperism and of crime, and to the many signs of English industry and enterprise in every quarter of the globe, and, rolling out their columns of magnificent statistics, they expect the world to be convinced! But working men, particularly in Australasia and America, know well that this is not the last word upon the subject! The matter of concern to them is not so much that goods should be produced in plenty, as that they should have an opportunity to use their skill; and, even in England, the working classes care more for a policy which promises high wages than for one which promises cheap goods. It is hardly reasonable to expect that a man, who has but sixpence in his pocket, should be greatly moved by hearing that the price of silk has been reduced to half-a-crown!

Accordingly, Free Trade must be justified in young countries and to working men in quite another way than by a catalogue of its effects upon production. It must be shown that Free Trade has also an effect in raising wages; that, whilst suggesting desires, it gives means to satisfy them by cheapening most articles of common use, and by bringing about the conditions which are most favourable to a fairer distribution of wealth, and most conducive in any community to a lasting rise in the average standard of comfort. In making this investigation, the real effect on wages of any fiscal policy will have to be considered, and the futility of attempting to raise wages by merely altering a customs tariff ought to be made plain. It is certain that, until such an inquiry is attempted, the Free Trade arguments will fly above the heads of those whom it is intended to convince.

§ 3. Partly in consequence of having directed so much attention to the effect of Free Trade upon capital, and partly for other reasons to be mentioned, Free Traders have incurred the charge of being hostile to the working-classes. No one, who has lived in a country where the fiscal controversy is active, can have failed to notice the strong and bitter feeling with which Free Traders are denounced by those who aspire to a political position by the aid of the working-classes. This feeling is, no doubt, to a great extent fictitious. It is necessary at times for the "friend of the working man"—and "friendship for the working man" is a recognised profession in most English-speaking countries—to use strong language if he would not have his sincerity suspected. Free Trade and Free Traders offer a convenient object of attack, the more so that Free Trade has been identified with an unpopular party both in Australasia and America. The Free Traders in Victoria, where the fiscal battle was first fought, were land-monopolists and Tories. The Free Traders in America were Southern slave-owners. It has taken a whole generation in both countries to dissociate Free Trade from these unpopular causes.

§ 4. Independently, however, of these local causes of ill-feeling, there is a more general ground for the popular idea that Free Traders have no sympathy with the aspirations of the working-classes. This arises from the attitude which has been adopted by many Free Trade writers towards the measures of reform demanded by the working-classes.

Most of those whom the public regard as the champions of Free Trade, from Ricardo to Professor Fawcett (with the two notable, but often unperceived, exceptions of Richard Cobden and John Stuart Mill), have been pedantically attached to that declining school of political thought which would restrict the action of the State within the narrowest bounds. In consequence of this, Free Trade has come to be identified with the general principle of "Laisser faire." Indeed, so deeply rooted is this confusion of ideas, that it is not uncommon, even in Radical journals, to find Trade Unions denounced as a violation of Free Trade principles, and a system of unregulated competition between masters and men justified by an appeal to the same authority.

Rightly or wrongly, however, working-men have believed that their condition could never be permanently bettered until the Government should interfere actively and widely upon their behalf; and they have accordingly demanded and obtained a long series of Acts of Parliament, to regulate and protect labour, of which the Factory Acts are the best-known examples.

All these measures have been opposed in the name of Free Trade, although (as will be shown later in these pages) Free Trade is an influence which works in the field of Production, and offers no argument either for or against the interference of Government within the field of Distribution. What wonder, then, that working-men, when they have found Free Traders confronting them at every effort to alleviate their lot by law, have ceased to take an interest in the promised benefits of Free Trade, and have regarded it as a middle-class doctrine, comforting enough to the well-to-do, but offering no help to them in their especial needs.

If, therefore, we would justify Free Trade to working-men, we must break away from the ancient argument and show the true relation of Free Trade to a general scheme of government. This will be attempted later in these pages. At present the misconception which exists upon this point is only mentioned as one reason for the prevalent mistrust of Free Trade doctrines, and as a special reason for their discredit among working-men.

§ 5. Not less dangerous to the influence of Free Trade than its supposed hostility to the interests of the working-classes, has been its supposed indifference to the evils of the competitive system.

Philanthropists and writers of the type of Mr. Ruskin have exhausted themselves in denunciation of the immorality and narrowness of the Free Trade system.

It is needless to say that these denunciations have been for the most part ignorant and misdirected. But they have had so much influence on a large class of benevolent people, who do not reason closely or at all on economic questions, that it is necessary to give them a passing attention.

It is said that Free Trade is indifferent to everything except material wealth, and that its last word is "to buy in the cheapest and sell in the dearest market."

This is a charge which, from the modicum of truth which it contains, has been peculiarly destructive.

Free Traders have, no doubt, written with only one object—that of showing the effect of a Free Trade policy upon national wealth; and it may be, that in looking at this single point, they have seemed to attach an excessive importance to material wealth. But this limitation of view no more justifies the assertion that Free Traders have no regard for the higher objects of national life, than the omission to mention pictures in a work on mathematics would justify a charge against its writer of ignorance of art. Because a Free Trader advocates the abolition of taxes on imports, it does not, therefore, follow that he regards this measure as a panacea for every industrial evil; nor, because he urges the advantages of free exchange, must he be supposed to hold that the highest social ideal is reached by merely buying in the cheapest and selling in the dearest market. The very silliness of a contrary supposition ought to be its own refutation. Yet, no one who has read Protectionist literature, or Mr. Ruskin's writings upon economics, can deny that even patent silliness is no impediment to the popularity of a groundless charge.

The only excuse for this wild vilification is a misapprehension of the attitude of Free Traders towards the doctrine of free competition.

§ 6. The Ricardian assumption of the existence within the industrial field of an universal and ever-active competiton—an assumption which was in accordance with facts at the time Ricardo wrote—has been taken by newspaper writers and others to be an assertion of principle. This imaginary principle has been erected into a "natural law," which is supposed to have been discovered by political economists! Then, by a confusion in the use of the term "law," political economy has been invoked by way of protest against every attempt to regulate or interefere with competition!

In fact, however, as every economist has pointed out, the "laws" of political economy are mere expressions of the regular sequence of certain events under certain assumed conditions. The most important of these conditions is that of free competition. It is assumed that there is a never-ceasing competition between the units of every industrial system, although it is admitted that this assumption only applies in fact to the wholesale trade and the great articles of commerce. Nor is this the whole of the assumption. The competition of abstract political economy is not the competition of masters and men as we see them in every-day life, but it is the competition of certain imaginary industrial units. These units are spoken of sometimes as individuals, and at other times as groups of individuals; but they are always supposed to have this characteristic—the units are equal to one another. It cannot be too often repeated that the competition of abstract political economy—that competition through which alone political economy has any pretension to the character of a science—is a competition between equal units. This is no place to consider whether this assumption still holds true in these days of "pools and combinations," (¹) or whether it was not always too far removed from facts to be of great practical value. It is enough to point out here how a misconception of its true nature has prejudiced the progress of Free Trade. It has been imagined that Free Trade being a doctrine founded upon political

---

¹ See, for a discussion of this point, an article by Prof. John B. Clark in the *Political Science Quarterly* for March, 1887, vol. ii., p. 62.

economy, justified the universal reign of lawless and unregulated competition. Nothing could be further from the truth.

§ 7. So far from justifying the universal reign of competition, the doctrines of Free Trade have no application outside of their own limited sphere. Free Trade is simply an expedient for carrying the principles of division of employment into international commerce. It is merely a means of facilitating the greatest possible production of wealth through facilitating exchange. Having accomplished that, its work is ended, and it leaves to other agencies the work of distribution.

Free Trade, in other words (using the term in its proper sense, to mean "the absence of protective duties"), operates exclusively within the field of production. Now, within the field of production there happens to be a competition between equal units. There is, as a general rule, an equality between those who buy and those who sell commodities, since both goods and capital can be removed from place to place, and the postponement of a sale or purchase causes at the worst a loss of money.

But once within the field of distribution, circumstances alter. The wages of labour and the price of goods are not in fact now, nor have they ever been, determined by the same forces; nor is that condition of free and equal competition, which political economy assumes to exist when it determines the laws of production and exchange, generally, or often, present at the time of the division of the product between those who have co-operated to produce it. That effective competition, which is the fundamental assumption of abstract political economy, does not as a rule exist between a labourer on the one side, and an employer on the other; and, therefore, to rigidly apply the principles which determine the price of goods to a determination of the rate of wages, would be in a high degree misleading. Buyers and sellers may, for the purposes of an abstract argument, be presumed to stand towards each other on a footing of equality; but to assume that the competition between the employer on the one hand, and the wage-earners on the other, when the latter are unorganised and unprotected by law, is a competition between equal units, is so fanciful and contrary to fact, that any conclusions drawn from such an assumption can have little value under present circumstances. Unfortunately, however, many Free Traders have not recognised this fact, but have attempted to apply maxims—which are true when applied to the production of wealth, where there is an effective and equal competition between buyer and seller— to the case of labourers seeking to obtain for themselves a higher rate of wages, although the determinant of the rate of wages is composed of such incalculable elements as the habits, desires, and customs of human beings.

It follows, from the fact that the laws of the distribution of wealth are less absolute and more changeable than those of its production, and from the fact that Free Trade operates chiefly within the field of production, that, although it may be demonstrable that government ought to leave men free to produce and exchange commodities when and how they please, it does not follow that the same policy should be applied to proportioning the distribution of commodities among those who have produced them. Unlimited competition may be good in the one case and evil in the other, without Free Trade giving us any guide for pronouncing a judgment.[1] The evils, therefore, of unlimited competition within the field of distribution offer no argument against the removal of protective tariffs.

§ 8. The last cause which may be mentioned as having had an influence in the revival of Protectionism, is the discontent with existing industrial conditions, which is a prevalent sign of the times.

It is not easy to trace this cause in actual operation, but no reader of Protectionist literature can fail to recognise its

[1] See further on this subject *infra* Part II., chap. 7.

presence. The jealousy of wealth, the dislike of "laisser faire," the pressure of the competitive system, all give rise to a profound dissatisfaction with existing social conditions. The evils of the day are felt to be intolerably irksome, until it seems as if the wished-for blessing might be found in any change of policy. There can be no question that, as the labour party in America, under the leadership of Henry George, is turning against Protectionism, so in England and Australia, discontent creates antagonism towards Free Trade.

It ought to be needless to point out that the remedy for the evils which create this discontent lies altogether outside the influence of Protection or Free Trade. Neither Free Trade nor Protection is a panacea for industrial evils, nor will either policy satisfy the wants of working men. Irregular employment, crowded homes, an existence without pleasure, an insecure old age—these are causes of complaint which cannot be removed by any changes in a fiscal policy. No mere tariff reform will give the poorer workmen regular employment, nor build them healthy dwellings near their work, nor find them openings for secure investment, nor relieve the monotony of their dull existence. All that can be done by the agency of taxation is to mitigate as far as possible the evils which exist, and to guard against creating others. Free Traders hold, that under their policy the remedial agencies will work with the greatest force; but they do not say that Free Trade has of itself the power to remove industrial grievances.

§ 9. To sum up the conclusions of this chapter, we have noted that the revival of Protection is largely due to the following causes, viz. :—

> 1. To the fact that Free Trade writers have directed their chief attention to the effect of the policy in increasing wealth, instead of considering its effect on wages.

2. To the discredit which has attached to Free Trade through being associated with unpopular or aristocratic parties.
3. To the idea that Free Trade is identical with a general policy of "laisser faire."
4. To the idea that Free Traders are indifferent to the evils of the competitive system.
5. To the prevailing discontent with existing social and industrial conditions.

The mere enumeration of these causes proves the necessity for a restatement of the Free Trade case. We have to deal with a new class of opponents, variously prejudiced against us, and suffering from real grievances, to all of which they imagine Free Traders are indifferent, and some of which they trace directly to the policy.

We have, therefore, to be careful to show that we do not gloss over any facts, nor disregard any interest. We have to be careful, also, to look at many facts from the standpoint of working-men and yet not to raise excessive hopes in the minds of those whom we address. Above all, we have to dissociate Free Trade from the policy of *laisser faire*. Some Free Traders may be advocates of *laisser faire*; but there are many, and their numbers are growing, who look upon Free Trade simply as an instrument which destroys one form of State interference, in order to leave the ground clear for more effective action by the State in new directions.

Nor are Free Traders necessarily wedded to the present social system. Free Trade is merely voluntary trade: a Free Trader only maintains that men should be allowed to buy and sell where and what they will. But he does not say that men's freedom should in no case be controlled by voluntary association, nor by public opinion. There is nothing inconsistent with Free Trade in a body of men agreeing to pay more than necessary for any article, provided they do not force other people to follow their example. Finally, there is nothing in the doctrines of Free Trade which requires their disciple to make a fetish of universal and unregulated competition. A Free Trader can admit as evils many things of which Protectionists complain. He can join with a Protectionist in his protest against labour being bought and sold like a bale of goods. He, too, may refuse to believe that masters and men can never be secured against the misery of fluctuating trade, and can prefer that the evils of dependence should be lessened, rather than that the number of millionaires should be increased with an unparalleled rapidity.

In short, the final aim of an honest Free Trader differs but little from that of an honest Protectionist, however much they may dispute with one another as to means. The ideal of both is, or ought to be, the same, namely :—to prevent the labourer sinking into the mere drudge of a machine, and to make him once again a craftsman with an artistic love and knowledge of his work.

But, while thus recognising the evils of our present industrial system, a Free Trader would desire it to be understood by those who suffer that, if Free Trade has proved an imperfect remedy, Protection is a poison. The grievances of the Protectionists are real enough, but their hostility is misdirected. The remedy, as will be pointed out later in these pages, is independent either of Protection or Free Trade. But, while Protection aggravates existing evils, Free Trade not only does much to mitigate them, but also brings about many conditions under which these evils can be more easily removed.

CHAPTER III.

THE SIGNIFICANCE OF A PROTECTIONIST REVIVAL.

§ 1. In the inquiry which has been conducted through the last two chapters into the nature and the causes of the Protectionist revival, no direct reference has been made to its extent or its significance. Yet both of these are so often overstated or misunderstood, that it is desirable to give them some attention before entering upon a discussion of the merits of the rival fiscal policies.

The impression of many Protectionists—if we may judge Protectionist voters by the speeches and writings of their political leaders—would appear to be that Great Britain stands alone, among civilised nations, in her acceptance of the doctrine of Free Trade, and that all other countries have deliberately declined to follow her example. From this it is argued that, if the policy were good, its merits would have been so decisively established by Great Britain's forty years' experiment, that the fact of its universal rejection is conclusive against it.

It is hardly necessary to point out that this is both an incorrect statement of facts and an unsound argument.

§ 2. In the first place it is not true that England is the only Free Trade country. Neither Holland, Norway, Belgium, Switzerland, nor Denmark can be called protected countries; and some of them—notably Holland—have tariffs very little higher than that of England. These countries are, of course, not to be compared in extent of territory with their Protectionist neighbours; but they are not one whit behind them in the other elements of national greatness. They are free, wealthy, peaceful, and progressive: Can any of the European countries which have adopted Protection be characterised in the same terms? Without over-estimating the importance of a fiscal policy, it is at least noticeable that those European countries, which are most free from clerical and military domination, are precisely the countries which most incline towards an unrestricted commerce; while the military and reactionary governments favour Protection.

§ 3. Suppose, however, it were otherwise, and that England stood absolutely alone in her adherence to Free Trade—it is surely plain that this fact would not justify a conclusion that the policy was unsound, unless we first knew the reasons which induced other countries to adopt or retain Protection? It might be that these had no reference to the fiscal controversy, but were local and special reasons of a political and temporary character. If, for example, one country imposed protective duties, for the purpose of retaliating upon a hostile neighbour, or another imposed them because the Custom House offered the easiest means of raising a large revenue for wasteful expenditure—it could hardly be contended that the action of either of these countries raised even a presumption against the expediency of Free Trade in a country of different industrial and political conditions. The fiscal problem is emphatically one which cannot be decided by the method of counting heads. Every country must work out a solution for itself according to its own conditions and its own needs. The experience of one country, although it may be valuable as a test of theory, is seldom useful to other countries as a guide to practice, since the necessary conditions of a just comparison are seldom, if ever, present.[1]

[1] Mr. Giffen, in his paper on "The Use of Import and Export Statistics" ("Essays in Finance, Second Series, p. 200), makes the following remarks in this connection:—

"To make any statistical comparison at all possible between different *régimes*, it would be necessary, either to find two countries practically alike in their economic and industrial circumstances, and in the character of their people, subject them to the opposite *régimes*, and then ascertain and compare their relative material progress; or, to find a particular country subjected at different

[Pt. ⅴ., Ch. iii., § 4.]

§ 4. Thus, although the results of either fiscal policy in any particular case can never be ignored, yet the greatest caution must be exercised in drawing inferences. Still more is caution necessary, when it is proposed to draw an inference, not from results, but from motives. There is no better instance of want of caution in this respect than the familiar Protectionist cry which we are now considering.

There is, indeed, no doubt but that the disinclination of many countries, both new and old, to abandon their Protective policies, and the inclination of others to adopt Protection, is a phenomenon, which requires careful explanation in view of the signal and incontestable success of the British experiment. But while giving full weight to any inference that can be legitimately drawn from the conduct of the citizens of one country for the guidance of citizens of another, and recognising that Free Trade has not spread so rapidly as might have been expected, it would be a mistake to assume that the doctrine of Free Trade has been impeached in any material point, either by the experience of Great Britain after forty years of a Free Trade policy, or by the Protectionist proclivities of other countries.

---

periods to the two opposite *régimes* without any other differences, and then compare the different results, if any such are appreciable. Experience does not supply us with such cases. No two communities are sufficiently alike to be comparable in strict logic. The slightest differences in the race or moral condition of the two communities, which are to outward appearance much the same, might make a great deal of difference to their material progress. If the two are subjected to different economic *régimes*, how are we to tell whether the inferior progress of the one materially—even when we are sure about the inferiority—is due to the *régime*, and not to other differences in the character of the communities which we cannot so well appreciate? The same with a community at different periods of its own history. How can we tell that there is no moral difference of a serious kind to affect the economic progress of the community between one period and another? External economic circumstances are, besides, incessantly changing, and may affect two communities apparently of much the same character and position quite differently. If it were possible to institute many points of comparison and exhibit an uniform result in all, it might be safe to infer that it was the *régime* which did make the difference, no other uniform cause of difference being assignable; but this condition, of course, it is impossible to fulfil."

The contrary is rather the case. English experience has indisputably shown the wisdom of a Free Trade policy, so that there is hardly an intelligent American or Australian Protectionist, who does not readily admit that Free Trade is a necessity for a manufacturing or commercial country in the situation of Great Britain. Nor are the Protectionist inclinations of other countries really an impeachment of Free Trade, when the circumstances attendant on their origin are understood. Moreover, so far from English example having carried no weight, it will be found, that after the adoption of Free Trade by Great Britain, there was a marked and steady movement in the same direction throughout the continent of Europe. It is true that this movement has been interrupted during the last twenty years, but an examination of the facts reveals that every country, with the exception of Canada and Victoria, that has adopted a Protectionist policy during this period, has done this under the stress of war, and that the influences which have been at work in favour of restriction have already begun to wane.

The truth, accordingly, is that this so-called revival of Protection has very little significance in the fiscal controversy. It has proceeded from circumstances which have only a remote connection with Protection and Free Trade, and has seldom been due to any deliberate rejection of a Free Trade policy. In every case, moreover, even when it has proceeded from an avowed adherence to Protectionist doctrines, it has originated under the stress of exceptional and peculiar difficulties, arising from a morbid and abnormal industrial condition. Thirdly, in most cases, it has been an interruption of an earlier and well defined movement in the direction of Free Trade, which, according to present indications, is likely to be renewed. Under these circumstances the much vaunted Protectionist revival is not likely to be of much use to logical champions of commercial restrictions. As, however, the Protectionist voter attaches great importance to the argument from numbers, it will be advisable to make a more detailed examination of the causes which have led the principal countries to raise their tariffs, because it must be admitted that, if these causes vary, or if they are mutually inconsistent, or if they have no application to the conditions of the country in which the example is quoted, the strength of the Protectionist's assertion, that all the wisdom of the world is upon his side, becomes considerably diminished.

It will be convenient, in pursuing this inquiry, to deal separately with the examples of Great Britain, the continent of Europe, the United States of America, and the British Colonies.

CHAPTER IV.

ILLUSTRATIONS.

SECTION I.—GREAT BRITAIN.

§ 1. It is not easy to understand the fashion in which Protectionists treat Great Britain's forty-five years' experience of a Free Trade policy. At one time they admit that it has been such as to establish once for all the superiority of Free Trade for a country situated like Great Britain. At another they assert, that Free Trade was adopted under a mistaken view as to the probable effect of English example upon foreign nations; and that, if the leaders of the Anti-Corn Law League could have foreseen that, after forty-five years, England would stand almost alone in the practice of commercial freedom, they would never have begun their famous agitation. Forgetful of the Free Trade maxim that "the best way to fight hostile tariffs is by free imports," these disputants assert that the Free Trade, which the exertions of the Liberal party won for England, is not the Free Trade for which the leaders strove, but a "one-sided" Free Trade, which Bright and Cobden in their earlier days would have regarded as little less pernicious than a close Protection.

Either of these methods of treatment allows the Protectionist orator to put English experience upon one side.

§ 2. If all Protectionists agreed that Free Trade had proved a great success in England, there would be no need to insist upon this fact in any controversial work. Unfortunately, however, the native-born Australian, and, in a less degree, the native-born American, often prides himself upon his indifference to the history of other countries. Absorbed in the great work of making a new nation, and rightly impatient of the vapid affectation of English ways and indiscriminate reliance upon English taste, which seems inevitable in a subordinate community, he is apt to confound the callow criticisms of the English traveller with the solid teachings of English experience, and dismiss each with the same contempt. This tendency has, until quite recently, been fostered in Australia by the omission from the school and university curriculum of any teaching of history—the reason assigned for this being the remarkable fear that to teach history might wound religious susceptibilities! The consequence is that, in spite of the disavowals of responsible Protectionist writers, voters are still found in Australasia and America who believe that the condition of England has not materially improved either subsequently to or in consequence of the adoption of Free Trade.

§ 3. It may be doubted whether any fact of industrial history is capable of easier or more conclusive proof than that Great Britain has enormously advanced in every direction of national progress since the adoption of Free Trade. All the evidence points to the same conclusion, and is, as Mr. Giffen has insisted, cumulative; so that it must be disproved in each particular item, if any doubt is to be thrown upon the impression created by a survey of the whole. "To justify the belief," says this eminent writer, "that there has been no great general advance, every one of the propositions stated [by him] would have to be disproved, and an opposite set of statements, all hanging together and all supporting the view of retrogression, or no advance, or very little advance, would have to be made good. There are too many facts to permit the setting up of a plea of ignorance, or impossibility of arriving at any conclusion."[1]

Nor, indeed, is the one fact of a stupendous growth in material wealth denied by any but a few fanatics—the signs of it are too manifest to the eye to admit of question or to require demonstration by figures [2]—but those who desire to depreciate the English example, content themselves with making the assertion that the chief benefit of their improvement has gone to the rich, while the poor have been growing poorer year by year. Such a statement naturally appeals to many prejudices, and often finds acceptance among men who do not know the facts.

In reality the assertion is almost unsupported by evidence. All the facts tell the other way. Official and private records of rates of wages and hours of labour show, that the workman receives to-day from 50 to 100 per cent. more money for 20 per cent. less work than was the case under Protection; and that, owing to a large fall in the prices of the chief articles of consumption, the purchasing power of his wages is considerably increased. In addition to this improvement in his relations with employers, the workman to-day gets the benefit of largely increased Government expenditure. He not only pays less taxes, but he gets more—much more—from the Government than he ever received under the Protective system. He is now better fed, better clothed, better housed, better educated, better cared for in his health and amusements

---

[1] "Essays in Finance"; Second Series.
[2] The paper by Mr. Medley, printed as a note to this chapter, contains some of the more striking facts.

than at any other period in English history. All the facts agree to prove that the poor have not grown poorer. Pauperism has diminished; crime has diminished; the deposits in the Savings Bank have increased; the funds of the Friendly and Benefit Societies have increased; the investments of small savings are greater than they were; life is in every direction longer, easier, and more comfortable; even the rate of mortality has declined, so that on an average a man lives two years, and a woman three and a half years longer than was the case before Free Trade. Is, then, the other part of the assertion true, and have the rich grown richer? The facts again agree to support a negative answer! The returns to the Income Tax and to the Probate Duties demonstrate conclusively that the number of the moderately rich has been increasing, and that the increase of capital per head of the capitalist classes is by no means so great as the increase of working-class incomes.

It may be that Protectionists will take exception to the value of the evidence by which these facts are sustained; and, no one would deny that the relations between evidence and conclusions in matters of this nature are always difficult to determine. But is any other kind of evidence forthcoming? Is it possible to get any other accumulation of facts, whether of the same or of a different character, to support the conclusion that the condition of the working-classes in Great Britain has become worse, instead of better, since the introduction of Free Trade? And if it is not possible to do this, it must surely be admitted that the experience of Great Britain has a certain bearing on the fiscal controversy. No doubt Protection may be supported by different arguments in different countries; but English experience is at least of so much value, that it justifies Free Traders in putting Protectionists to proof of their assertions. They tell us that Free Trade creates monopolies; that it increases profits at the expense of wages; that it produces paupers; that it destroys manufactures! The contrary has been the case in England; let them, therefore, prove their statements.[1]

[1] It will be apparent to all who are familiar with the subject, that the passages in the text about the condition of the working-classes are only a summary of Mr. Giffen's two Essays on the "Progress of the Working-Classes," since re-published in the author's second series of "Essays on Finance." This masterpiece of statistical investigation is supported in its conclusions by the analysis, which the late Mr. Brassey has made public, of the pay-sheets of his enormous business as contractor. This gives a faithful record of the rise and fall of wages, during that period, in the two great trades of the builders and the engineers (*see* "Work and Wages"). In addition to this there is a collection of statistics made in 1866 by Professor Leone Levi and Mr. Dudley Baxter under the title of "Wages and Earnings of the Working-Classes." These are collected chiefly from private sources, and most of the information appears to be drawn from the more favoured trades, so that, without questioning the accuracy of the figures, it is possible to believe that these gentlemen have made too high an estimate of the average earnings of the working-classes. Another useful source of authentic information is the annual return furnished by the Chamber of Commerce in different centres to the English Board of Trade, which are published among the miscellaneous statistics of the United Kingdom. The *Board of Trade Journal* now contains regular returns of wages, compiled from the best official and private sources.

In a note to this chapter the writer has put together the results of some independent investigations which he made in 1883 on the variation in wages in the four great English industries—the cotton, woollen, worsted, and iron trades—which, together, employ about one-half of the artisan population, to which the reader is referred for further information.

There is especial reason at the present time for emphasising the fact of the great and continuous advance in the well-being of the poorer classes, because a most active section of Free Traders have been misled by Mr. Henry George into an assertion to the contrary, and have thus considerably weakened the force of their attack upon Protection. Mr. George's work on "Progress and Poverty," which was his earliest important writing, begins, as is well known, with the assertion that "the poor have grown poorer and the rich richer." Although this is the fundamental proposition of the work, no tittle of evidence is advanced in its support. Its truth is quietly assumed. Yet all the known evidence as to the condition of old countries tells the other way. It may indeed be the case—although Mr. Giffen doubts this—that the agricultural labourers in Great Britain were better off in the middle of the last century than they ever have been since; but there is ample evidence to show that the condition of the great body of labourers was worse (*e.g.*, *see* Eden's "State of the Poor"). Mr. Giffen quotes from M. Yves Guyot ("Principles of Social Economy" [English Translation], Swan Sonnenschein & Co.), to show that there has been a similar improvement in France and Germany. Perhaps Mr. George in penning the phrase only had in mind the Western States of America, with regard to which it is probably true.

It is, indeed, possible that the arguments of those who insist upon the great improvement which has taken place in the condition of the working-classes under Free Trade are open to criticism upon one point, viz.—that the increase in money wages is sometimes exaggerated. Mr. Giffen estimates that the average rate of wages in England has doubled since 1830. This may be the case—and no one can differ from Mr. Giffen on such a matter without hesitation—but the average advance in wages as disclosed by the Board of Trade returns from 1830 to 1833, in the four principal English industries—the cotton, woollen, worsted, and iron trades—does not appear to have been so great. The question is dealt with in detail in the note at the end of this chapter, so that it will be sufficient here to summarise the conclusions.

Mr. Giffen's statement appears to be borne out by the figures returned for those four trades as the wages paid to skilled labour. The increase in these cases has often been more than double. But among the body of unskilled labourers, the increase, so far as can be gathered from the Board of Trade Statistics, is not more than from twenty-five to fifty per cent. In fact, it is a remarkable illustration of the truth that the stronger the labourer, and the better he is able to protect himself, the more likely is he to obtain good wages, that these figures show, that not only is it the class of skilled labourers who have benefited most, but in almost every case they have been the first to get the advantage of a rising market. Indeed, the figures of the cotton, woollen, worsted, and iron trades lead to these two conclusions : first, that the increase of wages has been largest among the best-paid class of artisans, less among the class of medium ability, and least among the common labourers ; and, secondly, that a rise in wages comes earliest to the best-paid class, later to the middle class, and latest to the unskilled workman. These assertions are not put forward as the invariable laws of rising wages, but they are certainly conclusions from a large number of important observations.

But it may be said, the unskilled labourers form the mass of the community, and since it is the poorest classes that suffer most, it is in their prosperity that the country is most interested. This leads to another branch of our inquiry, viz., whether wages have increased beyond the greater cost of living? There can be no doubt that even the poorest workman receives more money than he used; but does a sovereign in England go as far now as it did thirty years ago? In the hands of a workman it does. If anyone will make a table of the articles of a labourer's consumption, and, by a reference to any book on prices, estimate the cost of living, say thirty years ago, and at the present time, he will find that in respect of most items of a labourer's expenditure there has been a marked decrease of price, and that in respect of only two items has there been any increase. These two are meat and house-rent. The price of meat has nearly doubled, and rent has increased one and a-half times. But none the less, it is not true, as has been written, that rent has swallowed up the whole of the increase in workmen's wages. Theoretically, Mr. George's views are sound enough. Imagine a country with entirely unrestrained competition, with a limited quantity of land in private hands, shut out from all foreign trade, and its people prohibited from emigrating—then undoubtedly rent would increase at the expense of both wages and profits. But these theoretical conditions do not prevail in any country in the world, not even in Ireland, and in a Free Trade country least of all.

In fact, neither the rise in rent,[1] nor the greater cost of meat has reduced the workman's real income below what it was under Protection. By making a table of the average necessary expenses of a workman, with a wife and three children, in 1840, and at the present day, it will be found

---

[1] Part of the rise in rent is due to improved house accommodation.

that, while in 1840 an unskilled workman seldom had meat more than once a week, now, allowing for meat every day, and also for the rise in rent, he has a larger balance than he used to have.[1] That is to say, under Free Trade, even when the rise in wages has been lowest, namely, among the class of unskilled labourers, it has at least outpaced the increase in the cost of living. Other facts point to the same conclusion. The consumption of tea and sugar, for example, per head of the population, is four times what it used to be in the days of Protection. It is the same with the consumption of rice, tobacco, spirits, and similar luxuries. What better evidence could be given that the prosperity of the last forty years has been diffused among the masses? The articles named are emphatically poor men's luxuries, and not such that an increased consumption of them by the rich could make much difference to the quantity consumed. But, as has already been observed, all the facts agree. There is no test by which improvement in material prosperity can be measured, which does not bear out the

---

[1] Weekly necessary expenses of a carpenter, with a wife and three children:—

	1840.		1890.	
	s.	d.	s.	d.
8 quartern loaves	5	8	4	0
8lbs. meat	4	4	6	0
1½lbs. butter	1	6	1	9
1lb. cheese	0	7	0	8
2lbs. sugar	1	2	0	4
¼lb. tea	1	6	0	4½
1lb. soap	0	5	0	4
1lb. candles	0	6	0	5
1lb. rice	0	4	0	2
2 gals. milk	0	4	0	8
Vegetables	0	6	1	0
Coals, firing	1	0	1	6
Rent	4	0	6	6
Clothes and sundries	3	0	3	0
	24	10	26	8½

The increase on a wage of 24s. 10d. since 1846 has been to at least 28s., and in most cases to 30s.

assertion that there has been a great and general advance in well-being among the masses of Great Britain since the abolition of a protective tariff. No one would say that the advance has been sufficient. The condition of the poor in England is terrible, and their improvement has been little enough, even when measured by a low ideal, so that it is hard to see things as they are without desiring something like a revolution for the better. Still, the fact of an enormous progress must be kept in view, progress which may not be recognised until comparison is made with the former state of things. As Mr. Giffen warns us, " discontent with the present must not make us forget that things have been so much worse."

§ 4. The prosperity of Great Britain under Free Trade is logically fatal to the protective dogma, that the only way to secure prosperity is by means of protective duties against foreign imports. The prosperity of a protected country is not, by a parity of reasoning, fatal to Free Trade, because Free Trade is not a dogma, but a mere negative assertion of the errors of Protection. Protection, on the other hand, not only asserts the wisdom of protective duties, but justifies its action by the tacit and expressed assumption that national wealth cannot be produced or diffused without them. Hence, as Professor Sumner has pointed out, "either prosperity in a Free Trade country, or distress in a Protectionist country, is fatal to Protectionism; while distress in a Free Trade country, or prosperity in a Protectionist country, proves nothing against Free Trade."[1]

Nevertheless, it is frequently asserted that the prosperity of Great Britain proves nothing in the fiscal controversy, because the credit of it cannot be claimed entirely for Free Trade, but must be shared by the mechanical and scientific improvements which have characterised the period since Protection was

[1] "Protectionism—the -ism which teaches that Waste makes Wealth." New York: Holt & Co., 1885; p. 26.

abolished. It is plain that this argument effectually prevents Protectionists from taking credit to their system for the progress of the United States, since not only has the invention of machinery played a most important part in their industrial development, but it has been aided by unparalleled natural resources. In the United States are millions of acres of fertile land, with soil thirty feet deep; there are minerals of every kind in useful proximity to each other; there are coal-fields, oil-wells, and every sort of natural product in astonishing abundance; and all these resources are not locked up in inaccessible regions, but are brought near to the markets of the world by a most extensive system of railway and river communication. Add to all this, that on an average half a million immigrants are being poured into the country every year, representing each of them a capital expenditure of £200, or, in a body, a total increment of one hundred million pounds per annum to the national capital; that there is little or no expenditure for military purposes, and that there is an unrestricted system of Free Trade from one end of the vast continent to the other, and we have a combination of every circumstance which is most favourable to the increase of wealth. Under such conditions, it would be miraculous if America had not become a great manufacturing country. Her present inferiority in this respect to Great Britain is probably solely due to her protective tariff.

Disregarding, however, the logical irrelevance of the inquiry, and admitting that an assent to its necessity cuts both ways, it is expedient, for controversial purposes, to ascertain, if possible, what portion of Great Britain's prosperity has been due to Free Trade, and what portion to other causes.

No one can deny that railways, telegraphs, and every other improvement in the means of intercourse and production, have had a great influence in every part of the world in extending commerce and increasing wealth; but, nevertheless, it can be shown, with as much certainty as such an investigation admits, that a chief part of the increase in the wealth of Great Britain during the last forty years has been due to the abolition of the protective system. It can also be shown by *à priori* reasoning, that a nation cannot reap the full advantages of improvements in locomotion and mechanical processes under any system which restricts the intercourse between its citizens and foreigners.

There are two methods of conducting this inquiry. The first is by comparing the condition of trade in the year immediately preceding the remission of a tax on imports, with its condition in the year immediately following. If, then, it is found, that in every case a dose of Free Trade has been followed by an otherwise inexplicable increase in the volume of commerce, it may be fairly concluded that there is a connection between this increase and the legislation which preceded it. The second method is to estimate the influence of the mechanical or locomotive agencies, when they are at work without Free Trade, in order to deduct what ought to be assigned to them from the total increase of wealth. This method is extremely complicated, and not, perhaps, altogether satisfactory, owing to the difficulty of making an accurate estimate of the value of the mechanical and locomotive factor.

Both methods, however, have been used by Mr. Gladstone, in an article which is now lost in the kaleidoscopic pages of a monthly magazine.[1] It may accordingly be useful to indicate the character of Mr. Gladstone's conclusions, without attempting to summarise his article.

He first estimates the average annual increase in the volume of British trade, from the date of the first use of railways up to 1842, which was the first year of any large instalment of Free Trade, by the following method:—He finds that, for the twenty years from 1810-1830, English trade was almost stationary; but that in 1830, with the use of railways, there came a sudden increase, which continued year by year as new railways were opened. Consequently, he sets down the growth of trade from

[1] *Nineteenth Century*, February, 1880.

1830 to 1842 to what, for the purposes of this calculation, he terms the locomotive factor.

Assuming this method to be correct, and that the period is not too short to form the basis of such an estimate, the difficult question still remains, how to use the figures, which have been thus obtained, for the purpose of comparison with other periods.

Mr. Gladstone attempts to get over this difficulty in the following way:—He takes the number of miles of railway open during the years 1830–42, together with the mileage receipts during the same year, and, on the assumption that the increase before referred to during that period was owing to the locomotive agencies alone, he arrives at a rough estimate of the effect of each new mile of railway upon the volume of English trade. Then he calculates from this basis the deductions which have to be made from the yearly increase in that volume subsequently to 1842, on account of railways, and making an equal allowance on account of telegraphs and ocean steamships, and recognising that the influence of these factors has been increasing, and not constant, he reaches the conclusion that by far the larger portion of the increase in English trade during the last forty years must be assigned to other causes than improvements in the means of locomotion.

This conclusion is, at best, imperfect; but it is at least as worthy of attention as the unsupported statements of Protectionist orators and letter-writers, that the whole of the improved condition of English trade in recent years is owing to mechanical improvements in the means of intercourse.

Mr. Gladstone also attempts the first of the two methods, which have been already mentioned as suitable to an enquiry into the causes of the growth of England's trade, and which, although it is not so strictly scientific as the other, enables us, to arrive at more accurate results, and estimate with a greater degree of precision the effect upon trade by the removal of Protectionist restrictions.

[Pt. I., Ch. iv., § 4.]

Mr. Gladstone takes the fluctuations in the export trade as an index of prosperity, because any increase in the export of home-made articles is an unerring indication of general industrial activity; and because any increase in the export trade of a country which lends, and does not borrow capital, is always accompanied by all those other signs of progress for which an explanation is being sought in this inquiry. He begins with the period 1816–30, when railways were not invented, and Protection had the field to itself. It is instructive to find that during those fifteen years of peace, down to 1830 inclusive, although mechanical invention was in constant growth, the value of British exports remained almost stationary at about £36,000,000, or, if account were taken of the growth of population during that period, that there was an actual decline in the value per head of the population. Well may Mr. Gladstone say that during those years Protection proved itself to be, in the United Kingdom at least, but another name for paralysis!

The first instalment of Free Trade legislation was granted in 1842, by which time, thanks to the growth of railways, English exports had increased to £51,400,000, but the remissions of duty did not take effect until 1843. That year is consequently the first in which the influence of Free Trade can be perceived. The concession to freedom was very slight, consisting almost entirely of a permission to import certain articles, which had previously been prohibited, at reasonable duties; yet, slight as the concession was, the three years, 1843–45, showed an average export of £57,000,000, an aggregate growth, that is, of £6,000,000, and an annual growth, one year with another, of two millions.

The second instalment of Free Trade was given by Sir Robert Peel in the year 1845. By the tariff of that year all export duties were abolished, and 430 out of the 813 articles of raw material were admitted free of duty; but the Corn Laws, the Navigation Laws, and the Sugar Duties remained untouched. The three years during which this tariff was in force were marked by three great calamities. The first, scarcity in England and famine in Ireland; the second, commercial panic with the suspension of the Bank Charter Act in 1847; and the third, in 1848, wars and revolutions on the continent, which in one year drove British exports down by £6,000,000. In the days of more stringent Protection, any one of similar occurrences had caused a disastrous decline; under Free Trade, however, the result of all of them combined was little more than a stoppage of growth. The average of the exports for the three years, 1845-8, was £56,500,000, as compared with £57,000,000, which had been the average of the period from 1842 to 1845.

The third dose of Free Trade was given in 1849, by the total cessation of the Corn Duties at the beginning of that year, and the abolition of more than 100 other taxes upon imports, together with the repeal of the Navigation Acts later in the Parliamentary session. For that year the exports rose suddenly from £52,800,000 to £63,500,000. The rise steadily continued, so that the average annual value of exports for the three years, 1849 to 1852, was £72,000,000, representing an increase of £15,000,000 per annum over the preceding triennium.

The fourth instalment of Free Trade legislation began with the new tariff of 1853. The three years from 1853-55, notwithstanding the Crimean War, show an average export of £97,000,000. From 1853, a very flourishing year, with an export of £78,000,000, we pass to 1854, with the enormous increment of £20,000,000, and a total export value of £98,000,000. The effect of the war is seen during the next two years by the exports remaining about stationary; but, in spite of this, the average for the three years, 1853-55, is £94,000,000, or an increase of £22,000,000 on the previous triennium. This increase continued steadily up to 1859.

The fifth and last Free Trade period is marked by Mr. Cobden's French Treaty, and by the Customs Act of 1860, which finally established the principle that no protective duties should be charged, and by the repeal of the paper duties. This was again followed by an increase in our exports; but it is not possible to estimate the quantity of this increase for any purpose of comparison, since we have no limit provided by any fresh epoch of Free Trade legislation. It is, however, very noteworthy that, since the removal of the Free Trade stimulus—if we leave out of account the exceptional years 1870–75, when, owing to the consequences of the Franco-German war, trade advanced by leaps and bounds—the increase in English exports tends to become more regular and steady, as if it were henceforward to be attributed mainly to the growth of population.

It may be that these figures are not rigidly conclusive, because social problems do not admit of being demonstrated like a rule of mathematics. But let any candid man put this question to himself—"Supposing that in any other case but one in which Protection was at issue with Free Trade, I found that legislation of a certain character was always followed by the same results, for which no other cause can be suggested, must I not therefore conclude that there is a close connection between this legislation and the subsequent events?" This is a test which would be recognised in every other matter of political experience; why, then, should Free Traders have to ask that the same openness of mind, and readiness to look at facts, should be displayed by everyone who enters upon the fiscal controversy?

§ 5. Protectionists, who cannot deny the fact of English progress under Free Trade, adopt, as has been observed already, another method of disparaging the value of her example. They insist that the anticipations of the Free Trade leaders have not been realised, and that, as the struggle was conducted under the belief that other nations would be compelled to follow England, if she adopted Free Trade, the whole case is now re-opened, and the old arguments cease to apply.

The motives and anticipations of the leaders of the Anti-Corn Law League are, of course, wholly immaterial to the question, "Whether Free Trade or Protection is the better policy for Australasia or America?" Nevertheless, the statement that Cobden only fought for universal Free Trade, and that, being disappointed of this, he would have ceased his efforts, has obtained a vogue in both these countries, which would be surprising in any other controversy. It is used in two ways—first, as an easy justification for abuse of the Free Trade leaders; and, secondly, as an excuse for disregarding English experience. No one, therefore, who defends the Free Trade cause in either Australasia or America, can afford to treat this statement as it deserves; he must show once more that the Corn Laws fell by their own weight, and that the disappointment of any expectations, that the restrictive laws of any other countries would fall in the same way, has in no degree weakened the significance of the British uprising against the misery and injustice of a protective tariff. To assert the contrary, is one of those perversions of historical fact which are, unhappily, only too frequent in the fiscal controversy.

The basis of the charge is a speech of Mr. Cobden's in the House of Commons on January 15, 1846, in which he said, "I believe that if you abolish the Corn Laws honestly, and adopt Free Trade in its simplicity, there will not be a tariff in Europe that will not be changed in less than five years to follow your example." Speaking again at a public meeting in 1852, he made a similar prophecy; and on these two passages, Protectionists have raised a structure of abuse and ridicule, every one of them, from Mr. Serjeant Byles to Mr. James G. Blaine, contributing his little stone!

Yet, after all, what do the words amount to, even reading them literally and without the explanation of surrounding facts? They are, at most, an impeachment of Mr. Cobden's political judgment. To take them as expressive of the general opinion of his party, and then to say that it was this opinion which stimulated the party to its exertions, is to disregard the whole weight of evidence upon the other side. Quotations might be multiplied to fill a volume, to show from the pages of *Hansard*, and from the speeches of the Free Trade leaders as reported in *The League*, which was their organ in the Press, that the English people were under no misapprehension as to what would be the conduct of other nations, when they adopted Free Trade; but that they deliberately abandoned Protection, because, after a fair trial, it had proved, in the words of Lord John Russell's resolution, "the blight of commerce, the bane of agriculture, the source of bitter divisions between classes, the cause of poverty, fever, mortality, and crime among the people."[1] No fact in history is more certain, and few are more easily demonstrated, than that the Corn Laws were abolished because they injured England, and that the advocates of industrial freedom were indifferent to the course which other nations might pursue so long as Englishmen obtained bread.

Thus Sir R. Peel, in a speech on the Corn Laws, in the House of Commons, Jan. 27th, 1846, said:—

"I fairly avow to you that, in making this great reduction upon the import of articles—the produce and manufacture of foreign countries—I have no guarantee to give you that other countries will immediately follow our example. I give you that advantage in the argument. Wearied with our long and unavailing efforts to enter into satisfactory commercial treaties with other nations, we have resolved at length to consult our own interests, and not to punish those other countries for the wrong they do us in continuing their high duties upon the importation of our products and manufactures by continuing high duties ourselves, encouraging unlawful trade. We have had no communication with any foreign government upon

---

[1] See note at end of this chapter (p. 65) on the condition of England under Protection.

the subject of these reductions. We cannot promise that France will immediately make a corresponding reduction in her tariff. I cannot promise that Russia will prove her gratitude to us for our reduction of duty on her tallow by any diminution of her duties. You may, therefore, say, in opposition to the present plan, what is this superfluous liberality, that you are going to do away with all these duties, and yet you expect nothing in return? I may, perhaps, be told that many foreign countries, since the former relaxation of duties on our part—and that would be perfectly consistent with the fact—foreign countries which have benefited by our relaxation, have not followed our example, nay, have not only not followed our example, but have actually applied to the importation of British goods higher rates of duties than formerly. I quite admit it. I give you all the benefit of that argument. I rely upon the fact as conclusive proof of the policy of the course we are pursuing. It is a fact that other countries have not followed our example, and have levied higher duties in some cases upon our goods. But what has been the result upon the amount of your exports? You have defied the regulations of those countries. Your export trade is greatly increased."

On July 6th, 1849, with reference to Mr. Disraeli's assumption, "that you cannot fight hostile tariffs with free imports," Sir R. Peel said :—

"I so totally dissent from that assumption that I maintain that the best way to compete with hostile tariffs is to encourage free imports. So far from thinking the principle of Protection a salutary principle, I maintain that the more widely you extend it, the greater the injury you will inflict on the national wealth, and the more you will cripple the national industry.

* * * * * *

"To re establish duties upon the import of foreign produce to be regulated by the principle of reciprocity, would be accompanied with insuperable difficulties. You have, in my opinion, no alternative but to maintain that degree of Free Trade you have established, and gradually to extend it so far as considerations of revenue will permit."

Finally, if further evidence be wanted, there is this statement from a letter from Mr. John Bright to the writer, dated shortly before his death :—

"I never," he says, "held the opinion that the reform of the tariff would be at once followed by a like change of policy in other countries. If Mr. Cobden expressed such an opinion, of which I have no recollection, I can only say that he had more faith in the common sense of other nations than I had."[1]

---

[1] The whole of the letter is worth publishing—

One Ash, Rochdale.
December 10th, 1887.

MY DEAR SIR,—I never held the opinion that the reform of the tariff would be at once followed by a like change of policy in other countries. If Mr. Cobden expressed such an opinion, of which I have no recollection, I can only say that he had more faith in the common sense of other nations than I had. As to the changes of circumstances since the year 1846, it is every way in our favour, for we have had forty years of Free Trade, and all the facts are wonderfully on our side. Further, I would assert without fear of error, that our adherence to our Free Trade policy is the more necessary and advantageous to us seeing that other countries have not yet followed our example. Surely, if other nations injure us by their high duties, it would be no compensation to us to put difficulties in the way of our buying what we want. It would be better if we were free to buy and to sell, but to make it difficult to buy by high duties in our tariff, because foreign tariff makes it difficult to sell, seems to me an idea that can only be entertained by men who are totally unable to reason.

The high tariffs of European countries are in great part the result of the great armaments of those countries. The tariff of the United States is breaking down, and must break down. If the Protectionists of America could persuade or permit the Government to spend annually twenty millions sterling on a great army, and a great navy, their tariff might be sustained, but that being impossible, the tariff must be reformed, and some approach will be made in the direction of Free Trade. As to your Colonies, their true interest is in the adoption of the Free Trade policy. In our individual life every man is a Free Trader. He buys as cheaply as he can, and sells at the best price he can get. Why should not multitudes of men do the same?

In America there are some forty States, and there is no tariff between these States — there is a perfect Free Trade between them—why should not the same

The matter might fairly rest here.[1] But the disappointment of Mr. Cobden's hopes is such a constant source of satisfaction of Protectionists, and has so disturbed the minds of many of the faithful, that it will not be waste of time to pursue the investigation further, and, if possible, discover the sources of Mr. Cobden's error. Those who regard the reputation of its great men as the most precious heritage of the English-speaking race will be the less averse to this inquiry because it will be incidentally the means of vindicating the sagacity of Mr. Cobden from many undeserved reproaches.

Let us proceed, therefore, to discuss the causes of that Protectionist revival upon the Continent of Europe which is supposed by some to be a proof of the foolishness of Free Trade anticipations.

SECTION II.—THE CONTINENT OF EUROPE.

§ 1. The full significance of the Protectionist revival on the Continent of Europe cannot be understood without some reference to the circumstances under which Great Britain entered on her Free Trade policy. How came Mr. Cobden, who was the most sagacious of men, to indulge in his sanguine hopes, and why were they not fulfilled? Few subjects of historical inquiry better repay investigation.

---

freedom prevail between the States and Canada, and between both and the United Kingdom? And why not between your Australian Colonies and between them and this, their Mother Country?

Free Trade is the policy of wisdom and peace between nations.

I am, Sir, yours faithfully,

JOHN BRIGHT.

To the Hon. B. R. Wise, Sydney.

[1] Sir T. Farrer in his "Free Trade v. Fair Trade," refers to the following further passages from the speeches of Free Trade leaders:—

Hansard, vol. 68 of 1843.
,, vol. 73 of 1844.
,, vol. 106 of 1849.

During the years of the Free Trade agitation and triumph in Great Britain the European world was in a dream of universal peace. There had been no great war since the conclusion of the second Treaty of Paris in 1815; while the revolutionary explosion of 1848 only seemed to most onlookers to have ended those dynastic struggles which had been the principal cause of war for many centuries. It was not then perceived that the growing force of nationalism would prove even more fruitful than the jealousies and intrigues of rival potentates in creating international hostilities. The peaceful enthusiasm culminated in the International Exhibition of 1851, when people for the first time realised the enormous strides which Europe had made in its industrial progress since the Napoleonic wars. The praises of industry and commerce were in everybody's mouth: and it was thought incredible that, after so plain a proof of the paramount interest which the toiling masses have in the preservation of peace, their rulers would ever again be able to induce men to record their votes in favour of aggressive war. Commerce was thus naturally regarded as the handmaid of peace, teaching nations to know each other better, and breaking down the prejudices which the interests of selfish rulers had sedulously fostered. The interests of the people were to overcome the ambition of princes, and all the nations of the world were to be joined together by the golden tie of peaceful trade.

§ 2. Nor were these only the idle dreams of a few enthusiasts. Men most competent to judge saw no reason for believing that the frequent and rapid intercourse between people of foreign countries, which railways and steamships were rendering possible, could have any other result than that of destroying international enmities, and creating a common commercial interest in the continuance of peace. Even Mr. Cobden, as we have seen, yielded to the influences of his time, and ventured on that prophecy which, in all his copious forecasts of the commercial future, is the only one that can be quoted to his discredit, and which is always quoted by Protectionists who know nothing else of all that Mr. Cobden wrote or spoke. Everything else which he anticipated as a result of Free Trade has been realised in the manner and by the means which he foretold. Surely, if he had been a mere quack, this could never have happened? Correct judgments upon politics and accurate forecasts of the course of commerce during many years must be something more than lucky guesses.[1] If the matter in controversy were anything else except Protection and Free Trade, we should not hesitate to say that Cobden's accurate prognostications of the future arose from his firm grasp of a principle which rested upon sound knowledge, and was in accord with the deepest sentiments of human nature. The controversy being as it is, we will merely note the fact of his general accuracy, and, admitting that he was wrong in one instance, proceed to examine into the causes of his error. Perhaps at the end of such an inquiry it may be seen that it is sometimes better to be wrong with Cobden than to be right with his critics.

§ 3. The face of the scene suddenly changed. The thirty-eight years of peace came to an end, and the Crimean War and the growth of the new spirit of nationalism destroyed for a time all hopes of its return.

The Crimean War was followed by the American War, the Danish War, the Austrian War, the French War, the Turkish War, and no one can say at what time another war may not be added to this gloomy list. Profoundly peaceful Europe was thus suddenly changed into an armed camp; and contemporaneously with this, the Europe which was advancing

---

[1] If the famous saying, that a copy of the *Times* was of more value than the whole of Thucydides, is to be taken literally, it is an error of literary and not of political judgment.

towards Free Trade has gone back towards Protection. The weapons of commercial warfare have been called to the assistance of national armies.

§ 4. In the year 1879 a return was moved for in the English House of Commons, by Lord Sandon, of the changes which had been made by foreign nations in their tariffs since the year 1850. It was perhaps expected that this return would prove to demonstration the absurdity of Mr. Cobden's expectation and the rapid progress of Protection.

In fact, it proved the opposite.

The information collected showed beyond a doubt that, until the results of the Franco-Prussian War began to be felt in their full stress, there had been a steady progress towards Free Trade on the part of almost all civilised nations.

From 1850 to 1874 the alterations in the tariffs of Russia, Germany, France, Italy, Holland, Belgium, Sweden and Norway, Austria, Spain, and Portugal, had been steadily in the direction of Free Trade.

It was about the year 1874 that Europe entered into the full enjoyment of the legacy of evil left behind by the war of 1870. In that year the prodigious armaments of European countries seemed to have reached a limit; yet still they increased, and still it was necessary to raise taxes for their support. Direct taxation was resorted to in many forms; and when the wealthy classes came to the conclusion that this means of raising revenue was exhausted, resort was had to the Customs House.

In this way the progress towards Free Trade has been checked, and been perhaps delayed for two generations. Military rulers cannot be expected to have sympathy with freedom in any form: while the vested interests which have grown up under the Protection thus incidentally conferred form another force to bar the path of commercial liberty. Yet even now the peaceful, liberal, and progressive nations—such as

Holland, Switzerland, Belgium, Norway, Italy, and Denmark —are also nations which incline towards Free Trade.[1]

§ 5. It is no part of this treatise to inquire how far the rulers of these different countries were justified, from their own points of view, in fighting their neighbours by means of retaliatory duties, or in selecting the Customs House as an easy means of raising revenue for a wasteful expenditure. It is only intended to draw attention to the reasons which falsified the sanguine expectations of some of the early Free Traders. It would no doubt have been a gain to Mr. Cobden's reputation if he had foreseen the tremendous change which was about to take place in international relations. But that he failed to do so, and that, in consequence, some of his hopes were disappointed, is no reflection on the soundness of his views, nor any reason for depreciating the wisdom of his policy.

[1] The Protective reaction on the Continent has also been assisted by the changed conditions of agricultural production. The development of the American, Australian, and Indian wheat fields not only shut the farmers of Eastern and Central Europe out of the English market, of which they had had possession since the Peace of 1815, but also exposed all European agriculturists to a new and fierce competition, to which they have been slow to adapt themselves. Simultaneously with the development of these new sources of production, came the cheapening in the cost of transportation both by sea and land, which is perhaps the most notable industrial phenomenon of the present century. The Protective duties imposed since 1873 in France, Germany, Austria, and Italy, are in part due to an attempt to stave off or mitigate the effects of these great changes. The process is thus described by M. Alexandre Peer in an article on the fiscal situation in the February number of "La Revue d'Economie Politique" of the year 1891 :—" Alors commença la stagnation sur le Continent. À l'est, les produits russes et roumains exerçaient une pression ; a l'ouest, les marchés étaient en partie fermés et en partie occupés par les produits meilleur marché d'outre-mer. L'Europe Centrale commença à se sentir mal à l'aise : l'Empire d'Allemagne, repoussé par l'Angleterre, interdit les transports de l'Autriche-Hongrie, et l'Autriche-Hongrie, de son côté, ferma ses frontières à la Russie et à la Roumanie ; il s'ensuivit un mouvement pareil à celui que provoque l'arrêt subit d'un train, quand les wagons sont successivement un à un refoulés en arrière." Professor Taussig, on p. 326 of the first volume of the *Economic Journal*, has some suggestive remarks upon these occurrences, which need not, however, be referred to at greater length in the present connection.

[Pt. I., Ch iv., § 5.]

The tariff changes of the Continental States since 1850 have also another bearing on the fiscal controversy. They show that the example of these States is of little or no value to Australasia or America. The inclination of mankind towards war must, no doubt, be taken into account by politicians; but the fact that nations when disposed towards war adopt Protective tariffs is no reason why peaceful nations such as the Australian Colonies should do the same. When a Protectionist orator in Sydney or Melbourne proclaims, in his large and disdainful way, that nine-tenths of the civilised world agree with him,[1] we may fairly remind him that nine-tenths of the civilised world is also in favour of the conscription. And if he should reply that that coincidence has nothing to do with his argument, we may call in the aid of Lord Sandon's return,[2] and point out the close connection which exists in Europe between the growth of Protection and the advance of militarism.

Protection is, in fact, the natural weapon of military rulers. It is a system which flourishes in proportion to the strength of militarism, and everywhere decreases in favour as a people becomes freer and more peaceful. Such is the system which, in the name of "Liberalism," certain politicians introduced into Victoria.[3] But the growth of Protection in that Colony is a subject for another chapter. Let us first, however, treat of the United States.

[1] The Free Trade minority is always overlooked in these ingenious calculations.

[2] This is dealt with in detail by Sir T. Farrer in his "Free Trade *v.* Fair Trade."

[3] The Protectionists in Victoria call themselves "Liberals." In New South Wales, as in Canada, the nomenclature of parties is more appropriate and the Liberals are the advocates of industrial freedom. It would be strange indeed if the party which fought for civil and religious freedom should try to put fetters upon freedom of industry.

SECTION III.—THE UNITED STATES.[1]

§ 1. One of the most instructive economic works which yet remain to be written is an adequate history of the Protective movement in the United States. The difficulties of such a work are enormous. The tariffs, as enacted from time to time, have always been extraordinarily complex; while the large powers of construing Acts of Congress conferred upon the Customs Boards have still further increased the complexity of legislation. The consequence is, that an adequate treatment of the subject would not only require a knowledge of the processes of manufacture in all branches—which can hardly be possessed by any individual, since no one is acquainted with the secrets of every trade—but would also involve an accurate consideration of the fluctuations in prices, the conditions of trade, and the course of industrial development during the last hundred years ; and even if the initial difficulty were overcome of understanding the precise nature of tariff legislation, the obscure problem of tracing its effects would still present itself for a solution. The tariff in the United States has seldom, if ever, worked alone, but other influences have almost always obscured its operation. Currency delusions, war, the development of the interior, immigration, improvement in the means of locomotion, have all, at one time or another, rendered the precise effect of a tariff difficult to trace, either by prejudicing its working when it has been low, or hiding its injurious influence when it has been high. The one fact which stands out plainly from this intricate confusion is, that in all periods of American history high tariffs have resulted from a morbid condition of national affairs.

§ 2. No one, for instance, could contend that the circumstances

---

[1] For the contents of this section the writer is largely indebted to Professor Sumner's " Lectures on the History of Protection in the United States," and to Professor Taussig's " Tariff History of the United States," two admirable works which are too little known in England and Australia.

[Pt. I., Ch. iv., Sec. III., § 2.]

which led to the passing of the first Tariff Act of 1789 have any application to the present time. That measure had two objects—the first was to raise a Federal revenue from the only source then open to the Federal Government; the second was to re-establish the natural industries of the United States, and to restore them to the same position which they would have held if they had not been crushed for many years by the protective legislation of Great Britain. The revolt of the American Colonies was very largely a revolt against Protection. It was an effort on the part of the Americans to secure the benefits of a larger commerce. The policy of the British Government had been to cramp American trade, and thwart the development of American industry. Bancroft, the great American historian, says: " American independence, like the great rivers of the country, had many sources, but the headspring that coloured all the stream was the British Navigation Act. . . . This odious measure provided that no commodities whatever, being the growth, product, or manufacture of Asia, Africa, or America, should be imported into England or her Colonies except in ships belonging to English subjects, and of which the master and the greater part of the crew were also English. Subsequently, the ordinance was re-enacted with additional clauses, virtually excluding foreign ships from American harbours, and sacrificing to English monopoly the natural rights of the Colonies."

Nor were the efforts of the English Protectionists directed only against external commerce. Their despotic regulations were equally directed towards the suppression of manufactures and the destruction of internal trade.

" In 1699 the British Parliament prohibited the Colonies from exporting wool, jam, or woollen fabrics, and from carrying them coastwise from one Colony and place to another. In 1719 Parliament declared that the erection of manufactories in the Colonies tended to lessen their dependence on the Mother Country; and the English manufacturers memorialised

Parliament that the Colonies were carrying on trade and erecting manufactories, with a view to obtaining legislation to arrest it. In 1731 the Board of Trade were instructed to inquire as to the Colonial laws made to encourage manufactures, as to manufactories set up, and as to trade carried on in the Colonies, and to report thereon. In 1732 they reported that Massachusetts had passed a law to encourage manufactures; that the people of New York, Connecticut, Rhode Island, and Maryland had fallen into the manufacture of woollen and linen for the use of their own families, and of flax and hemp into coarse bags and halters, all of which interfered with the profits of the British merchants. The Board recommended that the minds of the people of those Colonies should be immediately diverted, and a stop be put to it, or the practice would be extended. The same year Parliament prohibited the exportation of hats from the Colonies, and trading in them from one Colony to another by ships, carts, or horses. No hatter should set up in business who had not served seven years, nor have more than two apprentices; and no black person should work at the trade. Iron mills for slitting and rolling, and plating-forges, were prohibited under a penalty of £500. This system of prohibition and restriction continued to increase till the Colonies rebelled, and declared independence in 1776."

As might have been expected after such a history, the first effort of the independent States was to retaliate upon Great Britain by cutting off the trade which she had endeavoured to preserve by such injurious measures.

§ 3. The first Tariff Act was passed in 1789. The preamble of this Act limited the duration of the Protective duties to seven years, that being the time after which, according to the Protectionists of that day, the infant industries would be able to stand alone. Before the seven years expired, the Act had been altered many times, and every alteration was in the direction of higher duties; while, it is almost needless to say, the infants of that day continue to be infants still. After one hundred years of Protection, not one of them can walk alone. In spite, however, of the alterations in the original Act, the tariff remained for twenty years a revenue measure. The duties were in all cases moderate, ranging from five per cent. *ad valorem* to fifteen per cent. on articles of luxury, and the ostensible ground for such increases as were made was the necessity for raising a larger revenue.

The first great change occurred in 1808, when, as Professor Taussig says, "the complications with England and France led to a series of measures which mark a turning-point in the industrial history of the country." The Berlin and Milan Decrees, the English Orders-in-Council, the Embargo, the Non-Intercourse Act (1809), practically destroyed all foreign commerce. War with England followed in 1812. Then, as always, tariffs provoked war, and war in its turn provoked still higher tariffs. The first serious agitation in favour of Protection dates, in the opinion of Professor Taussig—who has made a more careful study of the question than any other writer—from the period of 1808-15, when measures of overt hostilities terminating in open war, fanned that flame of discord and suspicion in which the fetters of a tariff are always forged. The conclusion of peace led to a slight reduction in duties; but in 1816 the manufacturers' agitation was successful, and duties of twenty-five per cent. were imposed upon iron, wool, cotton, and other articles of domestic manufacture.

The next alteration of the tariff occurred in 1824, and was due, as has often been the case, to the pressure of a financial crisis. The termination of the Continental wars caused commercial unsettlement throughout the civilised world, so that it was many years before trade flowed again in its natural channels. The period of transition from war to peace was necessarily attended with much distress. This was aggravated in America by an excessive issue of paper money, until a crash occurred in 1819, from which the country did not recover for four years.

During that period the Protectionists were active. Periods of national distress are always the opportunity of financial quacks. Defeated only by the vote of one State in 1820, they obtained a high tariff in 1824, which they again increased in 1828, being aided in the latter undertaking by the English crisis of 1825–26.[1] In the tariff of 1828 the Protective movement reached its highest point before the Civil War. The measures which followed in 1832 and 1833—the year of Clay's compromise tariff—moderated the peculiarly offensive provisions of the Act of 1828, and provided for the gradual reduction of duties to a uniform rate of twenty per cent. by the year 1842. In that year, however, the tariff, instead of being reduced, was again raised. Again we can trace in this fresh instalment of Protection the influence of currency delusions. The crisis of 1837 is described by the Hon. Hugh McCulloch, who was Secretary to the Treasury in three Administrations, as the most severe ever experienced in the United States, both in its immediate and its after-consequences. Every bank in America, except the Chemical Bank of New York, suspended specie payments, and the country did not recover from the disaster until 1843. The collapse was due, said Mr. McCulloch, in his first report to Congress, as was the great expansion of 1835 and 1836, which immediately preceded it, to "excessive bank circulation and discounts, and an abuse of the credit system, stimulated in the first place by Government deposits with the State Banks, and swelled by currency and credits until, under the wild spirit of speculation which invaded the country, labour and production decreased to such an extent that the country which should have been the great food-producing country of the world became an importer of bread-stuffs."[2] The Act of

---

[1] A graphic description of this crisis, which was largely due to wild speculation in South America, and was one of the fiercest ever experienced, is contained in Martineau's "History of the Peace," book ii., chapter viii.

[2] See "Men and Measures of Half a Century," by Hugh McCulloch (Sampson Low & Co., London, 1888), a work of extreme interest, which throws many side-lights upon economic questions.

1842 continued in force for ten years, when it was superseded by the Act of 1846, which greatly lowered the range of duties. In 1857 duties were again reduced, and remained low until the Morrill Tariff of 1861. This was passed in 1859–60, when Congress was once more under the influence of the feelings inspired by a commercial crisis. This had occurred in 1857 as a consequence of similar causes to that which had produced the crisis of 1837—namely, the unhealthy extension of various forms of credit. The Morrill Tariff, however, made only slight increases in existing duties, and professed to make the increases even less than they were. Its chief effect, according to Professor Taussig, was to alter the mode of collection. Hardly had this tariff come into operation when the Civil War began. From that moment dates the orgie of Protectionists. The exigencies of the war were everywhere seized upon as an excuse for the foundation of tariff monopolies; and the history of tariff legislation since that date is one of the most disgraceful examples ever offered to the world of the methods by which organised wealth is able to corrupt a legislative body. The framing of a tariff has been aptly described as a game of grab, in which every interest tries to steal some public money, and in which one robber assists another in return for the permission to do more plundering on his own account. The world, perhaps, has never afforded a more striking instance of the inherent evils of a Protective system than is offered by the debasement of American politics, and the unhappy condition of the industrial classes during the last five-and-twenty years. Fortunately, the writing on the wall is plain. The system of Protection cannot last for many years, now that the adoption of the Australian ballot system has restored freedom of voting to the mass of American citizens.

§ 4. It would unduly protract this inquiry if any attempt were made to investigate the connection between the fluctuating tariff legislation of the United States and the general prosperity of the country. Both Free Traders and Protectionists have asserted that such a connection exists; and each has claimed, with much parade of facts, that the tariff which they favour has produced prosperity, and that depressions have been due to changes in an opposite direction. Professor Taussig, in his chapter on "The Tariff, 1830—1860," has summarised all that can be said upon this point by either side with an impartiality which is as rare in tariff controversies as it is commendable. He concludes his remarks as follows :—

"In truth, there has been a great deal of loose talk about tariffs and crises. Whenever there has been a crisis, the Free Traders or Protectionists, as the case may be, have been tempted to use it as a means for overthrowing the system they opposed. . . . But the effect of tariffs cannot be traced by any such rough-and-ready method. The tariff system of a country is but one of many factors entering into its general prosperity. Its influence, good or bad, may be strengthened or may be counteracted by other causes; while it is exceedingly difficult, generally impossible, to trace its separate effect. Least of all can its influence be traced in those variations of outward prosperity and depression which are marked by 'good times' and crises. A Protective tariff may sometimes strengthen other causes which are bringing on a commercial crisis. Some such effect is very likely traceable to the tariff in the years before the crisis of 1873. It may sometimes be the occasion of a revival of activity, when the other conditions are already favourable to such a revival. This may have been the case in 1843. But these are only incidental effects, and lie quite outside the real problem as to the results of Protection. As a rule, the tariff system of a country operates neither to cause nor to prevent crises. They are the results of conditions of exchange and production on which it can exercise no great or permanent influence. . . . There is no way of eliminating the other factors and determining how much can be ascribed to the tariff alone." [1]

§ 5. These conditions prevent the example of America from being of much value to other countries. The conditions of the United States, both physical and political, are unique. In no other country in the world is there an extent of territory so great or of such varied resources; and over no other portion of the globe of equal extent is trade so perfectly untrammeled. When Protectionists point to American prosperity as a consequence of Protection, they forget that no other country offers such an example of the wisdom of Free Trade. Over an area of 3,547,390 square miles there is no Customs House, and goods can pass as freely from New York to San Francisco, as they can from Birmingham to London. The rapid development of new countries, the growth of arts, the enormous influx of immigrants, have all combined to obscure the influences of the American tariff. No other country is so well adapted both by nature and art to endure the burdens of high taxation. But such a fact gives little warrant for the assertion that high taxation is a universal good. America is a country by itself, whose conditions are so peculiar, and whose growth has been so rapid, that it affords but little instruction to tariff disputants in other lands. All that this chapter has endeavoured to make plain is, that in America, as in Europe, high tariffs have originated in an unhealthy condition of the body politic. Sometimes this condition is the result of war, sometimes of speculation, sometimes of delusions about currency; but whenever it exists, from any cause, Protection flourishes. (Quack doctors have no chance when the patient is in health.[2]

---

[1] "Tariff History of the United States," Taussig, pp. 121, 122. (G. P. Putnam's Sons, New York and London, 1888.)

[2] Colonel Grosvenor's "Does Protection Protect?" contains a mass of information on this subject. The tracts of the Tariff Reform League and

SECTION IV.—THE BRITISH COLONIES.

§ 1. WHILE the causes which have contributed to the revival of Protection in Europe and the United States have not been such as to give rise to permanent anxiety for the ultimate success of Free Trade, no candid supporter of that policy can view without disquietude the fiscal legislation of the British Colonies.

Colonial tariffs have had two distinguishing characteristics—in having been adopted more deliberately for the sake of Protection than has been the case elsewhere, and in being the direct result of those misapprehensions and mistakes which have been noticed in an earlier chapter as inducing a mistrust of Free Trade among the working classes.

This has been especially the case in the Colony of Victoria. The first restrictive tariff in Victoria was passed in 1865. Since that date it has been altered four times—without counting unimportant modifications—namely, in 1870, 1872, 1880, and 1889. On each occasion the scale of duties has been raised and their scope widened, until duties averaging 30 per cent. *ad valorem* are now levied on nearly a thousand

---

the " Economic Monographs," issued by G. P. Putnam's Sons, are also well worthy of attention.

Of the authors who have tried to deal with this great subject, Professor Taussig, and Professor Sumner of Yale, appear to have been the most successful. Professor Taussig, in his "Tariff History," gives an admirable survey of the course of fiscal legislation; while Professor Sumner, in his "Lectures on the History of Protection," aims rather at illustrating the effects of the various tariffs upon the condition of the country. In addition to these principal works, much information is contained in the tracts of the Tariff Reform League. The reports presented by Mr. Secretary McCulloch during his terms of office at the Treasury are also very valuable in showing the intimate connection which exists between Protection and currency delusions.

It would lie outside the scope of the present work to enter upon any detailed inquiry into the causes or effects of Protection in the United States. All that is desirable in the present connection is to indicate the special nature of the crises which in America, as in Europe, have led to an apparent and (as events will prove) a temporary abandonment of the principle of industrial freedom.

articles of commerce. The tariff occupies twenty-five pages of close print; and no visitor can pass from Sydney to Melbourne —although these cities are as closely related by ties of business and friendship as Liverpool is to Manchester, or Boston to New York—without being subjected to a tiresome delay of thirty minutes while his person is inspected by detectives and his luggage searched as if he were a suspected thief. Such is commerce as it is understood in Victoria, and this is the way in which Protectionists testify to their belief in the unity of Australasia.

§ 2. Unfortunately for the interests of Free Trade, Victoria was the foremost Colony in the Australasian group at the time when she entered upon her reactionary policy. She then held the lead in population, wealth, trade, commerce, shipping, manufactures, agriculture; and although she has for several years lost her position of supremacy in all these signs of material progress, except agriculture, to the Free Trade Colony of New South Wales[1] she exercised in 1865 a dominating influence throughout Australia. The effect of this extended even into New South Wales, so that shrewd observers like Sir Charles Dilke, visiting the Mother Colony in 1866, could publish the opinion that "the pastoral tenants of the Crown stood alone in their support of Free Trade."[2] It is a striking instance of the difficulty which must beset even experienced publicists in attempting to catch the drift of foreign opinion that, within twelve months of this sentence being penned, one of the strongest Colonial Ministries that ever existed—that under the leadership of Sir James Martin—was so hopelessly beaten at the polls upon the straight issue of Protection that the Protectionists did not exist again as a party in New South Wales until 1886. In spite of this reversal of his expectations, Sir Charles Dilke has had the

[1] See Appendix No. III.
[2] "Greater Britain," First Edition, vol. ii., p. 59 (London, 1868).

courage, in the last edition of his work, published in 1890, to repeat his gloomy forecast of the prospects of Free Trade in New South Wales in almost the same language which he used in 1866.[1] A stopped clock must point to the right hour at least once in a day; but it has yet to be seen whether, in spite of an accidental victory, the permanent triumph of Protection in New South Wales is not even farther off from 1890 than 1890 was from 1866.

The younger Colonies of South Australia and New Zealand were necessarily more exposed than New South Wales to the influence of Victorian opinion. Not only were they largely developed by Victorian capital, but many of their press-men and politicians received their earliest training in the Protectionist struggles of the Southern Colony. The consequence was that both in South Australia, Queensland, and New Zealand, there was a steady drift of opinion in favour of Victorian views. At the same time the movement towards Protection was assisted by the totally different feeling of antagonism to Victoria. The policy of extreme provincialism which that Colony has pursued, not only in her Customs tariff, but in other departments of administration, naturally aroused a bitterness of feeling in the neighbouring Colonies, which gave rise in South Australia and Queensland to an

[1] The portion of Sir Charles Dilke's book which deals with New South Wales is full of strange errors, both in the estimate of persons and of policies. He appears to have written the Australian portion of his work entirely under Victorian influences, and to have looked at everything through Protectionist spectacles. It is a great pity that a work which contains so much valuable matter, and gives so admirable a survey of the institutions and development of the English dominions, should be so unreliable when it treats of the progress and opinions of the Free Trade Colony of New South Wales. It is natural that Protectionists should strive, by all means in their power, to decry the progress of a Free Trade country, and to conceal the fact of its supremacy; but it is surprising that an English statesman should not have informed himself more accurately of the reasons which have induced New South Wales, alone of the Australian Colonies, to adhere to a policy of commercial freedom. Sir Charles Dilke, however, appears in all parts of his work to hold a brief for Protection.

irresistible demand for retaliation. New South Wales up to the present time has been sufficiently powerful to treat the jealousies of her southern neighbour with a good-humoured indifference; but even in New South Wales the desire to retaliate upon Victoria is the strongest element in the Protectionist cause.[1] This is especially the case among the farmers.

§ 3. The friends of Victoria were naturally unable to resist this legitimate application of their favourite doctrines; and thus, by a strange irony of fate, Victoria has been confined on every side, except that bordering upon New South Wales, by fetters of her own forging. The limits thus placed upon her trade have reduced her to a condition of grave financial difficulty. Her exports have failed for many years past to keep pace with the increase of population. In the meantime her debts have been increasing by leaps and bounds. She has borrowed twenty millions of pounds upon her public credit during the last ten years; while the increase of her private indebtedness during the same period has been enormous.[2] Naturally the expenditure of so much capital in a compact community of less than a million souls, produced that boom of which Sir Charles Dilke has written in such glowing terms. The boom, however, has ended as booms will; and at the time of writing (1890) the Colony of Victoria, which, according to Protectionists, is the paradise of working men, is suffering from a protracted agony of hard times. The Protectionist Ministry proposes the familiar remedy of more borrowing. Railways are to be made with English money at a cost of fourteen millions! Should this proposal be adopted, and should England be inclined to lend the money, the crash may be postponed. But in the mean-

[1] Thus all the constituencies along the border return Protectionist members.
[2] *See* Appendix.

time, unless the experiment of irrigation succeeds beyond the most sanguine expectations in giving the Colony new articles of export, or unless her hot-house manufactures can expand into new commercial channels, the necessary payments of interest to her foreign creditors will form every year an increasing proportion of the total value of her exports. It is no wonder that Victorian Protectionists have so suddenly become converted to the merits of Federation!

§ 4. The desire to retaliate upon a Protectionist neighbour which has stimulated the Protective movement in Australia, has operated in the same direction in the case of Canada. Although the Canadian tariff was adopted mainly as a revenue measure, the commercial tactics of the manufacturers of the United States undoubtedly affected the result. Secure within their own market, it was a common practice of the New England and Pennsylvania manufacturers to treat Canada as a useful outlet for surplus stock. This was sold at any price that would secure a buyer, until Canadian manufacturers complained that they could find no market for their goods in the face of competition of this nature. The Canadian people were appealed to by their pride not to allow their country to be the dumping-ground of American rubbish, but to establish for themselves a firm and national system of trade and manufacture. How far the attempt to do this by means of Protection has proved to be successful is an inquiry that would lie outside the province of this work. It is enough to state that while Canadian trade has developed since the tariff of 1879 in some directions, the signs of progress in others are by no means satisfactory.[1] A full examination, however, into Canadian progress under Protection would require a detailed investigation of many complicated figures, the value of which would diminish as each year added new facts and fresh

[1] See extract in note at end of this section from "The Tariff on Trial," by Sir Richard Cartwright (*The North American Review*, May, 1890).

statistics to Canadian history. All that is desired in the present connection is to indicate the causes which have led to the adoption of Protection, and not to estimate the results of the system.

§ 5. But, although retaliation was a powerful motive in inducing the acceptance of the Canadian tariff, it is doubtful whether the measure was not finally accepted rather for revenue than for fiscal reasons. It is certain that the leaders of both political parties evaded a contest upon the strictly fiscal issue. Thus the Hon. Edward Blake, leader of the Liberal or low-tariff party, used the following words in his electoral manifesto in 1882:—" Our adversaries wish to present to you an issue as between the present tariff and absolute Free Trade. That is not the true issue. Free Trade is, as I have repeatedly explained, for us impossible; and the issue is, whether the present tariff is perfect, or defective and unjust."

Similar views were expressed in 1877 by Mr. Mackenzie, then the leader of the so-called Free Trade party:—" My honourable friend (Sir J. Macdonald) has stated very correctly the position I have taken up—that is, that we have not really the questions of Protection and Free Trade as political principles of action to define or expose in this country."

Similar extracts might be made from the speeches and writings of other Canadian politicians; but enough has been quoted to show that the Canadian tariff was regarded by many of its friends and opponents as an exceptional piece of legislation, demanded by the circumstances of the country, and was not a deliberate rejection of the principles of Free Trade. Without entering into details, which would lie outside the scope of this work, it is enough to say that the supposed exceptional circumstances which justified the tariff were those physical and national characteristics which were thought to render impossible any form of direct taxation.

§ 6. The same difficulty of obtaining revenue without resorting to the Customs House has been felt very strongly in Australia. Direct taxation must always be a matter of difficulty in young and sparsely settled countries. If land is taxed, the cry is raised that the development of the country is being retarded; if realised wealth is taxed, the Government is denounced for discouraging the investment of foreign capital. And whether the taxes are levied on land or personalty, it must always be difficult in a young country, where local and personal feeling runs so high, either in friendship or enmity, to obtain satisfactory assessments without incurring the charge of favouritism or needlessly exposing private affairs. The consequence is that every Government, whatever may be its fiscal creed, is tempted to raise taxes by the easy method of the Customs House. Directly this is attempted the "interests" combine; and, sometimes before the country has had time to realise what is being done, and contrary to the intention of the Ministry, a Protective tax is sneaked into the tariff. One tax of this kind soon leads to another, until the country finds itself committed to a Protective policy.

This explains why the Free Trade party in the Australian Colonies is everywhere the party of economy. The aim of Protectionists is to increase public expenditure beyond the annual revenue, in the assurance that the difficulty of raising fresh taxation by any other means, except through the Customs House, will be so great as to necessitate a revision of the tariff. They then anticipate a general scramble, in which the highly organised manufacturers' rings will be able to obtain an ample share of public money. The Protectionists have hitherto been assisted in this object by the Colonial Upper Houses, which give the wealthy land-owning class a degree of influence far greater than that which is possessed by the same classes in communities whose form of government is outwardly less democratic. Thus, the Upper House in New South Wales, although it contains a large majority of Free Traders, has consistently thrown out every measure to impose direct taxation. The fiscal struggle in New South Wales has thus entered on a new phase; it has become a struggle of the masses against the classes, and the men of wealth are being driven slowly but surely into the camp of the Protectionists.

§ 7. This has not always been the case in the course of this controversy. In Victoria, indeed, the position of parties in the early days of the struggle was quite the opposite. The landowners and men of wealth were the Free Traders, the masses were Protectionists.

This was not owing to any special characteristics of either of the rival doctrines, but to the political accidents of the time. The real struggle in Victoria in 1865-6 was not between Free Traders and Protectionists, but between the landowners and the people.

It happened that the landowners were closely connected, both socially and by their financial relations, with the banking corporations and the mercantile classes, and thus the merchants and the banks were drawn into the struggle in self-defence. But primarily the movement was against landowners and not against merchants. As the contest continued, the issue of Protection was put more plainly forward, both in order to attract the manufacturing classes to the popular side, and because the anti-popular party happened to hold Free Trade views. The feelings generated in this bitter struggle have spread from Victoria to the rest of Australia, and the Protectionist party in that continent endeavours by every means in its power to associate Free Traders with Conservatism.

In truth, however, except in New South Wales, where parties are divided by their fiscal opinions, and where Free Traders are the democratic and popular party, there has been no straight fight upon the simple issue of Protection and Free Trade. Protection has been adopted for a variety of differing and sometimes inconsistent reasons, among which positive hostility towards Free Trade has had but little influence.

In practice it matters, of course, very little with what object Protective duties are imposed—whether it is to maintain costly armies or to save property owners from bearing their share of the national taxes. But when the conduct of a nation in adopting Protection is quoted as an example, then the motives which induced it to take that step become of the utmost importance; because if the motives are such as might reasonably affect our minds, then the case of that country is in point for us; but if the motives are altogether exceptional and far removed from those which either do or ought to operate upon us, then the example is of no value, except in so far as it illustrates the working and effect of the policy in question. The issue, whether Protection or Free Trade should be adopted in any particular country, is not one that ought to be decided by counting heads. But when an appeal is made to the conduct of other nations, it is necessary to bear in mind the facts and circumstances by which they have been controlled.

As a result of our inquiry we see that there has been no deliberate rejection of Free Trade as a sound principle, but only an abandonment of its practice under the stress of great and exceptional difficulties. It has still to be proved whether the rulers of many of the now Protected countries would not have acted more wisely by adhering under all difficulties to the natural policy of allowing men to buy and sell wherever they please; and it has yet to be seen whether, in the crash of the first great civil commotion, these childish impediments to human intercourse will not tumble to the ground.

There are already many signs that the evils which arise from a disorganisation of industrial relations are the greatest in those countries which have strayed the farthest from the path of freedom.[1]

It is not, however, intended to investigate the working of

---

[1] Thus the report of the English Royal Commission on the Depression of Trade (*circ.* 1883-7) shows that the depression was greater in the Protected than in the Free Trade countries.

Protective tariffs in this treatise. The materials for such an investigation are very voluminous and of uncertain value; while the circumstances which have to be taken into account in drawing a comparison between the industrial conditions of several countries are so numerous and impalpable that no sound practical conclusion can be based on such an inquiry. There are indeed a few points in which comparisons can be drawn between Great Britain and the United States, and between the Colonies of New South Wales and Victoria; while if the comparison is limited to particular industries, other countries may be added to the list. But, for the most part, each country must stand by itself; and the question between the rival policies must be decided upon facts drawn from its own history, and conclusions based on its own conditions. It is generally waste of power and a cause of confusion to draw arguments from the circumstances of other countries for any other purpose than that of estimating with correctness the actual operation of a fiscal policy. A knowledge of the industrial conditions of other countries is more generally useful as a check upon rash inferences than as a guide for our own conduct.[1]

[1] *See* Appendix III.: Comparison between the Progress of Victoria and New South Wales since 1866.

NOTE I.

THE CONDITION OF ENGLAND UNDER PROTECTION.

(Extract from Martineau's "History of the Peace.")

In Carlisle the Committee of Inquiry reported that a fourth of the population was in a state bordering on starvation—actually certain to die of famine, unless relieved by extraordinary exertions. In the woollen districts of Wiltshire the allowance to the independent labourer was not two-thirds of the *minimum* in the workhouse; and the large existing population consumed only a fourth of the bread and meat required by the much smaller population of 1800. In Stockport more than half the master-spinners had failed before the close of 1842; dwelling-houses to the number of 3,000 were shut up; and the occupiers of many hundreds more were unable to pay rates at all. Five thousand persons were walking the streets in compulsory idleness; and the Burnley Guardians wrote to the Secretary of State that the distress was far beyond their management; so that a Government Commissioner and Government funds were sent down without delay. At a meeting at Manchester, where humble shopkeepers were the speakers, anecdotes were related which told more than declamation. Rent-collectors were afraid to meet their principals, as no money could be collected. Provision dealers were subject to incursions from a wolfish man prowling for food for his children, or from a half-frantic woman with her dying baby at her breast, or from parties of ten or a dozen desperate wretches who were levying contributions along the street. The linen-draper told how new clothes had become out of the question among his customers, and they bought only remnants and patches to mend the old ones. The baker was more and more surprised at the number of people who bought halfpennyworths of bread. A provision dealer used to throw away outside scraps of bacon; but now respectable customers of twenty years' standing bought them in pennyworths to moisten their potatoes. These shopkeepers contemplated nothing but ruin from the impoverished condition of their customers. While rates were increasing beyond all precedent, their trade was only one-half or one-third, or even one-tenth what it had been three years before.

* * * * * *

At Leeds the pauper stone-heap amounted to 150,000 tons; and the Guardians offered the paupers 6s. per week for doing nothing, rather than 7s. 6d. per week for stone-breaking. The millwrights and other trades were offering a premium on emigration, to induce their "hands" to go away. At Hinckley one-third of the inhabitants were paupers; more than a fifth of the houses stood empty; and there was not work enough in the place to employ properly one-third of the weavers. In Dorsetshire a man and his wife had for wages 2s. 6d. per week and three loaves; and the ablest labourers had 6s. or 7s.

* * * * * *

There were riots of nailers and miners at Dudley and Stourbridge, and tumult over the whole district, requiring the active services of the military. The rioters resisted a reduction of wages, and hustled some of the masters, as did other rioters in Wales, where a gentleman of property had a narrow escape with his life. In the Potteries a force of 6,000 malcontents, spread over an extent of seven miles, and occasionally committing violence on recusant masters or men, kept Staffordshire in alarm. Troops were encamped on the Pottery racecourse, and magistrates tried to conciliate and mediate, but with little effect. In Manchester the influx of malcontents became alarming in August, 1842. Mills were stopped, and in some the windows broken and machinery injured. The Riot Act was read four times in one day, and prisoners were taken by scores at once. A large attendance of military was necessary, as there were threats of tearing up the railings and cutting the gas-pipes. At one time all the chief towns in the manufacturing district seemed to be in the hands of the mob.

* * * * * *

Further and detailed information on the subject is to be found in Karl Marx's "Essay on Capital" and in Engel's "Condition of the Working Classes in 1844." The novels of "Sybil" and "Yeast" also give an insight into the true nature of the time.

Mr. Medley has collected some of the more striking facts in a leaflet which is published by the Cobden Club, and is here in part reprinted :—

"During these thirty years (1815-45) the state of the country was simply awful.

"At one time, one out of every eleven of the population was a pauper.

"Some idea of the state of things may be gained from the *facts* which follow :—

"In 1816, at Hinckley, Leicestershire, the Poor Rate was 52s. in the pound.

"In 1817, at Langdon, Dorsetshire, 409 out of 575 inhabitants were receiving relief; while in Ely three-fourths of the population were in the same plight.

"In 1819, 1820, and 1822, agriculture was in a state of universal distress, and petitions for relief were presented to Parliament.

"During the time these laws were in force, there were no fewer than five Parliamentary Committees to inquire into the cause of the distress.

"Farmers were ruined by thousands. One newspaper in Norwich advertised 120 sales of stock in one day.

"In 1829 the workhouses in some parts of the country were so crowded that at times four, five, or six people had to sleep in one bed.

"Sheffield had 20,000 and Leeds 30,000 people dependent on the rates.

"Whole families were reduced to live on bran. In Huddersfield 13,000 people were reduced to semi-starvation.

"In 1839-42, in Stockport, one-half the factories were closed ; 3,000 dwellings unoccupied ; artisans were breaking stones on the road ; the Poor Rate was 10s. in the pound ; and outside scraps of bacon were bought in pennyworths by respectable people to moisten their potatoes.

"At Leeds the pauper stone-heap amounted to 150,000 tons.

"In Dorsetshire a man and his wife had for wages 2s. 6d. a week and their house, and the ablest labourers had but 6s. or 7s.

"In 1839, in Devonshire, the whole of a poor man's wages would scarcely produce dry bread for a family of four or five children.

"As to meat, in those times it was scarcely ever touched.

"In 1840 Lord John Russell told the House of Commons that the people were in a worse condition than the negroes in the West Indies.

"In 1842, in Bolton, there were 6,995 applicants for relief to the Poor Protection Society, whose weekly earnings averaged only 13d. per head ; 5,305 persons were visited, and they had only 456 blankets amongst them, or about one blanket to every eleven persons.

"In one district in Manchester there were 2,000 families without a bed.

"In Glasgow 12,000 people were on the relief funds.

"In Accrington, out of a population of 9,000, only 100 were fully employed.

"The reports of the factory inspectors showed that 10 per cent. of the cotton mills, and 12 per cent. of the woollen mills of Lancashire and Yorkshire were standing idle, and that of the rest, only one-fourth were working full time. As Cobden showed, in answer to Sir Robert Peel, the stocking-frames of Nottingham were as idle as the looms of Stockport ; the glass-cutters of Stourbridge, and the glovers of Yeovil, were undergoing the same privations as the potters of Stoke and the miners of Staffordshire, where 25,000 men were destitute of employment. He knew of a place where 100 wedding-rings were pawned in a single week to provide bread, and of another place where men and women subsisted on boiled nettles, and dug up the decayed carcase of a cow rather than perish of hunger.

"Such was the state of things which existed under a system which was called Protection.

"In those days the population of Great Britain was about fifteen millions ; it is now over thirty millions.

"In 1884, under Free Trade, there is not a man, woman, or child who is not better off than he or she would have been under the old starvation laws.

"Labourers get higher wages than they did under these laws, and with the same money they command more of the necessaries and conveniences of life than they could then.

"With these facts before them, they will not listen to those who, under pretence of protecting their interests, would induce them to vote for putting a duty on Foreign Wheat—that is, levying a Bread Tax."

NOTE 2.

FACTS SHOWING THE PROGRESS OF ENGLAND UNDER FREE TRADE.

BRITISH PRODUCE AND MANUFACTURES EXPORTED.

UNDER PROTECTION.			UNDER FREE TRADE.		
Year.	Total Value. £	Per Head of Population. £ s. d.	Year.	Total Value. £	Per Head of Population. £ s. d.
1815	51,603,000	—	1846	52,786,000	2 1 3
1821	36,659,000	1 14 7	1856	115,826,000	4 2 10
1831	37,164,000	1 10 7	1866	188,917,000	6 5 7
1835	47,372,000*	—	1876	200,639,000	6 1 3
1842	47,284,000	1 15 0	1884	232,927,000	6 9 6

This increase was caused by fiscal reforms, duties upon more than 700 articles being reduced and modified between 1831 and 1834.

Pt. I., Ch. iv., Note 2.

ANALYSIS OF IMPORTS AND EXPORTS FOR 1884.

	Imports. £	Exports of British Produce and Manufactures. £
Living Animals, Food, Spirits, Wine, Tobacco, Seeds, and Oil Cake	172,104,684	11,076,558
Raw Materials, and other Materials of Manufacture, including Cotton, Wool, Ores, Hides, Skins, Coal, &c.	146,489,696	13,469,551
Leather	5,411,253	2,016,136
Cotton, Linen, Jute, Silk, Woollen, and other Textile Manufactures, including Yarns	21,813,819	109,844,281
Metals in Various Stages of Manufacture	14,773,281	37,162,152
Steam Engines, Machinery, Tools, Hardware, and Cutlery ... ... (Import trifling, not stated separately)		13,051,028
Alkali Chemicals and Drugs	2,362,093	7,839,516
Other Manufactured Articles	23,337,202	38,468,353
Miscellaneous Articles	3,482,521	
Total Exports, British Produce and Manufactures		232,927,575
Exports of Foreign and Colonial Produce		62,443,715
Total real value of Imports and Exports	389,774,589	295,371,290
Gold and Silver Bullion and Specie	20,321,853	21,999,222
	£410,096,402	£317,370,512

BRITISH SHIPPING UNDER PROTECTION AND UNDER FREE TRADE.

TOTAL TONNAGE BELONGING TO THE UNITED KINGDOM.		TOTAL TONNAGE ENTERED AND CLEARED WITH CARGOES.	
UNDER PROTECTION. Tons.	UNDER FREE TRADE. Tons.	UNDER PROTECTION. 1845. Tons.	UNDER FREE TRADE. 1884. Tons.
1816 . 2,504,000	1845 . 3,123,000	British 6,617,000	British 40,156,000
1845 . 3,123,000	1880 . 6,574,000	Foreign 2,715,000	Foreign 13,814,000
Increase 619,000	Increase 3,451,000	Total 9,332,000	Total 53,970,000

It was prophesied that the repeal of the Navigation Laws would ruin British shipping, but it still maintains its supremacy.

CONSUMPTION OF ARTICLES OF IMPORTED FOOD PER HEAD OF THE POPULATION.

Under Protection, 1840.		Under Free Trade, 1883.	
Bacon and Hams,	a small fraction of 1lb.	Bacon and Hams ...	nearly 11lbs.
Butter	1lb.	Butter	above 7lbs.
Cheese	nearly 1lb.	Cheese	above 5¼lbs.
Wheat and Flour ...	...42½lbs.	Wheat and Flour ...	nearly 251 lbs.
Eggs	...3½ in number	Eggs	above 26 in number
Rice	nearly 1lb.	Rice	nearly 12½lbs.
Sugar, raw	...15lbs.	Sugar, raw	nearly 62lbs.
Tea	nearly 1¼lb.	Tea	above 4¾lbs.

Protection Prices, 1841.		Free Trade Prices, 1884.	
Tea	5s. per lb.	Tea	2s. per lb.
Coffee	2s. per lb.	Coffee	1s. per lb.
Sugar	9d. per lb.	Sugar	2d. per lb.

SOCIAL AND ECONOMIC RESULTS OF FREE TRADE.

The number of paupers relieved in England and Wales on the 1st of January, 1849, the first year of the present statistics, was 934,419, the population being 17,564,000; on the 1st of January, 1884, the number of paupers was 774,310, and the population 26,951,000. In 1849 the proportion relieved to population was 1 in 18; in 1884 it was 1 in 34.

The amount expended in poor relief per head of the population was the same in 1883 as in 1845—viz., 6s.—a fact largely attributable to increased humanity in the treatment of the poor; but the rateable value of the property assessed to the Poor Rate increased from £62,540,000 in 1841, to £141,407,686 in 1883.

The total capital of the savings banks was £24,474,000 in 1841; it was £86,756,000 in 1884.

The total traffic receipts of railways were £4,535,000 in 1843, and £71,062,000 in 1883.

The total assessment of Income Tax in Great Britain in 1842 was £251,000,000; in 1882 it was £565,251,000.

NOTE 3.

NORTH AMERICAN REVIEW (vol. cli., No. 5). May, 1890.

Extracts from "The Tariff on Trial," by Sir Richard J. Cartwright, K.C.M.G., and Thomas G. Shearman.

One of the most remarkable, and in many ways one of the most important, results of the Protectionist propaganda which was preached very successfully in Canada in 1877 and 1878, and which was actually reduced to practice in 1879, was that the good old wholesome dislike to taxation (and consequently to undue and extravagant expenditure) was for the time being completely rooted up from the minds of the majority. As very often happens, the indirect and secondary result of a false theory is not the least mischievous. In this case it has practically removed all check on expenditure by the Government.

Once imbue the minds of a large section of the people with the idea that wealth can be created by imposing taxes, and it is obvious that they have no longer any reason for opposing the imposition of new taxation, and that when the Government wants money it need only profess that it desires to encourage new industries to find a ready excuse for refilling its coffers. The present Government of Canada have not been slow to learn and profit by this lesson.

Under a system of taxation for purposes of revenue only, the total expenditure of Canada for the year 1874 was $23,316,316. In 1878, under the same system, it had increased to $23,519,301, being an increase of barely $203,000 in *four* years, in spite of the fact that a very large sum of money had been

[Pt. I., Ch. iv., Note 3.]

expended in the interval upon public works. Under a system of taxation for Protection the total expenditure of Canada for the year 1889 was $36,917,834, having increased by an amount of $13,398,531 in *eleven* years. So in 1878 the actual taxation of Canada was $17,841,938, though, as there was a deficit in that year, the necessary taxation might be placed at $19,000,000. In 1889 the actual taxation was $30,613,522, being an increase of $11,613,522, taking the necessary taxation (so-called) of 1878 as a basis.

* * * * * *

Unfortunately there is a yet darker shade to the picture. What the result may have been in other countries I cannot say, but in Canada (over and above the extravagant expenditure above referred to) one most important consequence of the introduction of the Protective system has been at the same time to make provision for a large and permanent corruption fund, to be applied with the effect and regularity of a machine to debauching the Press and Electorate as occasion serves.

It is probable that this result is inherent in the system. Speaking with knowledge, I say deliberately that I can conceive no more effectual method of installing and intrenching corruption in the politics of any country than to give a large number of active, energetic business men—frequently persons possessed of great wealth, and almost always having a large control of money—a direct pecuniary interest in controlling legislation and in supporting any particular political party. Of course they will do it, and there is but one way in which they can do it. Being subsidised, they must subsidise in return. It is quite impossible to pause to point out the innumerable ways in which this corrupt system works for evil at all times and periods; but I will give one notable example. Shortly before one of our General Elections the present Premier of the Dominion (Sir John Macdonald), being pressed for funds, deliberately summoned some eighty or ninety of the principal Protected manufacturers in Canada to meet him at the Queen's Hotel in Toronto; and then and there, in good set phrase, told them that as the Government had helped them to enrich themselves at the public expense, they in return must help the Government to keep in place; nor did he dismiss them till they had assessed themselves in a large amount for the purpose of providing a fund wherewith to corrupt the electors of the Dominion.

* * * * * *

To put the matter briefly, the results of the introduction of the Protective system in Canada have been :—

1. To remove all check on the expenditure of the Government, and to encourage a reckless extravagance on their part which has resulted in an annual expenditure for Federal purposes of nearly 50 per cent. more (after making all deductions), for a population of less than *five* millions, than the sum required by the United States for the like objects when their population was over *twenty* millions.

2. To systematise and intensify the tendency (always so perilous to the welfare of representative Governments) to use corrupt means for the purpose of influencing the Press and the Electorate, and to make it the direct pecuniary interest of a very active and influential class to provide a regular and large fund for such purposes.

3. To aggravate and accelerate the tendency to accumulate large fortunes in few hands, and at the same time to increase the indebtedness and depreciate the value of the property owned by the mass of the community, more especially in the case of the agricultural class.

4. To favour the growth of a few large towns at the expense of the smaller ones and of the rural population, which latter has been reduced to an absolutely stationary condition over very large portions of the Dominion, in spite of a large (alleged) immigration and of the fact that much new territory has been thrown open.

* * * * * *

Part XX.

PREPARING THE ARENA.

CHAPTER I.

DEFINITION OF FREE TRADE.

§ 1. THE discussion which has been carried through the first four chapters upon the nature and the causes and the significance of modern Protectionism ought, at least, to have suggested the reflection that there is nothing new in the Protectionist doctrine as it is preached in America and the British Colonies. These countries have not been perverted through the discovery of any new economic doctrine, but simply from indifference to the old, under the stress of new political conditions. Men who have no knowledge—either by personal experience or through books—of the appalling misery of England under its Protective policy have accepted in an unthinking way the general tenets of Free Trade; but they have not reasoned for themselves upon the application of these tenets, nor traced them to the facts on which they rest. Consequently many inhabitants of a young country have come to think that Free Trade is something peculiarly British and belonging to the Old World, with which they themselves need have nothing to do. They see that all the conditions of production are different from what they are in Europe; that instead of labour being abundant and land scarce, labour is scarce and land abundant; that capital is dear and wages are high, where in older countries capital is cheap and wages are low. Under such circumstances they are inclined to take a merely academic interest in discussions on Free Trade and to lend a ready ear to those who tell them that the old truths have no application to their new conditions.

It is therefore desirable, even at the risk of going over often-trodden ground, to re-state the economic argument in favour of Free Trade, in order to show that in all its bearings it has the same application to the circumstances of all countries.

§ 2. But first let us be sure in what sense we are using the term Free Trade.

In its political and controversial sense Free Trade simply means *the absence of duties of a Protective character.*

It is sometimes used, in a wider sense, to denote the absence of all Customs duties; but this is not the meaning which it bears when it is used in opposition to the term "Protection." In that sense it is simply *the absence of duties of a Protective character.*

It is no mere pedantry to insist upon this simple definition, because much of the confusion and heat of the controversy between Free Traders and Protectionists arises from neglecting to remember it.

How often, for example, in New South Wales, have we not heard Protectionists maintain their arguments against the differential railway rates! And in England trades unions have been frequently declared, even by those who ought to have known better, to be a violation of the principles of Free Trade. Now differential railway rates and trades unions may be in themselves good things or bad things; but neither the one nor the other has anything to do with the imposition of Customs duties. It would be just as logical to denounce them in the name of Gothic architecture as in the name of Protection or Free Trade! Of course, if the term Free Trade is used in an altogether different sense, and extended to mean "a general principle of non-interference in industrial matters either by the Government or by organised public opinion," the complaints to which reference has been made are logical enough. But not only is the term not generally used in this wide sense, but it would be impossible to carry on an argument upon the fiscal controversy if the meaning of the words "Free Trade" were so indefinite and large.

§ 3. Cobden, with his usual sagacity, perceived this long ago, when replying to the argument (which is one that seems to exercise a strange fascination over a certain class of minds) that because the commerce of no country is absolutely free, it is justifiable to make the commerce of any particular country less free than it is, he used the following words: "We do not want to touch duties simply for revenue, but we want to prevent certain parties from having a revenue which is of benefit to themselves, but advantage to none else. On the contrary, what we seek for is the improvement of Her Majesty's revenue; what we wish to gain is that improvement. We say that your monopoly gives you a temporary advantage—a temporary, not a permanent advantage, and that you thereby cripple the resources of the revenue."[1]

And again: "One of your candidates actually says that Free Trade means the abolition of all Customs House duties. We have said, thousands of times, that our object is not to take away the Queen's officers from the Customs House, but to take away those officers who sit at the receipt of custom to take tithe and toll for the benefit of peculiar classes."[2]

§ 4. The practical importance of recognising that Free Trade is not inconsistent with a tariff for revenue purposes has become greater by reason of the growing political power of those who earnestly advocate the abolition of all indirect taxes. Cobden himself belonged to this party, and his last political

[1] House of Commons, May 15th, 1843.
[2] London, Oct. 13th, 1843.

utterance was in favour of its views; but Cobden was preeminently a man of practical sagacity, who recognised, as the more far-seeing members of the single-tax party ought also to recognise, that in politics only one thing can be done at a time. It is idle to rail against revenue duties when an active agitation is on foot to replace them by Protective duties; and it can only encumber the supporters of Free Trade to have to fight in a double controversy.

It cannot be too clearly recognised that the present struggle between Free Traders and Protectionists is being fought upon a single issue. We are not now discussing the respective merits of direct and indirect taxation, but we are endeavouring to clear the ground for such a discussion by beating out of the field those who maintain as the cardinal maxim of their creed that duties of a Protective character must exist. Until this belief is destroyed, it is idle to argue the larger question whether there should be any Customs duties at all. Protection is wholly inconsistent with direct taxation; Free Trade is not inconsistent with it, but it stands apart as an independent fiscal principle.

But if it is important to bear in mind that the question at issue is not between direct and indirect taxation, it is even more important to remember that we are not disputing about rival principles of government. Free Trade, as opposed to Protection, in the sense in which it has been defined, is not a principle of government, but a principle of sound finance. It is a commercial expedient for securing the easiest interchange of commodities. A discussion of Free Trade need not, therefore, raise the question whether individualism ought to prevail in all industrial matters to the exclusion of any direction or control either by Government or by organised opinion, but only the small question whether Customs duties ought to be of a revenue or a protective character. If politicians and newspaper writers would once perceive within what narrow limits this controversy should be waged, there would be less exaggeration in the language upon either side, and the working of either policy would be better understood.[1]

CHAPTER II.

DIVISION OF THE ARGUMENTS INTO CLASSES—ECONOMIC AND POLITICAL.

§ 1. It is of the highest importance in the fiscal controversy to keep in mind a division of the arguments into two classes—the political, and the economic. The omission to observe this fundamental distinction has been the source of much confusion and ill-feeling.

No one can read discussions about a tariff without being struck by the tendency, which exists on both sides, to underestimate either the intelligence or honesty of opponents. There would seem at first sight to be no reason in the nature of things why Customs duties should not be discussed with as much calmness as any other form of taxation. Yet no one will deny that this is not the case. Probate duties, stamp duties, house duties, taxes upon income, taxes upon land, are gloomy subjects of discussion in the most exciting times; but let a word be dropped about an increase or reduction in the tariff, and sober men on either side are smitten with an almost fanatical frenzy.

---

[1] The necessity for keeping strictly to this definition of Free Trade is illustrated by a common Protectionist argument, which seems to be used partly by way of exhortation to Protectionists and partly by way of depreciating Free Traders.

The argument is this:—"No country," it is said, "is a Free Trade country. Even England levies Customs duties."

It is difficult to see how the violation of a principle in one point is an argument in favour of further violations, nor how the imperfection of a Free Trade system justifies its total overthrowal. Yet such is the enthusiasm of some advocates of free exchange (who, it may be remarked, generally vote with Protectionists), that because our commerce is not absolutely free, they are prepared — out of pure regard for consistency—to make it less free than it is!

Free Traders consider the unwillingness to accept what appears to them to be elementary and axiomatic truths, demonstrable as any proposition in Euclid, to be a sign of perverseness or stupidity; while Protectionists do not hesitate to attribute the most sinister motives to all the advocates of free exchange.

This curious state of affairs is no doubt partly owing to the fact that fiscal arguments are still enveloped in the atmosphere of party controversy, in which the doctrines of Free Trade were first carried into practice; but it is also, in no small degree, the result of a failure to perceive that fiscal controversies involve several distinct issues, which require to be dealt with by different classes of arguments. Thus, whatever the cause may be, it is quite certain that, after years of controversy, the issue is no clearer than it was, nor the end nearer. Each party is still fighting in the air, and neither meets the other's arguments.

§ 2. One way to make an end of this confusion is to state the point which is at issue.

Neither Protection nor Free Trade can be discussed as a purely economic question. Each policy involves political as well as economic considerations. Each may therefore be supported by political as well as economic arguments.

Free Traders, as a rule, confine their attention to the economic arguments—that is to say, they demonstrate that Protection causes a diminution of material wealth, and are then content; Protectionists, on the other hand, without openly ignoring economic conclusions, rest their advocacy almost entirely upon considerations of politics.

Now, it is true that economic and political considerations are in practical life inextricably interblended; and that no one can form a sound opinion whether Protection or Free Trade is good for a particular country without taking both into account. Nevertheless, it does not require much reflection to see that the two considerations must be kept apart in argument; and that one of two disputants can never convince the other if each is looking at a different side of the shield.

What, then, is the broad distinction between the economic and the political aspects of the fiscal controversy?

It is this:—Viewed as a question to be settled by economic arguments, the test of either policy is its result upon the production of wealth—using the term "production" in its largest sense to include exchange and every other form of wealth-creation. If it increases the aggregate of wealth possessed by a country, a fiscal policy is *economically* good; if it lessens the aggregate, it is *economically* bad.

Viewed, however, as a question of politics, the test of a fiscal policy is not so simple, because it depends upon the determination of the question, "What is best for the well-being of the nation as a whole?" Some politicians, for instance, may desire to divide the aggregate of wealth among a greater variety of industries, even at the risk of lessening the total amount to be divided; others, again, may have such a dread of the interruption of commerce by war as to wish their country to be independent of all foreign supplies, and with this end in view may be indifferent to the quantity of wealth produced or the cost of its production. And in many other ways political considerations may be brought forward to override conclusions of economic reasoning.

§ 3. It will accordingly be conceded at the outset of this argument that no mere economic demonstration is able to solve the fiscal problem.

The welfare of a nation is composed of many elements, and the paths towards it are extremely numerous, so that many aspects of a political question must of necessity lie beyond the range of any purely economic argument.

Everyone who has had to come to a reasoned conclusion upon political questions must have felt himself pressed by these considerations. Even the most extreme Free Trader—using the term in its wide Spencerian sense, to mean an advocate of universal and unrestricted competition—would hesitate before he allowed a foreign line of steamers to have the exclusive carriage of the ocean mails between Great Britain and her Colonies. Yet it might be that the foreign company wou'd carry the mails for nothing, while an English company would charge a high price for the same work. It is obvious that mere economic considerations hardly enter into a case of this kind.

Another familiar instance of the overriding of economic by political considerations is offered by the salutary practice of subsidising ocean-going merchant steamers of a high class on condition that they comply with certain requisites which will enable them in time of war to take their place as cruisers in protecting commerce. An incidental result of these subsidies may be to keep up freights by excluding competition, and to that extent they will be harmful to commerce. But nevertheless the nation may gain from them more than it loses, because every such subsidised vessel is in reality part of the naval reserve. Consequently, if the net result be that a larger sum is saved on the naval estimates than the total cost of the subsidies—including in their cost the indirect losses which they cause to merchants and producers—the transaction is on balance profitable.

Occasions must also arise in the history of a nation when motives of humanity, regard for safety, or other urgent reasons, compel wise rulers to subordinate considerations of economics. The Irish famine was such an occasion. Cobden thought that another had arisen in his lifetime owing to the congested state of population in the English towns. He proposed to correct this consequence of bad land laws by employing the Queen's ships in the free transport of emigrants from Great Britain to the Colonies. Whether this temporary measure of alleviation would have been successful is open to argument, but there is no inconsistency between such a proposal and a most vehement opposition to Protective taxes.

Pt. II., Ch. ii., § 4.]

§ 4. Let us now apply these distinctions to arguments about the tariff.

The economic argument—which will be developed at length in later chapters of this work—is exclusively directed to a consideration of the effect of Free Trade upon the production and accumulation of material wealth. It starts with the assumptions of the Individualist school of political economy as to the strength and universality of the desire for wealth, and as to the existence of an ever-active competition between equal units. It then proceeds to show that under natural conditions trade will develop according to the requirements of a country, without any encouragement from Protective tariffs; that every industry which rests upon Protection must divert labour and capital from the more to the less profitable employments, and that, consequently, Protection must be less favourable than Free Trade to the accumulation of material wealth.

The political argument passes by these economic conclusions, and, ignoring the effect of tariffs upon the production of wealth, considers them as means of securing a more equal distribution of advantages and comforts among the labouring classes, and of encouraging the developement of latent national resources.

If the Protectionist argument were stated with reference to economic conclusions—which is seldom or never the case—it would read something as follows: "We admit your demonstration to be correct. We allow that under Free Trade wealth is produced most rapidly and accumulates in the largest quantities; but we say that Protection gives other advantages which Free Trade does not give, and which more than compensate a country for its lessened wealth."

This is a fair and logical position if it can be held. Unfortunately Free Traders are not always willing to attack it with any but economic weapons. Yet it is idle to expect to make much impression with the weapons of economics upon the mind of a man who is impervious to all considerations except those which are political. Free Traders, therefore, if they are to make converts, must go beyond their economic demonstrations and fight the battle on the ground which the Protectionists themselves have chosen.

The question then will be "Whether there is any good reason for the opinion that Protection, though it reduces wealth and lessens national productiveness, adds to a nation elements of strength and happiness which greater riches could not give."

In order to answer this it will be necessary to consider separately each of the advantages which Protection is supposed to confer.

If as a result of the inquiry it shall be found that these advantages are either non-existent or illusory—*cadit quæstio;* but, on the other hand, it will by no means follow that the question must be answered in favour of Protection, even although it be found that some substantial advantages are given by that policy. The only consequence of such a discovery will be to necessitate a further inquiry, "Whether Protection does not bring with it certain political or social disadvantages which far outweigh the benefits which it may be supposed to confer."

Whenever political considerations enter into the inquiry, the question in every case—whether it relates to a whole tariff or to a single duty—will always be one of a balance of advantages. The absolutely best is never possible in politics. Every political measure, whether it relates to industry or not, must steer a middle course between the evils which it remedies and those which it creates. The utmost certainty a statesman can obtain will rest upon a reasonable hope that he is not making a mistake. He will assure himself of this in the first instance by evidence; and where evidence fails, by reference to principles and experience. But even with all precautions, the wise application of scientific conclusions to the facts of daily life must be to a large extent the result of empirical knowledge. When it is otherwise—and when it is possible to frame exact rules for the constitution and working of political societies—human nature will have become less variable or more accurately known.

§ 5. Free Traders have, accordingly, to prove two points:—They must show first, that Free Trade is more efficient than Protection as a means of increasing national productiveness; and, secondly, that it is more conducive to the general well-being of the nation as a whole. They must prove the economic issue by economic reasoning, and defeat the political objections which Protectionists may urge to the economic conclusions by political reasoning.

It is sometimes, however, contended that the political considerations should be dealt with in the first instance, and that economic reasoning ought only to be brought into play when political arguments have failed. The ground of this contention is the paramount importance of the political considerations which are involved in the tariff controversy.

There is no doubt that these considerations are paramount to anything which can be urged on purely economic grounds, since the right distribution of wealth and the due development of national powers are of far greater importance to a State than the mere possession of riches. It does not, however, follow that the economic argument upon the tariff can be subordinated to the political. The contrary is the case.

In the first place, it happens that most of the political arguments in favour of Protection tacitly assume an economic basis—that is to say, they really depend upon the assumption that Protection is more favourable than Free Trade to national productiveness.

A Free Trader says that a high tariff must lessen wealth. The Protectionist replies that the effect of a tariff on the production and accumulation of wealth must not be considered by itself; that the real object of inquiry is as to its effect upon the national welfare. Free Traders will accede to this statement of the case; but having done so they are entitled to call for some evidence, even if proof be not forthcoming, that a policy which increases the aggregate of wealth can in any way diminish the general happiness. When once it is proved or admitted that Free Trade is more favourable than Protection to the production of material wealth, a strong presumption arises that it is also more conducive to national welfare. This presumption may be overcome ; but while it stands, it puts a heavy burden of proof upon Protectionist shoulders. If the sum to be divided among all citizens is increased by Free Trade, the share of each is not likely to be diminished by an increase in the dividend. No doubt it may be shown that an increase in the aggregate of wealth gives rise to inequalities of distribution, but no one is entitled to assume this result. Therefore, although for purposes of controversy it is necessary to consider all Protectionist arguments—even when they are mutually destructive—such a concession ought not to be interpreted as a waiver of the demand that Protectionists should first show "How and why a policy which increases wealth injures the national welfare."

There is also another reason why the economic argument should take priority.

Suppose that each party agree that the final test of any measure is its effect upon the national welfare, still its effect upon the production and accumulation of material wealth must be considered first, because there is no available test of national well-being except material prosperity. The only known measure of national progress or retrogression is increase or decrease of material wealth. No one suggests that this is a perfect measure, or that it supplies a final test, but it is the first test, and none other can be used without it.

Suppose, for instance, that Free Traders accept the standard proposed by Protectionists, that the comfort and happiness of a nation is greatest when its wealth is most equally divided among all its citizens, so that the standard of comfort among the producing classes is highest, still the question will be,

[Pt. II., Ch. ii., § 6.]

"What have the producing classes got to spend?" It is true that their standard of living can be tested by statistics of crime, education, and disease, and is not always indicated by the rate of wages. But all these tests are, in their final analysis, in so far as an analysis of such things is possible, dependent on the material prosperity of the classes with reference to which they are used. A poor man may be virtuous and well educated; but a virtuous and well-educated class of wage-earners is always a symptom of a high relative standard of material comfort. Consequently after all political arguments on the tariff question have spent their force, and even before one of them can be applied, the economic argument must be considered; because the production of material wealth is both a necessary foundation and the only available test of progress in national well-being. Accordingly, whenever the political considerations which are urged against the economic conclusions, either expressly or impliedly assume that Protection increases national wealth, then the economic argument in favour of Free Trade has first to be disposed of.

§ 6. It may be thought that these concessions to the Protectionist side of the controversy materially weaken the force of the economic argument in favour of Free Trade.

This belief, as will be seen later in these pages, rests upon a misapprehension of the true nature of the fiscal controversy, which, although it must be affected to a large extent by considerations of politics, is yet determined in its final issue by the effect of either policy upon the material wealth-producing power of the community in question. A correct perception of this is of so much importance to a right handling of the arguments on either side that it will be desirable to clear the ground still further before making use of them.

We shall see, as the lines of the controversy become clearer, that the distinction which has been insisted upon in the preceding pages between the economic and political arguments is very seldom regarded. We shall find also that when it is regarded in name it is ignored in practice, and that the attempts which have been made to evade the sledge-hammer blows of economic reasoning by the construction of a new theory of economics have really ended in throwing a few political catchwords—such as "national welfare," "the comfort and happiness of the people," "national development," and the like—into a large phrase, and pretending thus to have obtained a new basis for a scientific system. But this is to anticipate the remaining chapters of this part, which will be devoted to an inquiry into the relation of economics to politics as a whole, and to a tariff in particular, in order to understand better how an economic argument upon the tariff is likely to be modified by that class of political considerations which peculiarly affect fiscal problems. Next an attempt will be made to ascertain whether it is possible to frame an economic defence of a Protective tariff upon any other basis than that upon which the Free Trade argument is usually erected. Finally, this being done, the economic and the political aspect of the controversy will each be separately considered.

At present it is sufficient to bear in mind that if the combatants would really grapple with each other—which they seldom, if ever, do at present—they must meet economic arguments with economic arguments, and political with political. And if Protectionists should say that they have all along been willing to adopt this course, and that none of their recognised leaders attempt to defend Protection upon economic grounds—as the term "economic" is understood by the followers of Adam Smith—the answer is, that they are right in their statement, but that the leaders cannot control the rank and file of Protectionist voters. No doubt most Protectionist writers admit that Free Trade is unassailable if the postulates and definitions of Individualist political economy are once admitted —this is what the unlearned voter means when he says, "Free

Trade is good in theory, but of no use in practice "—but even learned writers, after making this admission, often drop into vulgar errors, and talk about "the excess of imports," or "the drain of gold," or the need for "keeping the money in the country," or some other catch-phrase, which has no meaning apart from the arguments and conclusions of that form of economic science which they have openly disavowed. Thus, then, is the necessity great for clear distinctions, if we would avoid confusion in this very dusty fight.

CHAPTER III.

ECONOMICS AND POLITICS, OR THE VALUE OF THE ECONOMIC ARGUMENT.

§ 1. THE last two chapters ought to have disclosed the object of the controversy, and the lines upon which it has to be conducted. The time, however, is not yet arrived for entering upon the argument. The ground must first be cleared of those objectors who insist that economic argument is, from its nature, of no value in a practical discussion. The next four chapters will, accordingly, be devoted to considering the limitations which attach to any economic argument, and to an inquiry into the application of the economic argument in favour of Free Trade to a tariff controversy. In other words, we must see whether those Protectionists are right who object to the use of any economic conclusions in a discussion about Protection.

This objection takes a double form.

First, it is said that economic assumptions are of such an abstract character, and so far removed from the facts of life, that they can never have much importance for practical men;

and, secondly, it is denied that the tariff is in any aspect an economic question.

The latter of these objections plainly depends upon the question whether the political arguments in favour of Protection not only override the economic argument in favour of Free Trade, but are wholly independent of economic considerations. This can only be determined after each of the political arguments have been considered, which will be done in the later chapters of this work.[1]

The first objection, however, plainly strikes at the root of all economic discussions, by denying the utility of political economy in affording any aid to the comprehension of practical problems. It will accordingly be necessary, even at the risk of covering familiar ground, to examine briefly into the relation between politics and economics, as it is understood by those who claim to defend Free Trade by economic conclusions.

§ 2. Political economy, as the term is understood in England, rests upon two fundamental assumptions—viz., First, that the universal and dominant instinct of human nature, in its relation to non-human and material objects, is to endeavour to satisfy desires by the least possible expenditure of time and labour; and, secondly, that the struggle for existence in the industrial world, as it is at present organised, necessitates competition, and that the competing units—whether the unit be an individual or a group of individuals—are equal.

Starting from these assumptions, political economy attempts a scientific investigation into the influences which affect the production and the distribution of wealth. Sometimes the inquiry into the influences which affect the exchange of wealth is made a third division of the science; but, properly speaking,

---

[1] *See* infra, Part III., Chapters 6 and 7.

exchange is a method of production, similar in its action, with regard to completed articles of commerce, to the method of division of employment with regard to articles in process of completion. Exchange is, in fact, only a manifestation on a large scale of a well-known method of facilitating production by the co-operation of different sorts of labour.

Political economy is thus a formal science, which occupies towards the art of politics much the same relation as the formal science of jurisprudence occupies towards the art of legislation. Its principal function is analysis. It analyses, first—distinguishing the action of each—the three factors (land, labour, and capital) which co-operate in the production of wealth; and secondly, it analyses the causes which affect the distribution of wealth after it has been produced. In every process, however, its method rests upon the assumptions already mentioned; and its conclusions derive their practical value from the nearness or remoteness of the assumed conditions to actual facts.

This is the point of attack.

Political economy—in the sense of the English or Individualist school, which owes its paternity to Adam Smith—is declared to be an idle study, for two reasons:—First, it is said, "Its fundamental assumption is untrue, since men are not, in fact, dominated by the desire for gain."

Secondly, it is said, "Even if the desire for wealth is universal and supreme, the term 'wealth' is incapable of definition."

There is, unquestionably, much truth in both these criticisms. The question, however, is whether they destroy the value of economic conclusions. Let us examine them in detail.

§ 3. The first of these objections is expressed with great force and lucidity by Mr. Henry Sidgwick in a passage of his "Political Economy," which is much relied upon by an able opponent of economics whose work will have to be considered later in some detail, Mr. H. M. Hoyt.[1] The passage is in these terms:—

> "The first and most fundamental [assumption] is that all persons engaged in industry will, in selling or lending goods, or contracting to render services, endeavour, *cæteris paribus*, to get as much wealth as they can in return for the commodity they offer. This is often more briefly expressed by saying that political economy assumes the universality and unlimitedness of the desire for wealth. Against this assumption it has been argued that men do not, for the most part, desire wealth in general, but this or that particular kind of wealth; in fact, that 'the desire of wealth' is an abstraction] compounding a great variety of different and heterogeneous motives, which have been mistaken for a single homogeneous force. .... There are other things obtainable by labour, besides wealth, which mankind generally, if not universally, desire, such as power and reputation; and it is further undeniable that men are largely induced to render services of various kinds by family affection, friendship, compassion, national and local patriotism, and other kinds of *esprit de corps*, and other motives. The amount of unpaid work which is done from such motives in modern civilised society, forms a substantial part of the whole, and political economists are, perhaps, fairly chargeable with an omission in making no express reference to such work—with the exception of the mutual services rendered by husbands and wives, by parents and children."

§ 4. The soundness of this criticism may be at once admitted. But what does it amount to? Simply to this:—That many matters lie beyond the ken of economic science, and that of those that come within it, none can be completely dealt with in every aspect. But to admit that great caution must be exercised in applying economic conclusions to the facts of industrial life is very different from denying that they

---

[1] "Protection *versus* Free Trade. The Scientific Validity and Economic Operation of Defensive Duties in the United States." By Henry M. Hoyt. 3rd Edit. New York: D. Appleton & Co. 1886.

It must be remembered that the term "political economy" in this and the following chapter always means English or Individualist political economy.

can have a practical value under any circumstances. As a rule, those writers who, like Mr. Sidgwick, are most keenly alive to the imperfections which are charged against political economy, are the very men who insist most strongly on its practical advantages. Granted that men desire other things than wealth, and that this desire is in some instances stronger than the desire of wealth, this does not invalidate the assumption that when men are engaged in acquiring wealth, their desire for it is universal and unlimited.

The economic man, whose structure has been the butt of much cheap derision, is admittedly an abstraction moved by one idea; and in real life men do, no doubt, move and have their being in a multitude of other motives and desires. Love of country, family or reputation, pride, comradeship, artistic impulses, charity, politeness, loyalty to class or tradition—all these are influences which are unquestionably more potent in many cases than the desire of gain. But have any of them the same effect upon the production of material wealth? Protectionist critics of political economy appear to forget that economics only profess to deal with material wealth. Of what use is it, then, to point out that certain motives impel men to neglect wealth, if there is one powerful and universal motive which urges men to its production and acquisition? So far as motives of the former class prevail, by so much will the scope of economic science be diminished; but wherever wealth is not neglected, but pursued, there an example is presented of the operation of the economic motive. It would be absurd to apply economic tests to the decision of questions of conscience or duty; but it does not therefore follow that it is absurd to eliminate all motives but the desire for profit, when we are treating of men's conduct in trading with each other. Suppose, for the sake of argument, that an individual here and there starts a business from philanthropic motives, so that he is pecuniarily indifferent to its success or failure, can such a rare instance justify the statement that men are not as a rule dominated by the desire for gain when they enter upon commercial enterprises? When men are brought into a direct relation with the tangible material objects which we call "wealth," either by way of producing them for others or of acquiring them for themselves, what motive has a wider range or a more powerful influence than self-interest? Certainly, there can be no valid objection in such a case to eliminating all other motives for the purposes of scientific study, provided that due caution is exercised in applying any conclusions arrived at by this process. And the test of applicability will be the nearness or remoteness of the assumption to the facts of the particular case. Where self-interest dominates, economic conclusions apply; where it is overridden by other motives, they must be corrected. What, then, is the applicability of economic conclusions to a discussion about tariffs? This is a subject which it will be convenient to defer until the next chapter, in order that we may continue our examination into the objections which are urged against the applicability of economics to any practical case.

§ 5. The second objection to the use of political economy in practical discussions is that the term "wealth" is incapable either of analysis or definition. Here, again, the criticism is best expressed in the words of a Free Trade economist of high repute, the late Mr. Walter Bagehot:—

> "Just as this science [political economy] takes an abstract and one-sided view of man, who is one of its subjects, so it also takes an abstract and one-sided view of wealth, which is its other subject. Wealth is infinitely various; as the wants of human nature are almost innumerable, so the kinds of wealth are various. Why man wants so many things is a great subject, fit for inquiry; which of them it would be wise for men to want more of, and which of them it would be wise to want less of, are also great subjects, equally fit. But with these subjects political economy does not deal at all. It leaves the first to the metaphysician, who has to explain, if he can, the origin and order of human wants; and the second to the moralist, who is to decide to the best of his ability which of these

tastes are to be encouraged and when, which to be discouraged and when. The only peculiarity of wealth with which the economist is concerned is its *differentia specifica*—that which makes it wealth. . . . . He regards a pot of beer and a picture, a book of religion and a pack of cards, as all equally wealth, and therefore, for his purpose, equally worthy of regard."

§ 6. Thus the defect in the scope of political economy which Mr. Ruskin believes himself to have discovered was not after all unknown or disregarded by the professors of the science! It is not, however, quite correct to say, as Mr. Bagehot does, that an economist does not concern himself with the sort of wealth which is produced, or the uses to which wealth is put. It is true that wealth is defined simply by reference to its possession of an exchange value, and that whatever possesses an exchange value is, economically speaking, "wealth;" but the nature and uses of wealth are important considerations in dealing with the methods of production. It certainly falls within the purview of the economist to discuss how the accumulated wealth of a society can be most effectively employed in the creation of more wealth.

Nevertheless, the criticism is, in the main, sound. It is a limitation to the practical value of economics that it is unable to differentiate the various forms of wealth. But this is just one of the limitations, already referred to, which necessitate the correction of economic conclusions by reference to political considerations. It is clear that "wealth," which means one thing to the economist, may mean another to the politician. The love of gin, for example, is the desire for one kind of wealth, which, as Mr. Cliffe Leslie has observed, "often competes in the mind of a poor man with the love of a decent dwelling." Yet the moralist and the politician will obviously regard it as a matter of very unequal importance, both to the individual and the State, which of these desires be satisfied. In short, while the economist fixes his attention on the production and exchange of material wealth, and deals with distribution only as a part of the process of its production, the politician has further to consider what kinds of wealth should be produced, and to what uses it should be put. On these questions a purely economic argument, although it is not quite silent, offers very little guidance. It deals with the uses to which wealth should be put, only in so far as it attempts to prove that unproductive expenditure checks the further production of wealth, while a different mode of expenditure would encourage it; and it deals with the manner in which wealth is distributed, only as a question which arises in the course of production, when the rules have to be determined under which the portions of wealth in process of production will be divided between those who are actually engaged in producing it. It does not, however, decide the ends of civil society; nor does it say anything as to the uses to which wealth may be put in any other direction than that of wealth-production. It is probable that this defect in the range of economic science ought to be remedied. Such, at least, is the opinion of Professor Walker, the eminent American economist and Free Trader, who thus emphasises the Protectionist criticisms of the point now under discussion :— [1]

> "It is," he says, "in the use made of the existing body of wealth that the wealth of the next generation is determined. It matters far less for the future greatness of a nation what is the sum of its wealth to-day, whether large or small, than what are the habits of its people in the daily consumption of that wealth; to what use those means are devoted, whether to ends which inspire social ambition, which restrict population within limits consistent with a high *per capita* production, which increase the efficiency of the labourer and supply instrumentalities for rendering his labour still more productive; or to ends which allow the increase of population in the degree that of itself involves poverty, squalor, and disease, which debauch the labourer morally and physically, striking at both his power and

---

[1] Lest any reader might think it unfair to express Protectionist criticisms in the words of Free Trade economists, it may be stated that all the quotations in this chapter have been adopted by Mr. Hoyt as correct expressions of, to his mind, fatal defects in the value of Individualist economics.

disposition to work hard and continuously, and which waste in idle or vicious indulgences the wealth which should go to increase capital.

"To trace to their effects upon production the forces which are set in motion by the uses made of wealth, to show how certain forms of consumption clear the mind, strengthen the hand, and elevate the aims of the individual economic agent while promoting that social order and mutual confidence which are favourable conditions for the complete development and harmonious action of the industrial system; how other forms of consumption debase and debauch man as an economic agent, and introduce disorder and waste—here is the opportunity for some great moral philosopher to write the most important chapter in political economy, now, alas! almost a blank."

§ 7. Professor Walker's words will close the subject for most Free Traders.[1] Individualist economics are admittedly defective upon that side which deals with the consumption of wealth. But is this a proof that the science is inapplicable to political discussions? Or—to carry the matter a step further—has it any bearing at all upon the applicability of economic conclusions to a tariff controversy? Has a tariff more to do with the manner in which wealth is used, or with the manner and the quantity in which it is produced?

[1] In the following passage from a little volume by R. R. Bowker, entitled "Of Work and Wealth," which is published at New York in the "Questions of the Day" series, the distinctions in the text are thus referred to:—"The wealth of nations with which, as a state-craft, economics deals, is of two orders—wealth potential, and wealth produced. Potential wealth is, in truth, 'abundance of life:' to a nation, the amount of living vigour, present and prospective, applicable, within the limits of over-population, to produce work; as to each man, health, length of years, natural capacity for production increased by skill. Every 'able-bodied' immigrant is thus said to be worth to the United States, whose land still invites labour, a thousand dollars. It is this wealth which Ruskin regards, fulminating against economists for their narrow definitions; and Adam Smith himself included it in reckoning the capital of a country. It is this with which a statesman largely concerns himself in his economic direction of the State. But this wealth cannot be exchanged; like all higher things, it is beyond value and 'without price.' Produced wealth alone has value, in the economic sense of power in exchange; and it is this with which economists, as such, primarily deal. When, then, we speak of wealth, we mean usually the fruits of work, not the possibilities of it; wealth is labour stored by combination with materials."

To neglect the conclusions of a science which deals with the production and distribution of wealth, because it does not also deal adequately with its consumption, is to ignore the importance which the possession of material wealth has always played in the political development of an industrial people. The mere possession of wealth in large quantities does not, it is true, make a nation great; nor does extent of territory; but just as extent of territory is often a powerful influence in liberating the forces which contribute to national greatness, so is the possession of wealth. And wealth is even more important to the national welfare of an industrial State than is extent of territory. "Man," it is true, "does not live by bread alone"; but without bread the existence of an industrial community would at least be cramped! Riches alone cannot give a nation happiness or greatness; but without riches a nation will have difficulty in obtaining either! In fact, as political societies are now constituted, the possession of material wealth is the basis of all national development. The days of the hardy barbarian are gone by; and though abuse of wealth may still create effete societies, the want of it will certainly prevent the full realisation of all the capacities—whether moral, intellectual, or material—which are latent in an industrial community.

To refuse, therefore, to consider the economic effect of any political measure, on the ground that economics only concerns itself with the production and accumulation of wealth, and not with its uses, is equivalent to a refusal to regard the operation of the measure upon that which underlies and stimulates the beneficial influence of every quickening force of national life. It is true that a nation is the resultant of many forces; but it is not true that the economic is the least important.

It is beside the mark for Protectionists to take up time by ridiculing the imperfections and limitations of political economy. No one is more alive to these than the economists themselves. It is admittedly impossible to obtain precision in the postulates and definitions of the science except at some sacrifice of reality. But in that department of its investigations which deals with the production and exchange of wealth, the postulates and definitions of political economy do square fairly with facts. While men are engaged in buying and selling, they are dominated by the desire to make good bargains. Such persons, too, while they are so engaged, do compete with one another upon terms of practical equality; and the object of their desire is capable of being defined by its "*specifica differentia*"—the possession of exchange value. Consequently, an analysis of the influences which affect the production of wealth may suggest practical tests of the value of any political measure which is designed to make a nation richer. It remains to consider how far a Protective tariff is a measure within this category, and with what degree of correctness its pretensions may be tested by the conclusions of economic reasoning.

CHAPTER IV.

ECONOMICS AND THE TARIFF.

§ 1. It has already been observed that the economic test of any political measure is its effect upon the production and accumulation of material wealth. Can this test be usefully applied to a tariff? If it can be, then economic analysis will help to a decision in the tariff controversy; if it cannot be, then Protectionists are right in saying that, so far as the tariff is concerned, political economy is an "idle study."

Now a tariff is essentially a measure which is designed to affect in some way the production of material wealth; and therefore, since economics is the science which deals with the production of material wealth, economic conclusions must influence a right decision on tariff questions, if they can have any weight in politics at all. If this were not so, the framer or supporter of a tariff might logically refuse to consider its effect upon the production of wealth. Let any Protectionist, then, who questions the applicability of economics to tariff issues truthfully answer the questions, "Whether he would dare to disregard the possible effect of any tariff upon national productiveness." Whether he supports Protection because it "diversifies industries," or because it gives a "home market," or because it encourages "infant industries," or for any other reason—the basis of his argument must always be that it affects, by increase or decrease, or alteration in kind, the actual or potential wealth of the community.

The direct object of a Protective tariff is to induce some citizens to follow a certain calling. Why have they held aloof from that calling previously? Because it would not have returned them a sufficient profit. The tariff is to remedy this. By the imposition of a Protective duty it is to give a profit where there was none before. Bearing in mind, then, the argument of the last chapter, it is clear that, since a Protective tariff is primarily intended to operate upon the production of wealth by appealing to the motive of self-interest, all tariff arguments will have an economic basis. Whatever may be the political or social benefits which are supposed to accrue from tariff legislation, these must all depend upon a previous acquisition of material wealth. Consequently, the extent to which a Protective tariff affects the aggregate of national wealth can never be disregarded by those who advocate a tariff with the immediate object of encouraging new forms of productiveness. The supposed advantages of a tariff all spring from the fact that wealth is produced. It is the qualities which arise from labour in wealth-producing, and the power of enjoyment which arises from the profits of wealth-producing, that the Protectionist legislator seeks to conserve. The kind of wealth which he seeks to produce is also, no doubt, important in his eyes; and to this extent he is entitled to modify an economic conclusion by reference to the political considerations which may determine his selection of desirable occupations for his fellow-citizens. But he cannot ignore the science which deals with every form of wealth-production, by saying that he desires to encourage only certain forms of it. The larger must include the less.

Admitting, then, that it is a question of the first importance whether Free Trade or Protection gives more effective help in producing and accumulating wealth, the next matter for consideration is the applicability of economic methods in discovering the answer.

§ 2. Now the practical utility of economic analysis depends, as has been seen, upon the reality of the two assumptions of an active and dominating self-interest, and an active and equal competition. Are these mere assumptions true in the case of tariff problems? If they are, the economic analysis can be used in their solution; if they are not, it must be discarded.

Let us examine first the suggestion that the postulate of economics is unreal, when the subject of consideration is the motives which induce men to support a Protective tariff.

The denial that men as a rule are moved by the desire of gain is, as has been already mentioned, probably open to question, since it is difficult to see what other motive has a wider range or a more powerful influence. But when we are dealing only with tariff discussions it is many times harder to understand what possible objection there can be to eliminating other motives than self-interest, for the purposes of scientific study. It is unquestionable that *in the pursuit of material wealth*, the desire for gain, or (what is the same thing in other words) the impulse to gratify desires with the least possible expenditure of effort, is so largely predominant over all others that it may fairly be considered by itself. As has been said by an American writer[1] :—" Between one dollar and two dollars a man has

---

[1] Mr. John Bascom, quoted by Professor Perry.

no choice—he must take the greater; between one day and two days of labour he must take the less; between the present and the future he must take the present. This is not a sphere of caprice, or scarcely even of liberty—the actions themselves present no alternative." But the effect of a tariff upon the production and accumulation of material wealth is admittedly of great importance. There cannot, therefore, be much unreality in assuming that the citizens of the community whose tariff is in question desire to produce and retain wealth with as little sacrifice as possible; nor is it unpractical, in considering the effect of a tariff upon wealth, to eliminate from the discussion all the motives which may influence those who pursue wealth, except that which is everywhere supreme in prompting to the pursuit. To quote again from Mr. John Bascom:—"Whichever one of a thousand motives engages man in the pursuit of wealth, once in that pursuit these all conform to one method, and acknowledge one law." If the elimination of all motives save one is ever permissible—and it is only by such means that abstractions can be formed—it must be so where the motive which remains is that which predominates so largely in the majority of concrete specimens that all others are reduced to insignificance. This is the case with the motive of self-interest when the citizens of a State desire a Protective tariff.

§ 3. Assuming, then, that the first postulate of economic science as to the predominance of self-interest is sufficiently close to the truth to justify it being taken as the basis of a scientific abstraction for purposes of tariff disputes, let us see whether the second postulate as to the equality of the competing units is also applicable.

The competition which political economy assumes to be ever active—a competition the existence of which alone gives political economy a claim to be regarded as a science—is a competition of equal units. These may be individuals or groups of individuals, but they are always assumed to be equal to one another. In practice, no doubt, an exact equality does not exist. In many cases—such as the competition between landlords and tenants in Ireland, or usurers and peasants in Eastern Europe—the superiority of one side or the other is so marked that the parties can never discuss a bargain upon equal terms. This was the chronic condition of whole classes in earlier periods of European history—a fact which explains the inapplicability of modern economic ideas to the industrialism of the Middle Ages. It is the condition now of all classes in the East, where economic ideas are equally inapplicable. It is the condition still of many individuals even in the most advanced communities. The progress of society from status to contract, which Sir Henry Maine has lucidly illustrated, is not yet complete. The environment of an individual citizen has not yet become the result of his own choice, although the tendency in every democratic country is to enlarge the sphere of individual freedom. Even now, however, class traditions, oppressive customs, bad land laws, lack of education, difficulties of locomotion, mere localism, and many other causes, tend in a greater or less degree to impede the exercise of a free volition by classes or by individuals. Nevertheless, political economy takes no account of these fetters upon individual freedom. It assumes that every man is or may become equally equipped for the struggle of existence, and that as a fact the active combatants do engage upon equal terms. This assumption is true, for all practical purposes, as regards the competition of wholesale traders.

Men who buy and sell on a large scale, whether as merchants or producers, do practically stand upon a footing of equality. Unlike the artisan, who (unless he belong to a trade union) must accept work when it is offered or starve, the capitalist merchant or manufacturer can afford to let his prices be determined by the higgling of the market. Such compulsion as may exist in certain cases to buy or sell is the consequence of abnormal causes, and does not permanently or materially affect the general range of prices. The only modification which is required in the assumption of an equality of the competing units, before it is made the basis of an economical analysis of tariff questions, is owing to the effect produced on competition by the existence of trusts and combines. But even in this case the modification is more apparent than real—at least, so far as it affects the dispute between Protection and Free Trade ; because, although trusts and combines, when favoured by Protection, may destroy competition in a particular trade within the Protected country, they do not invalidate the assumption upon which the economic analysis is based—namely, that free competition would exist if it were not for the Protective tariff. Moreover, even if trusts could be formed in a Free Trade country—and no trust has been permanently successful when it is exposed to foreign competition—they could, *ex hypothesi*, be formed in all trades ; so that their only effect, so far as the economic assumption is concerned, would be to alter the nature of the competing units.

§ 4. It remains to be seen whether the refusal to submit a tariff to economic tests can be justified by the objection to political economy that it treats the acquisition of wealth, which is really a matter of minor importance, as if it were a matter of the first importance.

This may be a perfectly valid objection in certain cases—as, for instance, where the question was the desirability of forming a State collection of pictures, or of subsidising a National Theatre—but it can have little or no applicability where the material advancement of a country is the special object aimed at. But every one of the advantages which a Protective tariff is supposed to give is, in its ultimate analysis, material.

"Men are to develop their various faculties." How, but by being encouraged to follow profitable trades ? "Men are to have a home market." How, but by producing something to sell? "All the capacities and faculties of a nation are to be developed." Upon what other foundation than material prosperity is this development to rest?

It is true that, after economic arguments have been considered, a wise politician should direct his mind to the best uses to which wealth can be put; but it would surely be the height of absurdity so to fix attention on the mode of spending as to render a community neglectful of the best means of acquisition. Protectionists who attack economic arguments on account of imperfections and limitations which nobody denies, omit to notice that their own political arguments assume an economic basis. They begin by declaring that the narrow field of political economy renders it an "idle study;" and yet the moment they test their own conclusions, they take their stand within the much-derided limits of economic science, and cannot move a step outside without falling into an unfathomable bog. It is not sufficient in a tariff controversy to attack economic arguments in general terms; Protectionists should go further, and prove that the particular economic argument in favour of Free Trade is overridden by political considerations. In other words, although circumstances may render economic reasoning inapplicable to all the facts of life, it does not follow that the existence of these circumstances can be assumed, in order to invalidate the economic argument against Protection.

§ 5. To sum up, then, the results of this inquiry into the relation of economics to the tariff, we may say that those who condemn the use of economic analysis in the solution of tariff problems are, as might have been expected, partly right and partly wrong. They are right in insisting that economic methods should be used with extreme caution; but they are wrong in saying that they cannot be used at all. The arguments for or against any tariff are in part economic and in part political; and while the economist cannot safely refuse to qualify his abstract conclusions by considerations of politics, the politician cannot find a basis for any of his arguments against Free Trade unless he openly or tacitly adopt the methods and conclusions of an economic science. Economic conclusions therefore, so far from being valueless, possess a high importance as a test of fiscal legislation.

But when it is once conceded—and few disputants would refuse the concession were it openly demanded of them—that no sound political judgment can be formed about a tariff if its effect upon the increase of wealth is disregarded, a very significant factor has entered into the fiscal controversy— namely, the contrast between the attitudes of Protectionists and Free Traders towards economic arguments.

The Free Traders have never been afraid to frame a scientific statement of their case. They have, indeed, erred in the other extreme of making their arguments too scientific. They have proved, with a wearisome iteration, that Protective tariffs cannot increase wealth, and have insisted, until the world is tired, that it is mathematically demonstrable that their effect is to diminish wealth. The unanimity of condemnation has, indeed, been remarkable. Mr. Mongredien, in his admirable essay " Free Trade and English Commerce," mentions (p. 32) that in 1883 the British Museum Library, under the catalogue title " Political Economy," contained the names of seventy-seven authors of various nationalities and languages; of these, only *two* advocated Protection !

Such a consensus of expert opinion can only be set aside in one of two ways—namely, either by denying the applicability of economic reasoning, or by impeaching its validity. Some Protectionists adopt the former course, by insisting that although Free Trade may be economically sound, the political advantages of Protection more than countervail its economic inferiority. Others take a more courageous stand, and, denying the scientific value of Individualist economics, proceed to determine the laws of national well-being by a new economic system of their own construction. A consideration of the views of the former class may be deferred until the political aspect of the fiscal argument comes under review. For the present we may confine our attention to an inquiry into the nature of this new system and its application to tariff disputes. This will form the subject of the next chapter.

CHAPTER V.

NATIONALIST ECONOMICS.

§ 1. It has been implied in the argument of the preceding chapter that no systematic defence of Protection upon economic grounds has been attempted. As this statement might be denied by the more ardent partisans of a restrictive policy, some further explanation of its meaning is desirable.

The term "economic" has already been defined as "that which relates to the production and accumulation of material wealth." An economic argument is, thus, an argument which is directed exclusively to the consideration of the effect of a fiscal policy upon wealth in its production and accumulation. The necessity for considering this has been already pointed out, and it has also been observed that Protectionists have usually directed their attention to other matters.

In taking this course, Protectionists often claim to be making use of the conclusions of political economy. They have founded, they say, a political economy of their own, the conclusions and methods of which are free from all the objections that are urged against the school of Ricardo and Mill. From this study they deduce general rules of policy which, as they maintain, are a sufficient economic justification for Protective tariffs.

As it would be idle to dispute about terms, and make

differences where none exist, there can be no objection to assenting to a new use of the term "political economy," if the methods and conclusions of Protectionists can justify the change. This, however, is a fitting subject for inquiry—"Are there any other modes of economic reasoning? Is it possible to frame any general argument in favour of Protection, which shall be independent of empiricism and expediency, by applying the conclusions of a new science of economics with different definitions, different methods, and different scope?" Should Protectionists succeed in doing this, they will, undoubtedly, have turned the flank of their opponents.

§ 2. The first point to be observed about the new science is that the meaning of the word "economic" has been changed. Economic, with writers of the Individualist school, always connoted material wealth. With writers of the new school its meaning is enlarged to include everything which has any relation to national well-being.

> "Political economy," says the Hon. Thomas Reed, Speaker of the House of Representatives, in one of the tersest and most complete defences of Protective tariffs which have ever been penned,[1] "is an idle study except when it concerns itself with everything that adds to the comfort and happiness of the people."
>
> "The political economy of a nation," says List,[2] "is a compound of the economy of the people and the financial economy of the State, when the State embraces a whole nation fitted for independence by the number of its population, the extent of its territory; by its political institutions, civilisation, wealth, and power—and thus fitted for stability and political influence." The economy of the people is thus defined: "Those institutions, regulations, laws and conditions on which the economy of the individual subjects of a State is dependent, and by which it is regulated." The financial

---

[1] *Belford's Magazine*, Oct., 1889. The article was intended as a Protectionist manifesto, addressed to the educated classes of the Western States.

[2] "The National System of Political Economy." By Friedrich List. English translation, p. 195. (Longmans & Co., London, 1885.) The first German edition of this work appeared in 1841. It has had a vogue in America which is quite out of proportion to its merits.

economy of a people is thus defined : "That which has reference to the raising, the expending, and the administration of the material means of government of a community."[1]

The same author expresses this idea in another passage in the following terms :—

"National economy is that science which, correctly appreciating the existing interests and the individual circumstances of nations, teaches how *every separate nation* can be raised to that stage of industrial development in which union with other nations equally well developed, and consequently freedom of trade, can become possible or useful to it" (p. 127).

It will be apparent from these extracts that an economic argument, in the language of writers of this school, no longer means an argument which is exclusively devoted to the consideration of changes in the degree of national productiveness of material wealth, but one which takes within its purview every fact—whether it be an intellectual concept, or a tangible phenomenon, or a condition of the senses—which may, either directly or indirectly, promote the well-being of the citizens of a State.

§ 3. It follows from this use of terms that economic investigation ceases to be conducted by abstract processes, and becomes an historical inquiry into the social, political, moral, and religious conditions of a nation. The opposing methods are thus contrasted by Professor Sumner and Mr. H. M. Hoyt :—

"We have," says Professor Sumner, "to understand that an *economic* investigation may be carried on just as independently as

---

[1] Mr. H. M. Hoyt ("Protection *versus* Free Trade. The Scientific Validity and Economic Operation of Defensive Duties in the United States." By Henry M. Hoyt. New York : D. Appleton & Co. Third Edition, Revised. 1886) adopts a similar view of the meaning of the term. (*See* pp. 74, 79, 391, 396.) This is the most elaborate defence of Protection yet published.

Professor Thomson, a disciple of List, without rejecting Individualist economics, treats its conclusions as valueless. ("Political Economy, with Especial Reference to the Industrial History of Nations." By R. E. Thompson, M.A. Philadelphia : Porter-Coates. 1882.)

a chemical or physical or biological investigation. The economist does not need to be on the look-out all the time to correct his results by reference to some outside considerations, or to the dogmas of jejune and rickety systems of metaphysical speculation. On the contrary, he should regard the introduction of extraneous elements —no matter under what high-sounding names of *moral, political*, and *social*—as sure signs of impending confusion and fallacy (*Princeton Review*, March, 1882).

To this Mr. Hoyt replies (p. 74 [n.]):—

"Professor Sumner's form of economic investigation might be adequate to effect the immediate exchange of commodities existing on a given day. It would not account for the existing stock, nor would it furnish a clue to the nature or amount of to-morrow's supply, or where to-morrow's supply was to come from. A given kind of moral, political, and social man must, at last, be a definite kind of economic man in correspondence with himself. His wants are peculiar to his traits, and the preparations to meet them must grow out of his environment. You cannot expect a human being with one sort of aptitudes, to go off and live in a part of the world and in pursuits which do not engage those aptitudes. He will make the arena of his struggle such that it will engage his best efforts—physical, mental, and moral. Then the economic results will take care of themselves."

It will follow, also, from this change in the scope of "economic" science, that if the new subjects introduced into it are capable of scientific treatment, fresh tests must be devised of the value of any fiscal policy. It will not be enough to demonstrate that Protection lessens national productiveness, because Protectionists will apply some other formula by which to estimate the influence of tariffs upon the political, moral, social, and religious environment of a whole nation. It will be matter for inquiry later whether it is possible to frame a satisfactory formula for this purpose.

§ 4. It is, as has already been admitted, quite legitimate for Protectionists to adopt any basis for their science that they please. Nevertheless, it must not be forgotten, in following their attempt to establish a new economic science, with different definitions, methods, and scope, that its conclusions, whatever they may be, will not answer the conclusions of the Individualist political economy. They may justify a busy man in passing these by as verbal conceits, but they cannot meet them, because they stand on a different plane. If it be once admitted that the effect of a tariff upon the production of wealth is an important element in its success, then a scientific demonstration that a tariff lessens the wealth-producing power of a community is not disproved by showing that the same tariff advances national welfare in the direction of morals, politics, or religion. It may have such an effect, and the Individualist arguments may, in consequence, be overridden; but, for what it may be worth, the economic demonstration, as such, remains unassailed. But we have seen in a previous chapter that a Protectionist cannot ignore the influence of a Protective tariff upon national productiveness. If, therefore, he wants to disprove the proposition that Protection lessens the aggregate of national wealth, he must do more than show that his policy carries with it other advantages which compensate for its impoverishing influence; he must himself demonstrate that Protection increases national wealth. But where is the man courageous enough to maintain the simple proposition that the best way to increase the aggregate of material wealth in any community is by preventing or restricting international exchange?

Professor Sumner has pointed out, in the article in the *Princeton Review* which has been already quoted from,[1] what the work is which lies before any ambitious man who is desirous of becoming a Protectionist Ricardo. Such an one " must boldly declare that there is a science of wealth based on restrictions; that he can discover the principles of it, and reduce them to a theory; that trade between countries is a mischievous thing—at least, if it runs on parallels of latitude;

---

[1] *See* above, p. 108.

that isolation and antagonism of nations is the law of Nature upon which wealth and civilisation depend; and that there is therefore no universal science of wealth, but only a national science of wealth, and that this science is, in its final analysis, only a generalisation from certain empirical maxims of economic policy." And when our aspiring theorist has reached this point, he must then frame his tests of the effect of a tariff upon national productiveness. To use again the words of Professor Sumner, he must answer these questions:—" Does a tariff enable the population of a country to command greater material good for a given effort?" and "Does it lessen the ratio of effort and sacrifice to comfort and enjoyment?"[1] It is only by this means that any direct answer can be given to the economic solution of the fiscal problem as it is arrived at by the Individualist.[2]

It will be necessary to keep these considerations in mind, in order to understand the logical significance of the Protectionist theory of economics and its proper use in a tariff dispute. After these preliminary explanations we are in a position to begin a critical examination of the theory and precepts of "Nationalist economics."

§ 5. The essential divergence between the Nationalists and

---

[1] Professor Sumner also suggests two other test questions: "Does the statute enacted by the Legislature alter the distribution of property so that one man enjoys another man s earnings? Has the State a law in operation which enables one citizen to collect taxes of another?" and "Does the tariff prevent me from supporting myself and my family by my labour as well as I could do if there were no Protecting taxes?"

[2] "If Protection be good, it is good in and of itself; if it is bad, it has no business to be begging to lean on something so respectable as revenue. The burden of proof, at any rate, lies upon the man who brings in a theory interrupting the play of natural laws. Let him bring forward and prove his theory of restriction. Let us hear the arguments and see the grounds that justify the prohibition of an advantageous trade." (Professor Perry, quoted by Mr. Hoyt, p. 196.) So Professor Walker. [The Protectionist must give] "an analysis of the conditions of production, which shall disclose the law which makes trade within the lines of sovereignty beneficial, and trade across the boundaries of separate States deleterious to one or both parties."

Individualists is, as the terms import, that the one adopts the nation as the industrial unit, the other the individual. This leads to a radical difference of scope and method.

The "Nationalists" (as the members of this school like to designate themselves) view every nation as a whole, and treat of its national development. In their eyes a political community is not a congeries of individual atoms, but a sentient living organism, with roots in the past and branches reaching to the future. The scope of economics, as these writers understand the term, is to discover the laws of national growth, and to define the rules by which each nation may achieve its complete development. This body of laws and rules may differ for different peoples, since they are determined by the history, temperament, and capacities of each political community. The "economist" will, however, deal primarily with the economics of his own country, and will endeavour to indicate the measures by which the acquired and latent capacities of the whole body of citizens may be most fully and harmoniously developed.

As a consequence of this widened scope, the method of the science alters. It no longer deduces the industrial movement of a nation from a consideration of the industrial movements of its individual citizens; but starting with the nation as the unit, and explaining its existing industrial condition by reference to historical, political, moral, and religious considerations, it proceeds to discuss the power of free industrial movement which the individual has from time to time possessed, and the power which, in the present interest of the State, it is desirable to give him. The following extracts will make the contentions clearer:—

> "Every distinct community," says Mr. Hoyt, "society, state, nation, every *political entity*, is to be discussed as *an industrial entity*.[1] It is impossible to conceive of the terms of an industrial economic problem except under the condition of nationality. . . . .

[1] The italics are in the original.

The difference between civilisation and barbarism lies in the desires to be satisfied, the things to be exchanged, and their mode of production. These depend on moral, intellectual, and political considerations, as well as economic" (pp. 79, 80).

And again he says:—

"No real scientific results can be obtained by the atomistic view of the co-workers in a given society or nation. . . . The attempt to deal with the individuals as units involves us in the vicious error to which Mr. Herbert Spencer has called our attention—that of 'mistaking a part for a whole,' and thus 'its relations to existence in general will be misapprehended.' By this discrete treatment the whole is completely lost sight of, and the aggregates which the whole involve disappear from our investigations" (p. 234).

The problem which is to be solved by this repudiation of Individualist economics is thus stated:—

"The real problem is, then, to ascertain how the industry of a nation may be made to yield the greatest annual product" (p. 89).

List expresses the same ideas in more sonorous language:—

"The system of the school [of Adam Smith] suffers," he says, "from three main defects: firstly, from boundless *cosmopolitanism*, which neither recognises the principle of nationality, nor takes into consideration the satisfaction of its interests; secondly, from a dead *materialism*, which everywhere regards the mere exchangeable value of things without taking into consideration the mental and political, the present and the future interests, and the productive powers of the nation; thirdly, from a *disorganising particularism* and *individualism*, which, ignoring the nature and character of social labour, and the operation of the union of powers in their higher consequences, considers private industry only as it would develop itself under a state of free interchange with society (*i.e.*, with the whole human race) were that race not divided into separate national societies.

"Between each individual and entire humanity, however, stands the nation, with its special language and literature, with its peculiar origin and history, with its special manners and customs, laws and institutions, with the claims of all these for existence, independence, perfection, and continuance for the future, and with its separate territory; a society which, united by a thousand ties of mind and of interests, combines itself into one independent whole, which recognises the law of right for and within itself, and in its united character is still opposed to other societies of a similar kind in their national liberty, and consequently can only under the existing conditions of the world maintain self-existence and independence by its own power and resources. As the individual chiefly obtains by means of the nation, and in the nation, mental culture, power of production, security and prosperity, so is the civilisation of the human race only conceivable and possible by means of the civilisation and development of the individual nations.

"Meanwhile, however, an infinite difference exists in the condition and circumstances of the various nations: we observe among them giants and dwarfs, well-formed bodies and cripples, civilised, half-civilised, and barbarous nations; but in all of them, as in the individual human being, exists the impulse of self-preservation, the striving for improvement which is implanted by Nature. It is the task of politics to civilise the barbarous nationalities, to make the small and weak ones great and strong, but, above all, to secure to them existence and continuance. It is the task of national economy to accomplish the *economical development of the nation*, and to prepare it for admission into the universal society of the future."

§ 6. Let us pause a moment to estimate the value of this new "science" by reference to its avowed range. We recall that the main objection to Individualist economics was the difficulty of making any useful abstraction of a being so infinitely mixed and various as "the individual citizen." Yet an abstraction of some sort must be made if the "science" of political economy is to be anything more than the study of history. If generalised conclusions are to be reached as to the laws of national progress, or if a scientific analysis is to be attempted of the elements of national greatness—and it is only by performing both these tasks that Nationalist economics can justify its claim to being scientific—the variant and accidental elements must be eliminated from the object of study. But let any one attempt to eliminate the variant and accidental elements from "a nation." How is he even to make a beginning in such a task? Merely to enumerate the forces which compose the stream of a nation's life would be hardly possible without a wider range of knowledge than mankind as yet possesses; while even if the difficulties of enumeration could be successfully overcome, the work of separating the permanent from the transitory elements would prove insuperable. Who is to decide upon the precise degree of influence to be given to any of the constituent elements of national greatness? Take only one example. Religion has been at all times a powerful factor in national development; but could any one estimate its influence in any but the vaguest terms? If Individualist economics were objectionable because its scope was too narrow, Nationalist economics manifestly errs upon the other side by covering an illimitable field. The "welfare of a nation" is a conception of so vague a character that it cannot be submitted to any scientific analysis. Its elements are not only doubtful, but illusory; because, even were it possible to come to an agreement upon the nature of national well-being, still the things which admittedly go to make a nation great and prosperous—such as morality, high spirit, orderliness, capacity to govern, love of beauty, obedience, spirituality, intellectual force, and many other qualities and conditions—are of a character which cannot be measured by any known standard, or reduced to any common denomination. Were it not that large phrases possess an irresistible attraction for a certain class of minds, it might be thought unnecessary to pursue this subject further. But this so-called science wraps itself in such high-sounding jargon—and, as Professor Sumner says, "masquerades under such an affectation of learning and philosophy"—that it has met with more than the ordinary success of economic quackery. Take away, however, all verbiage, drop such talk as "the operation of the union of powers in their higher consequences," and present the theory for consideration in the simple language of Mr. Reed! It becomes at once apparent that a science which deals with everything that adds to the "comfort and happiness of the people" is defining its objects in terms of the unknown. Who shall say in what "the comfort and happiness" of a nation consist? Or are there to be as many sciences of political economy as there are professors? Certainly, it would seem that if practical conclusions of precision cannot be obtained from the science the scope of which is limited to a consideration of the individual, none can be looked for from that the range of which is boundless. The unscientific character of the inquiry is further illustrated by also putting into plain language the problem which is proposed for investigation—" Analyse the causes and expound the nature of national well-being." Such a problem may be studied historically, and history may often suggest an empirical solution, just as the historical studies of the Nationalist school have been particularly fruitful in throwing light upon the complexities of modern industrialism. But an attempt in our present state of knowledge to treat this problem scientifically can only result in the creation of utterly useless abstractions, or the pronouncement of a series of inconsequent dogmas.

Let it, however, be assumed, for purposes of argument, that the subject-matter of Nationalist economics is capable of scientific treatment—still Individualists, whose studies are so contemptuously cast upon one side, will want to know what measure of national happiness and comfort these new philosophers desire them to adopt; because if no such measure can be found, students have no means of testing the conformity of a legislative act to the scientific rule. But we have only to run over in our minds a few of the constituent elements of happiness or comfort to see that they consist of things which are quite immeasurable. What means exist by which we can estimate the value of different qualities, conditions, or ideas? And yet these things enter very largely into the concept of national well-being. Or, again, suppose that any of these things could be measured separately from the others, to what common denominator can they all be reduced in order that their values may be compared? Yet it is upon a " science " such as this that Protection rests—as if the framing of a large and general statement were the same thing as the construction of a scientific theory. No wonder that Professor Sumner, after many years of active battle with "scientists" of this school, denounces their pretensions as "an arrant piece of economic quackery." Our business, however, is to investigate this science further, without resort to terms of contumely. Let us test it again by reference to its practical conclusions.

§ 9. Nationalist economists profess to have discovered two fundamental rules for the guidance of their political disciples. The first of these is, "That every nation must be entirely self-supporting;" and the second, "That the development of productive powers, and not the increase of national wealth, is the object of wise statesmanship." Let us treat of each of these rules in turn.

The notion that every nation must be self-supporting is worked out by List in the following series of propositions:—

> "The idea of independence and power originates in the very idea of 'the nation'" (p. 181).
>
> "Nations have to pass through the following stages of economical development: original barbarism, pastoral condition, agricultural condition, agricultural-manufacturing condition, and agricultural-manufacturing-commercial condition" (p. 177).
>
> "In a country devoted to mere raw agriculture, dulness of mind, awkwardness of body, obstinate adherence to old notions, custom, methods and processes, want of culture, of prosperity, and of liberty, prevail" (p. 197).
>
> "Manufacturing occupations [on the other hand] develop and bring into action an incomparably greater variety and higher type of mental qualities and abilities" (p. 199). "They are at once the offspring, and at the same time the supporters and nurses, of science and the arts" (p. 200).
>
> [Statesmen must accordingly encourage manufactures by preventing the competition of any nation in a higher manufacturing stage than has been reached in their own country (Chaps. XVII.—XX.).]

Mr. H. M. Hoyt expresses the same idea thus:—

> "It is indispensable, if a given nation is to live on a given area, that opportunity should be afforded them to render mutual services to each other, or to somebody else somewhere else. If there were no such opportunity, the nation would be non-existent. There is no

existing or historical nation in which the vast mass of services by which men satisfy each other's desires have not been rendered within the lines of the political entity. To that extent the political entity and the industrial entity, as a matter of fact, do correspond" (p. 361).

And again :—

"The external relations of nations have not grown out of economic movements" (p. 362). "[If they had] no *economic* reason could be given why the industrial entity should correspond to the political entity" (p. 367). "[But in fact] the people of a nation are bound together by sentiments different in degree, not in kind, from those which bind together the members of a household. In the nation, as in the family, there is a vast multitude of services exchanged between its members which are not economic. The economic and non-economic services are grounded in the same substratum of humanity; and the effort to separate them, and render one here, and the other with people in another family, simply means disintegration. It is the union and mutual exchange of these two kinds of services which result in our welfare and create the sentiment known as patriotism. It is a genuine emotion, and is a true economic force. It reconciles us, also, to accept the averaged results of our efficiency expended on our own physical conditions. It engenders that sense of community which operates with such force in family and nation. Thanks to this feeling for the commonweal, the eternal and destructive war—the *bellum omnium contra omnes*—which an unscrupulous self-interest would not fail to generate among men engaged in the isolated prosecution of their own economic interests, ceases in the higher well-ordered organisation of society. On it are based the various forms of economy in common—family economy, corporation or association economy, municipal economy, and national economy. And these forces of economy in common are so essentially the condition and complement of industrial economy, that the latter without them could either not be maintained at all, or at least only in the very lowest stage of civilisation."

From these considerations it follows that—

"The problem is simply to provide the opportunity of economic labour for a population born or thrown together on a given geographical area, on which area there are overruling political motives for maintaining a political entity. The industrial entity must then be made to conform to the political entity, or both perish. Drop all considerations of patriotism, social ties, kindred, politics, and submit to the economic forces alone, and I grant there would be no economic reason for any correspondence of the industrial and political entities. But then there might be no economic reason for the existence of Germany or France " (p. 369).

Again there is reason to complain of the unnecessary use of pompous language. All this talk about the necessity for a correspondence between the political and the industrial entity only means that it is desirable, for political reasons, to develop every national resource, and that this object is best achieved by a policy of Protection. We may agree with the object, and dispute the efficacy of the means; but we cannot now project this political discussion into the middle of an economic argument. That must be reserved until a later chapter.[1] But an admission that it is desirable, in the interests of a nation, that all the capacities of all its citizens should have an opportunity of coming into play, does not require us to prohibit trade with any nation more developed than ourselves. Nor is it by any means clear that a nation advances most rapidly by concerning itself exclusively with its own affairs, at the cost of an industrial warfare with all the rest of the world. Yet, according to List, " Each nation, like each individual, has its own interests nearest at heart. Russia is not called upon to care for the welfare of Germany; Germany must care for Germany, and Russia for Russia" (p. 93). Nor must your Nationalist statesman stand upon the fear of war. " War," says List again, " acts on a State like a prohibitive tariff system. It thereby becomes acquainted with the great advantages of a manufacturing power of its own. . . . A war which leads to the change of the purely agricultural State into an agricultural-manufacturing State is therefore a blessing to the nation." Notable conclusions these for a philosopher who repudiated the economics of Adam Smith because they took no notice of religion or morality !

The mischievous idea that every nation must be independent of all others—like the Stoic idea that every individual

---

[1] *See* below, Part III.

must be self-sufficing—is best refuted by history and experience. Such an achievement, even if it be desirable, has never yet been possible. Nations, like men, grow stagnant by non-intercourse; their latent capacities wither, and the impulse of ambition dies.[1]

Mr. Hoyt may be right in his assertion that "considerations of patriotism, social ties, kindred and politics," require a nation in its best interest to trade as little as possible with the inhabitants of other countries. No one can dispute an *ex cathedrâ* statement; but in that case the Chinese reached the perfection of economic wisdom when, in the true spirit of Nationalist philosophy, they built a wall around their territory in order to maintain, by the most efficient means possible, the "correspondence of their political and industrial entities." And how distressing is the lack of correspondence between these "entities" in the case of Great Britain!

The Nationalist champions have, at any rate, this advantage—their rule is unassailable by logic. Let who will declare, with numerous rhetoric and sonorous phrase, that the interests of the State require an independence of the foreigner—no one can say him nay. He has Providence behind him, and natural rights, and knowledge of the future, and, failing these, he is at least entitled to his own opinion. Those who are not of the faithful can only wonder and look at a map.

§ 8. We pass now from the Nationalist rules for international dealings to those for internal statesmanship. These are summed in the maxim "That it is the duty of statesmen

---

[1] The commercial, rather than the manufacturing, nations have been in the forefront of civilisation: e.g., Carthaginians, Hanseatic Towns, Venice and Holland, in older times; while European nations might fairly be ranked according to their civilisation by looking at the magnitude per head of the population of their foreign trade.

"If trade pinches the mind," says Lowell, in his "Essay on Josiah Quincy," "the influence of commerce is liberating and enlarging."

to develop a nation's productive powers." This is thus expounded by its author, List :—

> "The prosperity of a nation is not greater in the proportion in which it has amassed more wealth (*i.e.*, values of exchange), but in the proportion in which it has more *developed its powers of production.*[1] Although laws and public institutions do not produce immediate values, they nevertheless produce productive powers; and Say is mistaken if he maintains that nations have been enabled to become wealthy under all forms of government, and that by means of laws no wealth can be created" (p. 144).

Mr. Hoyt says, in effect, the same thing in answer to the well-known Free Trade inquiry, "How can taxes create wealth?" :—

> "The Protectionist proposes to create nothing. He can create neither matter nor material forces. The energy he proposes to set free is already in the men and things he deals with. . . . The Protective statute renders possible the formation of the structural organisation peculiar to a given country through which the productive forces take effect" (pp. 380, 383).

The theoretical basis of this maxim is a denial of Adam Smith's proposition that "Industry can only be increased by the increase of capital."[2] This is thus expressed by a Protectionist writer, Mr. George Basil Dixwell, in a passage quoted by Mr. Hoyt (p. 388) :—

> "To make the proposition [that laws and government cannot increase industry] a vast gap has to be filled. It requires to be proved that in a normal condition of things there is no unemployed capital and no funds which, although intended for unproductive consumption, are capable of being instantly turned to the support of production the moment that a new industry introduced by a Protective law presents a profitable field of employment."

This is simply the old economic exposure of the fallacy of Mill's statement that "a demand for commodities is not a

---

[1] The italics are in the English translation.
[2] "Wealth of Nations," Book IV., Chapter II.—"The industry of the community can only be augmented in proportion as its capital increases, and the capital of the community can only increase in accordance with the savings which it gradually makes from its income." (*See* List, pp. 225 and 597.)

demand for labour;" and it is perfectly sound. The Nationalists are right in asserting that the development of productive powers is a most important element in national greatness, which, under certain circumstances, may be of greater importance than the accumulation of exchange values. Their error consists in failing to observe that, on the Individualist theory, there is a necessary connection between the accumulation of exchange values, or "capital," and the development of new industries; and that as capital accumulates, the self-interest which prompts to its profitable use will direct it into new channels of productiveness. Nationalists admit that self-interest will endeavour to use capital in this way, but they deny its power to do so without Government assistance. They assert that the competition of more highly developed nations will prevent the establishment of the desired industry; and that, therefore, this competition must be prevented by restrictive duties. The difference between the two parties is, therefore, largely one of fact, not theory:—"Does foreign competition in fact prevent the development of a nation's productive powers?" And, secondly, "If so, are restrictive laws the best means of encouraging this development?" But these are plainly questions of politics, which are out of place in a discussion about the value of a scientific theory. They will be examined fully in a later portion of this work, when the time comes for dealing with the political arguments in favour of Protection.

The maxim—which, for the sake of brevity, may be termed "the productive powers maxim"—is also supported on another ground. It is said that the self-interest of individuals cannot be relied upon to develop natural resources without aid from the Government. The reason given for this assertion is so curious and difficult to understand that it will be better to express it in the words of List:—

> "It is a further sophism," he says, "arrived at by confounding the theory of mere values with that of the powers of production, when the popular school infers from the doctrine that '*The wealth*

> *of the nation is merely the aggregate of the wealth of all individuals in it, and that the private interest of every individual is better able than all State regulations to incite to production and accumulation of wealth,*' the conclusion that the national industry would prosper best if only every individual were left undisturbed in the occupation of accumulating wealth. That doctrine can be conceded without the conclusion resulting from it at which the school desires thus to arrive; for the point in question is not that of immediately increasing by commercial restrictions the amount of the *values in exchange* in the nation, but of increasing the *amount of its productive powers*. But that the aggregate of the productive powers of the nation is not synonymous with the aggregate of the productive powers of all individuals, each considered separately—that the total amount of these powers depends chiefly on social and political conditions, but especially on the degree in which the nation has rendered effectual the division of labour and the confederation of the powers of production within itself—we believe we have sufficiently demonstrated in the preceding chapters" (pp. 169, 170).

Nothing could illustrate more clearly than this passage the danger of confusing an empiric statement of facts with a scientific argument. But it will be well to defer criticism until the maxims of the school are fully stated. It remains to point out how the object of the Nationalists is to be achieved. This is also explained by List.

The care of a statesman, as has been said, ought to be not so much the increase of wealth as the development of a nation's productive powers. This is to be achieved by the temporary sacrifice of wealth.

> "The nation must sacrifice and give up a measure of material property in order to gain culture, skill, and power of united production; it must sacrifice some present advantages in order to secure to itself some future ones" (p. 144).

To this end it must restrict its trade with foreign countries, and prevent individuals from following their own interests. If a statesman should permit citizens merely to concern themselves with getting rich, he is like an improvident landowner who—

> "puts out his savings at interest, and keeps his sons at common hard work, instead of foregoing his interest and submitting to a present loss in order to give his sons the benefit of education" (p. 138).

The above extracts will have given a brief but sufficient summary of the practical conclusions of Nationalist economists. Do these confirm its pretensions to be regarded as a science? Certainly they do not commend themselves to unassisted reason.

In the first place, they utterly repudiate the notion that the maxims of morality have any place in international transactions. Every nation is to be for itself, at whatever cost of injury to others. Secondly, they display the utmost mistrust of the individual citizen. They treat him in all industrial matters as a person who cannot be allowed a free choice. He is to be driven into this trade or that, as the changing wisdom of lawgivers may determine; and in no case is it to be conceded that he is the man of all others who is most likely to know and pursue his own interest. Legislative restrictions trammel him on every side, and Parliament, and not himself, determines what pursuits he is to follow and what avoid. In all this Nationalists are, of course, determined by the highest considerations for the well-being of the person whom they so insult; just as slavery was never supported for any other reason than because it increased the happiness of the slaves!

Time can be the only judge of such expedients; but while waiting for the verdict of posterity, it is not out of place to remind these doctors of human character that a narrow and vulgar provinciality is not patriotism, and that human nature reaches its highest development when it consciously, *and of its own free will,* enjoys at all times that which is best.

The question, however, which we are now discussing is not about expediency, but about principles.

§ 9. We are now in a position to pass judgment on the scientific character of Nationalist economy. We have traced this system through its definitions, scope, methods, and conclusions; but are we any nearer the perception of a single general principle? The scope of the science is ludicrously vague; its method is empiric; its conclusions are immoral according to the prevalent ideas of morality. At best, it has furnished a few political arguments by which to test the conclusions of Individualistic economics; but it has never really grappled with economic problems, while its criticisms generally fall short because it misconceives the character of the individualistic science.

Take, for instance, its cardinal maxim: that the increase of the wealth of all individual citizens is not the same thing as the development of productive powers! This is valueless as a scientific statement, although it may lead to useful political results, while as a piece of criticism it is beside the mark, because it ignores the limitations of the scientific school. It is idle to impeach the validity of the individualist methods by mentioning the social and political conditions under which the work of a nation can be most effectively performed, and then complaining that the Individualistic science does not take all of these into account. No Individualist would deny that the efficacy of a labourer depends in a great degree upon his social and political environment. In fact, this is the reason why economic conclusions about the products of labour have constantly to be corrected by reference to the conditions of the workman. But this admission is not inconsistent with a belief in Individualist methods.

The "individual" of Adam Smith's political economy is not, as Mr. Hoyt imagines, "a masterless, clanless man," but a citizen. His citizenship is assumed, so that there is no necessity to devote chapters to discussing its component elements. And not only is citizenship assumed, but that kind of citizenship which is only possible in highly civilised communities of the modern type, and which is described as citizenship in an industrial community. It is true that these assumptions are not made in so many words in every economic writing, but they are implied in the postulates. The free play of self-interest and the equality of competing units are only possible in a highly organised industrial State. Consequently, the tests of economics which Nationalists affect to make by applying its conclusions to conditions of savagery and isolation have no reference to the case.

Nor do Nationalists fare any better when they accuse the Individualist of ignoring the productive force of civil and social organisation. The theory of man's economic perfectibility runs through the whole scheme of economic study. It may be that, in fact, the individual's efforts are hampered, either because he cannot, for some reason, use his full productive powers, or because capital cannot find a safe investment in developing a latent national resource; but the only scientific consequence of this is a necessity in such a case of correcting an economic conclusion. The inability of the "economic" individual in certain cases to do all that he desires does not invalidate the scientific investigation of what the results would be if he were able to have his way. Indeed, the practical utility of economics often consists in indications of legislative hindrances to the free and most effective exercise of human industry.

So, on the other hand, the mere enumeration of the social and political conditions under which the work of a nation can be most effectively performed is in no sense the construction of a science. It is, at most, a useful study in history or politics.

The conclusion is inevitable to anyone who reads Nationalist writings, that every attempt to found an economic science on any other basis than that of Individualism inevitably becomes empiric, both in its scope and method. Whatever may be the value of the arguments and the conclusions of the Nationalists, they are at best historical; they establish no general principle, but depend upon varying conditions of local circumstances. This is not necessarily an impeachment of their bearing on the fiscal controversy. It may yet turn out that Protection and Free Trade are only, after all, matters of expediency, and not of principle: in which case the political investigations of the Nationalists may possibly correct our economic conclusions almost beyond recognition. At present, however, we are only considering the claim of Nationalist economics to be regarded as a science, and we have come to the conclusion that it cannot be substantiated.

NOTE TO CHAPTER V.
THE CHARACTERISTICS OF NATIONALIST WRITERS.

No attempt has been made in the present chapter to estimate the importance of the Nationalistic school of writers, or to exhibit all their characteristics. The references to their writings have been strictly limited to the requirements of the present argument—that is to say, only those passages have been referred to which seemed to affect the validity of the methods and conclusions of individualist economics as applied to tariff controversies. This leaves a large part of their work untouched.

It would be absurd to deny that many writers of this school—of whom Röscher may be considered the head—exhibit in a notable degree many of the best attributes of scientific investigators. Their historical investigations have been particularly fruitful in showing the modern character of economic ideas and their inapplicability to undeveloped communities, such as those of Europe in the Middle Ages or of Asia at the present time; while their analysis of existing social conditions has thrown a clearer light upon many of the complexities of modern industrialism. It is now, for instance, generally recognised that the growth of trusts and combines has materially qualified the old assumptions about competition, and that within the field of distribution these assumptions were always so wide of the mark as to possess very little scientific value. But it is in the change of temper in which economics are studied that the influence of the school is most perceived. There is no longer any inclination to include all phenomena in a few neat theories, and judge of facts by them; but in its place is a readiness to test theories by fact and observation, and a growing caution in applying them.

But this recognition of the services rendered by some Nationalist writers to the study of economic questions must not blind us to the serious evils of their influence. They have caused the pendulum to swing so far upon the other side, that it is hardly possible to obtain a respectful hearing for deductive reasoning. The recent publication of Mr. Marshall's "Principles of Economics" will, it is hoped, have a corrective influence; but no lapse of time can impair the merits of John Stuart Mill's epoch-making work. Sober wisdom, whether in economics or politics, is at a discount in this age of fanatics and cranks, but every succeeding generation, for many years

Pt. II., Ch. v., § 9]

to come, will testify to the sound judgment, foresight, and sagacity of that great thinker.

Nor must we forget that a wide distinction exists between the greater and the lesser writers of this new school. Just as in time past every newspaper writer had "The Laws of Political Economy" always on his pen, and was ready to say, with Mr. Lowe, "Political economy belongs to no nation : it is of no country. . . . It will assert itself, whether you wish it or not. It is founded on the attributes of the human mind, and no power can change it"—so the Mr. Lowes of to-day exhaust their stock of vituperative epithets in condemnation of the idea that any scientific analysis of economic facts is ever possible. Chief among offenders of this sort are List and H. B. Carey; while as for Mr. Ruskin, it were only charitable to assume that his writings upon economics ought not to be taken seriously.[1] One characteristic of these writers, and the swarm of pamphleteers they have created, is the infinite variety of their topics. They write voluminously on every subject, human and divine, except economics ; they indulge freely in misty speculations on the nature and the destiny of man ; they discourse upon distinctions of race and climate, and know exactly what the world was intended to be and what it is going to become ; and in every case their authority is unimpeachable by human reason, because all of them are believers in "natural rights," and some of them are theologians ! This is not pleasantry, but a literal statement of facts. The intrusion of theology and transcendentalism into reasonings upon economic subjects is a distinguishing feature of the Nationalist school. Sometimes the result is most grotesque. Mr. Carey, for instance, who has been regarded as a prophet in America for many years, has attested that "Trade between nations is illegitimate if it runs along parallels of latitude, but legitimate along meridians of longitude." No one can dispute this astonishing discovery, because Mr. Carey makes it under the express authority of "Providence" and "Nature" !

Fortunately, the best work in economics is now being done in America under the influence of the political science schools in more than one university,[2]

---

[1] Mr. E. T. Cook, in "Studies on Ruskin," p. 29 (n.), has ingeniously suggested as an excuse for Mr. Ruskin's worst extravagances of vilification that he was criticising not the teachings of political economy, but—"*what is the same thing—what it was believed to teach.*" A plain man, who was not of the brotherhood, might be disposed to think that a special duty was cast upon a teacher of the gospel of "truth, sincerity, and nobleness" to ascertain what, for instance, J. S. Mill did really teach, before terming him "a one-eyed flat-fish" on account of what "he was supposed to teach"—which in this case was not by any means "the same thing."

[2] *The Political Science Quarterly*, *The Economic Science Quarterly*, and the studies of the Johns Hopkins University, are the current sources of information as to what is being done in the United States in the prosecution of economic studies.

so that it may be hoped that before many years have gone by the class of literature of which Mr. Carey's writings are a sample will only possess an antiquarian interest; at present it is a melancholy fact that they are regarded by many voters as scientific revelations.

The elucidation of those matters of universal interest which occupy the province of economics requires the exercise in an exceptional degree of the rare, but humble, qualities of patience and sagacity. In no intellectual pursuit is it more dangerous than in political economy to give rein to the imagination. In tracing the working of society through all its manifold connections, brilliance, enthusiasm, sympathy, and even genius, must always be subordinated to an accurate regard for detail and a more than judicial hesitancy in the adoption of conclusions. This is especially necessary in dealing with questions of international commerce, because, owing to the minute and ever-changing inter-dependence of trades, no one can be sure that he sees any commercial transaction in all its bearings. There is a tendency to give undue weight to the facts which first meet the eye, although these are often of less importance than those which are concealed from the general public, and known only to the experts of the particular trade. Nor must the student of commerce ignore the danger of mistaking local and passing for permanent phenomena. Even ten years is but a short time in the industrial history of a nation; yet, let any country pass through only a three years' depression of trade, and how many quack remedies and revolutionary schemes will be put forward by its inhabitants, and gravely considered by so-called economic writers!

These dangers to the scientific character of economic studies are increasing as civilisation becomes more complex and a survey of the whole more difficult. Added to this is a temporary cause of danger from the wave of mere expansive benevolence, which is based on no reflection and holds before itself no definite aim, that threatens now to submerge all serious and detailed treatment of social problems. On the one side, the intellect of the country is being repelled from the study of politics and driven into the pursuit of physical science; on the other, the sentimentalists, without knowledge, are encouraging disturbance and aggravating difficulties. The risk of such a state of affairs is only dimly perceived at present; but it may yet be that Liberal institutions will go under before the indifference of one class of their supporters and the ignorance of another. The forces of reaction are always organised and watchful, and every social trouble or disorder makes in their favour. The greater, then, is the reason for showing that political economy is capable of scientific treatment, and that, while not ignoring the just claims of sentiment to find legitimate expression in an organised national existence, its conclusions are capable of being expressed in general terms, which are something more than abstract generalities.

CHAPTER VI.

NATIONALIST ECONOMICS AND THE TARIFF.

§ 1. It will be remembered that, before entering upon the economic argument in favour of Free Trade, it became necessary to clear the ground for a fair fight by getting rid of a contention that economic arguments could not lead to any results in the present case. This contention was supported by the statement that there was a new science of economics, with a different definition, scope, and method, the results of which completely invalidated all the investigations of Individualists. Inquiry has proved that this claim cannot be justified; but it will be well to probe the pretensions of the science still further by showing how its so-called principles are applied to the issues in the tariff dispute.

This task is fortunately rendered easier by the admirable monograph of Mr. H. M. Hoyt, to which such frequent reference has already been made.[1] Most Nationalist writers touch incidentally upon the question of the tariff; and it is believed that all of them, except Röscher, advocate Protection.[2] But, so far as the writer is aware, no one, except Mr. Hoyt, has devoted a separate treatise to a justification of Protection by reference to Nationalist principles. But whether Mr. Hoyt stands alone or not, his work is certainly an elaborate, careful, and ingenious statement of the Protectionist case, expressed with a temperateness of language that is unhappily rare.

He begins with a criticism and repudiation of the Individualist doctrines, then states the doctrines of the Nationalist school, and then finally applies these to the tariff controversy.

[1] "Protection versus Free Trade.—The Scientific Validity and Economic Operation of Defensive Duties in the United States." By Henry M. Hoyt. Third Edition, Revised. New York, 1886.

[2] See note at end of chapter.

His illustrations and arguments are, naturally, directed principally to American voters; but they are, nevertheless, of a sufficient general application to interest a foreign reader. In fact, the treatise is regarded as a text-book in Australia; and that it has largely influenced American thought would be apparent to any reader of the *Forum*, *Belford's Magazine*, the *North American Review*, and the *Atlantic Monthly*, during the Presidential campaign of 1888. A less connected view of the Protectionist argument is afforded by the Congressional speeches on the tariff question. The six best of these on either side have been collected and published in a cheap form, under the title of "An Appeal to the American People as a Jury," which forms an invaluable handbook of the fiscal policy from an American standpoint. It naturally, however, lacks the consecutive character of Mr. Hoyt's treatise, and is more useful for its graphic illustrations of the actual working of the tariff in the United States.

The argument has three steps:—(1st) That a high degree of manufacturing skill is necessary to the best national development; and (2nd) That this cannot be obtained without Protection; (3rd) That the loss in money values which Protection causes is more than recouped by the advantages which it confers.

List expresses the whole argument in the following passage:—

> "The nation must sacrifice and give up a measure of material property in order to gain culture, skill, and powers of united production; it must sacrifice some present advantages in order to ensure to itself future ones. If, therefore, a manufacturing power, developed in all its branches, forms a fundamental condition of all higher advances in civilisation, material prosperity, and political power in every nation (a fact which, we think, we have proved from history): if it be true (as we believe we can prove) that in the present condition of the world a mere unprotected manufacturing power cannot possibly be raised up under free competition with a power which has long since grown in strength, and is protected on its own territory: how can anyone possibly undertake to prove by

arguments only based on the mere theory of values that a nation ought to buy its goods, like individual merchants, at places where they are to be had the cheapest: that we act foolishly if we manufacture anything at all which can be got cheaper from abroad: that we ought to place the industry of the nation at the mercy of the self-interest of individuals? that Protective duties constitute monopolies, which are granted to the individual home manufacturers at the expense of the nation? It is true that Protective duties at first increase the price of manufactured goods, but it is just as true, and, moreover, acknowledged by the prevailing economical school, that in the course of time, by the nation being enabled to build up a completely developed manufacturing power of its own, those goods are produced more cheaply at home than the price at which they can be imported from foreign parts. If, therefore, a sacrifice of *value* is caused by Protective duties, it is made good by the gain of a *power of production*, which not only secures to the nation an infinitely greater amount of material goods, but also industrial independence in case of war. Through industrial independence, and the internal prosperity derived from it, the nation obtains the means for successfully carrying on a foreign trade and for extending its mercantile marine; it increases its civilisation, perfects its institutions internally, and strengthens its external power. A nation capable of developing a manufacturing power, if it makes use of the system of Protection, thus acts quite in the same spirit as that landed proprietor did who, by the sacrifice of some material wealth, allowed some of his children to learn a productive trade."

§ 3. Each step in this argument is open to dispute. It is beside the mark to "prove from history that a manufacturing power, developed in all its branches, forms a fundamental condition of all higher advances in civilisation," because there is no civilised country at the present time which is not far superior in its manufacturing power to the most completely developed manufacturing countries of the days before steam-power. History furnishes no guide under these altered circumstances. The question now is, not "Whether manufactures are necessary to national greatness?" but "Whether the best interests of the particular country whose tariff is in question would be advanced by the establishment, through the agency of Protection, of this or that manufacture?" List's arguments give us very little aid to a correct answer. He dwells at great length on the superiority of an artisan in character and intelligence to an agricultural labourer, and argues from this that it is to the advantage of a country to over-balance its "dull-witted" agriculturists by a greater number of manufacturing hands. But those who live in younger countries, where the rural labourer's intelligence is not depressed by traditions of caste or exclusive land laws, will be very slow to believe that the monotonous drudgery of tending a machine inside the walls of an unwholesome factory is more conducive to the cultivation of intelligence and character than the healthy open-air and self-dependent life of the Australian bush or the Western prairies. The increasing number of "larrikins" and "hoodlums" seems rather to suggest the opposite remedy of distributing the city populations. Yet the argument that Protection will increase the number of factory hands at the expense of the agricultural part of the community lies at the very foundation of the Nationalist defence of Protection. Are Protectionists prepared to take this step? Does any number of them in a young country seriously believe that the urban population is not already excessive in number and inferior in character?

§ 4. Let us, however, grant that the first step in the argument can be established, and that it is desirable to establish certain manufactures, does it follow that this cannot be done without Protection? The Individualist answer is an emphatic negative. The establishment of manufactures (he says) may safely be left to private enterprise, because so soon as capital accumulates it will be eager to find investment. Mr. Hoyt, however, and his school, entertain a profound mistrust of undirected individual effort. They will not believe that any hope of profit can be relied upon to attract capital into an industry that is exposed to the competition of a foreign country. It may face the competition of a countryman, but it would be dangerous to the community to let it run the risk of the competition of a foreigner! Here are his words :—

> "While considered as individuals, men may be trusted to pursue the industry which seems to offer the best returns; when we come to international exchanges, we must abandon this atomistic view of the co-workers in an organised nation. Our scientific standpoint must be at an elevation which places the given nation in proper perspective with all the other political and industrial units which compose the commercial nations of the world, who also have 'desires' which they wish to gratify. The wants of a nation as a whole, and its powers of supplying them as a whole—whether by domestic production or foreign exchange, or by their joint operation—are aggregates. The nature of our surplus production and the relation of that surplus to the markets of the world, involve aggregate estimates. The amount of foreign products needed, and the nature of the purchase money which we carry in our hands, are to be treated as aggregates, and the means of buying their gratification is an aggregate. . . . So some one, statesman or layman, must take the trouble to sum up the details of a nation's industrial resources and liabilities into the correct aggregate" (pp. 234, 235).

Again words! Words!

"Men may be trusted as individuals to follow their private interest in internal commerce, but in international commerce they must be guided by legislation." But are the legislators any more to be trusted than the individuals? and if so, why? Is it not notorious that legislators are not chosen for their business knowledge, or their delicate appreciation of the higher spiritual and social necessities of the "individual citizen"?

Again, in what sense are the "wants of a nation" an aggregate, except that they are resultant of the wants of individuals? To supply the wants of a nation, "as a whole," is, surely, the same thing as supplying the wants of each individual citizen. Else could the parts be full and the whole empty? But let Mr. Hoyt speak in his own defence :—

> "If men could be born where they pleased, or if men could and would go freely from one country to another when the demand for the products of their industry in their native land failed, or when the

pursuit of an occupation in which they had special aptitude is incapable of being carried on—if men did not care where they lived and where they died—we might assent to speculations as to what would be. If, on the other hand, all the motives of life except economic ones keep him in his political home, the capacity and opportunity of a man to work at all may depend on governmental restraints on the products of foreign labour, and the industrial entity must be *conterminous* with the political entity. It is not a question of protecting the weak against the strong, or the high-priced labourer against the low-priced labourer. It is giving to the labourer of a given country the market for the products of his labour. It is to prevent the labourer himself from being removed from the country, and substituting therefor a trade in the product of his labour. The argument does go equally well with either end first. Germany successfully keeps its lower-priced labour in German industries on German soil by protecting her home market; and so does France. Otherwise, it might conceivably happen that there would be no occasion for a German to live in Germany."

And in another place :—

"The problem, therefore, is not 'How far for a given exertion and sacrifice to get the maximum of material good,' but rather, 'How we may so occupy our field of employment that we can expend upon it *all* the exertions and *all* the sacrifices which we, *as a people*, are *willing* and *able to make*. How we may get the maximum for all which is possible when all our *abilities* and *all our energies* are called into play'" (p. 201).

But again we ask, why cannot this problem be solved by the free play of enlightened self-interest? Why cannot individuals be trusted to use their industrial organisation to the best advantage of the whole? And if they cannot be trusted, who are the persons to direct them? Why should men lose their sense of what is best for their own interests when they engage in foreign trade? If every man knows his own interest best, and may be trusted to follow it, as, Mr. Hoyt admits, he may in internal trade, does not the presumption arise that national industry will be most wisely organised by leaving the producing class alone? But to Mr. Hoyt, the idea of organisation and the idea of individual action seem incompatible. He regards the "individual" as "a masterless, clanless man," fighting against every one else, and indifferent to everything but the momentary gratification of his desires. Yet there is no inconsistency between individualism and organisation; rather the organisation that is firmest and directed to the highest ends can only be created by freemen. Spontaneous recognition of the necessity for union is an essential condition of strength. But it will be just to hear Mr. Hoyt further. He thus works out the application of his conception to fiscal policies[1] :—

> "Under Free Trade, men would follow certain natural industries. The only natural industries are those connected with the land and the product of raw material." (This fundamental position is assumed without proof.) "The surplus of these is to be exchanged for foreign manufactures. A time, however, will come when the surplus of these industries will be more than foreigners can take, and, at the same time, the demand for manufactures may be greater than foreigners can satisfy. Under these circumstances, the theory of Exchange breaks down, and the surplus of the natural industries is unsaleable. To remedy this state of things, it is proposed to encourage the direct production in America of the goods which would, in a state of freedom, be purchased from abroad. By such a direct production, the market for the surplus of the natural industries is enlarged, and the supply of the qualifications which are desired by the producers of this surplus is rendered longer and more constant.
>
> "The effect of this direct production is beneficial in another way. It provides employment for the rapidly increasing stream of immigrants, and enables the State to utilise the various capacities which may be possessed both by the original inhabitants of the country and by the new arrivals. It calls into play all our abilities and all our energies."

§ 5. The time for criticising this argument will come later, when each of its parts is separately considered. It is sufficient, for the present, to point out that it rests on several unexpressed and unproved assumptions, of which the chief are, that without Protection, direct production would not have taken place; and that under Free Trade there would have been no manufacturing industries. A Free Trader, replying to the argument, would first require some proof of the assumption that manufacturing

[1] In this summary Mr. Hoyt's language has been adhered to very closely.

industries were not "natural" to a country of such unequalled wealth in raw materials as the United States; and he would ask next whether, if it should happen that, under Free Trade, foreigners could not supply the American demand, anything would stand in the way of the Americans supplying themselves? The "natural" course of events would be that, as population increased, and the demand for manufactured goods became sufficient to justify the erection of costly works, labour and capital would be employed in a great variety of manufacturing industries.

Mr. Hoyt's argument, however, whether good or bad, is clearly not "economic" in the sense in which we have used the term. It is, in fact, only the expression in larger terms of the two stock phrases of Protectionist manufacturers: "Keep the home market for the home labourer" and "Secure diversity of industry."

Mr. Hoyt himself seems to recognise the political nature of his argument at a later period of his work, when he admits that he is driven to his conclusions by considerations of "patriotism, social ties, kindred, and politics, and that, submitting to the economic forces alone, there would be no economic reason for any correspondence of the industrial and political entities" (p. 369).

It would be impossible to have a plainer avowal that the so-called "economic" argument in favour of Protection is, in all its attributes, political and moral. The admission is plain—that if it can be proved that the acquisition of material wealth is the principal element of national productiveness, and the most potent stimulus of latent energies, there is then no reason why nations should not trade with one another.

But that is the very proposition which is demonstrated by the Individualist economist, which Mr. Hoyt believes himself to be refuting.

The truth is that Mr. Hoyt and the economists are not arguing about the same point.

It is obvious that a purely economic argument cannot be refuted by a process of reasoning which starts with an assumption that the acquisition and production of wealth are matters of trifling importance. The utmost which Mr. Hoyt's method can achieve is to suggest reasoning for disregarding the economic conclusions. The questions which he raises are of great importance; but it is a cause of confusion to term them "economic." They are really the stock political arguments of the Protectionist armoury,—" Keep the money in the country," "Diversify employment," "Encourage infant industries," and "Preserve the home market for the home labourer." Any or all of these phrases may contain reasons for modifying the economic conclusions about the tariff; but we are not considering them at present in that aspect, but only inquiring into their effect in impugning, by economic methods, the validity of an economic argument. The conclusion is inevitable that they have failed to do this. The "economic" argument stands firm against all "economic assaults."

NOTE TO CHAPTER VI.
"NATIONALISM AND PROTECTION."

No reference has been made in the course of this chapter to the particular Protectionist conclusions expressed by the various writers of the Nationalist school; but those of List are particularly noticeable, in view of the importance attached to his pretentious work. He is a strong opponent to any protection of agriculture (p. 214), and advocates the free admission of all the raw materials of manufacturing industry (pp. 217, 316, and 324). He was also of opinion that "where any technical industry cannot be established by means of an original protection of forty to sixty per cent., and continue to maintain itself under a continued protection of twenty to thirty per cent., the fundamental conditions of manufacturing power are lacking" (p. 313). The length of time for which Protection was required for European nations was, he thought, "ten or fifteen years" from the date of writing (1841,: (p. 184.

List, like most Protectionists, has the prospect of war ever before his eyes. The bugbear of a general blockade scares him from one extreme to another, and is the chief reason for his anxiety to make every nation self-supporting. His morbid and diseased mind—he suffered from chronic ill-health, and died by his own hand—is also haunted by the spectre of "perfidious Albion"; he sees wickedness in every action of Great Britain, and seriously warns his countrymen that the Secret Service money is spent in bribing Continental countries to adopt Free Trade,—just as the average American voter is instructed to beware of "British gold" and the "Cobden Club." Such are the writers to whose judgment we are asked to entrust the delicate duty of adjusting the rival interests of the individual and the State!

Mr. Hoyt seems to have taken warning by the failure of List's prophecies,[1] and is more cautious of committing himself to any definite statement as to the amount of Protection that is needed, or the length of time for which it must be maintained. He also, however, objects to Protection upon raw materials; and in a noticeable passage admits the injury which the American tariff has inflicted on the welfare of the Southern States (p. 373).

CHAPTER VII.

FREE TRADE AND LAISSEZ FAIRE.

§ 1. The lists are not even yet clear for the entry of the contesting arguments. The obstacles have been removed, but the boundaries have still to be defined, lest the disputants might never meet each other in a field which stretches from the quicksands of Socialism to the arid waste of "*Laissez faire.*" Yet the real battle-ground on which the contest must take place is equally removed from each extreme. Unhappily, the champions on either side are so unwilling to observe the proper limits of their controversy, that it is necessary, if we would avoid confusion, to define, with as much exactitude as the subject will permit, the true relations of either fiscal policy to its cognate political system.

It has already been observed, in the chapter which defined the meaning of the term that Free Trade is not a principle of

---

[1] An instructive test of the soundness of List's principles is furnished by comparing his anticipations of the future with the actual course of events (see especially pp. 104, 158, 184, 191).

government, but an expedient of commerce. Commerce has many other aids to its enlargement and extension—of which bank-notes and a system of credit are two familiar examples. Each of these works within a special sphere by its own method, and under its own rules. The sphere of Free Trade is the production of exchange values, and its method is the extension of the principle of division of employment into international transactions. Not much room here, it would seem, for any wide excursion into the philosophy of politics!

It happens, however, that while exercising within its own province its especial functions of cheapening products, steadying prices, and equalising markets, Free Trade has established an important rule of political conduct, which is capable of being applied to many other departments of civil activity. This is the well-known rule of *Laissez faire*. The principles by which the practice of Free Trade is justified, and the practice of the policy itself, have both shown that, in the case of international exchanges, it is wiser for a Government to allow its traders to have a free choice in the selection of their articles of barter than to attempt to control their sales and purchases by the means of Customs duties. But that is a rule which is strictly limited by its terms to international exchanges. How has its extension been brought about?

The theory and practice of banking have established certain rules as to the right proportion which should be maintained between the value of a note issue and a gold reserve; yet no banker has thought of applying these rules without modification to the issue of Exchequer bonds. Why should not Free Traders and Protectionists be equally ready to confine their fiscal rules to fiscal matters? The answer to this question is to be found in the historical circumstances under which this rule was first pronounced and carried into practice.

§ 2. When Adam Smith wrote the first systematic explanation of the phenomena of an industrial and commercial society, labour and capital were hampered at every turn by regulations and restrictions. It requires a vigorous effort of the imagination to picture the conditions of industry prior to the great industrial revolution which marked the close of the last century. Wages, prices, processes of manufacture, migrations of labourers in search of work, meetings of workmen, the transport of goods, the wholesale trade, and all international commerce, were either forbidden or regulated by law or custom down to the minutest detail. Some industries were forbidden to be carried on except by certain persons or at certain places. Over-sea goods were only allowed to be carried in English ships, or in ships of the nation whose product they were; while a high, and often prohibitive, tariff closed our ports still further. The trade guilds, although their influence was on the wane, still exercised a legal and customary right of hindering the processes of manufacture, by applying their old rules to the altered conditions of production by machinery and steam-power.[1] But if the position of employers was rendered irksome by their wide-reaching system of restraint and regulation, the position of the workman was hardly that of a free man. Whatever may have been his happiness in the possession of regular employment and sufficient food—and there is a tendency now to over-estimate his condition of prosperity and contentment—he had little or no hope of ever altering his mode of life. He worked, it is true, in a cottage instead of a factory, and breathed pure air, and he fed at his master's table, and served no other all his life; but behind this idyllic picture is another—of a gross animal, unable to leave his parish because he lacked the means of gaining a "settlement" in another by forty days' continuous residence, subject to the brutality of a master hardly more refined than himself, his wages fixed for him by Justices in Quarter Sessions, prohibited by the laws of apprenticeship from trying his hand at a new trade, without

---

[1] *See* Brentano's "Essay on Trades Unionism."

[Pt. II., Ch. vii., § 3.]

interest, without hope, sunk in ignorance, bestiality, and vice.[1] In the meantime, the conditions of industry were everywhere changing. Even before the period of great mechanical discoveries (1770—90) the old system of domestic industry was breaking down before the growth of foreign trade and the accumulation of capital. At the conclusion of the Seven Years' War (1763) industry required new outlets in all directions. The old order was passing away, but the old rules remained. It was the aim of Adam Smith's great work to show how the industrial organisation should be made to correspond to the existing needs.[2]

§ 3. It is a mistake to regard Adam Smith as a deductive economist, theorising from abstract postulates. On the contrary, he was essentially an observer of the things about him, and his method of study is chiefly, although not exclusively, historical. He did so far yield to the influences of his time as to take the doctrine of "natural liberty" as the philosophical justification of his attacks upon the existing restrictions; but he nowhere developes this into the extreme theory "that every man in pursuance of his own advantage at the same time furthers the good of all!" This later growth was due almost entirely to the success of Adam Smith's proposals. The doctrine of "natural liberty" gained a reflected glory from the

---

[1] The pictures of the condition of the poor given in the novels of Smollett and Fielding are very instructive, and should be read as a corrective of the often quoted passages from Defoe's "Tour through Great Britain."

[2] Toynbee's "Industrial Revolution" gives the best, although fragmentary, account of the industrial changes during this period.

Professor Thorold Rogers' "Six Centuries of Work and Wages," and his "Lectures on the Economic Interpretation of History," contain, perhaps, the greatest quantity of systematised information upon the subject; while Professor Ashley's "Introduction to English Economic History and Theory," and a useful Compendium, prepared by Mr. Gibbins for the University Extension Series, under the title of "The Industrial History of England," are two notable additions by Oxford men to a study which the University of Oxford is making peculiarly her own.

Eden's "State of the Poor," Nichol's "History of the Poor Law," Baines' "History of the Cotton Trade," and Scrivener's "History of the Iron Trade," are indispensable as works of reference.

immediate and striking results which followed its practice. As restriction after restriction fell before the force of law or custom, the belief gained ground that some new principle of policy had been discovered or revealed.

The same work was proceeding in France as in England, only that the need for it was greater. From the time that the merchant Legendre returned his famous answer to Colbert's question, "How he might best protect French commerce?" —"*Laissez faire, laissez passer*"—until the Revolution, the aim of every wise ruler was to lessen the restrictions upon the passage, manufacture, and exchange of goods. The odious ingenuity of these impediments, and the vigour with which they were supported in the name of religion and order, caused Turgot to adopt Legendre's saying as the cardinal maxim of sound administration. From France it passed to England, where it was received for a time as a new gospel by all those— and at that time they were many—who suffered in their fortunes or their ease in consequence of the corrupt and injudicious interferences of Government with the private affairs of citizens. It has not, however, been accepted as a scientific principle by any economist or writer of repute, except Mr. Herbert Spencer. This will probably be a hard saying to many Nationalists; yet, in truth, the reputation of the older economists has suffered by the indiscretions of their thoughtless followers. They never did, in fact, teach, *as a scientific truth*, that "the road to national prosperity lies in the unchecked and competitive pursuit of material wealth,"[1] in spite of the belief of many estimable persons to the contrary. Their conclusions were strictly limited by their premisses, and were only applicable to the facts of daily life, when the conditions, which were assumed to exist universally, were present. Their so called "natural laws" were mere statements of the regular

---

[1] "Studies in Ruskin," by E. T. Cook (p. 30). It is only fair to mention that this is Mr. Cook's summary of Mr. Ruskin's opinion of economic teaching, not a statement of his own.

sequence in which certain results would follow from certain combinations of ascertained facts.

Journalists and politicians, however, who were anxious to clinch an argument, and busy men who wished to avoid one, used the economic conclusions as statements of a natural law. Ignoring the limitations under which their masters wrote, and forgetful of the nature of their assumptions, these incautious disciples treated a scientific deduction as if it were a formula for daily use; and, not perceiving that the reforms which had been carried by the influence of Adam Smith were purely negative, and that the abolition of the antiquated legislation of restriction would become useless if the labourer was prevented by the changed conditions of his life from exercising his newly won freedom of movement, they applied the arguments of Adam Smith to every species of Protective legislation. Yet, in fact, the position had entirely altered. The watchword, which had been "Remove the shackles!" had become "Prevent the forging of new shackles!"

It happened that Ricardo and many other economists—although John Stuart Mill was not of the number—honestly believed that many of the efforts to preserve the working-classes against the dangers of their new condition would be ineffective and mischievous; and Ricardo gave evidence to this effect before a Committee of the House of Commons. The general public, not unnaturally, failed to discriminate between these political opinions and the conclusions to which the same men had arrived as scientific economists. It happened also that most of the Free Trade manufacturers, who were the backbone of the Anti-Corn-Law League, took the same view of the new legislation, under the impression that legal equality and freedom of contract were the only conditions that were needed to secure the working-classes in their just rights. Here, again, the greatest of the Free Traders, Richard Cobden, held aloof. But the public have been in no mood to discriminate, and Free Traders have been joined with the economists in a general condemnation.

The same display of feeling is observable in the United States, and is to some extent justified by the writings of Free Traders. Not only have most American Free Traders been unswerving devotees of *Laissez faire* as a political maxim—moved thereto, no doubt, by the wonderful achievements of Individualism in the United States and the frequent corruptness of Government action—but they have assumed the universality of the maxim as the basis of their justification of Free Trade. Professor Sumner—of whom all lovers of clear thought and precise expressions must speak with unfeigned respect—has been the leader of this school,[1] of which Professor Fawcett, whose work upon Free Trade has been largely circulated in the United States, is an English disciple. On the other hand, Professor Walker and the younger school of economists—among whom may be named Professor Clark, Professor Ely, Professor Richmond Mayo Smith, and Professor Taussig—have never supported *Laissez faire*, either as a political or scientific doctrine. It is to be feared, however, that some time must elapse before the new school of writers can clear the reputation of Free Trade from the effects of its unfortunate association with an unpopular doctrine.

We are now in a position to understand the combination of influences under which the notion has grown up—to which reference was made in the second chapter of this work—that Free Traders were fanatical adherents of *Laissez faire*, and that "Administrative Nihilism" (to use Professor Huxley's expressive synonym) was the last word of economic teaching.

---

[1] In the present state of the law as to international copyright, American writings on political and economic subjects are almost unknown in Great Britain or Australia. Yet no one has ever penned a more lucid statement in a shorter space, of the economic argument against Protection, from the standpoint of a believer in *Laissez faire*, than is contained in Professor Sumner's little book entitled "Protectionism - the ism which teaches that waste makes wealth."

[Pt. II., Ch. vii., § 4.]

No reader of Protectionist literature can entertain a doubt of the wide influence of this misapprehension, to which the rejection of the individual as the industrial unit, and the adoption of Nationalism, is almost entirely due.[1] The dislike of *Laissez faire*, which is the governing inspiration of Nationalists, is so intense that it prevents a fair appreciation of the meaning of the maxim. The same blindness of rage obscures the vision of the fighting Protectionist. Remembering that many prominent Free Traders are ardent believers in this maxim, he has come to regard it as an essential part of Free Trade, and as the logical outcome of Individualist political economy, and has consequently sought for a new basis for economics which will not lead to such an unworkable conclusion. Popular impressions die hard; and it will probably be as difficult to persuade Protectionists and Socialists that *Laissez faire* is not a necessary part of economic teaching as it is to persuade Individualists that Socialism does not mean either a re-distribution of private property or the abolition of capital. Nevertheless, the attempt must be made.

§ 4. Whatever may be the merits of *Laissez faire*—and, according to Mr. Herbert Spencer, they are great—the maxim is certainly not an expression of a scientific principle. It is at best only the correct application of a principle—being a term of political art which does not belong to science.

An attempt has been made earlier in these pages[2] to define the limits within which the maxim may be safely applied; and it was suggested that within the field of the production of wealth, where the economic postulate of an ever-active competition between equal units is practically in accord with facts, the best results were obtained under a policy of strict non-interference; but it was pointed out that, within the field of the distribution of wealth, the conditions of competition were so altered that no such general rule could be safely adopted.

[1] *See* List: Book II. *passim*. Hoyt: Chaps. II., IV., V., and *passim*.
[2] *See* above, p. 11-13.

It is not to be expected that so fragmentary a discussion of a large question should carry conviction to the minds of those who are already believers in the universal applicability of *Laissez faire;* nor is it desired in this treatise to enter upon any long discussion of the subject. We are not now concerned with principles of government, but with the smaller question of a fiscal policy. There is no need to do more than show the independence of the Free Trade argument of this or any other political theory.

The Free Traders who have pressed into their service the doctrine of *Laissez faire* have certainly adopted a most convenient course; because, if it can once be proved that Governmental interference is always wrong, any argument against the particular kind of interference known as Protection becomes a work of supererogation. But although most Free Traders who give up *Laissez faire*—such as Mill, Cobden, Jevons, and Toynbee in England, and Professors Walker, Clark, Mayo Smith, Ely, and Taussig in the United States—undoubtedly yield a great advantage to their opponents, it would be idle to expect to convince Protectionists of the futility of Protection by any demonstration that the individual always knows his interests best in the sense in which they are identical with the interests of society. The mistrust of the doctrine of Administrative Nihilism is so widespread and deep-rooted that it may be doubted whether any Protectionist writer could be induced to read a refutation of Protection which rested on a proof of this kind. Accordingly, from motives of controversial expediency, if for no other reason, it will be well to meet Protectionists upon their own ground, and discuss the interference of a Government in matters of trade and tariffs as if there were no presumption either against or in favour of interference in that or any other case. A few words more in explanation of the reasons for taking this course are, however, due to a deserved respect for the eminent names of those who have conducted the dispute on other lines.

Pt. II., Ch. vii., § 5.

§ 5. The political maxim of *Laissez faire* is arrived at partly by a process of induction, and partly by deduction from economic principles. But since economic principles rest upon an assumption of an ever-active competition between equal units, no rule of practice can be founded upon economic reasoning where there is either no competition at all or a competition between unequal units. Now, it has already been observed that the peculiar province of economic reasoning is the production and accumulation of material wealth. Accordingly, if the merits of a fiscal policy depend to an appreciable extent upon its effect upon the production and accumulation of material wealth, they can be tested to that extent by economic rules. This is the justification of applying the "let alone" maxim to all commercial dealings between foreign countries.

When, however, we enter the province of the distribution of wealth, and have to deal not with goods and prices, but with human beings and wages, we are confronted by a totally different set of facts. Our postulate becomes at once of questionable accuracy. The competing units are not, in fact, upon a footing of equality.

There is some approach to an equality between those who buy and sell commodities, because goods and capital can both be moved from place to place, and the postponement of a sale or purchase only leads to a loss of money. But between the labourer who is unaided by a union and unprotected by law, and his employer, equality rarely exists. He is seldom, if ever, in a position to make terms as to the price at which he shall sell his labour. Being seldom capable of more than one occupation, he must find work at that or starve. This disadvantage is to some extent removed by the institution of Trade Unionism, which is to the labourer what capital is to his employer, in that it enables him to delay the sale of his services until the market for them rises. But even trade unions do not bring about a sufficiently real equality between labourers and employers to justify the use of economic rules in regulating their mutual relations. The value of human labour cannot under any circumstances be determined, like that of a commodity, simply by the higgling of the market, because labour cannot be stored, moved, or sampled, like a bale of goods. Mr. Frederic Harrison[1] has very happily expressed this difference. "For those," he says, "who have commodities to sell there is a true market. Here competition acts rapidly, fully, simply, fairly. It is totally otherwise with a day-labourer, who has no commodity to sell. He must be himself present at every market—which means costly personal locomotion. He cannot correspond with his employer: he cannot send a sample of his strength: nor do employers knock at his cottage door. Moreover, when buyer and seller meet, the bargain is made; his price is paid, the goods change hands, they part; the contract is complete—the transaction ends. But the relation of employer and employed is permanent, or at least continuous. It involves the entire existence of one at least; it implies sustained co-operation. This is no contract to sell something; it is the contract to do something: it is a contract of partnership or joint activity: it is an association involving every side of life."

These words contain the kernel of the labour question, which Free Traders who believe in *Laissez faire* are apt to overlook. And yet, if we would persuade the working-classes to support Free Trade, it cannot be too often repeated that such sentiments are not at variance with the practice of that policy.[2]

[1] *Fortnightly Review*, 1878.
[2] Professor R. T. Ely, whose work on "The Labour Movement in America" was not known to the writer when he penned the text, expresses the same idea with admirable perspicuity (pp. 101-3). "The labourer," he says, "must offer labour in the labour market in which he resides, and cannot seek the best market, or even a better market, like others who sell commodities. He is often too uneducated to know the conditions of the labour market in other localities, and too ignorant to be able to pass judgment on such data as are at his command. When he does know, his poverty frequently prevents his removal; for he cannot sell his commodity in a remote place unless he removes his own person thither, nor can he ship, as others do, a sample of his commodity.

"If the demand falls, labour cannot be withdrawn from the market, like other

Pt. II., Ch. vii., § 5.]

There is also another reason why economic conclusions can seldom be applied with any confidence to a discussion about wages, besides the unreality, in such cases, of the economic postulate: namely, the paramount importance of the political considerations by which they must be modified. These arise from the very nature of the subject. Human beings cannot be wares. On the contrary, as the demand decreases the supply must increase, by reason of competition of a greater number of labourers. There are several causes for this. Members of the family who before did not work outside the home—chiefly children and women—will seek labour to eke out the father's income. A decreased demand usually occurs at time of a general depression, and the ranks of the working-men are enlarged by accessions from other social classes. Competition may thus increase in severity almost to an unlimited extent between labourers to secure what little work there is. Thus it happens that when demand for labour diminishes, the fall in wages is apt to be more than in proportion to this diminution in demand.

"The cost of production is the limit below which the price of other commodities cannot permanently fall, for the production is diminished as the price falls, and at times ceases almost altogether. But the individual labourer cannot diminish his supply of labour so long as he lives, and misery and death [1] are the factors which must bring about a decrease in the supply of his commodity, and raise its price to the cost of production: in other words, to what it costs the labourer and his family to live and to maintain the customary standard of life among the members of his class.

"Closely connected with the foregoing is the fact that the price of labour does not at once rise when the demand increases, as is usually the case with other commodities, for the first effect is that the unemployed receive work; and after the 'reserve army' finds employment competition among purchasers of labour raises its price.

"Finally, the only way to diminish the supply of the commodity labour in the market in the future is, by prudence in marriage, to diminish the birth-rate. But to accomplish this, will and intelligence are necessary, and some probability that the labourer would reap the fruits of his self-denial. No such guarantee exists, because the folly of his fellows will render his prudence of no avail. In addition to this, the labourer in America can hope to influence the supply of labour offered in the market of the future only when he gains some control over immigration."

[1] "The way these operate is so simple that it ought to be better understood. Few now starve outright; but a large number, especially of the young, starve gradually as has been abundantly shown by recent investigations; but many more deaths are occasioned in other ways. A carpenter is ill, and previous hard times have exhausted his resources. He dies; whereas a more generous supply of delicacies, better nursing, and more skilful medical attendance, would have saved his life. A second mechanic is so poor that he feels that he cannot afford an umbrella. In a severe rain storm to which he is exposed the seeds of consumption are laid. A third is unable to afford new shoes, and wet feet at a

argued about as if they were inanimate objects, but account must be taken of their variations in desires, capacities, and action. It is impossible to argue about labour as if it were a commodity, both because the labourer himself is a conscious being, who may at any time refuse to act according to our conclusions, and because the State has an overwhelming interest in the character of his actions. The purchaser of wealth fulfils his purpose when he buys his goods; and the final end of the goods themselves is to be used. But the purchaser of labour buys that with which he desires to enter into relations of a more or less permanent character. His object is to keep the labour for future use. The object of the labourer, on the contrary, is to sell his labour upon such terms that he may be able to use it afterwards in furtherance of his own purposes. And by the side of both employer and labourer stands the State, whose interest is that neither party should be injuriously affected in his power to perform the duties of citizenship. But if the bargain is unrestricted, the employer might gain such a control over the other's labour that he would be able to defeat the object of the seller by dictating all or most of the uses to which it might afterwards be put. This is a necessary consequence of the relationship of employer and employed, so that it is the duty of the State to watch, lest the terms of the bargain should be such as to destroy or stunt the moral or political existence of its actual or unborn citizens.

Professor R. T. Ely suggests a third distinction between labour and other commodities in " the uncertainty of existence, which, more than actual difference in possessions, distinguishes

---

time of feebleness, and insufficient nourishment, cause his death. The most distinguished statistician of our day, Dr. Engel, calls the causes of most deaths ' social.' The difficulty is not to prescribe a remedy, but to apply it. A physician cannot tell a man earning a dollar a day to take a trip to Egypt for weak lungs. No current fiction is more widely removed from the truth than the common assertion that working-men and their families enjoy exceptionally good health. The exact opposite is the truth; and statistics have established the fact beyond controversy that labourers are shorter-lived by many years than those who belong to the wealthier social classes. Dr. Lyman Abbott quotes some interesting statistics on this subject in a recent article in the *Century Magazine*."

[Pt. II., Ch. vii., § 5.]

the well-to-do from the poor." The whole passage in which Mr. Ely criticises the "natural liberty views" of Adam Smith is worth quoting. ("The Labour Movement in America," pp. 97-100.)

"The economic philosophers of the time believed that legal equality and freedom of contract were the sole conditions needed to enable the working-classes to secure a share of the product of national industry sufficient to serve as a basis for their physical, ethical, and spiritual development. This theory was based on two fallacies: the first was the assumption of the natural equality of men. The differences found among men, in their opinion, were not due to original native qualities, but were the result of education, legislation, and government. . . . . The second fallacy was the assumption that labour was a commodity just like other commodities, and the labourer a man with a commodity for sale just like other men who offer their wares to the public. It is true that labour is a commodity, for it is bought and sold, but there are peculiarities about it which distinguish it from other commodities, and that most radically.

"While labour is a commodity, it is an expenditure of human force which involves the welfare of a personality. It is a commodity which is inseparably bound up with the labourer; and in this it differs from other commodities. The one who offers other commodities for sale reserves his own person. The farmer who parts with a thousand bushels of wheat for money reserves control of his own actions; they are not brought in question at all. Again, the man of property who sells other commodities has an option. He may part with his wares and maintain his life from other goods received in exchange, or he can have recourse to his labour-power. The labourer, however, has, as a rule, only the service residing in his own person with which to sustain himself and his family. Again, a machine—a locomotive, for example—and a working-man resemble each other in this: they both render services, and the fate of both depends upon the manner in which these services are extracted.

But there is this radical difference: the machine which yields its service to man is itself a commodity, and is only a means to an end, while the labourer who parts with labour is no longer a commodity in civilised lands, but is an end in himself, for man is the beginning and termination of all economic life. The consequence for the great mass of labourers possessed of only average qualities are as follows, provided there is no intervention of legislation, and provided the working-classes are not organised: While those who sell other commodities are able to influence the price by a suitable regulation of production, so as to bring about a satisfactory relation between supply and demand, the purchaser of labour has it in his own power to determine the price of this commodity and the other conditions of sale. There may be exceptions for a time in a new country, but these are temporary, and often more apparent than real. Even now in the United States the right of capital to rule is generally assumed as a matter of course, and when labour would determine price and conditions of service, it is called dictation. The reason is that man comes to this world without reference to supply and demand,[1] and the poverty of the labourer compels him to offer the use of his labour-power unreservedly and continuously. The purchase of labour gives control over the labourer, and a far-reaching influence over his physical, intellectual, social, and ethical existence. The conditions of the labour contract determine the amount of this rulership. Again, while illness, inability to labour by reason of accident, or old age and death, do not destroy other commodities, or their power to support life, when these misfortunes overtake the person of the labourer, he loses his power to sell his only property, the commodity labour, and he can no longer support himself and those dependent upon him."

[1] "There are certain qualifications to what is here said which the limits of this book will not allow me to enumerate. It would be far too large a work for present purposes were every topic to be treated exhaustively. I always take it for granted that my reader is possessed of common sense, and will not raise trivial objections; also that he is to do some thinking himself.

For these reasons, and for others which will readily suggest themselves to a reader's mind, it follows that there is a radical distinction between the ideas which may be applied in the production of wealth and those which may be applied in its distribution. Working-men have always insisted by their actions, if not by words, that this distinction existed, although it must be confessed that many Free Traders have been slow to perceive that this contention was no less sound in theory than it is true in fact. The wages of labour and the price of goods are not in fact now, nor have they ever been, determined by the same forces; nor is it possible to use the processes of economic reasoning in a discussion of this topic without adopting the most fanciful assumptions.

§ 6. The ideas which are expressed in the foregoing observations were only slowly recognised by politicians and economists; but in this respect the politicians led the way.

What is termed the great industrial revolution, consequent upon the invention of machinery and the use of steam as a motive power, came upon England with appalling suddenness. The centres of industry shifted when its methods changed, and great towns grew up upon the sides of what only ten years previously had been silent valleys. Population naturally followed to the new workshops, and, once there, changed every habit of its ancient life. The system of domestic industry under which men worked in their own homes, employing a few apprentices or journeymen, whom they treated as members of the family, vanished utterly, and almost in a moment, before the institution of the factory. The consequence was that all the old relationships of industrial life were wrenched asunder, and for the first time in English history the labourer was left entirely unprotected in making terms with his employer. Before this date he had always been strengthened by some support, whether of legislation or custom. Even the laws which he was beginning to find oppressive, such as those against apprenticeship or those which fixed wages, operated not infrequently to his advantage; while when laws failed custom intervened. "Custom," as Mill observed, "has always been the great protector of the weak against the strong." In England it had turned the villeins into copyholders, and to this day it forms the basis of that benevolent despotism which the best of squires and parsons exercise in many English parishes. Among the artisans it had worked principally through the Trade Guilds, whose customary regulations, harassing as they were beginning to become, were originally designed to help the labourer to a better footing, and to prevent unscrupulous employers from taking an advantage of his weakness. All these safeguards disappeared at the inauguration of the new industrial era. A new set of employers grew up, having no high traditions of their class, and subject to the restraints of no public opinion in their dealings with workmen. The consequence was that for some sixty years—from 1770 to 1830—the relations between employers and employed were largely determined by an unrestricted competition, with a result so frightful in its cruelty and horror that the experiment will never be repeated.[1] Whatever

---

[1] The story is well known, and would in any case be out of place in the present treatise. It may be read in the works of Karl Marx, or in the pages of "Yeast," "Sybil," or "Alton Locke." One phase of it will illustrate the whole, and may be told in the words used by Mr. Gibbins in his "Industrial History of England" (pp. 178-9) :—"When factories were first built there was a strong repugnance on the part of parents, who had been accustomed to the old family life under the domestic system, to send their children into these places. It was, in fact, considered a disgrace so to do: the epithet of 'factory girl' was the most insulting that could be applied to a young woman, and girls who had once been in a factory could never find employment elsewhere. It was not until the wages of the workmen had been reduced to a starvation level that they consented to their children and wives being employed in the mills. But the manufacturers wanted labour by some means or other, and they got it. They got it from the workhouses. They sent for parish apprentices from all parts of England, and pretended to apprentice them to the new employments just introduced. The mill-owners systematically communicated with the overseers of the poor, who arranged a day for the inspection of pauper children. Those chosen by the manufacturer were then conveyed by waggons or canal-boats to their destination, and from that moment were doomed to slavery. Sometimes regular traffickers would take the place of the manufacturer, and transfer a number of

[Pt. II., Ch. vii., § 6.]

may be the evils of State interference, freedom of contract in the determination of wages inevitably leads to industrial anarchy. The working-classes instinctively felt that their only

> children to a factory district, and there keep them, generally in some dark cellar, till they could hand them over to a mill-owner in want of hands, who would come and examine their height, strength, and bodily capacities, exactly as did the slave-dealers in the American markets. After that the children were simply at the mercy of their owners, nominally as apprentices, but in reality as mere slaves, who got no wages, and whom it was not worth while even to feed and clothe properly, because they were so cheap, and their places could be so easily supplied. It was often arranged by the parish authorities, in order to get rid of imbeciles, that one idiot should be taken by the mill-owner with every twenty sane children. The fate of these unhappy idiots was even worse than that of the others. The secret of their final end has never been disclosed, but we can form some idea of their awful sufferings from the hardships of the other victims to capitalist greed and cruelty. Their treatment was most inhuman. The hours of their labour were only limited by exhaustion, after many modes of torture had been unavailingly applied to force continued work. Children were often worked *sixteen hours* a day, by day or by night. Even Sunday was used as a convenient time to clean the machinery." The author of the "History of the Factory Movement" writes :—"In stench, in heated rooms, amid the constant whirling of a thousand wheels, little fingers and little feet were kept in ceaseless action, forced into unnatural activity by blows from the heavy hands and feet of the merciless over-looker, and the infliction of bodily pain by instruments of punishment invented by the sharpened ingenuity of insatiable selfishness. They were fed upon the coarsest and cheapest food, often with the same as that served out to the pigs of their master. They slept by turns and in relays in filthy beds which were never cool, for one set of children were sent to sleep in them as soon as the others had gone off to their daily or nightly toil. There was often no discrimination of sexes, and disease, misery, and vice grew as in a hotbed of contagion. Some of these miserable beings tried to run away. To prevent their doing so, those suspected of this tendency had irons riveted on their ankles with long links reaching up to the hips, and were compelled to work and sleep in these chains, young women and girls, as well as boys, suffering this brutal treatment. Many died, and were buried secretly at night in some desolate spot, lest people should notice the number of the graves; and many committed suicide. The catalogue of cruelty and misery is too long to recite here; it may be read in the 'Memoirs of Robert Blincoe,' himself an apprentice, or in the pages of the Blue-books of the beginning of this century, in which even the methodical, dry, official language is startled into life by the misery it has to relate. It is, perhaps, not well for me to say more about the subject, for one dares not trust oneself to try and set down calmly all that might be told about this awful page in the history of industrial England. I need only remark that during this period of unheeded and ghastly suffering in the mills of our native land the British philanthropist was occupying himself with agitating for the relief of the very largely imaginary woes of negro slaves

safeguard was Protective legislation. Being forbidden by law to combine in their own defence, or even to meet for the purpose of discussing grievances,[1] they were of necessity compelled to rely upon an outside power. Their demands were supported by the Tory party, in part from genuine sympathy, and in part from a feeling of hostility towards the class of manufacturers. The first ameliorative measure was passed in 1803, for the better regulation of the labour of children; and then began that long series of enactments designed to place the workman in a position of equality with his employer, which has been more characteristic of the legislation of Great Britain than of any other country, and which, even in Great Britain, is not yet completed. The Factory Acts, the Mining Acts, the Friendly Societies and Trades Union Acts, the Education Acts, the Employers' Liability Act, the Pawnbrokers' Act, the Ground Game Act, the Agricultural Holdings Act, the Truck Acts, the Irish Land Act of 1881, and many others, are illustrations of this movement. All of these were, in the strict sense of the word, Socialistic measures. They all invoked the intervention of the State to remedy artificial inequalities, and place the competitors in the industrial strife more nearly on a footing of equality. All of these, as has been said, were opposed in the name of Free Trade, and as an interference with freedom of

---

in other countries. He, of course, succeeded in raising the usual amount of sentiment, and perhaps more than the usual amount of money, on behalf of an inferior and barbaric race, who have repaid him by relapsing into a contented indolence and a scarcely concealed savagery which have gone far to ruin our possessions in the West Indies. The spectacle of England buying the freedom of black slaves by riches drawn from the labour of her white ones affords an interesting study for the cynical philosopher."

And yet proposals to remedy this state of things by means of legislation were opposed in the name of Free Trade. No wonder that the policy has a hard struggle to obtain a favourable consideration at the hands of working men!

[1] This state of the law was first modified in 1824, but workmen were not finally put upon an equality with employers in this respect until 1876. The first volume of the new series of "State Trials," now in course of publication, throws a most lurid light upon the oppressive character of this class of legislation.

contract; yet in reality they were an attempt to establish a real state of freedom, in which the stronger party to the bargain could not take advantage of the other's weakness. England has, in consequence, had her reward in being the country of all others which is most free from the fanatical spirit of revolutionary anarchism.[1] But this remedial legislation is not ended

---

[1] Any one who examines English social legislation will see that it is very far in advance of Australia in all respects except that of education. As illustrating the immense distance which England has advanced beyond the United States in her industrial legislation, it may be mentioned that of the sixteen demands contained in the platform of the Socialist Labour Party, which is one of the most radical organisations in the United States, no less than twelve (marked * in the subjoined list) have been wholly or in part granted by the English Parliament. Some of these have been enjoyed by English workmen for many years. The platform is published in full by Professor Ely, in his "Labour Movement in America" (pp. 366-70), and is as follows:—

* 1. The United States shall take possession of the railroads, canals, telegraphs, telephones, and all other means of public transportation.
* 2. The municipalities to take possession of the local railroads, of ferries, and of the supply of light to streets and public places.
  3. Public lands to be declared inalienable. They shall be leased according to fixed principles. Revocation of all grants of lands by the United States to corporations or individuals the conditions of which have not been complied with, or which are otherwise illegal.
* 4. The United States to have the exclusive right to issue money.
* 5. Congressional legislation, providing for the scientific management of forests and waterways, and prohibiting the waste of the natural resources of the country.
  6. The United States to have the right of expropriation of running patents; new inventions to be free to all, but inventors to be remunerated by national rewards.
  7. Legal provision that the rent of dwellings shall not exceed a percentage of the value of the building, as taxed by the municipality.
  8. Inauguration of public works in times of economical depression.
* 9. Progressive income tax and tax on inheritances; but smaller incomes to be exempt.
* 10. Compulsory school education of all children under fourteen years of age; instruction in all educational institutions to be gratuitous, and to be made accessible to all by public assistance (furnishing meals, clothes, books, &c.). All instruction to be under the direction of the United States, and to be organised on a uniform plan.
  11. Repeal of all pauper, tramp, conspiracy, and temperance laws. Unabridged right of combination.
* 12 Official statistics concerning the condition of labour. Prohibition of

yet. So long as there are any who are forced by external circumstances, in whose ordering they have had no voice, to start in the struggle for existence handicapped by want of education: so long as there are others who are weakened in the power of self-improvement by any alterable condition of society: so long as the State or public opinion maintains any institution which directly or indirectly causes to others physical misery or mental darkness—so long it will be the duty of Free Traders and Protectionists alike to agitate for a policy of action which may bring us nearer to the day when inaction can be justified.

§ 7. It would be easy to amplify these observations on the policy of "Let alone" into a treatise of many pages,[1] but enough has been said to illustrate the necessity of using the maxim with extreme caution in industrial matters. For the purposes of the Free Trade argument, it cannot be too often repeated, if we would persuade the wage-receiver to support Free Trade, that the most Socialistic sentiments in favour of an alteration in their industrial condition are not at variance with the teachings of Free Trade. The experience derived from the practice of Free Trade is no justification for the denunciation of State interference in other directions. The unrestricted competition

<blockquote>
the employment of children in the school age, and the employment of female labour in occupations detrimental to health or morality. Prohibition of the convict labour contract system.

* 13. All wages to be paid in cash money. Equalisation by law of women's wages with those of men where equal service is performed.
* 14. Laws for the protection of life and limbs of working people, and an efficient employers' liability law.
* 15. Legal incorporation of trades unions.
* 16. Reduction of the hours of labour in proportion to the progress of production; establishment by Act of Congress of a legal work-day of not more than eight hours for all industrial workers, and corresponding provisions for all agricultural labourers.

[1] Montagu's "Limits of Individual Liberty" and Sir James Stephen's "Liberty, Equality, and Fraternity," may be referred to in this connection.
</blockquote>

of private persons may be an expedient of great value in furthering the production and exchange of goods, without thereby becoming a general maxim of public policy. Free Trade acts within its own province, and within that province, but no further, it justifies an unrestricted competition. It may be that Professor Sumner and Mr. Herbert Spencer are correct in applying the principle to other departments of human activity. On this question Free Trade offers no guidance in the formation of a right judgment. Certainly, many Free Traders, who to all appearance form a majority of the party, vehemently repudiate the doctrines of Administrative Nihilism; while of those who are inclined to adopt it in a more or less modified form, none need be induced by any Free Trade leanings to deify the principle of competition and close their eyes to every instance of its ravages. Nothing in the theory or practice of Free Trade declares that competition ought to be the governing influence of social life. A Free Trader would rather be inclined to the opinion that competition is a force of nature, like a flood or a gale, which, in Bacon's phrase, "man must obey, so as to command." But the path of commercial freedom lies altogether apart from these large questions.

CHAPTER VIII.

PROTECTION AND SOCIALISM.

§ 1. IN the discussion of all political arguments, one of two theories of State action must be either expressed or assumed. Believers in *Laissez faire* will adopt the view that the State is a mere organisation for police purposes, with no constructive powers or moral duties. Others, on the contrary—among whom all Protectionists ought to be numbered—regard the

State as an organised expression of the popular will, which is capable of directing individual citizens to the achievement of many high aims. They believe that the power of combination can reach to many things which are not attainable by individual effort, and that the State is the greatest of all combinations for the realisation of a complete and harmonious development both of the individual and the nation. This view of State action, which admits of many varieties, is in its essence Socialism.

As we proceed to examine the political arguments by which Protection is supported, we shall find that all of them are really contained in the single contention that under Free Trade the rich *may* grow richer, but the poor *must* grow poorer! To prevent this, the State must interfere by regulating the nature and restricting the quantity of foreign exchanges.

What ought to be the attitude of Free Traders towards this line of argument?

We have seen in the last chapter that the argument for Free Trade is independent of either a belief or disbelief in the general wisdom of a policy of *Laissez-faire*. The same arguments can be used to prove its independence of a belief or disbelief in Socialism. But is it the part of a prudent controversialist to use them?

§ 2. If we want to strike at the opinions which really sway the judgment of Protectionists, we must attack them with considerations of unquestionable strength. Now, seeing that no Protectionist can admit that the "police theory" of State action has any validity, it will be necessary to conduct the argument against him from another standpoint. Accordingly, we must meet him once more upon his own ground, and, admitting the correctness of his Socialistic theory, demonstrate by his own tests that tariff taxes, although they are Socialistic in their method, do not accomplish the results which Socialists desire.

Many Free Traders—of whom the writer is one—would

readily—and from conviction—take this stand ; and, adopting the view that the State must energetically use its power to widen the sphere within which each man's will may work with complete freedom, would be prepared to prove that the influence of Protection is no less pernicious in its moral than in its material effects upon the development of a free people. Professor Sumner, on the contrary, and a large class of Free Trade writers, denounce Socialism in any form, and make the Socialism of Protection to be the head and front of its offending.

It is a curious instance of the hap-hazard inconsistencies of most political opinions that many Protectionists indignantly repudiate any connection between their views and those of the Socialists. In fact, Socialism generally finds its strongest enemies among Protected manufacturers. The men who most detest and fear the spread of Socialist opinions are those who owe their fortunes to Socialistic voters. Yet sincere Protectionists—who are also sincere opponents of Socialism—must either close their ears to all reasoning about principles or have very uneasy consciences.

Professor Sumner has pointed out the connection between these two policies with his usual terse lucidity :—

> "When I say that Protectionism is Socialism, I mean to classify it, and bring it not only under the proper heading, but into relation with its true affinities. *Socialism is any device or doctrine whose aim is to save individuals from any of the difficulties or hardships of the struggle for existence and the competition of life by the intervention of 'the State.'* Inasmuch as 'the State' never is, or can be, anything but some other people, Socialism is a device for making some people fight the struggle for existence for others. The devices always have a doctrine behind them which aims to prove why this *ought* to be done.
>
> "The Protected interests demand that they be saved from the trouble and annoyance of business competition, and that they be assured profits in their undertakings by 'the State': that is, at the expense of their fellow-citizens. If this is not Socialism, then there is no such thing. If employers may demand that 'the State' shall guarantee them profits, why may not the employés demand that 'the State' shall guarantee them wages? If we are taxed to

provide profits, why should we not be taxed for public workshops, for insurance to labourers, or for any other devices which will give wages, and save the labourer from the annoyances of life and the risks and hardships of the struggle for existence?—the 'we' who are to pay changes all the time, and the turn of the Protected employer to pay will surely come before long. The plan of all living on each other is capable of great expansion. It is, as yet, far from being perfected, or carried out completely. The Protectionists are only educating those who are as yet on the 'paying' side of it, but who will certainly use political power to put themselves also on the 'receiving' side of it. The argument that 'the State' must do something for me because my business does not pay is a very far-reaching argument. If it is good for pig-iron and woollens, it is good for all the things to which the Socialists apply it."

§ 3. It would be interesting to hear a Protected manufacturer in answer to Professor Sumner's convincing words. His reasoning, however, does not appeal with the same force to a large class of Free Traders.

It would unnecessarily interrupt the present argument to introduce a discussion on the attitude of Free Traders to the large questions of policy involved in the theory of Socialism. It will, however, not be out of place to remind those Protectionists—who are also Socialists—that the Free Traders who refuse to accept the maxim of "*Laissez faire*" as a scientific dogma are pledged to no rejection of a measure because it happens to be Socialistic. They are not to be scared by a nickname.

Recognising that the Factory Acts, the Poor Law, the Irish Land Act, and many of the most beneficial measures of this century, are Socialistic in their essence, they do not shrink from other applications of the same principle. They do, however, require to be satisfied on three points before they will support State action: viz., First—that the State is the best agency for the accomplishment of that which is desired; secondly—That this object cannot be obtained by private enterprise; and thirdly—that the result, when obtained, and when all its effects are taken into account, is worth having on a balance of advantages and disadvantages.

[Pt. II., Ch. viii., § 3.]

They say, further, that no satisfactory assurance can be given by Protectionists as to any of these three demands.

It is the subject of the following chapters to inquire whether this be true.

NOTE TO CHAPTER VIII.
THE LIMITS OF STATE INTERFERENCE.

This is not the place to elaborate a theory of State interference, but since Free Traders are accused of being fanatical adherents of that theory, which would confine the action of the State to keeping order and administering affairs, it is well, before mentioning particular cases, to state summarily, and without reference to other matters, the general principles on which Free Traders might justify a more active interference by the State.

The State exists in order to secure liberty : that is to say, to bring about conditions under which every citizen can, by a conscious exercise of will, at all times do that which is best. Having provided these conditions, the function of the State is at an end. Other influences must determine what is good or bad, and must supply the motive which would make men choose the former. Philosophy and religion begin their operations upon the ground which the State has cleared ; but the action of the State should not interfere with the work of either. It consequently becomes one part of the business of political science to define the limits within which the State can act without trenching on the province of moral agencies. It is not necessary now to show in detail where those limits reach. It is enough for our present purpose to mark them in rough outline.

Laws exist to prevent men unduly interfering with the individual freedom of their fellow-citizens ; or, looked at in another way, a law defines a sphere within which each man's will may work with complete freedom. What, then, determines the exact amount of interference with individual freedom which is necessary for the advantage of Society? To that we answer—"Experience," and a clear sense of what is needed by the individual, in order that he may attain to a full and harmonious development. Whether this clearer sense of what is needed is evolved by inherited instinct, or whether it is due to the inspired direction of sacred writers, matters not to the State. All that the State has to do is to see that such social conditions exist, that Society may satisfy its wants so soon as it becomes aware of them, and so soon as it is certain that their satisfaction is necessary to human development. This is the utmost which the State can do. It must not attempt to decide for Society what moral influence should guide its judgments ; still less must it interfere with the free determination by every individual of the guiding principles of his own life. Consequently, every act of the State is bad which weakens the motives to self-improvement, either by unnecessarily taking away a duty which is owed to others (as, for instance, the care of children), or by preventing the full play of the human instinct towards self-development. A law which forbids men to think as they like, and to express their thoughts with a due regard to the public order, is bad, on the same ground that a law would be bad which weakened individual self-reliance, or which removed the motives towards thrift and industry.

It would seem, then, that the principles by which any act of State interference should be tested may be summarised as follows :—

1. The State ought in no case to weaken the motives for morality.
2. The State should not do that which might be done as well by private persons.
3. The State should never act in such a way as to weaken individual self-reliance.

But where the object to be gained is one of national importance, which the efforts of individuals cannot accomplish, and when it can be gained without discouraging any from making efforts on their own behalf, or from entering into union for a common purpose, then all the conditions are present which are required to justify State action.

Part XXX.
THE ECONOMIC ARGUMENT.

CHAPTER I.

FREE TRADE IN ITS EFFECT UPON PRODUCTION.

§ 1. In estimating the economic value of any fiscal policy, the test to be applied is (as has already been mentioned[1]) the effect of the policy in increasing the national productiveness. The actual application of this test to the circumstances of a particular country is, no doubt, extremely difficult; but its theoretic value as a test of the economic efficacy of rival fiscal policies is, as we have seen, not on that account impaired.

The material prosperity of a country must, in the long run, depend upon the capacity of its citizens to produce wealth, so that whatever enlarges that capacity must, *per se*, be an advantage. Some men may take more interest in schemes for distributing wealth than in schemes for facilitating its production; but no one can say that an increase in the national productiveness can, of itself, and without the aid of any other influence, cause any diminution in the material welfare of the general body of citizens. The increase of wealth may be accompanied by a displacement of labour and capital from one industry to another, and such a displacement would probably cause much undeserved suffering to individuals; but if the result of the displacement were that more wealth was produced than had been produced before, no one could say that the nation *as a whole* had become poorer. Possibly, the increase

---

[1] See p. 79.

of wealth might be accompanied by such grave evils of a political character that many men might reasonably wish to keep their country poor. But this is a consideration of politics, and not of economics, which will be dealt with in its proper place.

When we come to deal with the political arguments upon the tariff, arguments will be advanced to show that Free Trade does not, and cannot, prejudicially affect the distribution of national wealth; but that, on the contrary, it assists the labouring and poorer classes to obtain a fairer share of the products of their toil by its efficacy in extending the area of employment, in steadying wages, and in reducing the cost of living.

At present, however, let us consider Free Trade solely as an influence upon the production of wealth, and, waiving every other consideration, follow the single inquiry, "How Free Trade affects the aggregate of wealth within a country."

§ 2. This is a matter which has already been so overlaboured by writers on Free Trade, that it is not necessary in this treatise to do more than indicate the heads of the argument.

Regarded in its influence on production, Free Trade is simply an expedient for carrying the principle of the division of employment into international commerce. As it is found in domestic industries that the largest quantity is produced when each man confines himself to a particular department, so it can be shown conclusively that wealth will accumulate most rapidly in a country which produces those articles in the production of which it has especial natural advantages, and exchanges these for the other things it needs. Just as a baker would waste his time by making his own clothes, so will a nation spend its labour uselessly by producing articles at greater cost than it can buy them from another country. Nature gives gratuitously to every country advantages peculiar to itself—to one it is coal, to another iron, to another wheat, to another wool; but, thanks to Free Exchange, men in every quarter of the globe can serve themselves of these free gifts.

Free Trade, as has often been remarked, is only another name for voluntary trade. If, therefore, every man follows his own interest, he will prefer to trade in whatever calling returns him the largest profits. Accordingly, if we find the citizens of any country in which capital and labour are abundant choosing certain occupations in preference to others, the reason must be that the occupations which they adopt are considered likely to return them a larger profit than those which they avoid. Following out these ideas, we reach the familiar Free Trade conception of industrial progress, which is, that as capital accumulates and labourers increase, the desire for gain is a sufficient motive to secure the developmen of every suitable industry.

CHAPTER II.

PROTECTION AND PRODUCTION.

§ 1. WE have next to consider the operation of Protection upon the production of wealth. If any quantity of labour is attracted from old and more profitable to new and less profitable occupations, it is plain that, unless there should happen to be a compensating increase in the productiveness of the labourer which is left in the old pursuits, there must be a decrease in the national productiveness.

Now, although an increase in the productiveness of an industry may, through an improvement in the process of manufacture, or through some other agency, occur simultaneously with the withdrawal of a portion of the labour and capital previously employed in it, the increase is seldom, if ever, occasioned by such a withdrawal. On the contrary, in most industries the greater the expenditure of labour and capital, the greater the result.

The conclusion is thus reached that a withdrawal of capital and labour from more to less profitable occupations must occasion a loss of national wealth equivalent to the difference between the profitableness of the natural and the artificial industries. Suppose, for example, that the average rate of profit under the natural conditions of a Free Trade country where no special inducement is offered to follow one trade rather than another, be ten per cent., and that an industry which is not yet established in the country would only return three per cent.: it is plain that unless these two rates of profit more nearly approach each other, the industry which returns the lower rate will be neglected; and that to attract labour from an industry which returns ten per cent. into one which only returns three would be a net loss of seven per cent.

So far, the argument has proceeded upon the assumption that the capital and labour which are required to establish a Protected industry must be withdrawn from some other employment. It remains to consider the supposition that these may be imported from a foreign country. If this should happen to any large extent, there will, undoubtedly, be an increase to the national wealth. Consequently, if Protection is to be carried out to the greatest advantage, each new industry that is established must be created and sustained by imported labour and imported capital. This has been the case in many industries in the United States, where the huge burden of the Protective tariff is only borne with such apparent ease on account of the enormous influx of labour and capital from other countries. In the cases of Canada and Victoria the influx has not been so marked; while in all the Australian Colonies those who most strongly advocate Protection most strongly oppose assisted immigration. It may, therefore, be taken as a fact that in most young countries, where the annual increase of population is not larger than can be employed in the natural development of the country, and where able-bodied persons willing to work are always in demand, the labour and capital required to start new industries must be supplied within the community, and must therefore be withdrawn from those industries which have grown up naturally and without State aid.

The cases, therefore, in which Protection induces an importation of labour and capital need not materially qualify the conclusion previously arrived at, that a transference of capital and labour from an industry which returns a satisfactory profit to one which would return a less profit, if it were not for the subsidy given indirectly by a Protective tax, must cause an immediate loss of wealth to the community.

In the most favourable view of the transaction the tax can only cause a transference of money from the pockets of one set of citizens into those of another; while what happens in actual practice is a transference of money from those who were using it reproductively to those who must use it unproductively unless they are assisted by a subsidy, together with a loss of many of the coins during the process of transfer, owing to the cost of maintaining Custom House officers to effect the operation. During the process of transfer many of the coins fall upon the ground, and become visible to every bystander. In such a case, if the bystander is a Protectionist, he at once exclaims that the wealth of his country is increasing; and the more often a display is made of the same coins the louder become his exclamations!

The experience of Canada offers an instance, which is cited by Sir T. Farrer, of the effect of a Protective tariff in developing some industries at the expense of others. In 1878, under Free Trade, Canada exported of her own manufactures to the value of £825,000. In 1884 she only exported them to the value of £700,000: in spite of the fact that her population had increased and the development of her natural resources had been improved during those six years.

§ 2. But the diminution of the productive power of a country which is occasioned by the transference of capital and labour from a more to a less profitable occupation is not the only prejudicial effect which Protection has upon the aggregate of national wealth.

The essential object of Protection is to draw people into industries which they have hitherto declined to enter. The inducement offered is, of course, pecuniary. The patriotic founder of a new industry is to be protected against the competition of anyone who lives inside the borders of another country; and this protection is to be afforded by means of a tax upon all imported articles of the same nature with those which he produces.

The first question which presents itself under these circumstances is as to the amount of the duty which it will be necessary to impose to effect this object. The duty must clearly be sufficient to enable the manufacturer to sell his goods at a remunerative price. Now, a remunerative price must be a price which will give the manufacturer the same return for his money, skill, and time as he could obtain by a similar expenditure in any other occupation which is carried on within the country. In other words, he must obtain the average rate of profit (whatever that may be) which rules in the community, taking into account the usual considerations, such as risk, agreeableness of occupation, &c., which determine the rate of profit with which a man will be satisfied. Suppose, for instance, the ruling rate of profit be ten per cent., and that the manufacture of iron would only return one per cent., no duty on iron would encourage the home manufacturers of that article unless it were sufficiently high to give a reasonable expectation to the manufacturer that he would obtain a return of ten per cent. upon his outlay.

There must, therefore, be such an expenditure of labour within the community as will produce a fund from which those who enter the new industries may be recompensed for the loss which they make in quitting the old. This labour is, economically speaking, as much wasted as if it were employed in digging holes in the sea-shore and filling them with sand. Had Protective taxes not attracted capital and labour into industries which did not pay without State aid, there would have been no necessity for any expenditure for the purposes of recompense. The operation of a Protective tax produces, therefore, a double loss:—It not only attracts men from the industries in which they can produce more, to those in which they produce less, but it compels those who continue in the old industries to pay for the support of those who enter the new.

This, however, is not a full catalogue of the economic evils of Protective taxes.

§ 3. Such taxes cause yet a third loss to the productive powers of a community, by reason of their effect in decreasing the fund which is available for the employment of labour.

Any increase in the prices of articles of general consumption soon tells its tale upon the purses of the bulk of a community. Their power of purchasing becomes restricted, and the employment which they can give to others is less than it was. Nothing re-acts more quickly upon the labour market than the impoverishment of the poorer classes, since this not only directly reduces the demand for labour, but very speedily increases the supply. When persons of small means find that a sovereign only goes as far as fifteen shillings used to go, they not only very sensibly contract their expenditure, but they are forced to look about more actively for opportunities to increase their income. The labourer is thus oppressed by Protection on all sides. The cost of his living is increased, and his opportunities of finding employment are diminished. If he belongs to a Protected trade, he employs a portion of his time in doing for himself what some one else in another country would do for him at a less price. If he is a member of that larger class who cannot be Protected, he pays away a portion of his earnings in support of his Protected brethren; while, whatever his position in the community, he has to pay more for what he wants than if he bought it in the open market, and has, therefore, less to live upon than he had before, and less to spend in giving employment to his fellow-workmen. Yet we are asked to believe that when the citizens of a State are exposed to these necessitous conditions, and when all these sources of loss are added together, the country as a whole will increase in wealth! Surely a more extravagant proposition was never submitted for the acceptance of intelligent men. Wealth is the product of labour, which may be directed by a tax from one channel into another, but which no tax, however cunningly devised, can call into existence.

If labour seeks one channel in preference to another, the reason for its choice is, plainly, the desire for greater profit. If the encouragement of a tariff is required to attract men from one occupation into another, that is an admission that the occupation into which it is desired to lead them is not, by itself, so lucrative as those which are of natural growth. As Mr. George has expressed it:—"If the time has come for the establishment of an industry for which proper natural conditions exist, restrictions upon importations in order to promote its establishment are needless. If the time has not come, such restrictions can only divert labour and capital from industries in which the return is greater to others in which it must be less, and thus reduce the aggregate production of wealth."

We have thus reached the first step in the economic argument in favour of Free Trade, and shown that Protection lessens a nation's power to produce wealth by attracting capital and labour from the more profitable to the less profitable occupations, and by taxing the majority of a community in order to provide a fund for keeping profits and wages in certain industries up to the average rate.

The precise extent of the loss which is thus inflicted will be a subject for a separate chapter.

CHAPTER III.

FREE TRADE AND PRICES.

§ 1. THE hardiest advocate of a restricted commerce has never had the courage to assert that Free Trade raised prices; the charge against a policy which permits free exchange has always been the opposite. This abhorrence of cheapness appears to be due, in a large degree, to the false idea that a low level of prices must be associated with a low rate of wages—a misconception of facts, which is among the earliest, as it is the longest-lived, of economic errors. The true relation between prices and wages will be the subject of inquiry when the effect of Free Trade upon the distribution of wealth comes under review, but such an inquiry is foreign to the scope of an argument directed only to the working of a fiscal policy within the field of production.

The exact relation between prices and production is both intricate and obscure. The economist says, and says unanswerably, that there can be no such thing as excessive cheapness, because the cheaper things become, the greater the number of people who will buy them. The practical man of business, on the other hand, asserts—and brings forward facts in support of his assertion—that falling prices always check production.

What is the explanation of this difference of opinion, and what is the truth?

A low level of prices may be due to one or more of three causes, viz. :—

1. To a lessened cost of production.
2. To a decreased power of consumption.
3. To a scarcity of gold.

Each of these causes acting upon prices may affect the production of wealth in a different way. Low prices, due to a scarcity of gold, may at first limit trade, and then abnormally extend it by encouraging inflated credit; low prices, due to a decreased power of consumption, give rise to that unhealthy over-production from which the industrial body is only relieved by the drastic remedy of a commercial crisis. Low prices, however, which are due to the lessening of the cost of production are a healthy stimulus to the productive power of the human race.

These differences in the causes of low prices are generally overlooked by those who raise an outcry against cheapness. This has been notably the case during the extraordinary industrial depression which prevailed over all parts of the civilised world during the six years 1883 to 1888. This depression was unparalleled in history, both in its extent and its duration, and it was, moreover, accompanied by a large and rapid fall in prices. The consequence has been a revival of the old fallacy that "Low prices make low wages," and an onslaught on the Free Trade doctrine that a cheapening of prices is for the general advantage. The circumstances, however, of this unprecedented and disastrous period afford no test for the guidance of voters in choosing between fiscal policies, and certainly throw no discredit on the teachings of Free Trade. On the whole, Free Trade countries came best out of the ordeal, but all suffered terribly.[1] The causes were complicated, and perhaps impossible to trace. One fact, however, is certain: that all the three causes which have been mentioned as affecting prices were at work simultaneously, with the result that in 1886 prices had fallen thirty-six per cent. below the average rate of 1873,[2] and that this fall continued until the middle of 1888, when it received a check.

[1] *See* Reports of Evidence taken before Royal Commission on Depression of Trade, 1883-6. According to the Washington Labour Bureau, one million men were out of work in the United States in 1886.

[2] *See Journal of Statistical Society, passim*, especially the papers read by Mr. Giffen and Mr. Sauerbeck.

It would fall outside the scope of this argument to examine in detail the many causes which have been believed to have originated or prolonged this great depression. It may, however, be mentioned that the report of the Washington Labour Bureau for 1886 classifies the causes assigned for industrial depressions by witnesses before Congressional Committees of Inquiry under 180 heads.[1] Free Traders will learn with pleasure that Free Trade was not considered to be the only cause of industrial evils. Some witnesses attributed them also to the use of tobacco, others to the neglect of female education; each of which explanations may serve to illustrate the danger of indulging in generalisations upon the effect of low prices!

Low prices may be both the cause and the effect of increased production. When the low prices are caused by an extension of the market, or by a cheapening of the cost of production, they give an immediate stimulus to the productive powers of a community; but when they are caused by a falling-off in the demand without a corresponding diminution in the supply, then they may mark a period both of low wages and small profits.

§ 3. Free Trade, however, is, as has been pointed out, an instrument of production, in that it cheapens and steadies the supply of raw materials, and permits the application of the principle of division of employment to the transactions of international commerce. It is, in other words, in itself a form of a cheapened process of production; and as it is applicable to every kind of article, it must, therefore, affect prices in that particular way which stimulates production. If the distinctions between the various causes of low prices have been correctly followed, and if the fact is once admitted that all these causes have been at work during the last six years, the futility of

[1] See paper by Professor R. M. Smith, *Political Science Quarterly*, I., p. 444.

the Protectionist alarm lest commodities should be too cheap in consequence of Free Trade will be at once apparent. Looking at cheapness simply as an influence upon production, we can say with certainty that a cheapness of the sort induced by Free Trade—viz., a cheapness which arises from the use of a wider area of production and a freer interchange of goods—can never be excessive. Whether it ever happens that a cheapness arising from this cause can (as Protectionists assert) so diminish employment that higher prices would be an advantage to the labouring classes, because they would be accompanied with more work, will be matter of inquiry when we come to deal with the influence of Protection in reducing wages.

For the present, treating the question merely as one of production, it must be apparent that a low level of prices, arising from a cheapening of the processes of manufacture, stimulates the productive power. The majority of mankind is still so far beneath the level of its aspirations in its enjoyment of material comforts, and the desires of all men are so constantly enlarging, that no definable limit can be placed to the extension of the present demand for the necessaries and luxuries of life. All that can be said is, that in respect of any particular article, the actual limit of demand is the price at which it can be profitably produced; and that, while everything which tends to lower the price of remunerative production increases demand, everything which increases demand reacts in turn upon prices by causing production upon a larger scale, and thus economising cost. Or, if this is thought by those who believe in the theory of Protection to be too abstract and vague, let them arrive at the same conclusion by asking themselves two simple questions:—" Would they think it an advantage if other countries were to give us everything we wanted, and took nothing in exchange?" If the reply is in the affirmative, then let them ask—"Whether, if a gift of everything we want is advantageous, a gift of a part is not also advantageous?"

[Pt III., Ch. iii, § 4.]

The difference between a free gift and a reduced price is only one of degree.

§ 4. Free Trade, besides lowering prices through cheapening the process of production, also steadies them, and in this performs a most important function.

The complexity of our present industrial system, and the universal practice of producing on a large scale for an unknown market,[1] has made it a matter of supreme importance to check as far as possible wide or sudden fluctuations in prices. Industrial depressions, whatever be the variety of their causes, resemble each other in this respect: that during their continuance the supply of commodities is greater than the effective demand for them. This may arise from over-production or under-consumption: that is to say, the supply may be unduly increased, or the demand may be unduly lessened. Possibly, as was the case during the last depression, these two things may happen at the same time. But, whatever the immediate cause, the result is always the same—that enterprise is stopped, labour is unemployed, stocks accumulate, and goods cannot be sold at a price which is remunerative. Production, however, cannot at once cease; mills cannot be closed, nor skilled workmen suffered to disperse. The adjustment of the supply of a commodity to the effective demand for it is always a slow process. It is therefore a matter of supreme concern to every producer that he should be able to anticipate with some

[1] "How does it happen that when enough of a commodity is produced, men should still go on producing? ... The explanation is that in our present industrial organisation we produce on a large scale for an unknown market. In old times the shoemaker made a pair of shoes for the man who ordered them; now our manufacturers make thousands of dozens in advance of the demand. If they can do this so as to undersell others, they have an unlimited market; but if another undersells them, they lose the entire market. It is the same way in agriculture. The American farmer ruined the English, and now the Indian wheat threatens to displace the American in the European market." (Professor Richmond Smith, in *Political Science Quarterly*, Vol. I., p. 447.)

M

degree of certainty the probable demand for his particular class of goods.[1]

Now, if prices fluctuate, the equation between supply and demand becomes more difficult to calculate, because both the supply of and demand for any commodity are greatly affected by the steadiness of its price. Men are always more ready to enter upon new undertakings or to increase their purchases when they can calculate the cost beforehand with some degree of confidence and exactitude. Whatever, therefore, steadies prices must tend to avert commercial depressions, and to lessen their severity, by enabling a more accurate adjustment to be made between supply and demand.

Free Trade operates in steadying prices by widening both the area of production and the area of consumption. It not only gives a larger supply of raw materials, but a wider market for the sale of the finished goods.[2]

---

[1] Of late years the power of production has enormously increased through the invention of new machinery; at the same time, the power of consumption has diminished in consequence of the displacement of labour caused by the adoption of mechanical processes. Professor Richmond Smith quotes from the Report of the National Bureau of Labour for 1886 (already referred to) many striking instances of this.

[2] In the days before Free Trade, the price of a quartern loaf in England was seldom steady for a month together. Every frost and every fall of rain might be, and often was, the presage of starvation. The price of a quarter of wheat often doubled within a year; while since the adoption of Free Trade the annual variation is between twelve and fifteen shillings. Or, to express the same fact in another way, the price of the quartern loaf, which in one year reached eighteenpence and in another sold for fourpence, has, since Free Trade, remained almost stationary between fourpence and sevenpence. And this is not all. While, under Protection, high prices were the rule, under Free Trade they are exceptional; so that in thirty years the average price of wheat has been reduced twelve shillings the quarter. It is difficult for those who have never lived in a country where poverty and want abound to realise the inestimable boon of cheap food. But those who have read the literature of the Chartist period—such tales, for instance, as Kingsley's "Yeast" or Disraeli's "Sybil" know well that in those days the varying price of corn continually drove the working-classes to starvation. Periodic starvation was, in fact, the normal condition of masses of working-men in England previous to the introduction of Free Trade; and if this statement seem exaggerated, the cruellest and most

A wide area of production must tend to steady, as well as to reduce, the prices of raw material, because it not only increases the sources of their supply, but tends to make the market independent of local disturbances. Suppose, for instance, that New South Wales were dependent for her supply of iron upon the furnaces of Lithgow: the price of iron might be doubled in a single day by a strike, a breakage of machinery, disease among the workmen, or any other accident. But when iron can be bought from England, Belgium, and America, the failure of one market would only have a slight effect upon prices in the others. The wider, therefore, the area of production, the less the risk to a producer, and the more constant his supply of raw materials.

Almost every article is, however, the raw material of another in some stage of its production. Consequently, whatever steadies the prices of raw materials affects production in all its forms, by enabling producers to calculate beforehand all the items of their outlay.

But in order that the supply of a commodity may not be disproportionate to the demand for it, something more is needed besides a regulation of the output. The probable purchasing power of the customers must also be capable of calculation. A producer must not only have an assurance that there will be no sudden rise in the price of his raw materials, but he must also be able to estimate the amount he is likely to sell. In making this estimate, a producer is again assisted by Free Trade. It is true that under Free Trade his market is larger, and therefore his calculations will be more complicated; but the same security against the ill effects of local disturbances which assisted him in his production will also assist him in his sales. Wars, pestilences, bad harvests, and all the other torments of producers, cannot have the same effect over a wide

rigid proof of its accuracy is given by the tables of mortality. The returns of the Registrar-General show an increase in the number of deaths with every rise in the price of bread.

area that they would have within the limits of a single country. But it has already been remarked, in considering the effect of Free Trade upon production, that there is always a danger, under a system of Protection, of over-supplying the local market. This danger is to a great extent obviated by a policy of Free Exchange; because, whatever widens the area of consumption gives a larger market for the sale of goods. This consideration explains why Free Trade countries are generally the last to feel, and the first to recover from, a trade depression. Their foreign trade affords them a speedier outlet for surplus stock, and helps the more rapid readjustment between supply and demand.

But it is not only by widening the areas of production and consumption that Free Trade is an agency in the prevention of commercial crises. It also acts in this direction by giving producers a more accurate knowledge of the wants and the position of their customers. Trade depressions, as has been said, are always marked by an accumulation of unsaleable goods. Sometimes this is owing to a mistake on the part of the producers, as was the case in 1825, when a cargo of skates was shipped to the Brazils, and grand pianos and diamond tiaras were consigned for sale to the South American Indians;[1] and in such a case it cannot be denied that the crisis might have been prevented, or at least alleviated, by greater knowledge. Even in cases where the error is not quite so gross, there must always be room for more accurate information. Can anyone doubt under which policy producers are less likely to mistake their markets?—whether it will be under a policy which encourages intercourse with foreigners, or under one which insists on isolation? It must be plain that the risk of producing goods which are not wanted at the time is lessened by everything which brings the inhabitants of distant countries nearer to one another. Free Trade, like telegraphs and

---

[1] See Martineau's "History of the Peace" for an entertaining account of this commercial crisis.

railways, tends to keep both producers and consumers better informed as to each others' needs.

§ 5. But, although Free Trade tends to steady prices, and therefore to prevent commercial crises, by equalising, disclosing, and enlarging markets, it cannot prevent these terrible disturbances. Fluctuating trade, with all its misery of wasted efforts, savings squandered, and homes destroyed, is an evil which lies beyond the range of any tariff. The causes of commercial crises cannot be removed either by Protection or Free Trade. Wars, excessive speculation, dishonesty, gambling in land values—to mention only the chief of such causes—are manifestly outside the influence of Customs duties. All that can be done by any fiscal policy is to lessen the frequency of trade depressions, and strengthen a community to bear them better. In this beneficial and remedial work, Free Trade has always played a most important part.[1]

CHAPTER IV.

PROTECTION AND PRICES.

§ 1. It was shown in the second chapter of this Part that Protection diminished the aggregate production of national wealth in three ways:—

1. By causing an artificial and compulsory transfer of money and labour from profitable to unprofitable industries.

---

[1] The Report of the Royal Commission on the Depression of Trade contains the following paragraph:—"There is no feature in the situation which we have been called upon to examine, so satisfactory as the immense improvement that has taken place in the condition of the working-classes during the last twenty-six years. At the present moment (1886) there is a good deal of distress, owing to the want of regular work; but there can be no question that the workman in this country [Great Britain] is, when fully employed, in almost every respect in a better condition than his competitor in foreign countries."

2. By causing a wasteful expenditure for the purpose of giving to those who were induced by Protection to change their employment a rate of profit in their new occupations equal to that which they might be making in the old.
3. By increasing the cost of living to consumers, and thus lessening the amount which, but for Protection, would have been available for the employment of labour.

Underlying the argument by which these conclusions were supported was the unexpressed assumption that Protection raised prices—an assumption which is so obviously contained within the terms of the propositions submitted about Protection, that it was not thought necessary to interrupt the argument by inquiring into its correctness. Those, however, who have lived in a country where Protectionists are active, will know that no proposition about commerce or finance is so plain that there will not be some persons who dispute it; and will not be surprised to learn that it is even denied on public platforms and in the columns of party newspapers that Protection has the effect of raising prices. A few words, therefore, as to the effect of Protection on prices will not be out of place in a work which is intended to be of direct practical assistance to those who are engaged in the fiscal controversy.

§ 2. Very slight reflection will show that if Protection does not raise prices it does not effect what is required of it. That much-regarded personage, the home producer, has complained that he cannot sell an article of his own make at the low price at which it can be imported, and the advocate of restricted commerce has given him, in consequence, a Protective duty. If, as some Protectionists assert, this duty will not increase prices, why, we may ask, was it imposed? If the only object of the manufacturer who asked for the duty was that he might sell his goods at a lower rate, why did he not proceed to do this without waiting for the imposition of a duty? He might have been sure that no one would have offered him a higher price than he himself asked.

Or, to express the same idea in a more general way, the competition against which Customs duties are designed to assist the home producer is the competition of low-priced articles. Now, there cannot for any length of time be two prices ruling at the same time in the same market for the same article. Therefore, if certain articles can be bought in the open market at a price which will not repay the home producer, no production of these is likely to take place within the country until their price rises to a height which will repay him. If, however, the importation of the low-priced articles is stopped, or if something is added to their price before they are allowed to be landed, their price may be sufficiently raised to make it worth the while of somebody within the country to attempt their production.

But the hypothesis with which the Protectionists start is that foreign competition keeps prices below the level which native capitalists regard as satisfactory. If, then, native capitalists do enter the lists of competition, and if they have been previously prevented from doing so by the low price of imported goods, they must sell the goods of their own make at a price which is higher than the price of the same quality of goods in the open market. In other words, since the Protectionist assumption is that home production is checked by the low prices of imported goods, native home production can only come into existence (if this assumption be true) when prices rise. This conclusion so nearly approaches to a truism that, did not experience teach the contrary, one would have pronounced it impossible that confusion should exist about it even in the minds of those who wish to be confused.

§ 3. In justice, however, to those persons who repeat in an authoritative way the assurance of Protectionist orators that

Protection will not raise prices, two facts should be mentioned which have given the statement a semblance of truth. These are the universal fall in prices which has taken place during the last thirty years, and the fall which often takes place in the price of a particular article, in consequence of the competition of Protected manufacturers one with the other.

The fall in prices, which is the marked commercial feature of the last thirty years, has been due to many causes which it is not necessary to enumerate here—the chief of these being the wonderful improvement in every process of manufacture and in the means of transport. This fall, however, has occurred contemporaneously with the introduction into many countries of Protective duties, consequent chiefly upon the revival of militarism as a result of the Franco-Prussian War, and has, of course, affected most of the Protected articles. Uneducated or unthinking persons, noticing an article has fallen in price since Protection was imposed, adopt the familiar fallacy of attributing this to the Protective duty, whereas in truth the price would have fallen still lower if the Protective duty had not existed. It is, for example, constantly asserted in New South Wales that a duty of sixpence per gallon on kerosene, which was imposed many years ago for revenue purposes, but which has now become Protective, has had the result of lowering the price of kerosene. The price of kerosene has no doubt fallen very much since the duty was imposed; but that has been owing to the immense discoveries of natural oil-wells in America and Southern Russia, and not in any way to the duty. This is made apparent at once by the fact that the price of kerosene at London, New York, or Batoum, after deducting freight and charge, is less than its price in Sydney by just the amount of the duty. It is, indeed, impossible that it should be otherwise. The price of an article of universal consumption, such as kerosene, is not likely to be determined for the whole world by its price in New South Wales.

The fall of prices in consequence of internal competition is another cause which has tended to obscure the operation upon prices of Protective duties. It cannot be denied that, although the immediate effect of Protection must be an increase in prices, it is possible that the competition of the home producers, one with the other, may, after a time, become so fierce, that prices will fall below their normal level. This, however, although it is a probable consequence of Protection, is by no means necessary; since a ruinous internal competition is generally checked by the facilities for combination which Protection offers. In the absence, however, of any combination among the Protected manufacturers to keep up prices by restricting their output, a Protective tax must, in the long run, cause excessive production. The home market, even in a country of the gigantic size of the United States, is necessarily more limited than that which is open to a Free Trade country. Industries which exist under Free Trade prove by the very fact of their existence their ability to hold their own against the competition of the world. Industries, on the other hand, which require for their support the fostering aid of a Protective duty, signify by this admission their inability to cope with foreign industries even on their own soil. How, then, can they compete with them in foreign countries? If the home manufacturer requires to be Protected against the foreigner when the foreigner is handicapped by all the costs and charges of transport, how can he hope to undersell the foreigner in a foreign market when he has himself to bear the cost of freight and other charges of exportation? Nowhere is a manufacturer situated so favourably as in his own market. If, then, under the most favourable circumstances, he cannot hold his own against the foreigner, he is not likely to be able to do so in a foreign market, where the circumstances are less favourable to him and more favourable to his rival. If a Protected manufacturer can sell his goods at a profit in a foreign country, it is proof positive that he wants no Protection in his own. If, however, he does want Protection in his own market—and it is on that assumption that the argument is being conducted—then he cannot sell his goods abroad except at a loss; and if he does sell them abroad, he must make up for his loss by charging more to the persons who have to pay for his Protection.

§ 4. Seeing, then, that Protection renders no service to an exporting country, and that no country which requires Protection can profitably export Protected articles, it follows that when the home market of a Protected country has been supplied there is no outlet for the surplus products. The consequence must be an immediate fall in prices, which producers will naturally endeavour to prevent. If no arrangement can be come to for the creation of a pool or trust, a cut-throat competition ensues. In either case the result is disastrous. The pool, by annihilating competition within the country, and being Protected against competition from outside, has both the labourer and the consumer at its mercy. The only limit to its power of raising prices or reducing wages is the untrustworthiness of its component parts. If high prices tempt some members to secede from the pool, prices may again fall; but so long as all the members hold together, a tyrannous monopoly exists against which resistance is impotent. If no pool is formed and a war of prices ensues, the workman is the first to suffer. Since each producer must undersell his rival, and since every one has a surplus of goods for sale, no expedient is spared for cutting down the cost of production; and the first item of this cost which is sure to attract attention is the wages of labour. If the native-born labourer will not accept a reduction, his place will be supplied by imported labourers from the most poverty-stricken countries in the Old World.

This has been the invariable course of Protection in new countries. At first prices rise, and all goes well in the Protected trade. The rise of prices soon attracts other capitalists to take their share of the plunder which the law allows them.

In time come over-production and a glutted market. There is no outlet abroad, for Protection has destroyed the trade with foreign countries; yet the goods which are constantly increasing have to be disposed of. Prices are then reduced and wages are cut down; strikes occur, and mills are closed; distress and famine at last cause outbursts of violence, which attract public notice and compel the manufacturers to combine together. A new period of combination is then entered upon, the end of which no one can foresee; but which in its inception has riveted the fetters of poverty upon the poor more firmly than ever, and given to the possessor of wealth wider opportunities for the tyrannous exercise of power than were ever dreamt of by despotic rulers.

CHAPTER V.

FREE TRADE AND WAGES.

§ 1. A STATEMENT of the theory of wages is beset with many verbal difficulties, but these may be avoided without distorting facts, if wages are defined as "The labourer's share of that which is produced." They are that portion of the product which remains after rent, profits, and taxes have been satisfied. Consequently, if these factors are constant, the amount of each man's wage will depend upon the proportion between the quantity of this remainder and the number of workmen engaged in the trade.

The theory may be expressed algebraically. Let R be rent, P the average rate of profit, having regard to all the circumstances, such as security, agreeableness of occupation, &c., which lead to the choice of one occupation rather than another. Let P also include cost of materials, interest or capital, wages of superintendence, wear and tear—everything, in fact, which is usually provided and allowed for by the capitalist employer. Let T be taxes; x the product. The amount divisible in wages will then be expressed thus: $x - (R + P + T)$. And if Q is the number of labourers employed in the given occupation, the share of each labourer will be

$$\frac{x - (R + P + T)}{Q}$$

Assuming, as before, that R, P, T remain constant—and we are entitled to make this assumption in an economic argument—the rate of wages depends upon the relative amounts of x and Q. So that wages may be increased either by increasing the total product or by diminishing the number of labourers. Mr. Edward Atkinson, of Boston,[1] who has made a special study of the wages question, has demonstrated by an elaborate process of induction from a great variety of authentic illustrations, that the tendency under the existing industrial system is to raise wages by both these methods: *i.e.*, by increasing x and lessening Q. This result is due to the marvellous improvements which have been effected during the last fifty years in the means of transport and in mechanical invention. Mr. David A. Wells, now happily again a senator of the United States, has pursued this line of investigation to the same conclusion in his lately published work on "Recent Economic Changes." All inquiries into the earnings of the working-class since the inauguration of the industrial era at the beginning of the present century lead by a series of cumulative proofs to the conclusion that the tendency of the competitive system of industry is towards the production of a steadily

---

[1] "The Distribution of Products." G. P. Putnam's Sons, New York, 1885. See also, by the same author, "The Industrial Progress of the Nation," Putnam's Sons, 1890. Further information on this deeply interesting economic phenomenon—which is the real cause of our recent trade depression and social movements—is to be found in Sir Lyon Playfair's recent volume of collected addresses, and in Mr. Mongredien's pamphlet, "A Neglected Chapter in Economics."

increasing quantity of things by means of a steadily decreasing number of labourers.

Accordingly, if we assume that there is no check to the increase of population (and the possibility of raising wages by this means need not be considered here), the conclusion is inevitable that there can be no general rise in the rates of real wages except by means of an increase in the quantity of things produced, nor of money wages except by means of a similar increase, coupled with the maintenance of the relative prices at which such products can be sold. Does it equally follow that an increase in the quantity of things produced is an essential requisite to the opening of new channels of employment, so that wages may be earned in fresh pursuits by those who have been displaced from their former occupations? Experience and theory alike reply in the affirmative. The accumulation of capital gives the best known stimulus to the establishment of new industries; while every increase in the efficiency of labour by raising wages and lowering prices creates new ranges of desire, which must be satisfied by the exertions of new labourers. Poverty may, for a time, ensue as a consequence of an invention; but labour adjusts itself in time to new conditions with a silence and rapidity which bear a striking testimony to the apparently inexhaustible productivity of human powers

§ 2. The action of Free Trade on wages becomes now easy to trace. Free Trade is, as we have seen, a device for increasing the number of things which can be made by a given quantity of labour through access to the natural advantages of distant countries. It is plain, therefore, if this be correct, that Free Trade cannot of itself cause any diminution in wages, and that it is *primâ facie* likely to raise them.

It does not follow, as we have repeatedly conceded, that the labourer will always get a proper share of every increase in national productiveness; but it is impossible to argue from the mere fact of an increase having taken place that wages are likely to fall. If it should happen that some other factor of the product gets an undue share of the increase at the expense of labour, this must arise from causes which are independent of the economic operation of Free Trade ; because (to put the case in its simplest form) an increase in the sum to be divided cannot, *per se*, lessen the quotient.

It thus becomes necessary to consider whether Free Trade has any other effect which may influence wages besides that of causing an increase in the aggregate of material wealth. Does it, for instance, unduly raise profits, or rent, or taxes; or does it by any means depress the labourer so that he cannot claim a fair share of the increase ? This is really an inquiry into the effect of Free Trade upon the distribution of wealth, which raises political rather than economic considerations.[1] There are, however, two ways in which Free Trade is alleged by Protectionists to lower the rate of wages, which may properly be considered in this connection.

It is said, in the first place, that the tendency of commerce between two countries in which the rates of wages differ is to depress the higher rate to the level of the lower ; and, secondly, that wage-earners are less able under Free Trade than under Protection to prevent the owners of natural monopolies, such as land or mines, from appropriating an undue proportion of any increase in productiveness.

These arguments are plainly expressions in another form of arguments, which are well known on the political side of the fiscal controversy under the titles of the " Pauper Labour" and the " Diversification of Industry" arguments. At present, however, we are not concerned with these arguments in their practical applications, but need only consider whether they have any theoretic value.

[1] " Protection now assumes a new form, and is advocated as a means of securing to the labourers a larger share in the distribution of wealth." (Prof. Patten's " Economic Basis of Protection," p. 20.)

§ 3. The notion that the rates of wages in two competing countries tend to an equality, so that a country of high wages ought to be protected against the competition of a country of low wages, depends upon the fallacy that the rate of wages is the true measure of the cost of production. This confusion of money wages with labour cost has always been a deeply seated and frequent cause of error in the economics both of external and internal trade. In former days it prompted the opposition to the use of new machines, just as to-day it prompts the opposition to the labour-saving institution of foreign commerce. The difference between the competition of machines and that of cheap foreign labour is only one of degree. That which the craftsman fears upon the introduction of new machinery is lest his services should be more costly to his old employer than those of the machine. That which the home producer fears at the first rumour of foreign competition is lest his employer should be able to import the foreign article at a less price than that at which it can be made by home labour. In each case the fear is lest the new competitor should be able to do more work at a less price: in other words, lest it should prove more efficient than the man who fears its competition. This fear is sometimes well founded. The hand-loom weavers disappeared as a class before the competition of the power-loom, and the Coventry watchmakers have been sorely injured by the competition of America and Switzerland. But when it is said that the foreign competition of a cheap-labour country tends to reduce the wages of a high-waged country, the statement is intended to have a general application, and not to be limited to the particular trade which is exposed to competition.

It is a truism of economic experience that no displacement of labour can take place without causing much unmerited suffering among labourers during the period that they are seeking new employment; and it is indisputable that during the last twenty years whole classes of skilled artisans have sunk into the reserve army of unskilled labour for no other reason than that the invention of a new machine has destroyed the market value of their special skill. But it is equally incontestable that the wages of workmen generally have risen during this period, and that the rise has been greatest in those countries, such as America and England, where the competition of machinery has been the keenest. It is the same with the competition of cheap foreign labour. If it is successful, and if it does, as in the Coventry watch trade, supplant a home industry, the reason must be that, either in consequence of the low wages of labour—or, more probably, in spite of it—it can produce the article which is the subject of competition at a less cost than this can be produced at home. To this extent, therefore, foreign competition is a labour-saving device to all those in the country who may desire to buy the finished article. The labourer which it supplants must find another occupation, and is assisted in doing so by the increased power of saving, which the reduction in the price of the article in the production of which it was formerly employed has given to his former customers. Thus, when the watch trade left Coventry, the trade in bicycles grew up; and the rate of wages is higher, and the number of artisans greater in that city than at any other period in her history. An extreme instance will test the soundness of these views.

Chemists tell us that honey can be manufactured in a laboratory which is indistinguishable from the work of bees. Yet should we on that account, and in order to employ labour, prohibit the keeping of apiaries in order to establish chemical works and their attendant industries in every country? The suggestion, says a Protectionist, is absurd. Yet, how does he act differently from this when he deals in the Legislature with another article of sweetness—namely, sugar? Sugar can be grown in New South Wales by white labour, and it is grown in Fiji by Kanakas. The white man says—and possibly he says truly—that labour enters so largely into the cost of producing sugar that it is impossible for a New South Welshman to compete against Fiji in its production without the aid of a Protective tariff. Protectionists accordingly insist that no one in New South Wales should be allowed to buy a ton of sugar from Fiji without paying £5 to the Government for every purchase. How, then, does this differ from the suggested action against the competition of the bees? The result of the competition is in each case the same—namely, that the product is sold at a less cost. What does it signify to the man who is competed with whether his competitor be a bee or a black-fellow?

§ 4. The fallacy of the argument against the competition of cheap labour lies in confusing the rate of wages with the labour cost of production.

Now, the rate of wages can only be a measure of the true cost of labour in those few industries in which the product is the result of almost unassisted hand-work. In such cases, as Mr. Atkinson points out, " both the materials worked upon, and also the product, may bear a very high price, but the work upon them not being aided by effective machinery, the quantity of labour will be very large, and the result of the sale may therefore leave but a very small sum to be divided among very many labourers, after the cost of materials has been set aside. . . . . For instance, after the pattern is drawn it takes merely manual dexterity to make Brussels lace. The material which is used in this branch of industry is fine and costly cotton-thread, which is converted into lace by hand, without the aid of any machinery whatever, but merely by the use of two or three simple tools. The lace-makers of Brussels are among the poorest of the poorer classes of European operatives. They work at the very lowest rates of wages, which will barely keep them in existence, but their product is of very high cost in money. The very best Lyons silks and German velvets are other examples. They are made upon hand-looms of the most primitive kind. Beet-root sugar is another example. Beets require constant hand-work in weeding. We cannot afford the time or labour for such work so long as we can exchange wheat raised by machinery for money, and with the money buy our sugar. In all handicrafts the quantity of labour is very great, but even at the high prices which such products bring, the total sum of money recovered from the sale leaves but a very low rate of wages to be divided among those who have performed the work."

Most industries, however, in a country of high industrial development, are assisted either by natural advantages or mechanical appliances. Accordingly, in all such cases high money wages become a necessary consequence of the low labour cost. In other words, since the labour of each wage-earner is rendered more efficient, the proportion between the value of the product and the number of workmen increases, so that there is both a larger quantity to divide and fewer labourers to receive. Reverting to the formula used on a previous page, if the wage of each labourer in a given occupation be—

$$\frac{x - (R + P + T)}{Q}$$

x is increased and Q diminished. Low wages thus become an indication of dear production; while a high rate of money wages is a necessary result of a low labour cost. "Low wages and cheap labour are not synonymous terms; but," as Mr. Atkinson further says, at the conclusion of his investigations, "that labour has, in fact, proved to be cheapest by which the largest product for each dollar expended was assured, and that has been the highest paid labour." ("Distribution of Products," p. 66.)[1] Low wages are rarely, if ever, the accompaniment of a degree of industrial efficiency.

---

[1] Mr. Atkinson's conclusions are as follows:—First: The rate of wages constitutes no standard even of the money cost of production: which cost must be made up by adding together the sum of all wages and dividing by the product, in order to establish a unit of cost in money by way of a unit of measure, whether by the yard, barrel, or pound.

Second: Low rates of wages are not essential to a low cost of production, but, on the contrary, usually indicate a high cost of production—that is to say, a large measure of human labour and a large sum of wages at low rates. Con-

It follows, then, from these considerations, that the pauper labour argument needs to be re-stated. It is not the competition of a low-waged country that Protectionists need fear; but what may become dangerous to particular industries is the competition of a country where production is carried on at high wages, and consequently at a low labour cost. In the latter case, individual industries may suffer, as individual industries have suffered, by the introduction of machines, but the country, as a whole, gains in wealth. The question thus becomes one of politics: "Whether, in the interests of the State, this injury to individuals ought to be prevented?" Later in these pages, when the political aspect of this argument comes to be discussed, it will be shown that the alarms at foreign competition are to a great extent illusory. Individual industries do not, in fact, suffer from the competition of other countries to such a considerable extent as to justify a politician in imposing the burdens of Protection upon other industries. Trade is mutually beneficial, and nations are dependent one upon the other; if in the rush of competition one country should gain an unfair profit for a

versely, high rates of wages may, and commonly do, indicate a low cost of production—that is to say, a small proportion of human labour and a small proportionate sum of wages at high rates in a given quantity of product.

Third: Cheap labour, in a true sense, and low rates of wages, are *not* synonymous terms, but are usually quite the reverse.

Fourth: An employer is not under the necessity of securing labour at low rates of wages in order to make cheap goods, but he may, and commonly does, pay high rates of wages, for the very purpose of assuring the production of goods at the lowest cost—that is, in order to be able to sell them on the lowest terms, or "cheap," in the popular sense.

The abuse of the word *cheap* leads to more mischievous fallacies than any other abuse of language. The cheapest labour is the best-paid labour; it is the best-paid labour applied to machinery that assures the largest product in ratio to the capital invested.

If these propositions can be sustained, it may be submitted that the more the capitalist increases his wealth and applies it to reproduction, the more the welfare of the labourer is assured. The competition of capital with capital tends constantly to a decrease in the ratio of the profit of capital to the total production, and of necessity tends also to a constant increase in the rate of wages of the labourer, thereby more than counteracting the tendency of the competition of labourer with labourer to diminish wages.

time at the expense of another, the evils of attempting to adjust the balance by the aid of a Protective tax are greater than the temporary loss. Experience shows that foreign competition, in the few cases where it is effective, is better met by studying the laws of nature, and laying to heart the reasons why rivalry has succeeded, than by looking to the laws of Parliament, and praying for relief at the expense of others. If Protectionists were right, and if the tendency of trade between two countries of unequal rates of wages were to depress the higher rate to the level of the lower, the rate of wages should vary in all European countries according to the magnitude of each one's dealings with the Asiatic or other uncivilised races. That is to say : wages should be lowest in England of all European nations, and in New South Wales of the Australian colonies. The contrary is notoriously the case. So is it equally notorious that the competition which the American or colonial Protectionists most fear is not the competition of the dark-skinned races, but the competition of the skilled and high-paid labour of Great Britain. No instance can be cited by Protectionists of any country whose rate of wages has been perceptibly affected by a foreign commerce with a low-waged race. Again, as often in this controversy, we must ask Protectionists to give us facts as well as theory.

§ 5. The second argument against Free Trade, as an influence in raising wages—that high wages depend upon a diversity of industry, which Free Trade discourages—will be best understood by reference to the economic condition of Ireland.

In that country there were no important manufacturing industries until very recent times—each one, as it came into existence, having been ruthlessly destroyed by the Protectionist measures of the British Parliament during the eighteenth century. Ireland thus became a country of practically one industry. An Irishman who would live in his own country must make his living out of the land. The consequence has been that rents have risen at the expense of wages. This process has been checked of recent years, partly by legislation, and partly by trades unions and emigration, but chiefly by the creation of new outlets for industrial activity.

But even now a Protectionist might fairly argue that a high rate of wages could be created and maintained in Ireland by a tariff upon imports. The result of this, he would say, being the creation of new industries, the labourer would be able to exercise a choice in the selection of his mode of life, so that the landowners would no longer be enabled to exact monopoly terms for the use of land.

It is quite conceivable that under these circumstances the decrease in rent and the increased demand for labour would more than compensate the wage-receiver for an increased price of manufactured articles, so that the burden of the tariff would be entirely borne by the owners of natural monopolies. But to concede this is not to concede the desirability of imposing a Protective tariff. As we shall see, there are other ways besides Protection of establishing a variety of industries. If Government aid is required at all—as would probably be the case in Ireland—in the establishment of a new industry, there is no method by which it can be given more wastefully, and with a less effective result, than by means of a tariff, and there is none which carries greater evils in its train.

This argument, which has some applicability to a country situated so unhappily as Ireland, requires to be used with great caution. Some Protectionists, not perceiving its necessary limitations, extend it to all countries without discrimination. Their mode of reasoning is as follows:—

"Free Trade," they say, "results in an interchange of those commodities which are the products of relative natural advantages, due to superiority of soil, climate, or location. The population increases, the available quantity of these diminishes, and the competition to obtain them raises the profits of their owners. Thus, when population is small, relatively to the available quantity of natural advantages, the price of the products of these is low in comparison to the price of manufactured commodities, as is evidenced by the fact that in a newly settled country food and raw materials are generally cheap, and other commodities are dear.

"With every increase in the population of a nation not increasing [by means of Protection] the variety of its consumption and the uses of its land, less fertile lands and poorer national resources are brought into use, and the price of food and raw material is raised. The increase of population, however, creates a keener competition among the producers of commodities, and as a result they bear a lower price. Every further increase in population adds to this contrast between the value of food and material and that of finished commodities.

"As all natural resources are limited in quantity, the surplus population cannot find employment upon them, but must seek work in competition with their fellows who are engaged in the manufacture of finished commodities. For these reasons a change in prices, due to increasing competition in a Static society, is not nominal. Any decrease of price of commodities does not result in an advantage to consumers— the advantage is secured by those who profit by the increased price of food and material. Competition lowers wages and interest, thus taking from those not exempt from its crushing power, and at the same time increasing the advantage of monopolies to a corresponding degree."[1]

These are the words of Professor Patten, the Wharton Professor of Political Economy in the University of Pennsylvania, and not of Mr. Henry George. Thus nearly do the extremists on either side approach one another.

[1] "The Economic Basis of Protection," by Professor Patten, Whartonian Professor of Political Economy in the University of Pennsylvania. Philadelphia: J. B. Lippincott & Co., 1890.

Yet the argument is undoubtedly a sound deduction from economic postulates. Given a country of limited area and a rapidly increasing population; given, too, that the population has no means of escape by emigration, and that the means of subsistence do not keep pace with the requirements of the people; given, too, that there is an effective competition between all classes—the result is an inevitable increase of rent, at the expense of wages and profits. Since all must have food, all must be at the mercy of the landowner. But where does such a country exist? The economic postulates cannot be applied literally even to Ireland, where the pressure of population upon the land has always been greatest.

The theoretical conclusion has, in fact, always been modified by practical conditions; and landowners have never been able for any lengthened period to extort monopoly prices for the use of land. Their theoretical power to do so has always been directly, or indirectly, limited in fact. Sometimes rents have been fixed by custom or by legislation; sometimes they have been forcibly lowered by a combination of tenants or by emigration; while the steady improvement in agricultural processes which has characterised the last three centuries has so largely increased the efficiency of agricultural labour, that the margin of profitable cultivation is continuously expanding. These considerations, however, plainly cannot affect the economic soundness of the argument. All that we have to consider now is its applicability to the fiscal controversy.

Is it the case that Free Trade assists the owners of natural monopolies, and aggravates the tendency of rent to absorb wages and profits?

Professor Patten boldly answers in the affirmative, relying on the reasoning already quoted. "A Protective policy," he says, "results not in general high values, but in the high value of commodities produced entirely by labour and capital, and a low value of the products of natural monopolies. Free Trade has the opposite effect. It tends to give a high value to the products of natural monopolies,[1] and increases the competition of producers of commodities, so that what they produce has a low value relative to the price of products of natural monopolies " (p. 38).

But is this so?

§ 6. A landlord can, no doubt, exact higher rents in a country of no manufacturing industries than he can where a variety of occupations attracts his tenants from the land; but, on the other hand, he is still more strengthened in his monopoly if his fellow-citizens are forbidden by law to purchase any of their food from foreign countries.

Let us, however, assume that Protectionists who use Professor Patten's argument are, like List and Hoyt, opposed to Protective taxes upon food or raw materials. The argument then depends on the assertion that Protection creates an industrial variety, while Free Trade preserves industrial uniformity.

This is an assertion which will have to be tested both by facts and theory when we come to consider its political application under the title of the Diversification of Industry. It is sufficient to point out at present that it rests upon two unproved assumptions, namely:—

1. That a sufficient variety of industry cannot spring up without Protection; and

---

[1] It is not an unfair introduction of the personal element to ask Mr. Patten what was the effect of Protection upon the natural monopoly of nickel, of which his pious founder, Mr. Wharton, was the owner in the United States. Was the price of nickel reduced when a tax of fifteen per cent. was placed upon that metal in 1864? or were not the American people, in fact, compelled, in consequence of that duty, to purchase all their nickel from Mr. Wharton, who owned the only nickel mine in the United States?

Perhaps Mr. Patten cannot be expected to answer these questions plainly, because he holds his chair upon the express condition, by the terms of Mr. Wharton's grant, that he preaches the doctrine of Protection. A strange notion this of University teaching—that Professors shall not be allowed to exercise an impartial judgment on the subject of their studies. And what sort of scientific investigation of facts or principles can be expected from men who are thus trammelled?

2. That Protection is the best method of creating the desired variety.

Both of these assumptions will be shown to be unfounded at a later period in this discussion. It is enough to concede at present that in pure theory it is conceivable that Free Trade might depress wages by increasing rent. In practice, however, this seldom occurs—although it has most nearly happened in the case of Ireland; and even if it did occur, Protection is not the true remedy. Rents have a tendency to increase either under Protection or Free Trade. If, under peculiar circumstances, they increase more rapidly under Free Trade than under Protection, the real remedy is not the temporary check of a high tariff, but the permanent use of a tax upon land values, which, by means of regular assessments at fixed periods, should give to the general body of citizens a due portion of the State-earned increment.

§ 7. The inquiry which has been conducted in the previous pages leads to the conclusion that the effect of Free Trade in raising the rate of wages by improving the efficiency of labour is not lessened by any other economic operation of the policy; except in the rare case where Free Trade acts as a discouragement of industrial variety, when it may possibly depress labourers to the profit of landowners. It remains to consider the effect on wages of a policy of Protection.

Before, however, entering upon this inquiry, some notice should be taken of the influence of Free Trade in the direction of steadying wages. Working-men make two demands in respect of wages—that they should be high, and that they should be steady. It is hard to say which of these requirements is of more importance; but it seems to be admitted that regular employment at a steady rate tends to greater security and independence than larger, but uncertain, gains.

Now, Free Trade, as we have seen, exercises a direct influence in steadying prices; this necessarily reacts on wages, because, since real wages consist not so much in money as in money's worth, whatever steadies the prices of articles in common use makes it easier to estimate incomes and calculate expenditure, and thus offers increased opportunities for saving.

Nor is the benefit of steady prices confined to workingmen. Employers also find it an advantage to know beforehand all the items of their outlay. From being able to make more certain estimates, they are encouraged to undertake more business; and they can undertake this at a lower cost, without reducing wages, because the risk is lessened. This activity in business soon reacts upon the wages of the labourer, until it is shown by yet another instance that Free Trade means Great Trade, and Great Trade means Prosperity. Moreover, through this steadying effect on prices, Free Trade proves itself to be a great security against commercial crises. Fluctuating trade, with all its misery of wasted efforts, savings squandered, homes destroyed, is an evil which lies far outside the range of any fiscal policy. But, although the cause of fluctuating trade is independent either of Protection or Free Trade, Free Trade can at least mitigate its evil. Wars, excessive speculation, dishonesty, gambling in land—these are among the causes of commercial crises which cannot be affected by Free Trade, and with regard to which Protection is most certainly as impotent. But Free Trade does at least remove one source of danger. It gives a larger area for the production of raw materials, so that no industry is now dependent upon the supply of a single country.

Closely connected with this virtue is the effect of Free Trade in giving a more accurate knowledge of the state of distant markets. A Free Trade country, which encourages intercourse with foreigners, is less likely to mistake its markets than one whose policy is isolation. The danger of producing goods which are not wanted at the time is plainly lessened by a closer intercourse with those who are your customers. Free Trade, like telegraphs and railways, serves to keep producers and consumers both informed as to each others' needs. Thus, although commercial crises will continue to occur in Free Trade countries, there is perhaps no risk of their resembling some of those in earlier times, when, for instance, a cargo of skates was shipped to the Brazils, and grand pianos lay upon the beach at Valparaiso for the want of storage-room, and diamond tiaras were consigned for sale among the savages of South America! Moreover, when the crisis comes, the workman will be more prepared to meet it in a Free Trade country. In the first place, owing to the greater accumulation of capital, employers will be able to keep business going for a longer time. Secondly, the larger foreign trade will afford a quicker outlet for the surplus stock, and bring the market sooner to its normal state; while, whether the spasm be prolonged or momentary, the workman's greater power of saving and the lower price of his domestic necessaries will both relieve the pressure of the harder times.

This is no imaginary picture. Between 1877 and 1880, England suffered from a trade depression as profound as any in her history. That time is near in all our recollections. It was the time of reaction from the artificial stimulus which followed the conclusion of the Franco-German War. It was also a time of war in Europe, Africa, and Asia. There was such a famine in Ireland as had not been known since 1846, and for seven consecutive years the English harvest had been bad. Events like these in former days produced the Luddite and the Chartist riots. Yet during those three years in England there was not one single outbreak. There were splutterings of disorder in France, Germany, and Spain, while in America the workers in the iron trade—the most Protected industry of that Protected country—suffered such extremities that they broke into actual riot, and occupied the town of Pittsburg.

But that is not all. Not only was England quiet when other countries were disordered, but, in spite of her difficulties, and in spite of the slackness of work during those three years, there was actually no perceptible increase in the number of paupers. The working-class largely lived upon their savings. It is hardly possible to offer a more pointed illustration of the working of a Free Trade policy.

Yet all the recent facts of English industrial history point to the same conclusion. Crime has diminished; pauperism has diminished; the deposits in the savings banks have increased; the funds of the friendly societies have increased; the consumption of domestic articles in common use, per head of the population, is nearly three times what it was in 1840; the rate of mortality has declined, so that on an average a man lives two years, and a woman three and a half years, longer than they used.

Where, we may ask again, is it possible to get an accumulation of facts like these to support the contrary conclusion of Protectionists that Free Trade has injured the working-classes, depressing wages?

CHAPTER VI.

PROTECTION AND WAGES.

§ 1. THAT Free Trade, unless some other and distinct influence should supervene, cannot lower wages we have already proved. That Protection must lower them, unless something supervene, should now be made equally clear.

Protection, as we have seen, must raise prices for a time, until the competition of the home producers has over-supplied the local market, or else it will fail of its economic purpose. At any rate, it must be admitted even by the most impatient partisan that Protection either will raise prices, or else it will not. And on that admission we may fairly ask—If it will not raise them, to whom is the advantage? If it will raise them, who will have to pay the piper?

[Pt. III., Ch. vi., § 1.]

The Protectionists' desire to tax the "foreigner" is well known, and is a laudable weakness that has seduced into the Restrictionist ranks many of the less clear-headed voters. But whatever confusion may exist in the minds of those who are willing to be confused, as to the incidence of Customs duties,[1] there can be no means even imagined of shifting on to strange shoulders the sum which is added by Protective duties to the price of home-made articles. Every penny of this must fall upon the purchasers of those articles who are the citizens of the "Protected country." But if Protection raises prices and the increase has to be paid by the "Protected" purchasers, where do these fortunate people get the money from to pay the higher prices?

This is the key of the economic attack upon Protection in regard to its effect on wages.

Assuming, as we have already assumed for the purposes of an economic argument, that rent, profits, and taxes remain constant, and remembering that wages are the remainder of the product after rent, profits, and taxes have been satisfied, so that the rate of wages depends upon the proportion between the quantity of the product and the number of labourers who are employed in its production, the conclusion is irresistible that if every one has to pay more for what he buys, and if the number of things produced is not increased, while the number of labourers keeps the same, the rate of wages must fall.

Or the argument may be expressed in another way.

Protection diminishes the efficiency of labour by depriving it of the assistance of the superior relative advantages which

---

[1] It is rarely, if ever, the case that a *Protective* Customs duty can be borne by the exporting country, because Protected countries are always pressed by an anxiety to export. A good illustration of the fallacy of the view that Customs duties are paid by the foreigner is given by the case of the salt duty in New South Wales. This is at the rate of 90s. per ton. Now, the price of salt in bond at Sydney is about 15s. a ton, and salt can be bought at the mine at from about 10s. to 12s. a ton. Yet it is gravely asserted that the foreign merchant who buys salt at 10s. a ton can afford to pay a duty on it of four times the cost price!

exist in other countries. It compels a man to do for himself what another person is willing to do for him at a cheaper rate, and so it compels the exertion of a greater effort to produce a given result. In other words, it lessens the quantity of things produced in the Protected industry by any given number of workmen working for a given time. The test is price. If ten workmen, working eight hours under Free Trade, can produce something which can be exchanged for a ton of foreign commodities, and if they cannot produce those commodities by working for themselves with less than ten hours' labour, any Protective tax which raised the price of the foreign commodities so that the workmen can no longer purchase them by eight hours' work must diminish the efficiency of labour by the amount of extra exertion which is required to overcome the new obstacle to the enjoyment of the foreign commodities which is created by the enhancement of their price.

"But," argue Protectionists, "even if Protection does weaken the efficiency of labour in one direction, it strengthens it in many others. Natural advantages are not all-in-all. It is true that Protection confines the labourer to using those natural advantages which exist in his own country, and shuts him out from those which exist elsewhere; but, by way of compensation, it makes him a brisker and more capable workman." For the sake of argument, grant the assertion. The only evidence of its truth must be a fall in prices. If the home labour has been made so efficient by means of Protection that it can dispense with the assistance which Nature has afforded to the producers of a similar article in other countries, all occasion for Protection vanishes. The Protection of the article at home is no longer prevented by the competition of the foreigner.

§ 2. The conclusion is thus reached, that so long as Protection is required—and the evidence of this is the higher price of the Protected article—it cannot raise wages, but must have a tendency to depress them. If, however, it be true that

[Pt. III., Ch. vii., § 1.]

Protection develops new industries and so creates an increased demand for labour, or if it be true that Protection stimulates new qualities in the labourer which greatly increase his efficiency, then it may be that the effect of Protection upon wages is not wholly bad. Nothing can be predicated of this with certainty, because the probability is that if Protection gives these compensating advantages to labour, there will be an influx of immigrants to share them, and the rate of wages will be again depressed by the competition of labourers with each other. At present, however, we are treating these advantages as non-existent. It will be our business later in these pages to inquire into the claim of Protection to be justified upon the score of encouraging new industries and diversifying the opportunities of employment.[1] At present we are only concerned with the operation of Protection upon wages, in consequence of its effect upon the aggregate of material wealth. And here we are met by two phrases which require a full consideration. The first of these is, "That high prices make high wages;" the second, that "More money makes more work." Both of these contentions are plainly independent of the Nationalistic argument in favour of production. They assume the economic postulates, but deny that the conclusions are unfavourable to a policy of restriction. They will be considered separately in the next two chapters.

CHAPTER VII.

DO HIGH PRICES MAKE HIGH WAGES?

§ 1. WE are now outside the citadel of the Restrictionists, and in the very centre of the battle. The true relation between prices and wages is the determining issue of the fiscal controversy. Low prices are, to the eye of the Protectionist, the true

[1] See, for a further discussion of the effect of Protection upon wages, Part IV., Chapter V.: "The Pauper Labour Argument."

cause of low wages. According to his theory, they prevent the establishment of new industries, and restrict the development of those which are already in existence by compelling manufacturers to exercise such great economies in production that the wages of the labourer are reduced to the lowest possible rate. He proposes, therefore, to raise prices by the operation of Customs duties. To the argument that this may press hardly upon slender purses, he has the ready reply that "it is much more important to the workman to have large wages than cheap commodities; that cheapness destroys employment, because commodities cannot be cheapened without somebody suffering; that commodities may be too cheap when they are below the price at which our people can make them profitably; that, in short, we must be careful lest, in our regard for the interests of consumers, we sacrifice the interests of producers." Such arguments really rest on the assumption that high prices make high wages, and low prices make low wages. Is this assumption true either in fact or theory?

§ 2. It has been already pointed out that prices may be raised in two ways: either by increasing the demand for goods or by diminishing their supply; and it has been shown that a rise in prices which results from an increased demand is often accompanied by an increase in wages.[1]

But this is not the way in which Protectionists propose to raise prices. Their plan is to restrict supply. They want to keep out the goods which are supplied from abroad in order to compel their fellow-citizens to purchase those which are made

---

[1] "What we want is abundance. We do not say that Free Trade necessarily brings low prices. It is possible with increased quantities still to advance prices; for it is possible that the country may be so prosperous under Free Trade that whilst you have a greater quantity of anything than you had before, increased demand, in consequence of increased prosperity, may arise, so that the demand will be more than the supply, and you may raise the prices on some articles. In some articles it has been the case. It has been so on wool and on meat; and we may not know yet what effect it may have on wheat itself."
—Cobden, House of Commons, December 13, 1852.

at home. What is this but to substitute an artificial scarcity for a natural abundance? And what is the whole argument against the low prices which are caused by the competition of foreign countries but a repetition of the arguments of those who fought against the introduction of machinery?

Free Trade is merely a device for cheapening the process of production. In its operation it may interfere with certain kinds of labour, and may possibly destroy some industries; but has not the invention of every new machine the same effect in a greater or less degree? The power-loom threw thousands of hand-loom weavers out of work by reducing the price of woven goods; but did the wages of weavers fall in consequence, or did the Luddites gain advantage by breaking their plan of the machinery? Yet the Luddites were true Protectionists. They, too, argued that employment was better than cheapness, and that the producer ought not to be sacrificed to the consumer; and they, too, like their modern representatives, ignored the interest of any section of the public but their own. Have times changed in this respect, and can it be that scarcity is now a greater benefit to labourers than abundance? Can the limitation of supply raise wages through the agency of prices?

§ 3. Certainly, the man who makes the assertion that this can be, starts, as Sir T. Farrer points out, with a strong presumption against him. He cannot, by "any of the laws which he proposes add one iota to the productive powers of the world. He cannot add an idea to the brain of the thinker, a muscle to the arm of the worker, a fertilising ingredient to the soil. All his implements are fetters on free action or weapons of destruction. To suppose that by preventing men from using their natural powers and satisfying their natural desires you can increase their capacity for production, and for earning wages by production, is in the highest degree improbable."

§ 4. Such an assumption is not only improbable—it is

contrary to fact. The theory that "high prices make high wages" is in flat contradiction to all experience. Cobden showed it to be palpably untrue by every modern instance that was open to examination. The facts of to-day disprove it to any one who chooses to investigate them; and the records of six centuries have recently borne witness to the same effect. Yet this vain and baseless theory, evolved out of the selfish imaginings of interested persons, still continues its delusive hold upon the minds of many working-men.

Let us test it first by reference to facts. Professor Thorold Rogers—than whom no one can speak with greater authority—recently published an inquiry into the condition of the English working-classes from the earliest times of which we have authentic record, under the title of "Six Centuries of Work and Wages." Nothing is recorded in this work which has not been taken from contemporary documents, with the result that all readers of the English language have before them now a complete and exact account of the movements of wages and prices during the last six hundred years. Surely, if the Protectionist theory were true, such an examination as this would furnish some facts in its support. It furnishes none. Every piece of testimony is the other way. Wages have not risen with prices, and they have not fallen when prices became low, but quite the contrary. Mr. Rogers, summing up the results of his investigations into the fluctuations of prices and wages during these six centuries, lays it down as an universal law that "wages have always increased absolutely—*i.e.*, in their money amount—and relatively—*i.e.*, in their purchasing power—when prices were low."[1]

[1] "Six Centuries of Work and Wages," p. 527. Compare also p. 428 and the following passage from p. 429:—"As, therefore, wages do not rise with prices, no crime against labour is more injurious than any expedients adopted on the part of Government which tend to raise prices. Unluckily for them, many working people have been misled by interested sophistry into believing that high prices for employers mean good wages for workmen. I do not deny that if an artificial stimulus is given to some particular industry, the demand

Modern experience tells the same story. "Do you think," said Cobden in the House of Commons on February 24th, 1842, "that the fallacy of 1815, which I heard put forth so boldly last week, that wages rose and fell with the price of bread, can now prevail in the minds of working-men after the experience of the last three years? Has not the price of bread been higher during that time than for any three consecutive years for the last twenty years? And yet trade has suffered a greater decline in every branch of industry during this period than in any preceding three years. Still there are hon. gentlemen on the other side of the House, with the reports of committees in existence and before them proving all this, prepared to support a Bill which, in their ignorance—for I cannot call it anything else—they believe will keep up the price of labour." Later in the same speech, Mr. Cobden referred to manufacturing wages:—"Have low wages," he said, "ever proved the prosperity of our manufactures? In every period when wages have dropped, it has been found that the manufacturing interest dropped also; and I hope that the manufacturers will have credit for taking a rather more enlightened view of their own interests than to conclude that the impoverishment of the multitude, who are the great consumers of all they produce, would even tend to promote the prosperity of our manu-

for the produce of which is limited, but continual, and the craftsmen in which are also limited, such a calling may get enhanced wages for a short time. But others soon crowd into the calling, and very speedily the thing is made dearer, and the producer remains no better off, having lost in the interval the knowledge which competition gives as to the best conditions under which industry can be exercised. But it is idle to argue that such an artificial stimulus can be given to every kind of industry. Were it universal, the country would be debarred from all intercourse with foreign commerce, and the legislature would raise a blockade round the ports far more effective than anything which the most successful belligerent could enforce. If it be partial, it will either affect all consumers or some. If all, it induces a universal scarcity without benefiting any one, for internal competition is sure to do its work on profits and wages; if some, it simply narrows the area of consumption, and with even more rapid results on profits and wages. These elementary principles, which one is almost ashamed to allege, could be illustrated by a thousand facts."

facturers. I will tell the House that by deteriorating that population, of which they ought to be so proud, they will run the risk of spoiling not merely the animal, but the intellectual creature; and that it is not a potato-fed race that will ever lead the way in arts, arms, or commerce. To have a useful and a prosperous people, we must take care that they are well fed."

The figures of English agriculture tell the same story. During the present century the price of corn has fallen from 98s. to 30s. a quarter, yet the wages of the agricultural labourer, reckoned in money, are almost a third more than they were ninety years ago; while his real wages have increased even more, owing to the greater cheapness of everything he buys. It would be wearisome to cite many other instances in contradiction to the unproved assertion of Protectionists—that wages and prices rise and fall together.[1] It is for them to bring forward proofs and illustrations in support of so incredible a proposition. One further example may, however, be pardoned on account of its instructive character. The economic conditions of Victoria and New South Wales are as nearly similar as those of any two countries can be, except that Victoria is a strictly Protected country, while New South Wales has almost a Free Trade tariff. Prices of "Protected" articles are higher in Victoria than those of the same articles in New South Wales. According to the Protectionist theory, wages in Victoria should be higher also. Yet, so far as there is a difference in the rates

[1] During the first twenty years of the century wheat was, on an average, 98s. a quarter. The average weekly wages of the agricultural labourer were 10s. from 1799 to 1803; 12s. from 1804-10; 12s. 9d. from 1811-14. They then sank about 17 per cent. from 1814-18, and about 20 per cent. more in 1819-20; bringing them down in the last year of the decade to about 8s., for which year the mean price of wheat is given by Mr. Tooke at 76s. Sir J. Caird, in his book on the "Landed Interest," states that in 1878, when wheat was 46s., the agricultural labourer's wages were 15s. a week. In 1886, wheat fell to 30s. a quarter, but the nominal wages of the labourer were only less by 10 per cent., while, owing to the fall in prices, his real wages did not alter. The agricultural labourer was better off during the recent period of low prices of agricultural products than at any other time in the century. [Summarised from Sir T. Farrer's address to the Cobden Club, July 30, 1887.]

of wages in the two colonies, it is in favour of New South Wales.[1] In short, the Protectionist assertion that wages and prices rise and fall together cannot bear the test of argument. It is, indeed, disproved by so many facts, that were it not for the extraordinary influence of this delusion, we might fairly decline to discuss it until some instance was brought forward in its favour. Unfortunately, such is the nature of the controversy between Protection and Free Trade that facts are seldom accorded their due weight on either side; but it may be doubted whether there is any feature in the Protectionist revival more surprising than that any number of persons at the present day should believe that wages vary with prices when that cannot be shown to have happened in any single instance, and when the records of industrial history point unanimously to the opposite conclusion. It must remain one of the marvels of human credulity that persons not deficient in intelligence should give credence to the bare assertion of interested parties, that "high prices make high wages," when an unbroken record of experience proves the contrary.

§ 5. We have hitherto been using the term wages with reference to the whole community, and not to any particular trade. This is the sense in which the term is used when

---

[1] I am aware of the controversy which rages on this point between the supporters of the two policies. Comparisons between rates of wages are notoriously difficult. It is, however, generally admitted that the nominal rates of wages— e.g., those fixed by trades unions — are higher in New South Wales. Victorians, however, assert that in their colony work is more regular, and rents are lower. The latter part of the assertion is undoubtedly true as regards Melbourne, where the natural features of the country make building easy and cheap, while in Sydney similar work is necessarily very costly. Moreover, in the older colony more of the land round the large towns is in the hands of large proprietors, having been acquired by them in early days. Nevertheless, the balance is in favour of New South Wales, so far as there is any difference between the two colonies. I have satisfied myself by personal investigation that from 1886 to 1888 the wages paid to bricklayers, miners, and railway servants were from sixpence to one shilling a day higher in New South Wales than in Victoria. (See Appendix III.)

appeals are made to the patriotism of consumers to submit to a rise in prices for the purpose of raising wages. Certainly, such an appeal is never intended to be understood with reference only to wages in Protected trades. Even a Protectionist might shrink from asking a community to tax itself for the benefit of the workmen in a few industries. Yet it cannot be denied that a rise in prices, such as Protection must cause, may for a time raise wages in the particular trade which is Protected. It does not follow that this will be the necessary result of the Protective duty; but if the result of the duty is to shut out foreign competition, and if the home producers are unable to meet the demands of the local market, and if the supply of the particular kind of labour which is required cannot be immediately satisfied, the artificial scarcity which is created by Protection may cause a temporary rise of wages in one or more of the Protected trades. This would unquestionably be an advantage to some classes of wage-earners, but from the very nature of its origin it cannot be permanent.

The transference of labour from one industry to another is much more rapid than it used to be; and there are now few manufacturing processes which cannot in their simpler stages be conducted by any person of ordinary intelligence. This important difference between manufacturing and other pursuits is often overlooked by the zealous advocates of manufacturers. An agricultural labourer, a seaman, a clerk, an artisan in any of the building trades, or a handicraftsman of whatever nature, has to learn his business by a long apprenticeship. The man who attends to a machine can almost learn his business in a week. It is true that the higher processes of manufacture require both skill and taste, but they only give employment to a small number compared with the large number of unskilled "hands" who perform the chief of the work. It follows from these considerations that any sudden rise of wages in one trade is likely to attract labourers very rapidly from others; and that this attraction will be strongest towards those branches of employment which require the least skill. The consequence of men thus crowding from other occupations into the Protected trades would be that the wages of the less skilled labourers would soon fall to their former level. Nor are the more skilled members of the trade likely to enjoy the benefits of their position for any great length of time. The smallness of the communities in which Protection is now being tried makes the competition among skilled labourers even more severe than it is among the unskilled. Unskilled workmen in young colonies can always command good wages in any occupation requiring physical strength. Skilled workmen, on the other hand, whether under Protection or Free Trade, are seldom so well off as they are in England. The smallness of the scale upon which business must be carried on in a small community prevents that sub-division of employment under which a man's peculiar talents acquire a special value. Wages of 20s., 28s., and 40s. a day, such as Sir Lowthian Bell mentions as the rate for certain classes of workmen in the ship-building and iron trades in the north of England, are unknown in Australia; and it is no uncommon thing to find among the passengers of the homeward-bound steamers skilled English artisans, who are returning to England because they cannot make the high wages that they used to earn, in any part of Australia—not even in Protectionist Victoria.[1]

In these colonies manufacturers can only give a limited employment to any class of labourers, and of those whom they do employ, only a small number require any special skill or training. Now, the skilled artisan is just the person who

[1] In a paper read before the Industrial Remuneration Conference in 1885 (see Report, p. 140), Sir Lowthian Bell, the President of the Iron and Steel Association, mentions a ship-builder who in one year paid from 8s. 0d. to 12s. 10½d. a day to all his skilled hands. Among these were ten who made 25s. a day, and thirty who were paid 20s. a day. They were at work for 313 days in the year. At the rolling-mills, furnace-men were paid 12s. 8d., and the head shearers 28s. 3½d. per day. The least experienced of the chief rollers received 17s. 5d., and the best 40s. 11d. per day. The average daily receipts of fourteen men employed at the rolls were 27s. 8d.

emigrates most readily, as he has both the means to take this step and the intelligence to appreciate its advantage. Consequently, most young countries have a superfluity of skilled manufacturing labour; while if there should not be any trade for which skilled labour was not available at a low price, nothing would be easier than for the "Protected" manufacturer to import as much as he required. Accordingly, whatever may be the effect of Protection in raising prices in a particular trade, the wages in that trade are not likely to rise for any appreciable length of time. They will be kept down both by the competition of the home labour market and the facility with which the manufacturers will be able to import labour from other countries.

§ 6. There is, however, another consideration which should not be overlooked in considering the effect of prices upon wages—viz., the difference between "nominal" and "real" wages. Very slight reflection will show that a rise in the money value of wages is of small advantage if the purchasing power of money is diminished. If a sovereign under Protection only goes as far as 15s. under Free Trade, the workman whose wages are raised from 15s. to 18s. is worse off by 2s. a week than he used to be. This diminution in real wages must not be forgotten by those who are attracted by the prospect of an immediate increase in their money wages. Prices will not be allowed to rise in one industry only.[1]

§ 7. Protection will never be submitted to unless its anticipated benefits are believed to be shared by all citizens

---

[1] The experience of Protected countries shows that this conclusion of abstract Political Economy accords with facts. Wages are not higher, either in the United States or in Victoria, in the protected than in the unprotected trades. Indeed, in many of the "Protected" trades in the United States wages have fallen so low that the native Americans have been displaced by labourers of a lower standard of living.

alike. Consequently the scheme of the Protectionist is to protect everything!

Buoyed up by their belief in the ability of Governments to regulate the price of goods and labour, Protectionists are ready to apply their nostrum to every form of industry, and indignantly repudiate the charge of wishing to confer a favour upon special trades. Have they protected the native industry of iron-producing? They will admit that by doing so they have inflicted hardship upon every one who has to purchase iron, such as machinists, boiler-makers, engineers, shipbuilders, &c., &c. Seeing, then, that they have made iron scarce and dear, they are willing to go further, and lay a duty on the importation of every substance made of iron. By this means, they say, the makers of iron-ware of every sort will be able to recoup themselves for the higher price of their raw material by charging higher prices to their own customers.

But here a new injustice would arise if our Protectionists were not so careful and far-sighted! The consumers of iron goods of all sorts—the manufacturers and householders who need boilers, fenders, pots, pans, and iron-ware of every kind— are they to go without Protection? They are hindered in their laudable desire to foster native industry by the high prices they have to pay for their requisites of production. Let them, says the Protectionist, accordingly obtain a tax to raise the price of all the articles which they produce; and if, directly this complicated business is concluded, there should crop up another lot of patriotic natives eager to have their industry fostered, let them, too, obtain a tax even as the iron-ware makers! So the process continues. Every man who can produce, or thinks he can produce, an article which is imported, is, under the Protectionist creed, entitled to a duty. No wonder that the politician who may have started on his career with the intention of protecting iron and nothing else, soon, in a despair of puzzle-headedness, cries out with iron producers, iron labourers, iron consumers, and all the deluding and deluded crowd, "Protect not only iron, but coal, cotton, bread, meat, tobacco, clothing, china! Protect everybody and everything!"—that every one may have the pleasure of robbing his neighbour to distribute to the poor, that the laying goose may be destroyed and one golden egg divided!

"If you tax corn," says Sir T. Farrer, "you must tax flour and everything made of corn; if you tax sugar, you must tax biscuits and jams; if you tax salt, you must tax chemicals; if you tax chemicals, you must tax dyed goods; if you tax leather, you must tax boots, shoes, gloves, harness, and gearing; if you tax wool, you must tax yarns and woollen goods; if you tax yarns, you must tax cloth and silk; if you tax iron or steel, you must tax everything made of iron and steel—from a ship to an umbrella." Generous indeed as is the impulse which leads the advocate of a restricted commerce in a young country to demand that Protection should be given equally to every one, it is to be feared that this all-round system differs only from that which they so boastfully despise in being more unjust and more impolitic. Could such a system be carried out in its entirety, it would result in a rise of nominal prices, which would leave the real rewards of labour exactly as they were.

§ 8. But the fundamental objection to a system of all-round Protection is its complete impracticability. The large majority of persons in any community can never be Protected, because, as consumers, they outnumber the producers; so that Protection weighs upon them with all its disadvantages, without being able to confer even an imaginary benefit. All those who are engaged in rendering services to make life and property secure—such as judges, soldiers, police, and civil servants in all their infinite variety—cannot fail to suffer unless with every rise in prices their fixed salaries are also raised. Another class which can receive no benefit is that which is engaged in what Mill calls, in the widest sense of the term, "unproductive" labour, whose duties might be better defined by borrowing from Bastiat—"*services immatériels*." This class comprises domestic servants, lawyers, clergy, schoolmasters, authors, artists, and all kinds of "professional men." Neither does the class of retail dealers receive from the system anything but injury. If we use "retail dealers" in its widest sense, to mean all who are concerned merely with the distribution of wealth, this class will comprise bankers, brokers, merchants (both wholesale and retail), railway servants, seamen, wharf labourers, carriers, and many others. There is yet a fourth class to whom Protection brings more hardship than aid, composed of all whose products are immediately consumed upon the spot, such as caterers, masons, carpenters, blacksmiths, gardeners, bakers, butchers, &c. In short, one may say that all those whose services or trades are such that they can never fear the competition of the foreigner are directly injured by a system of Protection.

Such persons form by far the larger number in every community. Probably not more than one person out of ten is engaged in an industry which it is possible to protect. Thus even all-round Protection turns out to be a favouring of special trades, although every fresh application of the principle may make it more difficult to trace its working.

The comparatively narrow sphere within which any Protective duties can operate leads to an important economic consequence, by increasing the rapidity with which Protection affects the labouring classes. Every loss which is inflicted on the non-Protected portion of a community by a rise in prices soon recoils upon producers. Increased prices result either in a less consumption or a diminished power of saving; and as a great part of the industrial enterprises of a country are carried on by the use of small savings, the result follows that as producers lose the assistance of that capital industry begins to languish.

§ 9. It is worthy of notice, in conclusion, that the argument that Protection ought to be supported because by raising prices it will raise wages is entirely inconsistent with the argument that Protection ought to be supported because it will in the long run bring prices down. No one who has been actively engaged in a campaign against Protection would feel surprise at noticing that any two Protectionist arguments were mutually destructive; but for the benefit of those whose happier fortune has led them into other paths, it may be mentioned that the two arguments are never intended to be addressed to the same audience. The argument that Protection will raise wages by raising prices is for the exclusive use of the working-classes; while the argument that Protection will lower prices is reserved with equal carefulness for the voter with a fixed income! As, however, the working-classes are the power behind all policies, it is with the arguments intended for their ears that Free Traders have the most to do.

In spite, therefore, of the fact that there never has been, nor can be, a general rise in wages in consequence of a rise in prices resulting from a diminution of supply, the idea that the contrary is possible is so deeply rooted in the minds of many working-men that no excuse is needed for devoting further time to its consideration. Let us assume, then, for the sake of argument, that the high prices caused by Protection can cause an increase of wages: where does the money come from to pay the increase? If everybody has to give more for what he buys, how comes there to be a larger sum available for wages? By whose labour is it created? These are questions which go to the root of the Protectionist argument. How far Protectionists succeed in answering them will be the next inquiry.

CHAPTER VIII.

DOES MORE WORK MEAN MORE MONEY?

§ 1. IF the argument of the last two chapters has been followed, it will be remembered that the inquiry at present is into the truth of the assertion that the higher prices caused by Protection may be beneficial to the working-classes.

At first sight, a man would not appear to be better off for having to pay a higher price for everything he wished to purchase; but the Protectionist explains that the benefit which is thus conferred is of a twofold nature.

First he says, "High prices mean high wages." With that theory we have already dealt.

Next he says, "More work means more money." It is with this portion of the explanation that the argument is now concerned.

Developed at more length, the Protectionist reply to the question by which Free Traders hoped to have posed their adversary—namely, "Where does the money come from to pay the higher prices?"—is of this nature:—

"True," it is said, "that Protection raises prices for a time; true that it draws labour and capital into industries which they would not enter if they were left to themselves; true that high prices cannot cause an all-round rise in real wages. Nevertheless, the encouragement which a judicious tariff will give to the starting of new industries, or the development of those which are already established, must so greatly increase the demand for labour, that the wage-earning class under Protection, even in the unprotected industries, will be better able to pay high prices than the same class under Free Trade was able to pay low prices."

The first remark which suggests itself as a criticism upon this presentation of the Protectionist case is that it is rather an assertion of fact than an argument. It is merely an expansion of the stock controversial phrase that "employment is better than cheapness," of which the underlying assumption is that Protection gives a wider and more regular employment than is given by Free Trade.

The first question, therefore, which arises is in reference to the truth of this assumption: "Is it a fact that a comparison between countries whose industrial conditions in other respects are in the main similar, shows that the employment of the working-classes is more constant in those which have adopted Protection than in those which have adopted Free Trade?" This is, plainly, a question of evidence. Yet, how. many writers or speakers think it necessary to obtain or weigh the evidence on either side before they hazard an assertion, one way or the other?

It is one of the many indications of the empirical character of most economic opinions that persons of eminence in other branches of science do not hesitate to generalise upon commercial or industrial phenomena, without even an elementary knowledge of the facts on which their reasonings rest. A man who would talk on law or physics with the assurance with which some lawyers and scientists talk of commercial phenomena, would be at once asked to produce some proof of his acquaintance with the facts of the subject upon which he was speaking. Yet men of education and intelligence, who are accustomed to weigh their words about other matters, will readily adopt a fixed opinion for or against Free Trade, without any apparent consciousness that opinions upon such a matter ought to rest upon accurate acquaintance with the industrial conditions of the particular country to which they relate, and require, before they can possess any value, at least a superficial acquaintance with the course and extent of its foreign commerce.

Although industrial and commercial phenomena are generally complex, on account of the variety and changeable character of the forces by which they are occasioned, and although any fiscal policy must be judged by its effect on industry and commerce, the number of persons who study the development of industry or the course of commerce, even as regards one country or during any period of years, is small indeed, as compared with the number of those who are prepared to pronounce authoritatively in favour of Protection or Free Trade.

It is surprising, for instance, how readily people will repeat the old fallacy that "Employment is better than cheapness," without inquiring whether the countries in which a low level of prices prevails are not precisely those in which—after making allowance for other diversities of industrial conditions, such as would arise from differences in the amount and distribution of capital, labour, and available land—the employment of the working-classes is the most regular and the most profitable. Such neglect in the observation of industrial facts certainly cannot be due to the difficulty of obtaining information.

The Reports of the Commission of Enquiry into the State of Trade in the United States, which was appointed in 1885 by Mr. Secretary McCulloch, collected a mass of authentic information as to employment and wages in other countries besides America; while the late Royal Commission on the Depression of Trade, of which Lord Iddesleigh was the Chairman, has compiled an almost complete body of testimony upon the industrial condition of every part of the civilised world between the years 1883-6. The results of these investigations are supplemented from time to time by Official Reports published by the Board of Trade in England and by the Labour Bureau at Washington.

Surely, if there existed anywhere any proof that the best way to give employment to the working-classes was to cause an artificial scarcity of the articles they wished to buy, these officials and commissioners would have discovered it. Yet nothing is more remarkable than the omission on the part of Protectionists to adduce even a solitary instance in support of their theory that employment is made more regular by the adoption of Protective duties.

It would be out of place, in a work which is intended chiefly as a guide to the understanding of principles and their application, rather than as a handbook of polemical illustrations, to enter upon any lengthy statistical investigations in order to compare the progress or condition of one country with another. The figures upon which such a comparison must rest change from year to year, so that it would be impossible to give any demonstration of the superior condition of the working-classes in a Free Trade country which would carry conviction to a reader two or three years hence. All that can be done is to indicate, so far as an extended range of reading will permit, that from time to time this demonstration has been made by Free Trade writers for the dates at which they wrote; but that, unless the newspapers and controversialists of his own side have been singularly oblivious of his work, no Protectionist writer has even attempted to prove the opposite.

The characteristic, indeed, of Protectionist utterances in Australia—where the controversy rages keenly—is a resolute ignoring of official records as to the condition of Protected countries. Free Traders are not so unwilling to look at facts. Their inclination to go for their arguments to men and markets is as marked as is that of their opponents to lean upon books and maxims. Dull as statistics must always be, they are the only evidence by which a fiscal theory can be put to the test of practice. Who will say that Protectionist orators and writers are willing students of the figures of trade, wages, and prices?

It may be that some believer in Protection is prepared to bring forward definite evidence in support of his theory that the best way of giving employment is to cause a scarcity of commodities. All that Free Traders say, at present, is that such evidence is wanting. When it is produced they will be prepared to consider it. Until it comes it is only by the courtesy of controversy that they give consideration to the strange theory. They are justified, however, in pointing out, before they discuss the theory as a theory, and without entering into details, that the body of testimony is against it. All the reports which have been already mentioned, together with the investigations of Mr. Giffen in England and Mr. Atkinson in the United States, and the evidence which is afforded by other official documents, show that, other things being equal, there is, in fact, at least as steady and as large a field of employment under Free Trade as under Protection. Commercial crises and interruptions of employment occur at least as frequently under Protection as they do under Free Trade.

§ 2. Let us, however, for the sake of argument, waive all objections founded upon want of evidence, and discuss the theory of the Protectionists that "More work means more money," upon *à priori* grounds. The allegation is that "Protection will give more employment."

Now, that the removal of a Protective duty might, at any rate for a time, deprive some persons of employment, cannot seriously be denied; and by a parity of reasoning it may be admitted that the imposition of Protective duties may cause some persons to be employed who were previously idle. But when Protectionists talk about giving employment, they have in their mind the general body of workmen. It is not employment in a particular trade which they profess to consider, but an increase in the total number of workers, and a more constant demand for labour in all its branches. The question accordingly to be considered is, "Whether Protection gives more regular employment to the body of wage-earners than is given by Free Trade?"

Let us recall for a moment what has been already shown to be the operation of Protection. The admitted object of

P

Protectionists, and the admitted effect of Protective duties, is to cause something to be made in one country which, in a state of freedom, would be made in another. The proposal is, by means of a duty, to bribe men into making for themselves at a greater cost, or—what is the same thing—by a greater expenditure of labour, the things which they had been in the habit of obtaining at a less cost by a process of exchange. In so far, then, as Protection increases the price of any article, it is a device for causing unnecessary labour; because the price of most articles of common use—which are the articles usually affected by Protective duties—is, under ordinary circumstances, a measure of their cost of production.

Now, it has been shown in previous chapters of this work that Protection causes a rise in prices—at all events for a time—and that an increase of prices from this cause is not accompanied by any general rise in the rate of wages. The effect, therefore, of Protective duties upon employment is that men have to work for a longer time before they can earn enough money to buy what they want. If Protective duties raise the price of boots by two shillings a pair, every one who wants a pair of boots must earn two shillings more before he can buy them. Now, as has been proved in the last chapter, the wages of workmen in other trades are not raised by a duty upon boots. He therefore will have to earn the additional two shillings which the boots will cost him by doing more work than he used to do previously. In this sense, and in this sense only, does Protection give more employment to the working-classes—they have to work a longer time before they can earn enough to purchase what they want. It has remained for Protectionists to assert that the short cut to general prosperity consists in compelling men to do for themselves what Nature has done for them gratuitously in other countries.

The idea that the employment which is given by the necessity of supplying the scarcity which is artificially created by Protective duties is advantageous and profitable to a community is in the same category with the idea that any one causing two labourers to be paid instead of one thereby doubles the amount of remuneration received in wages. The Protectionist ironmaster, who insists that it will give employment to the people if he is allowed to make iron at six pounds a ton, which persons can at present buy for three pounds, is (without always knowing it himself) in the same position as the temperance lecturer in the story, who—happening himself to be a manufacturer of bottles—always urged his audience to smash the bottles after they had drunk their ginger-beer!

§ 3. The plain truth is, that the matter of importance to a community is not the mere giving of employment, but that the employment which is given shall be profitable. Any number of men might be employed in digging holes in the seashore and filling them again with sand, but even a Protectionist might hesitate to say that this was a mode of employment that was advantageous to the nation—even though all the money spent in wages should be "kept in the country."

Yet simple and plain as these considerations are—so that it almost seems an insult to good sense to state them—they are not so simple and plain as not to be ignored by those who carry into practice the doctrines of Protection. Perhaps no better instance of the fatuity of those who think to benefit a country by putting unnecessary labour upon its inhabitants has ever been afforded than that which is offered by the kerosene industry of New South Wales.

Many years ago a duty of sixpence a gallon was imposed for revenue purposes on kerosene oil. At that time no kerosene was produced in New South Wales, but large deposits of shale have subsequently been discovered. A process was soon adopted of extracting oil from the shale, and the sixpenny duty has been for some time highly Protective. The abolition of the duty is, consequently, pressed for by Free Traders, but strenuously resisted by Protectionists upon the ground that its retention affords employment. No Free Trader can deny that this is the case. The question is, "Whether the employment is profitable?" The case stands thus:—Since the duty was imposed, great natural wells of kerosene have been discovered in America and Southern Russia, and the process of extracting oil from shale is almost entirely superseded by the gratuitous operations of Nature. When oil bubbles from the ground almost as if it were spring-water, one would hardly think, unless one were acquainted with Protectionists, that people would be found to urge that it was better to refuse the gift of Nature and make oil by the old process. Yet so it is in New South Wales. The oil is flowing from wells in Russia and America, so that if a man wants oil he has little more to do than dip a pannikin into the flowing stream. "But," argue the Protectionists, "what 'employment' is there in dipping a pannikin into a stream? Can we not in New South Wales get the same oil by the laborious process of squeezing it out of our own clay? And shall we not by these means be developing our natural resources and giving employment to our own people? Let us then shut out the oil which flows in natural streams, because Nature gives us that for next to nothing, and set our men to work at squeezing the oil which we require out of our own clay." Who can deny that such a policy, which is literally carried out in New South Wales, will give employment, and that, if the duty is removed, the employment may cease?

Let us, however, carry the investigation a little further, and inquire into the cost to the nation of providing this employment. The amount of kerosene imported in 1888 realised, in round numbers, about £25,000 in duty, and was a little more than half the amount consumed. The full cost of the tax, however, can only be calculated by adding to the amount collected at the Customs House another £25,000, being sixpence a gallon on the total quantity of home-made oil consumed in the colony. Fifty thousand pounds! That was the amount which it cost the inhabitants of New South Wales to give employment to the persons who were engaged in the year 1888 in extracting kerosene from deposits of shale.

It will hardly be credited by any one who has not had practical experience of the characteristics of a Protective system that the number of hands who were so employed in that year was only 299! Fifty thousand pounds to give employment to 299 persons! It would manifestly pay the Government, if the duty were removed from kerosene, to give £10,000 to some speculative individual to build an asylum, in which every one of these 299 persons might be supplied gratuitously with food, clothing, and lodging for the rest of their natural lives. Or if it is essential to the well-being of the State that these men should be employed, why not put a sum in the estimates which would give each of them eight shillings a day to sit still with folded arms, and do nothing—if only by that means they would consent to the free admission of kerosene oil? To refuse to accept oil which is manufactured by Nature in the bowels of the earth, because to do so would throw out of employment some three hundred persons who are engaged in manufacturing it by machinery, is no whit more absurd than it would be for a settler to refuse to draw his water from a running creek in order that he might have the employment of digging a well on its bank.

Yet this kerosene example is by no means an exceptional instance of the extravagant absurdity of a Protectionist tariff. The Victorian and American tariffs offer many similar cases, in which the amount raised by the tariff is altogether disproportionate to the employment which is given; and in which a far larger sum is collected by the tax at the Customs House —without taking into account the amount collected from the consumers by the local manufacturers in the shape of increased prices—than would be required to give the current wage to each of the workmen whom the tax allows to be employed, and leave a handsome surplus over.

§ 4. It must be remembered that we are not dealing now with the argument that Protection is desirable in order to cause a variety of industries or in order to collect revenue—both these arguments will be dealt with later—but only with the argument that Protection is *economically* sound because it gives employment.

The root fallacy of this argument lies in the assumption that the persons who are employed in the industries which the tariff calls into existence would be idle if the tariff were removed.

A moment's consideration will show that this assumption is baseless.

The labour which is caused by Protection is unnecessary labour, because (since the assumption is that, without Protection, the particular class of work in question would not be done) the only reason for that labour is that it may produce something which might be produced by far less labour in another country. To ask a nation to give more labour to produce for itself what it might obtain with less labour by a process of exchange is manifestly to cause an unnecessary expenditure of effort. It is no doubt true that this must in some industries cause an increase of employment, but the question to be determined is, Whether this indicates any economic advantages to the community? It would hardly be contended (to recur to our former illustration), except by a thoroughly logical Protectionist, that any one who by bungling workmanship or by extravagance caused two labourers to be paid instead of one, thereby doubled the amount of money which he expended in, directly or indirectly, remunerating labour. It is undoubtedly true that the necessity of employing two men to do the work of one does, for the moment, cause an increase in the amount paid to the labourers in one class of occupation; but inasmuch as, by the hypothesis, one-half of this expenditure is wasteful, it lessens, by the extent of its cost, the amount which the engager of the labour is able to direct to productive employment.

No one, for example, could imagine that it would conduce to the general prosperity gradually to poison all the wells and streams in England. Yet such an act might be defended by every argument advanced in favour of Protection. As thirst must still be quenched, another means must be adopted of procuring drink. A new industry—that which Protectionists so much desire—will accordingly spring up. Capital will be directed to the distilling of salt water—a great natural resource which will now be utilised. All fear of uniformity of occupation will then have vanished before the constant demand for builders of all kinds, carters, horse-dealers, railways, tank-makers, coopers, and fishermen, not to mention the number of retail water-sellers whose services will also be required. And in this case the industry will never perish. With every increase of population more fresh water will be needed, and so a profitable and permanent employment will have been provided for the poor!

An extreme instance like this reveals at once the underlying fallacy of the Protectionist assumptions. Those who claim that Protection gives more employment than Free Trade ignore the fact that this employment must be paid for. "You cannot," said Cobden, "go on for ever feeding a dog with his own tail." There must in time come a limit to the power of one class in a community to live upon another. Since a tax upon imported commodities cannot of itself create wealth, the higher prices which the tax allows must be paid for out of wealth already in existence. But if everybody has to pay more for the things he wants, the power of a community to save is necessarily lessened. Now, money is not, as a rule, hoarded. Men invest their savings either directly in productive enterprises or by depositing them in banks and kindred institutions. Every penny which is invested employs labour. Accordingly, whatever diminishes savings must diminish the power of employing labour. This is precisely the operation of Protection. By taking more from people in the form of increased prices, it leaves them less to spend in the form of invested savings. Protectionists see the labour which the tariff employs, but they omit to notice the labour which the tariff causes to be idle.

The decline in the export of Canadian manufactured produce, from £825,000 in 1878, which was the last year of Free Trade, to £700,000 in 1884, which has already been referred to, offers a good illustration of the double influence of a Protective tariff. The Canadian Protectionists who exult over the increase in the number of hands employed in a few weakly manufactures never speak of those who used to be employed in the produce of articles of export, and who lost their occupation on the introduction of Protection. It may be a good thing to be occupied in working for the home market, but it does not follow, without any evidence, that the home market will give more employment than the export trade. Any increase in the total of employment can only arise from an increase in the total of productiveness, which Protectionists have yet to prove can ever be the consequence of a restricted trade.

The argument thus comes round to the point from which it started. Other things being equal, employment will be greatest and most constant in the country where there is the most wealth. To cause a waste of wealth and an unnecessary expenditure of labour in particular directions cannot increase the aggregate number of men who are employed unless it at the same time reduces their wages. Once let it be recognised that Protection causes waste, and the absurdity of thinking that the working-classes are better off because wealth is wasted and labour is employed uselessly will be at once perceived. Protection can divert industry from one channel into another, but it can do no more. By the whole amount of labour which it causes to be employed needlessly does it lessen the productive employment of the rest of the working-classes.

The same argument may be stated in another way. Since

the aggregate wealth of a community is not increased because a change in the character of goods demanded alters the direction of capital, any apparent gain to one class of labourer must be a loss to others. The whole amount payable in wages can only be increased when the increased demand for those articles which are affected by the tariff is greater than the diminished demand for others. But to assent to this proposition is equivalent to an admission that employment can only be increased by an increase in the aggregate of wealth—and that, as has been proved, is not a result of Protection.

§ 5. It must, of course, be borne in mind that the argument of the preceding pages has been entirely economic: that is to say, it has proceeded on the assumption of a free movement of capital and labour, which is the postulate of all economic reasoning. There may, however, be circumstances in which this postulate cannot be conceded, and in such a case the conclusions must be qualified. What the full extent of the qualification must be, and what are the circumstances under which it must be made, are the proper subjects of the concluding portion of this work. All that is relevant to the present inquiry is a reminder that every abstract argument in the field of politics must be subject to practical limitations. No attempt has been made, up to the present point in the argument, to indicate the nature of the special limitations which, either rightly or wrongly, are sometimes thought to be required upon the economic argument against Protection; but an endeavour has been made by a variety of methods to enforce the homely truth that waste cannot make wealth, and the difficulty of the argument has been entirely caused by the simplicity of the conclusion. Even, however, if we assume that there may be circumstances under which, in a country of large but undeveloped natural resources which has at the same time a considerable quantity both of its labour and its capital unemployed, even a Protective tax may be one means of directing industry to a permanent and profitable channel, still the inquiry must be made whether such a tax would be the best means of effecting this result, or whether the temporary difficulty might not be more effectively dealt with by other means, such as the gift of a bonus or the placing of Government contracts with local producers at non-competitive prices. It is plain, also, that such a qualification of the conclusions of abstract reasoning, even were it practically justified, would in no way affect the validity of the previous reasoning which has been directed against those who maintain two consecutive propositions—1st. That without Protection prices must be unremunerative to the producer; 2nd. That with Protection the consumer will be better off, in spite of high prices, because he will obtain more constant and profitable employment. In order to probe these assertions, the questions have been put in a variety of forms. At what will the employment be, and who will pay for it?" And the old conclusion has been reached: that men cannot be employed except by the proceeds of labour. From which it follows that whatever diminishes the proceeds of labour—either by lessening its efficiency or imposing new and artificial obstacles in its way—must diminish employment. That this is the result of Protection cannot be denied by any one who believes that where labour is free and capital abundant, men will naturally follow the most profitable occupations. If Protective taxes are required to establish industries which cannot grow up naturally, that fact is conclusive evidence that the return of the Protected industries is less than that of those which are already in existence. Protection, by holding out the bribe of high prices, may draw labour from one channel into another; but by every penny which it takes from the consumer in the form of higher prices, by so much does it lessen the employment of those workmen who are not protected.

Whether or not it is a good thing that one class of workmen should live upon the contributions of another may be a fair subject for argument. All that Free Traders ask is that the recipients of public charity should acknowledge their obligation. Let it be fairly understood that when a Protectionist manufacturer asks for taxes in order to give employment, he is really asking the rest of the community to pay for the support of himself and his workmen; and we may be sure that it will become a matter for most critical consideration as to whether or not the case is a deserving one for public charity. Our present cause of complaint is that Protectionists have not the courage to plunder us openly. They take sixpence here and a penny there from every citizen who buys their goods, but instead of collecting it from him in a fair and open manner every time he makes a purchase, they disguise their operations by increasing prices. No one will deny that in taking this course the restrictionists are wise in their generation. For what length of time would a law remain upon the statute-book of a democratic country which should empower a constable to detain every man or woman as one left a shop, and then and there, for every pound's worth of goods which he or she had bought, to claim five shillings for the support of certain manufacturers? Yet a 25 per cent. duty takes more than 5s. in the £ from every purchaser of the Protected article for all the time that a duty of that amount is required in order to equalise the prices of home-made and imported goods. The only difference between taking the five shillings by means of a policeman as one leaves the shop and taking it over the counter in the form of an increased price, is that the former method is honest and open, while the latter is fraudulent and secret.

Track the Protectionist argument from point to point, and it must end in the admission that under Protection one class will live upon another. Let it assume what disguise it may, Protection, if it is effective, can never be anything more than spoliation under the forms of law. Every Protective tax, by whatever extent it operates to the exclusion of imported goods, is a licence to one class of the community to plunder another under the pretence of charity. Hard as these words are, there are times when the use of plain words is necessary.

Such a time has always arrived when benevolent but heedless men are moved by the sight of sufferings to countenance quack remedies. Such is the present situation of the fiscal controversy. The ravages of competition have been great, and the intelligence to hear the cry of distress is growing keener. What more easy and more satisfying to lazy emotionability than to denounce competition in all its forms, and to urge that a beginning should be made with the competition of foreign nations? If only the cure were so easy! Knowledge, however, and experience teach the contrary; and in the meantime, to those who despise knowledge in political affairs, and who have not the strength of character to possess their souls in patience, we may fairly say, as plainly as we can, "Not only will your policy of commercial restriction fail to remedy the evils of which you complain, but it is in every aspect a disgraceful policy, because it turns your workmen into beggars for public charity, and your manufacturers into thieves." Great indeed should be the advantages which are to compensate for evils such as these!

Part IV.

THE POLITICAL ARGUMENT.

CHAPTER I.

THE ARGUMENTS CLASSIFIED.

§ 1. ALL that can be said in favour of Protection on political grounds may be reduced, on analysis, under one of four heads, which may be conveniently designated by the names which the arguments bear in popular controversy. These are :—

1. The Infant Industry Argument.
2. The Variety of Industry Argument.
3. The Home Market Argument.
4. The Pauper Labour Argument.

§ 2. It is well pointed out by Professor Taussig, in his "Tariff History of the United States," that these arguments have a certain historical connection. The whole passage referred to is so instructive, and the work from which it is taken so little known to Australian and English readers, that no further excuse is needed for quoting it at length :—

"The system of Protective legislation began in 1816, and was maintained till towards the end of the decade 1830–40. The Compromise Act of 1833 gradually undermined it. By 1842 duties reached a lower point than that from which they had started in 1816. During this whole period the argument for Protection to young industries had been essentially the mainstay of the advocates of Protection, and the eventual cheapness of the goods was the chief advantage which they proposed to obtain. It goes without saying that this was not the only argument used, and that it was often expressed loosely in connection with other arguments. One does not find in the popular discussions of fifty years ago, more than in those of the present, precision of thought or expression. The 'home market' argument, which, though essentially distinct from that of young industries, naturally suggests itself in connection with the latter, was much urged during the period we are considering. The events of the war of 1812 had vividly impressed on the minds of the people the possible inconvenience, in case of war, of depending on foreign trade for the supply of articles of common use; this point also was much urged by the Protectionists. Similarly the want of reciprocity, and the possibility of securing, by retaliation, a relaxation of the restrictive legislation of foreign countries, were often mentioned. But any one who is familiar with the Protective literature of that day—as illustrated, for instance, in the columns of *Niles's Register*—cannot fail to note the prominent place held by the young-industries argument. The form in which it most commonly appears is in the assertion that Protection normally causes the prices of the Protected articles to fall,[1] an assertion which was supposed, then as now, to be sufficiently supported by the general tendency towards a fall in the price of manufactured articles, consequent on the great improvement in the methods of producing such articles.

"Shortly after 1832, the movement in favour of Protection, which had had full sway in the Northern States since 1820, began to lose strength. The young-industries argument at the same time began to be less steadily pressed. About 1840 the Protective controversy took a new turn. It seems to have been felt by this time that manufactures had ceased to be

---

[1] See, for instance, the temperate report of J. Q. Adams, in 1832, in which this is discussed as the chief argument of the Protectionists. Adams, though himself a Protectionist, refutes it, and bases his faith in Protection chiefly on the loss and inconvenience suffered through the interruption of foreign trade in time of war. The report is in "Reports of Committees, 22nd Congress, 1st Session, vol. v., No. 481."

young industries, and that the argument for their Protection as such was no longer conclusive. Another position was taken. The argument was advanced that American labour should be protected from the competition of less highly paid foreign labour. The labour argument had hardly been heard in the period which has been treated in the preceding pages. Indeed, the difference between the rate of wages in the United States and in Europe, had furnished, during the early period, an argument for the Free Traders, and not for the Protectionists. The Free Traders were then accustomed to point to the higher wages of labour in the United States as an insuperable obstacle to the successful establishment of manufactures. They used the wages argument as a foil to the young-industries argument, asserting that as long as wages were so much lower in Europe, manufacturers would not be able to maintain themselves without aid from the Government. The Protectionists, on the other hand, felt called on to explain away the difference of wages; they endeavoured to show that this difference was not so great as was commonly supposed, and that, so far as it existed, it afforded no good reason against adopting Protection.[1] About 1840, the positions of the contending parties began to change.[2] The Protectionists began to take the offensive on the labour question; the Free Traders were forced to the

---

[1] Some signs of the appeal for the benefit of labour appear as early as 1831 in a passage in Gallatin's "Memorial," p. 31, and again in a speech of Webster's in 1833, "Works," I., 283. In the campaign of 1840, little was heard of it, doubtless because other issues than Protection were in the foreground. Yet Calhoun was led to make a keen answer to it in a speech of 1840, "Works," III., 434. In the debates on the Tariff Act of 1842, we hear more of it; see the speeches of Choate and Buchanan, *Congr. Globe*, 1841-42, pp. 950, 953, and Calhoun's allusion to Choate, in Calhoun's "Works," IV., 207. In 1846 the argument appeared full-fledged, in the speeches of Winthrop, Davis, and others, *Congr. Globe*, 1846, Appendix, pp. 967, 973, 1114. See also a characteristic letter in *Niles*, Vol. 62, p. 262. Webster's speech in 1846, "Works," V., 231, had much about Protection and labour, but in a form somewhat different from that of the argument we are nowadays familiar with.

[2] See, among others, Clay's Tariff speech in 1824, "Works," I., 465, 466.

defensive on this point. The Protectionists asserted that high duties were necessary to shut out the competition of the ill-paid labourers of Europe, and to maintain the high wages of the labourers of the United States. Their opponents had to explain and defend on the wages question. Obviously this change in the line of argument indicates a change in the industrial situation. Such an argument in favour of Protection could not have arisen at a time when Protective duties existed but in small degree, and when wages nevertheless were high. Its use implies the existence of industries which are supposed to be dependent on high duties. When the Protective system had been in force for some time, and a body of industries had sprung up which were thought to be able to pay current wages only if aided by high duties, the wages argument naturally suggested itself. The fact that the iron manufacture, which had hitherto played no great part in the Protective controversy, became, after 1840, the most prominent applicant for aid, accounts in large part for the new aspect of the controversy. The use of the wages argument, and the rise of the economic school of Henry C. Carey, show that the argument for young industries was felt to be no longer sufficient to be the mainstay of the Protective system. The economic situation had changed, and the discussion of the tariff underwent a corresponding change."

§ 3. This brilliant survey of the history of the Protective movement in America might easily be illustrated from Australian experience. In that country, also, the pauper-labour argument has been the last to come into prominence.

The argument which was most frequently used in the early days of the Protectionist agitation in Victoria was drawn from the supposed necessity of providing new avenues of employment for the mining population as the yield of gold decreased.[1]

The same cry was raised in New South Wales when,

[1] Victoria adopted a Protectionist tariff in 1866.

owing to a reaction from a period of excessive expenditure on public works, and to the effect of a Land Act in stopping improvements on Crown lands, a number of "Unemployed" made their appearance in the streets of Sydney. Gradually, however, as the agitation in each colony settled down, and as industries began to be established in Victoria under Protection, in New South Wales under Free Trade, the necessity was felt for appealing to cupidity and self-interest by some other means. The pauper-labour argument was admirably adapted for such a purpose. Indeed, there is no other argument in the Protectionist quiver which offers a politician such a rare opportunity of doubling the parts of prophet and philanthropist. Cassandra-like predictions of desolation and ruin are exceedingly effective anodynes to the present inconveniences of higher prices. In Australia, however, as in America, no one argument has ever been used to the exclusion of others. The utmost that can be said is that in each country the influence of the various arguments has varied at different periods.

It will be necessary now to consider each by itself.

CHAPTER II.

THE INFANT-INDUSTRY ARGUMENT.

§ 1. THE political argument which came first into use in support of Protective tariffs is that which is generally known as the "Infant Industry Argument," and which may be stated in these terms: "Protection is desirable for a few years in order to establish the industries which are naturally suited to a young country."

It is apparent from its terms that this argument is not intended to be a defence of Protection as a permanent policy, but that it is addressed to those who may be frightened at the cost of a Protective tariff, or have other objections to it, in order to induce them to submit to a temporary sacrifice for the sake of a future permanent gain. The argument thus becomes in part an admission that Protection is an evil, and in part a prophecy that the evil will be temporary.

The admission is correct; the prophecy is not.

Before examining this, the first political argument submitted for consideration, a warning must again be given of the limited scope of our immediate investigation. We have to isolate each political argument, and consider it apart from others, if we would estimate its true value. In practice, of course, this is seldom done. Men pass almost imperceptibly from one argument to another, and are apt to be angry if they are pinned, even for a time, to the separate consideration of any. If, then, any Protectionist who may read these pages should be inclined at any point of the argument to charge the writer with unfairness, he should reserve his final judgment until he has perused the whole of the political discussion; and even then he should ask himself whether his own arguments and phrases are, upon analysis, anything more than a compound of two or more of those political fallacies whose nakedness he is ready to admit when each is separately exposed. Further, let it be remembered that a greater freedom of criticism is permissible in dealing with political than with scientific arguments, and that *ad captandum* statements may be fairly answered in the same measure.

With these few words of warning and deprecation, let us proceed to the consideration of the argument which owes its name to the advocacy of Infant Industries.

The notion is, as has been said, that certain industries cannot be established, under the circumstances ordinarily existent in a young country, if they are exposed at the outset to the competition of the older and stronger industries of other lands. It is then answered that if the critical stages of struggle and difficulty can be successfully passed, the industries in question will be able to sustain themselves without assistance against all competitors. And, finally—it being represented as a desirable thing that these industries should be established—the people who will have to pay for their establishment are exhorted to bear the burden for a short time, in the assurance that they will reap benefits a hundredfold when the period of pupilage is at an end.

§ 2. It is obvious that this argument assumes that after a reasonable time the Protected industries will be able to stand alone. Accordingly, the first question which a voter ought to ask when this argument is addressed to him is as to the length of time for which the assistance of Protection will be needed; because, as it must again be mentioned, this argument is not addressed to those who advocate Protection as a permanent policy, but to those who, regarding it as undesirable in itself, are nevertheless prepared to submit to its inconvenience in order to gain the advantages of new industries. It becomes, therefore, a matter of chief importance to test the assumptions of the argument by concrete instances, in order to form some idea of the amount of sacrifice which is demanded to obtain the promised benefits.

On this point let us first listen to Professor Sumner:—

"I know of no case," says he, "where the hope that infant industries can be nourished up to independence, and that they then become productive, has been realised, although we have been trying the experiment for nearly a century. The weakest infants of to-day are those whom Alexander Hamilton set out to protect in 1791. As soon as the infants begin to get any strength (if ever they do get any) the Protective system forces them to bear the burden of other infants, and so on for ever. The system superinduces hydrocephalus on the infants, and instead of ever growing to maturity, the longer they live the bigger babies they are."

The "infant-industry" argument has never been disposed of in fewer words, nor more completely; and the treatment is according to its deserts. Some persons, however, may require to know the evidence by which the statement is supported. This is given by the instances of the United States, Victoria, Germany, and every other country which has adopted the Protective system.

Let us begin with the United States.

§ 3. The history of the "infant-industry" argument in the country of its birth is a singular record of human blindness and popular forgetfulness. As might be expected, it first saw light in the discussions which preceded the Tariff Act of 1789, and had at once a complete success. Among the many and various motives which induced the framers of the American Constitution to submit to a federal tariff, not the least strong was the belief that by taking this step they would raise up new industries within their borders, and preserve them from the crushing competition of Great Britain. Thus the Tariff Act of 1789 contained a statement in its preamble that it was passed for "the encouragement and protection of manufactures." Nor was the preamble the only portion of the Act in which its framers displayed the honesty of their convictions. A subsequent clause provided that the Act should expire in 1796, and that the duties, which were fixed at eight-and-a-half per cent. *ad valorem*, should not be collected after that date — so confident were these clear-sighted men that at the expiration of seven years Protection would no more be needed! The infant industries were to attain their majority in seven years! This was the belief in 1789. Never was the vanity of Protectionist good-wishes more strikingly exemplified!

The very year in which the Act was passed the "infants" required a further assistance of two-and-a-half per cent., and two years later, in 1792, their Protection was raised to thirteen-

and-a-half per cent. The year 1796 arrived, but the coming of age was indefinitely postponed!

Between 1789 and 1816—a period of twenty-six years—seventeen Acts were passed affecting duties, which generally and steadily raised them.[1]

Some Protectionists have said that these successive increases in the rate of duty afford a proof of the beneficial operation of Protection; but those who assert this in Australia need to be reminded that the present argument is not whether Protection is permanently beneficial, but whether any period can be ascertained at which Protection can be done without.

The second great fight upon the tariff in the United States occurred in 1816. After the experience of previous years, it might have been thought that there would have been a certain disinclination on the part of Protectionists to fix beforehand any limits, either of time or amount, to the desire of manufacturers to get the most they could from a State that was willing to give. Still, in those days of inexperience in Protective legislation, it was felt that the claim to special privileges would have to be justified by some more plausible argument than the bare assertion of an abstract right to plunder the general body of citizens to the end of time. Consequently, the old appeals to sympathy were renewed; and the old promises were repeated, with even greater fervour, that the aid would only be required for a few years.

Two great industries were particularly insistent in their demands: viz., the cotton and the iron. Both of these had established themselves under Free Trade with a fair measure of success—the iron industry, even in the old colonial days, having been so profitable that its progress threatened the superiority of the English iron-masters, and led to the passing

---

[1] It will be obvious to all who are acquainted with the subject that I am much indebted for this record of the practical application of the infant argument in America to Professor Sumner's Lectures on the History of Protection.

of Acts of Parliament designed for its suppression. Changes, however, in the mode of manufacture, and the disorganisation consequent on the return of peace in 1815, had thrown these industries and several others into a condition of distress. This state of things led to the tariff of 1816, and furnished another example of the ease with which voters are misled by promises which from their nature are incapable of fulfilment.

Our illustrations may be confined to the two leading industries of cotton and iron.

The duty on cotton was fixed by the Act of 1816 at twenty-five per cent., but in order to conciliate purchasers it was enacted that this Protective duty should only be levied for three years.[1]

The end of the three years came, but the duties remained.

So far from being removed, they were increased in 1824. They were again increased in 1828, again in 1832; and from that date to this the manufacture of cotton in the United States, where the raw material for the world is grown, has been continuously protected by a tariff which is in some lines almost prohibitory. Yet so little vigour has this "infant" been able to obtain in seventy-three years, that the imports of cotton goods into the United States from Great Britain amounted in the year 1888 to £5,750,000 in value—or nearly twice as much as the total exports of cottons from America to all the world; in addition to which, Great Britain almost monopolised the open markets of the world.[2] Surely, if Protection was ever desirable, it would be in the case of the cotton industry of the United States? Yet if, after seventy-three years of Protection, that industry is still an "infant," and so weakly, even for an infant of those tender years, that,

---

[1] Taussig: "Tariff History of the United States," p. 30 (G. P. Putnam, New York, 1888).

[2] Taussig: "Tariff History of the United States," p. 40:—The exports of cotton goods from Great Britain in 1888 were £60,329,000; the exports of cotton goods from the United States in 1888 were £2,750,000.

although it has its raw material on the spot, it cannot compete with a little country like England, which has to convey the raw material three thousand miles and send the manufactured goods the same distance before they get into the market, it is difficult to see what the industry can be which requires to be nurtured into manhood by Protection.

But the loudest and most persistent beggar for Protective duties has always been the iron industry. Despite the fact that the manufacture of pig-iron was started in America in the seventeenth century, and that it was a firmly established, prosperous, and increasing industry before the first tariff, this hoary infant of 250 years still demands and receives a Protective duty amounting to sixty per cent. *ad valorem*.[1] The increment in the tax has been gradual. Up to 1816 there was no Protection on pig-iron, and the furnaces were numerous and increasing;[2] but the revision of the tariff in that year rendered the imposition of a duty inevitable. A duty on iron is necessarily the keystone of a Protective system, partly because of the close connection of that commodity with every form of manufacturing process, and partly because its industrial importance easily attracts attention. For many years the whole Protective system of the United States depended upon the retention of the duties upon iron.

In the fervent words of Mr. E. J. Donnell, "the tariff monopoly in iron is the tap-root of the upas-tree that has poisoned both our industry and our politics. With free iron the monopolies in other raw materials could not stand a day, and the tariff on manufactures would soon cease to have a single advocate, even among the manufacturers. In point of fact, the tariffs on coal, copper, lead, wool, timber, and many other articles which constitute the basis of various branches of our industry, had their origin in what is called

---

[1] See Taussig's "History of Protection."
[2] The iron products of the United States were valued at £14,000,000 in 1810.

log-rolling—they were supported by the iron monopoly as a buttress to the iron tariff. . . . Iron is the key to the arch of monopoly. Almost every branch of American industry can be liberated by emancipating the one article, iron."[1]

The iron industry in 1816 was quite as moderate in its demands as the cotton. Duties were fixed at twenty-five per cent.; but in 1819 these were to be reduced to twenty per cent.

When 1819 arrived, the reduction was postponed, and it is almost unnecessary to add that since that date the duties have been increased and not diminished, until they stand at the present, in some lines, as high as 100 and 250 per cent,[2] to the no small advantage of Mr. Carnegie and other enthusiastic champions of Protective legislation.

In 1832 the tariff was again revised in the Protectionist interest. At this date Protection had existed, in a greater or less degree, for forty-three years, and still the "infant" argument was not abandoned! It was only modified. That it should have been used in any form—and still more, that it should be used in any country in the year 1890—is a striking illustration of the great difficulty in the way of tariff reform which arises from the indifference of the popular memory to the details of so unattractive a subject. When, added to this indifference, we have on the part of some a willingness to be deceived by phrases, and on the part of others an intense wish to gain advantage by deceiving—the progress of Free Trade in the United States and other countries, slight as it is, becomes a matter of considerable surprise.

In 1832 the weakness of the "infant" argument was beginning to be felt, and Henry Clay, the Protectionist champion, abandoned the seven years' minority, and named twenty-five years as the period during which assistance might

---

[1] Since the passing of the McKinley Tariff, wool has taken the place of iron in this respect. (*See* article by Prof. Taussig in Vol. I. of the *Economic Journal*.)
[2] *e.g.*, nails.

be legitimately demanded by a "Protected" industry. The admirers of Henry Clay will not consider it an injustice to his intellectual powers to believe that he was sincere in making this prognostication. On the contrary, Mr. Horace Greeley, the modern defender of Clay's principles, expressly declares that Clay and all the earlier champions of Protection—including Hamilton, Carey, Niles, and the earlier presidents—"champion not the maintenance, but the creation of home manufactures."[1]

Possibly the modern champions of Protection would insist on placing themselves in the same category. After all, there is but a difference of degree between "the creation" of an industry and its "maintenance"; and who is more competent to decide whether an industry has passed from the growing to the mature stage than the manufacturer, who is to be paid for attending to the growth? This, at all events, seems to be the view of the most modern teaching on this Protectionist argument.

In the last edition of his "Political Economy" (p. 233), Professor Thompson, of the Pennsylvania University, tells us that "it will ordinarily take the lifetime of two generations to acclimatise thoroughly a new manufacture, and to bring the native production up to the native demand."

From seven years to two generations is a long step! Yet, if this is the latest exposition of the gospel, Free Traders only ask that it may be spread abroad. For, as Mr. George suggests, it would hardly be a popular argument to address to the present generation: that it should tax itself and its successor for the benefit of a third. To such a demand we might well ask, "What has posterity ever done for us?"[2]

[1] Horace Greeley: "Political Sermons," p. 34; cited by Mr. George: "Protection or Free Trade?" p. 103.

[2] The latest writer on Protection, Professor Patten (1890), boldly abandons the Infant argument, and takes his stand on the position that Protection ought to be a permanent policy. Free Traders, therefore, may surely use language of derision about this once famous argument without incurring odium.

§ 4. Were it not for the numerous instances which history offers of the truth of Dean Milman's theory of the immortality of humbug, it might have been thought impossible, after the experience of the United States, that this tattered and fact-riddled theory about infant industries should ever be dressed up again for use in other countries. But it appeared in Victoria in 1865 in all its old effrontery; and is still the favourite catchword of Protectionist audiences in New South Wales. Yet the history of Victoria has been in no whit different from that of the United States as regards the falsification of all prophecies that a time would come when a Protected industry could stand alone.

Although the framers of the first Victorian tariff were wise enough to fix no date for its repeal, they won for it no small measure of support by the assurance that it would not be needed for any length of time. Then, as in America in 1789 men believed—or affected to believe—that Protection might be adopted as a temporary expedient, in order to give a start to a few suitable industries. Then, as now, in New South Wales, most Protectionists professed themselves to be "moderate," or "discriminating." They would neither have high duties nor maintain any duties permanently.

The result of these expectations ought to be a significant warning to simple-minded people in other countries who allow themselves to be persuaded into similar beliefs. The "temporary" duties are in force to-day. The "moderate" duties have been three times revised, and have been raised on each revision. Protection has now been the law of Victoria for twenty-three years, and during all that time the reductions of duties have been almost imperceptible, while the increases of duties have been steady and enormous. It is not too much to say, if we accept the sincerity of the public professions of the "moderate" men, that the tariff of 1865 would never have become law if the same rate of duties had been asked for then which was readily conceded in 1889. Take the hat-making trade for an illustration. How many electors in 1865 would have voted for a duty of 5s. apiece on hats? And how many candidates would have ventured to support it? Yet in 1889 the hat-makers obtained a duty of 60s. a dozen on hats, and are grumbling still because they did not obtain one of 72s. What the tax may be on hats in 1900 it is dangerous to conjecture. Similar instances of the unappeasable appetite of the principal Victorian "infants" may be collected from every side.

The greatest cormorant is the woollen trade, which, in spite of its contiguity to the source of its raw material, is in chronic difficulties. In 1868 the duty on clothing imported into Victoria was 10 per cent. After three years the duty was raised to $12\frac{1}{2}$ per cent. In 1872 it was raised again to 20 per cent., at which figure it remained for eight years. But 20 per cent. was not enough for this struggling industry, nor twelve years sufficient to draw it from a state of pupilage. In 1880 the duty was again raised to 25 per cent. In 1886 it was raised again to 30 per cent.; and in 1889, after twenty years of a Protective tariff, the manufacturers of clothing, asking for a duty of 40 per cent., got one of 35 per cent. The duty on furniture, again, has increased from 10 per cent. in 1866 to 25 per cent. in 1888; and the duty on woollens has increased from $7\frac{1}{2}$ per cent. in 1871 to 35 per cent. in 1889.

The subjoined table shows the changes in the Victorian tariff from 1866 to 1889 upon a few of the commoner necessities of life:—

Article.	1866.	1868.	1872.	1880.	1886.	1888.	1889.
		p. c.	p. c.	p. c.	p. c.	p. c.	p. c.
Apparel and Slops	4s. per cub. foot	10	20	25	30	35	25
Furniture	10 per cent.	10	20	25	25	25	35
Hats and Caps and Bonnets	4s. per cub. foot	10	20	25	25	25	var.

Is there any reason to believe that we in New South Wales would have a different experience from that of America and Victoria? Would not any Protective duties, however low they might be at first, inevitably increase in this country, as they have done in others? Those who really are "moderate" Protectionists should learn a lesson from experience, and vote for Free Trade.

§ 5. The illustrations which have already been offered from the history of Protection in countries so different in their conditions as the United States and Victoria, indicate sufficiently the nature of the answer to the argument in favour of Protection—"that it may be temporarily useful in assisting infant industries." The fatal objection to this argument is its inapplicability to political facts. It takes no account of the imperfection of human nature. It assumes that every Government is incorruptible, and every manufacturer disinterested. Whereas the truth is, that Governments are squeezable, and manufacturers are very active in their own interests.

There is one great, plain, practical fact in respect to Protection to "Infant industries" which is itself a sufficient answer to all the arguments which may be advanced in its favour. "Temporary" Protection, or "moderate" Protection, or "diminishing" Protection never has existed, and never can exist while human nature continues as it is. There cannot be one single instance referred to in the history of any State, nation, or people in which the Protected classes have voluntarily abandoned the assistance of Protection when the purpose for which it was imposed has been achieved. This is owing partly to the unchangeable characteristics of human nature, partly to the economic consequences of all Protective legislation.

No matter with what honesty of purpose Protection may be first established, its continuance will always be secured by the selfishness of vested interests. The men who derive advantage from the right to tax their fellow-citizens, being few and powerful, will combine to support their privilege; while the majority of the people, being affected by the tariff in different ways, and often unable to perceive its operation, have no motive of equal strength to stir them into opposition.[1]

The vested interests have also the further advantage, in any contest, of being able to appeal to public sympathy with a force which is directly proportionate to their own weakness. When once Protection has been established, its continuance can be secured, not only by the illegitimate use of organised wealth and power, but by drawing harrowing pictures of the loss and hardship to innocent persons which would be inflicted by its abolition. This consideration is naturally strongest in a small community, where members of all classes are more or less acquainted with each other. Kind-hearted and impetuous persons, who would never have voted for the establishment of Protection, are easily moved to support its continuance by pictures of the miseries which would follow an " extermination " of the Protected trader—the ruined capitalists with useless plants, the thousands of labourers " robbed of their livelihood." Unfortunately, these good people do not stop to inquire whether the return to Free Trade will really cause the industry to stop, or whether the statement is not merely the unproved assertion of an interested party.

It has been asserted by the Hon. David A. Wells—and the statement has never been disproved—that from eighty to ninety per cent. of American manufacturers are able, from their

---

[1] The notorious corruptness of the Presidential election of 1888 illustrates the text. The investigations conducted by the New York *World* in January and February, 1889, revealed a complete organisation on the part of the Protected manufacturers for purposes of corruption. As one of the Republican organisers stated, "the fat was to be fried" from the manufacturers. The Democratic party were, no doubt, also corrupt; but not being able to stimulate their supporters by the same inducement, they could not collect the same amount of money, and so lost the election. The purchase of New York State by the corrupt agreement of the Democratic leaders for the sale of the Irish vote for the Presidency in consideration that a Republican vote should be cast for the Democrats in the State election, gave President Harrison the victory

natural advantages, to under-sell foreign competitors without assistance from the tariff; and that only ten to twenty per cent. of them are in any degree subject to foreign competition.[1]

Nevertheless, the question must arise in any country where Protection has been long established, whether a return to Free Trade would not destroy some of the existing industries; and Free Traders must admit that such might be the case. Industries which are unsuited to the country, either owing to the conditions of its civilisation—such as handicrafts in a country of highly developed mechanical appliances—or to the natural disadvantages of its climate—such as tea-growing in the United States—must suffer by a change from Protection to Free Trade if they cannot soon adapt themselves to the new conditions.

A Free Trader has two replies to those who urge the continuance of Protection upon this account :—

First, he says, "Industries such as these are not worth preserving—our country cannot afford to keep them. They belong to a lower grade of civilisation, in which our citizens ought not to be compelled to live."

Secondly, he would say, "Even under Protection industries such as these are never prosperous. From the conditions of their existence they can never export their articles of manufacture, and are therefore confined to a small and non-expansive market. Of such industries distress and suffering is a chronic complaint, and the continuance of the Protective system will, in most cases, only make the misery of those who work in them greater and more extended. The blame for this belongs properly to the policy which made this ruin inevitable, and not to that which sought to limit its effects. If a choice has to be made between the total abolition of Protective duties, after a reasonable notice, and their gradual reduction, the truer kindness, probably in every case, is to prefer the speedier

[1] *See* "Practical Economics" (p. 142). Putnam, New York, 1888.

process. Trade suffers less from a sharp shock than from a protracted agony."

§ 6. There is another reason for the want of finality in all Protective legislation, which has already been referred to incidentally in the discussion of the economic argument: namely, the close and often unforeseen dependence of one trade upon another.

It is obvious that Protective duties upon iron, steel, cotton, or any other raw material, necessitate compensating duties upon the finished products of any of these articles; but it is not always easy to trace either the amount of compensation which is requisite or the products which require it. The processes of manufacture are so complicated, and the interdependence of several trades upon each other is so intricate and variable, that even experts find it difficult to say beforehand on what lines, or to what amounts, compensating duties ought to be imposed. The compensating duties placed on woollen goods in the United States offer an illustration of this difficulty. These are so numerous, and so delicately graduated, that no person who is not in the trade can possibly understand either their amount or their incidence, and even manufacturers themselves have been disputing about them since 1869. The whole matter is fully discussed by Professor Taussig in his "Tariff History of the United States," in a chapter which will well repay perusal.

§ 7. But not only is there a legitimate connection between duties upon raw materials and duties upon finished products, but there is an illegitimate connection between all Protective duties. It is not in human nature to stand by while another person's industry receives Protection without demanding the same privilege for oneself. Such a demand is certain to receive considerable attention. In the first place, it appeals to the universal sense of fair play by asking that every class of industry should be treated alike; and secondly, it gives new allies to those who are already Protected. Thus is initiated the system known as "log-rolling," by which one set of manufacturers will help another set to get what duties they want on condition of receiving similar assistance for themselves.

Nor is this practice, although most destructive of political purity, altogether without justification. It is not the men who are to blame, but the system. For, as Professor Sumner has pointed out, "if one industry should be set out in free competition, while the rest were Protected, it would be found . . . . that machinery, raw materials, and labour supplies would be so dear that the exposed industry would have no fair chance in competition with foreigners. Hence one long-Protected industry, if it became independent by natural causes, could not be left free unless the whole system were abandoned. But then the cry goes up from those nurslings of recent beginning that they are not yet ready. If you defer the introduction of freedom for ten years longer on their account, a new company of infants is meantime brought into being, and the plea for further delay comes from them. Thus you go on for ever, and the theory is reduced to an absurdity." ("History of Protection," p. 44.)

A Senator of the United States—the Hon. Samuel S. Cox—has described the practices which result from the interdependence of Protected trades as "mutual brigandage and reciprocity of robbery." After making all due allowances for the warmth of the expression, we may still derive some profit from the graphic illustrations by which the senator supports it:—

> "Kentucky," he says, "wants cheap copper stills for her whisky. She gets even with the Michigan robber by demanding a tariff on hemp. . . . Maine steals on lumber to make up for the Massachusetts roguery on fabrics. Massachusetts hauls for cheap coal; Pennsylvania says no; and so Massachusetts goes out with a 'Home Market Club' [referring to a political association of that

name], and knocks down the West and South to rifle them of half their gains on raw cotton. Tennessee, Virginia, and North Carolina, being fleeced all round in clothing, sugar, and what not, go for goobers at a cent a pound. California demands a large reprisal for her lumber, because she is fleeced on salt by New York. . . . Pennsylvania, the Robert Macaire of the lot, steals boldly on all articles, from a plate-glass to a locomotive; and to make up for the general loss, the North-West masks herself behind her forests and demands timber reprisals; and so on. Nothing is sacred. . . . Oh, the beauty of reciprocal rascality!"

The same conflict of interests, pacified, if possible, by the same methods, is seen wherever Protection exists. The result is an impossible effort to satisfy a thousand Pauls by robbing a thousand Peters. In attempting this, Protection is perpetuated.

§ 8. The conclusion is inevitable. Whether the infant-industry argument be tested by experience or by *à priori* reasoning, its emptiness and the unreality of its assumptions are equally apparent. It is difficult, indeed, to understand how any man who is acquainted with the history of tariff legislation, or accustomed to reflect upon the springs of political action, can with any honesty of conviction continue to maintain or lend attention to the vain assertion that "Protection can be tried for a short time, and laid aside after trial if it either performs its object or proves unsatisfactory."

If Protection be once established, it will spread itself with a silent and irresistible growth, which nothing short of a convulsion of the State will be able to uproot. Each Protective duty is the seed-nut of a hundred others, some of which propagate themselves, while others are planted by industrious sowers. Nor is resistance to this pernicious growth of much avail. Self-interest, especially when it masquerades as patriotism and philanthropy, is almost irresistible in a conflict with disorganised justice. The nation, therefore, which adopts Protection stands on an inclined plane. Once let it be started on the downward path, it will slide inevitably to the bottom; but where that bottom is no one yet knows, because no one has yet fathomed the depths of human credulity and greed.

It is true that the foregoing considerations can have no weight with those who regard Protection as a scientific doctrine. To such persons the permanency of Protection is a thing to be desired for its own sake.

But it is the characteristic of a political argument, such as that at present under review, that it appeals differently to different people. Thus, the "infant-industry" argument is not directed to the true believers, but only to the doubters. That it has effect on these is plain to any one who has lived in the atmosphere of tariff controversies. Two-thirds of the Protectionist members of the present New South Wales Assembly have described themselves in their addresses as "moderate Protectionists," or have supported their views by making use of the "infant" argument. To such men and to their hearers the considerations which have been urged above ought to appeal with force.

The argument has also a certain weight with scientific writers on the tariff question—a fact which probably accounts for its political vitality. John Stuart Mill has notably given it an undue prominence in his consideration of the case of Protection in a young community. But it will be found upon examination that the cases which Mill imagines, although they are theoretically conceivable, are not such as have ever occurred in New South Wales; and that in any country his argument assumes the existence of that which has never yet been discovered: viz., a Government honest enough and powerful enough to resist all claims to illegitimate Protection, and to remove Protective duties directly they have done their work.[1]

---

[1] See Appendix II. for a full examination of J. S. Mill's view of the possible economic justification of Protection in a young country.

CHAPTER III.

THE "DIVERSIFICATION OF INDUSTRY" ARGUMENT.

§ 1. It is probable that Protection gains the majority of its supporters by appealing, in a more or less direct manner, to the sentiment of national sufficiency. There is a general desire—which is especially strong in a young community whose place among nations has not yet been recognised—to become independent of other countries by supplying all its wants through the labour of its own citizens.

The industrial characteristics of a new country are very visibly determined by its natural features. The attraction to settlers is, in almost every instance, the possession in an exceptional degree of some great natural advantage. The consequence is that in the early days of the community the population is fully employed in the production of raw material; and the high profit which this occupation returns enables it to satisfy its wants very easily by trading with foreign countries.

After a time, however, the extractive industries, as they are called, become less profitable. The virgin soil gives out, the surface ores are exhausted, the nearer forests are thinned, and the special natural advantages which were possessed by the young country grow gradually less. In the meantime, the influx of population—which is generally much behind the demand for labour—keeps up at the old rate, or probably increases. Two currents of opinion are thus set in motion, the one coming from the more far-seeing of the former inhabitants, who observe the increasing difficulty in carrying on the old pursuits; the other from newly arrived immigrants, whose expectations of an El Dorado are not realised. Each class wants to find new avenues of employment. The older settlers need openings for their children. The new-comers want work at the trades to which they have been accustomed.

Under such circumstances, it only needs the occurrence of a commercial crisis, or a disorganisation of industry from one of the causes to which young communities are especially exposed —namely, drought, over-speculation, or excessive borrowing —and the Protectionist manufacturer has ready to his hand the very best of opportunities. He can point out to the discontented the indisputable fact that a change is coming, and that industry cannot continue in the old paths. He will say that " it is the duty of the State to preserve the industrial organisation, and to see that the capital which has already been spent in the country be not wasted, or the labourers forced to go away to other lands." He will, therefore, urge the necessity of opening up new channels for employment and preventing the nation sinking into a state of stagnation. He will maintain that, although it may be cheaper to buy manufactures from abroad in exchange for raw produce, yet the gain thus secured would be dearly bought by the limits which this practice would impose upon the growth of population, and by the injurious influence upon national character which arises from a lack of variety in the occupations of a people. He would say that the " extractive industries " do not call forth the highest mental qualities; and that in any case they can only be followed by men who are suited to outdoor work. Accordingly, to confine the labour of the country to these pursuits would deprive many men who might excel in handicrafts of the opportunity to find employment, and thus to cause a waste of industrial power. Nor would he omit to mention that the establishment of manufactories means the growth of towns, and that the social development and progress of a country cannot be so rapid if the greater part of the population be employed in field work and live in scattered settlements. " Therefore," he would say, " seek a stimulus for new industries in a Protective tariff, in the hope that the home demand for manufactured goods may force home labour and capital into a variety of new channels, until every natural resource is developed to its full extent and no native talent is without a scope. The piteous cry of the farmer and miner, 'What shall we do with our boys?' will no longer be heard in the land;[1] but every lad, when he comes of age, will find a calling suited to his powers, and every immigrant, on landing at the wharf, can take a place in his own trade. By this means, though the individual may suffer temporary loss, the latent capacities of the nation as a whole will be developed, and its attractiveness to immigrants will be increased."

This is undoubtedly a clever picture, which lacks no feature of attraction for the public eye. Nor is the picture an incorrect representation of what might be. It is part of the truth, but not the whole.

§ 2. It is evident that the reasoning which supports Protection because it gives a variety of industries, rests upon three important but unexpressed, assumptions: viz.— 1. That there is, in fact, no sufficient diversity of industry in any young community which adheres to Free Trade. 2. That, without Protection, no sufficient diversity of industry can either be secured or maintained. 3. That, when a sufficient diversity of industry is secured and maintained by means of Protection, the country, as a whole, will be better off.

The burden of proving these assumptions to be sound clearly rests on the Protectionist, because it is he, and not the Free Trader, who proposes to interfere with the natural course of trade. Consequently, until he discharges this burden the diversity of industry argument counts for nothing. A pleasant escape, indeed, from a long discussion!

It is to be feared, however, that logic has very little

---

[1] This ridiculous question is really put to Protectionist audiences, and sadly passed by, as admitting of no satisfactory answer while Free Trade continues. An irreverent believer in freedom once suggested, when the question was being put in more than usually lugubrious tones, "Marry them to our girls"; but the advice, though it has become historic, has never been well received by the prophets of evil.

influence in a tariff controversy. Certain it is that the diversity argument loses none of its force by having its assumptions taken for granted instead of proved. What Protectionist orator or writer would stop, in his glowing catalogue of benefits to be derived from a variety of industries, for any dull inquiry whether this much-desired variety does not already exist to a sufficient degree; or whether, if some industries are still wanting, Free Trade is an absolute bar to their establishment? Yet these are, essentially, inquiries into facts, which cannot be ignored by any man who wants to form a reasonable judgment upon the value of this famous argument.

If, however, Free Traders ignore the diversity argument until its assumptions are proved, they will never convince voters. Let them, therefore, begin the attack. But first let them survey the position.

§ 3. The aim desired is a variety of occupations. Are Free Traders to admit this aim to be desirable or not? Professor Sumner answers sturdily in the negative. "It is not," he says, "an object to diversify industry, but to multiply and diversify our satisfactions, comforts, enjoyments. If we can do this by unifying our industry in greater measure than by diversifying it, then we should do, and we will do, the former." ("Protectionism," p. 116.) It would be difficult to find a more striking instance of the divergent scopes of an economic and a political argument. To Professor Sumner, "satisfactions, comforts, and enjoyments" are words of "economic" import. They are products or sensations which are obtainable in exchange for wealth. To the politician, and especially to the Protectionist, they convey a different meaning. The "satisfactions" are satisfactions of sentiment as well as of wants—and no serious politician will ignore the demands of national sentiment—while the "comforts and enjoyments" are not only of material things, but of everything which occupies pleasantly the life of a citizen, or relieves him from alarm. Vague, illusory, and unobtainable these " satisfactions, comforts, and enjoyments" may be in most instances, but they are sufficiently definite to be the subject of argument, when they are of the kind which are promised to the labouring classes through the establishment of a variety of industries. The ambition to rise, the love of change, the very difference of physical and mental qualities—all conduce to make men who have to live by wages look forward with pleasure to the possibility of obtaining different kinds of work for themselves and their children; while the politician may share with peasant and artisan the fear lest the temper of the nation may be lowered and its talents wasted by a dull, sluggish uniformity of occupation.

Accordingly, if we are to answer their political argument with a political answer, we must, at the outset, frankly recognise that the aim of the Protectionists in this instance is good; and that a variety of industrial occupation is, for many reasons, advantageous to a community.

We may even, indeed, go further on the path of conciliation, and also admit that, in some stages of national development, Protection is very likely to create industries which either would not otherwise come into existence, or would be delayed in their birth for many years.

We start, therefore, by admitting that Protection in this instance aims at effecting a good result, and partly succeeds in its aim. But we are still far from a final agreement. Protection may be one means to secure diversity of occupation, but Free Trade may be a better.

§ 4. As in every political question, the point to be considered in judging of the expediency of adopting Protection, in order to secure an early diversification of industry, is— "Whether, on a balance, the advantages exceed the disadvantages."

In order to ascertain this, the present condition of the country must first be examined. Thus, if the argument is being used to justify the abandonment of Free Trade, the question will be, "Whether, as a fact, the industrial occupations of the country have not already been so much diversified, under a policy of freedom, as to give a reasonable ground for the belief that no legislative interference is required to prevent stagnation?" If, again, it is used in a Protected country to resist a return to freedom, the question at the outset is equally one of fact: namely, "Whether Free Trade, although it might alter the kinds of industries, would really lessen their number?"

These facts having been ascertained to form the basis of discussion, the question then assumes a wider scope, and invokes a general consideration of the working of Protective policies. Every circumstance which attends the operation of Protection must be taken into account—its effect upon existing industries, as well as upon those which it seeks to create; its effect upon the relation between capital and labour generally in the community; its effect upon the industrial temper of the people, their energy, honesty, and self-reliance; its effect upon the purity of political life; its social effect in creating "vested interests" and privileged classes—in a word, its bearing generally on all the intricate relations of the industrial, political, and social life of the community in which the experiment is to be justified.

By thus considering, first, the actual industrial position of the country, and next, the actual or probable effect of Protection in all its bearings, some estimate can be formed of its wisdom or unwisdom as a means for encouraging a variety of industry.

It is the fate of every political measure to produce unexpected consequences of evil. Protection, as a political measure, cannot hope for better fortune; so that we may fairly assume that the results of a Protective measure in any country will not be wholly good. Therefore, when we are asked to support Protection because it causes a diversity of industry, we cannot fix our attention on the one good result of the policy and ignore all those that are bad. Admitting a diversity of industries to be a good thing, and admitting it to be attainable by Protection, still we must inquire, " Whether there is not any other means which would give the same, or almost the same, good, with less of the evil ? "

Applying these considerations to the particular argument now under discussion, it follows that, although it may be true, under ordinary circumstances, that Protection will cause an earlier diversification of industry than would be established naturally, that is not conclusive in its favour, even if it be further admitted that an early diversification is desirable. The Protectionist will also have to show that industry will not diversify under Free Trade—if not, perhaps, quite as rapidly, yet with sufficient speed, and with more advantage on the whole to the welfare of a young community.

The discussion of the validity of the diversity argument will then take the following order :—

First—Whether, in fact, any Free Trade country has suffered, or is likely to suffer, from an insufficient variety of industrial occupation ?

Secondly—Whether, if a country is so suffering, Protection is the only remedy ?

And thirdly—If Protection be the only remedy, whether, in any case, Protection is not too high a price to pay for the advantage of diversity ?

A discussion of these questions will occupy the remainder of this chapter.

§ 5. The first duty of a tariff disputant is to verify his facts. Yet, probably, in no other controversy professing to deal with facts is there such an outspoken contempt for accurate inquiry, or such a readiness to build large conclusions upon so slight a basis of verified evidence. No doubt each party to the controversy brings this charge against the other, but we may prove it against Protectionists in at least one instance.

The "diversity of industry" argument is intended to be used as a general defence of a Protective system. The assumptions upon which it rests are partly of existing facts and partly of theories. The assumption, for instance, that a country either is suffering, or is in imminent danger of suffering, from a lack of variety in its industrial occupations, is purely an assumption of present fact; while the assumption that Free Trade destroys or prevents diversity of occupation is a theory. No doubt, if the theory is true, it will be an inference from facts; but it does not give rise to an inquiry into evidence of the same direct and simple character as the assumption which was first mentioned.

Now, it is plain that the use of the diversity argument in a Free Trade country implies a belief, either proved or taken for granted, that the variety of industries existing at the time is insufficient to the wants of the community. It must also be admitted that, if it can be shown that there never has in fact been any country in which a sufficient variety of industries did not grow up naturally without Protection, such a proof should materially lessen the alarm of those who believe that a return from Protection to Free Trade will cause employment to be narrowed to a few extractive industries.

Let us, then, keep the argument to one point, and—setting aside for a moment the question whether it is conceivable that Free Trade could prevent the growth of industrial variety—let us examine the actual condition of the United States of America, Victoria, and New South Wales at the time when the argument was used in each of those three countries to justify the abandonment of industrial freedom. Is it, or is it not, the case that either of those countries ever suffered, or was likely to suffer, because the efforts of its population were limited to a few occupations? This is a simple matter of evidence.

§ 6. Look, first, at the industrial condition of the United States in 1789. During the existence of the British dependency all American industries were exposed to the crippling influence of the colonial system, under which the whole trade of the colonies was at the mercy of the English Parliament. This terrible power was used by the English Protectionists entirely in the interests of English manufacturers. Thus, not only were Americans forbidden to trade with any country except England, but the moment an American manufacturing industry showed signs of growth, it was suppressed by Act of Parliament.

Protectionists often ask what country ever reached the manufacturing stage without Protection? Seeing that the principles of Free Trade may be said to have been unknown until the close of last century, it would be just as reasonable to inquire for the name of any country which attained to manufacturing eminence without a system of communication by means of post-horses and hand-signals. Free Trade, like telegraphs and railways, is a modern device, and is directed to the object of all modern human invention: viz., the overcoming of natural obstacles. Still, if this silly question is to be pressed, an answer is easily found—the United States of America.

In the early colonial days, in spite of hostile legislation, many manufacturing industries had so firmly established themselves that their products were able to undersell the English manufacturer in his own market. The consequence in every instance was the same: viz., that the English manufacturer obtained an Act of Parliament prohibiting the export of the American article. A list of the Acts referred to can be found in Mr. Bancroft's "History of the United States," or in Mr. Lecky's "History of England."

Yet, so irresistible is the tendency in a growing community to diversify its occupations, that, in spite of this crushing system of legislative interference, Hamilton, the father of

American Protection, was able to enumerate, in his report on manufactures, no less than seventeen industries as being "firmly established" in the year 1792. The list of these speaks for itself. It is sufficient to note that the iron industry was one of those which had so become "established" without Protection.

§ 7. The recent history of the United States furnishes another instance of the spontaneous development of manufactures in a growing community, in despite of the competition of older and powerful rivals. The Western States of America, in their early days, stood towards the Eastern in precisely that industrial relation which, according to Protectionists, makes diversity of industry impossible without Protection. In the West the extractive industries were exceptionally profitable. In the East there were old-established and important manufactures. In the West the average rate of wages was, and still is in some States, about twice as high as that prevailing in the East. The rate of interest in the East was, and is, from six to two per cent. lower than in the West. The Eastern manufacturer thus has all the advantages which, according to Protectionists, are essential to the successful establishment of manufactures: viz., low wages, cheap capital, acquired skill, established business connections, traditions of manufacturing industry, a wealthy and settled population—everything, in short, which makes the competition of an older rival irresistible. If the Protectionist theories are true, the Western States would still be communities of miners, pastoralists, or farmers. They would never have enjoyed the blessings of a varied industrial life unless they had been able to Protect themselves by tariffs against the "inundation" of Eastern goods. That bracing and delicious life within factory walls, which (in Protectionist speeches) the farmer and the miner are always supposed to be desiderating, could never have been opened to the man of the West unless he had consented to reduce his wages or to take a lower return for his capital!

Yet, what are the facts?

There has always been absolute Free Trade between all the States of the Union. Goods pass as freely from Pennsylvania to California as they would pass from Pennsylvania to Toronto if the obstacles of legislation were removed. The Western manufacturer has always been "at the mercy of" his Eastern rival. In the meantime, the industry of the Western States has been steadily diversified. Towns have grown up, at first as reservoirs for agricultural produce or as mining centres; and as population has come together, manufactures have been established. At the present time a large number of manufacturing industries are carried on in California, giving employment to about twenty thousand persons. A similar development is taking place in all the Western States. Their manufactures of woollens, certain grades of leather and iron goods, are not only able to supply the local demand, but to hold their own in competition with the produce of Eastern factories in every part of the Union.

This instance of industrial progress in the Western States of America has a particular significance to Australians.

The only serious rival to Australian manufacturers is Great Britain—the imports from other countries being insignificant compared with those from the motherland. Now, the difference between the industrial conditions of Australia and Great Britain is no greater than that between the conditions of California and New York.

There is, no doubt, a greater difference between Australia and England in the rates paid to the lowest grade of unskilled labour than there is, in respect to the same class of labour, between any two States of the Union; but the difference between wages in manufacturing industries in England and Australia is not so great as the difference between the same class of wages in Pennsylvania and California; while in other respects, the comparison between Australia and England is strikingly similar to that between the Eastern and Western States.

What reason, then, can be suggested why England and Australia should not trade together, which would not equally apply to trade across the American continent? If in the face of Eastern competition the Western States develop a variety of industries, is not the alarm of Australian Protectionists lest manufactures can never be established here in the face of English competition, exaggerated and unfounded? Can any reason be suggested why the industrial progress of Australia should be different from that of the Western States?

If it be said that California and Pennsylvania are parts of a "political entity," to which the economic entity should be compelled to correspond, the reply is obvious. England and Australia are equally parts of a political entity! And if it be urged that the political connection between England and Australia is not likely to continue, the value of the reply is not lessened. The basis of any sound "political entity" must be a living sentiment of national unity; and, whatever may be the future of Australia, no one can pretend at present that she is not connected with England by ties of race, speech, and nationality, which are stronger than any political forms. The differences between the inhabitants of the Southern, Eastern, and Western States of America in race, manners, religion, even language itself, are far greater than the differences between Englishmen and Australians; yet a "Nationalist" economist allows Spanish Florida, French Louisiana, and Mexican Texas to trade with one another and with Puritan New England, but prophesies every sort of disaster if Australia continues to trade with England.

§ 8. Let us now turn from America to Australasia, and examine the actual conditions of the latter country, in order to ascertain whether they give any colour to the assertion that a young country cannot diversify its industries without Protection.

Australia furnishes a striking instance of two colonies, of

[Pt. IV., Ch. iii., § 8.]

similar industrial conditions, of no great inequality in natural advantages — since the physical advantages of New South Wales are more than equalled by the advantages of early development which Victoria owes to her concentrated and well-watered territory—living under similar forms of government, and resembling each other in all respects save that one has adopted Protection and the other has adhered to industrial freedom. No other countries, past or present, offer so excellent an occasion for studying the effects of different fiscal policies. At present we are only dealing with the supposed effect of Protection in securing and maintaining a diversity of industries. It is a striking illustration of the impotence of legislation to control in any material degree the operation of economic forces, that after twenty-five years of Protection in Victoria and Free Trade in New South Wales, there is no great difference between the two colonies in the diversification of their industries. If any difference exists, it is in favour of New South Wales. There is a greater variety of industry in the Free Trade colony than in the Protected. This is, no doubt, owing to the operation of other causes than the absence of Protection, but it is a very strong piece of evidence against the theory that industrial variety cannot exist in a young community without Protection.

Even in Victoria, Protectionists will find it hard to prove that the industrial diversification which now exists would not have been without the tariff. In 1866, the last year of Free Trade, there were no less than 735 manufacturing establishments within the colony, giving employment to 12,127 persons out of a population of 651,899.

Who can say, with the experience of the Western States of America before him, that the industries which have sprung up during the last twenty-three years are wholly owing to the tariff? And still more, who can count or estimate the industries which the tariff has destroyed or stifled in their birth? A comparison of the industries in existence in 1866 with those of 1889 shows that, whatever Protection may have done in the way of creating new industries, it has materially discouraged some of the old industries—notably the industries of ship-building and meat-preserving.

But if there is little or nothing in the history of Victoria to justify the belief that without Protection there must be industrial uniformity, there is still less in the history of New South Wales.

The "industrial uniformity" of Free Trade New South Wales in 1889 consisted of 109 distinct varieties of manufacturing industries. The number of establishments was 3,106, and the number of hands employed was 45,564, while the value of the plant was £5,743,025, and the horse-power of the machinery was 24,990. The list of manufactures in the official returns made by the manufacturers, whose interest it is to minimise their success, shows that, so far from New South Wales being in any immediate risk of becoming a purely pastoral community, the progress of manufactures has been such that most articles of common use can now be made in the country, from a pearl button to a steam-engine.

Still, it may be said, great as is the manufacturing progress of New South Wales, it might have been even greater under a system of Protection. Conceivably it might. But that is not the question immediately at issue. Time enough later to consider whether greater progress in that direction would have been possible or healthy. The pressing question is, "Are Protectionists right when they urge New South Wales to abandon Free Trade in order to secure diversity of industry?" Where, we ask, is the evidence that variety is lacking? Where is the proof that your alarms are well founded? The proportion of our manufacturing to our agricultural and pastoral population is well up to the average. The number of our industries is large and increasing. Where, then, are the signs that the cause of our inconveniences is an excessive concentration upon pastoral pursuits? Can they point to any country of

[t. IV., Ch. iii., § 9.]

modern times which was prevented from diversifying its industries for want of Protection? If they cannot, the first and principal assumption of the diversity argument, when it is used in a Free Trade country, is unsupportable by facts. There is not, in fact, any lack of variety in the industrial occupations of a Free Trade people who inhabit a young community whose resources are great and expanding.

Let us now test the argument by theory, in order to discover, if possible, to what extent it is probable that Protection can ever be a necessary condition of industrial variety.

§ 9. The first assumption of the diversity argument—viz., that without Protection there can be no sufficient industrial variety in a young country—has now been tested by reference to facts, and it has been shown that the assumption is, at least, not supported by evidence. All young countries with which we are acquainted have developed many natural resources without Protection, while there is no evidence that any of them has been prevented from doing so by the existence of Free Trade. It remains to test the assumption by reference to theory. Protectionists cannot complain of this test, for until they advance facts in support of their assertion it can only be tested by the probabilities which are derived from a consideration of general principles.

It has already been pointed out that when a State is first settled the energies of its people are so largely directed to the extractive industries that there is no supply of spare labour available for manufactures on a large scale.

It does not, however, follow that there will be no other avenues of employment. Even a pastoral community—and pastoralism is the simplest of the extractive industries—requires houses, clothes, tools, and conveyances; while, as Professor Fawcett, among others, has pointed out, "However purely agricultural the industry of a country may be, there must always be a great deal of work to be done which will provide

S

many different kinds of employment besides the mere tilling of the land. Houses and other buildings have to be erected, roads have to be made, agricultural implements and machinery have to be repaired, and the cost of carriage will make many articles, especially those of a bulky kind, so expensive to import that, although labour may be dearer in a new country, it will be found cheaper to make the articles at home. The various trades and handicrafts which are thus called into existence will create an increasing demand for skilled labour, and in this way that industrial uniformity about which the Protectionists express so much alarm will be avoided." ("Free Trade and Protection," p. 77.)

But none of the young communities of modern times is devoted exclusively either to pastoral or agricultural pursuits. They follow all the extractive industries simultaneously. Now, nothing more conduces to the concentration of the population and the growth of towns than mining. Consequently, in any country where minerals abound the domestic industries, which are inevitably created by the growth of towns, are sure to gain a firm footing.

It would therefore appear that under any conceivable circumstances the cry about a country suffering "from the stagnation of a single industry" is both exaggerated and ridiculous. No community can exist without a great variety of industries which no foreign competition can destroy. The true question, when the diversity argument is stripped of its exaggerations, is, "Whether a State can pass from the agricultural to the manufacturing stage without the assistance of a Protective tariff."

§ 10. Now, the successful prosecution of manufactures on a large scale depends upon the concurrence of two conditions, namely:—

1. A large and concentrated population.
2. A supply of available capital.

Pt. IV., Ch. iii., § 10.]

It is sometimes asserted that Protection encourages immigration, and thus stimulates the increase of population. This assertion, although it is not demonstrably incorrect, is not supported by proof. Such evidence as can be obtained points rather the other way. Since the adoption of Protection by Victoria there has been a steady stream of emigration from that colony to Free Trade New South Wales, as was disclosed by the often-quoted report of Mr. Hayter on the census of 1881.[1] The emigration of young men from the colony of Victoria is particularly noticeable, in view of the Protectionist assertion that Protection provides employment.

It will be imitating a Protectionist method of argument to assert that New South Wales gained the whole of this population from her southern neighbour on account of the superior attractions of her Free Trade policy. But the fact of the decrease in Victoria during ten years of Protection certainly does not predispose the mind to a ready belief in the unsupported prophecy of Protectionists, that their policy will increase population.

Nor does American experience justify Protectionists in this assertion. The figures of immigration into the United States have been analysed by Professor Sumner ("Protectionism," p. 122), with the result that nine-tenths of the immigrants are shown to be labourers, domestic servants, farmers, and others who belong to trades which are not Protected, and whose arrival cannot therefore be attributed to the operation of a Protective duty.

Suppose, however, for a moment that Protection does encourage immigration. This is a curious result to be brought about by those who invariably declare themselves the enemies of immigration. A tax to increase the supply of labour very soon becomes a tax to lower wages; so that there seems some inconsistency between the argument that Protection

---

[1] See below, Appendix III.

raises wages and the argument that it increases the number of the wage-receivers.

Moreover, it is worth considering whether any rapid increase of population—even although it causes the establishment of manufactures as one result—is altogether desirable to a young community. The absence of poverty, the easier conditions of life, the higher standard of comfort, which are characteristics of a young country, are owing in no small degree to the strong position which the labourer occupies in making his bargain with employers, in consequence of the limited number of his competitors. The man who desires to introduce the pressure of population into a young country must also be prepared to face the evils of an old.

But if it is conceivable (although unproved) that Protection may assist the encouragement of manufactures by stimulating immigration, there is certainly no ground for any fear that Free Trade will operate as a hindrance to new settlers. That which attracts population to a young community is precisely that which is an obstacle to the establishment of manufactures : namely, the profitableness of the extractive industries. So long as the natural fertility of the soil enables much to be produced with little effort, so long will immigrants pour into a country of high wages and large profits. It was the discovery of gold, and not the Protective tariff, that caused the rush of population to Victoria ; and it is the vast expanse of fertile land that draws the annual stream of immigrants to the United States.

The second requisite to manufacturing development is an abundance of capital. Now, the profits of capital in a young country are usually large, because the demand of the old world for raw produce is very great, and, owing to the assistance of nature, is easily supplied. But, as capital accumulates, and the natural advantages of the country become exhausted, new openings for investment will naturally be sought. Will these be sought in the country or outside ? Can the answer be in doubt ? At any rate, no one whose professed faith is belief in the nation as the industrial unit ought to hesitate a moment in his reply!

Let it, then, be granted that a time will come when the spare capital of the country can no longer find a satisfactory investment in the extractive industries—what is more likely to attract attention than a further development of natural resources, in order to supply the young community with articles that it has hitherto imported?

But the more vigorous the foreign trade, the larger is the home production; and the larger the home production, the greater the opportunities for saving money. Accordingly, a large import trade is the surest sign that foreign industries will soon be naturalised; and the fear of industrial uniformity is groundless so long as the capital of the community continues reproductive, and natural resources remain to be developed.

The conclusion is thus reached that, just as there is no known instance of industrial variety being prevented by Free Trade, so is there no *à priori* reason that such should be the case. Once grant that individuals seek their own gain, and are alive to their own interests, and that the conditions of a country are such as to encourage a rapid growth of population and a large accumulation of capital—and the tendency to develop new industries continues with gathering strength until every natural resource has been exhausted.

Manufactures will spring up in every State as need arises, for then the demand for their products will be sufficient to ensure a profit. Protection, by creating an artificial demand, may hurry their growth by a few years; but Free Trade is not an obstacle to manufactures, but rather an assurance that they will be planted in a healthy soil, and grow to maturity. "The development of society is as regular and as natural as that of a plant, and there is no more need of human interference than there is to make a bud burst into blossom at the proper time. It is a development, moreover, which cannot be hastened without injury. A new country cannot have the higher social development until its population begins to grow dense. It is so in America yet. We have not the literature, or the science, or the fine arts of the old countries; but we have not their poverty and misery. We must take our advantages and disadvantages together." (Sumner's "History of Protection," p. 26.) This is the answer to Protectionists in a young community who complain of its industrial uniformity. Free Trade is no obstacle to a natural diversity of occupation which is sufficient for the present needs of any growing country, and is free from the risks and disorders of that rickety diversity which is the untimely fruit of legislative labour.

§ 11. We have already considered the argument that Protection causes a diversity of industry by the tests of fact and theory, and endeavoured to show that young countries do not, in fact, suffer from industrial uniformity, and that, if they did, there is no reason why they should not find a remedy under a policy of unrestricted trade.

It remains to point out that, even if all the force is given to the argument which Protectionists demand for it, there are certain natural limits to diversity which no legislation can ever pass. It must never be forgotten, when Protection is extolled because it causes a diversity of industry, that there is an impassable limit to diversification set by Nature herself.

It has been well said that "there is a natural law in operation which as surely determines the number required for each great class of employment as do the natural laws which locally determine the times and relative heights of the tide. No social advancement . . . can ever alter the relative numbers of the various branches of human service."[1] That

[1] Extract from paper read by R. M. Johnston, Government Statistician of Tasmania, before the Australasian Association for the Advancement of Science, at Melbourne, 1890 (p. 9). Mr. Johnston gives (p. 11) a valuable table showing the proportional classification of the occupation of all persons engaged in the supply of home wants. The highest proportion employed in industrial occupations is in England: viz., 24·5, as against 7·6 in the United States.

which determines the numbers required for each class in any country is the condition of its leading industries.

In a country where dominating industries are pastoral or agricultural, the proportion of industrial employees must be comparatively small; while in a country like Great Britain, which is pre-eminently a manufacturing country, the number will be large. Until a country has exhausted the profitable occupation of its soil, whether in the cultivation of iron or search for minerals, no amount of Protection can draw labour and capital to other industries without inflicting a dangerous check to national development.

Even in the United States, where Protection has run mad, the proportion of industrial bread-winners is, according to Mr. Johnston's figures, only 7·6 of the entire population; while in England it is 24·5.[1] While, if "industrial" occupations are still further sub-divided so as to place manufactures in a separate class, it is usually estimated that not more than one person in ten can, under any circumstances, find employment in that channel. Nor can this number be safely anticipated in a country which, like the United States or Australia, is still in the agricultural stage. But, whatever may be the precise proportion which manufactures ought to bear to agriculture or to mining, the point to remember is that it cannot be safely exceeded. A country like England, which exports its manufactured goods to every corner of the world, can enlarge the proportion which its manufacturing employees bear to its own population, because they are engaged in supplying the wants of other countries. But a country which cannot export its manufactures can only safely permit the existence of a sufficient number of employees to supply its own wants.

The practical rule to be deduced from these obvious reflections is that manufactures should be allowed to find their own level. If an attempt is made to forcibly divert labour from agricultural to manufacturing pursuits, there is an almost

[1] In Free Trade New South Wales in 1889 it was 6·5.

certain danger of over-production; while if manufactures are allowed to grow up as they are required, they will be able, having originated under open competition, to extend their market as they increase their production. Nothing is more striking in commercial history than the inability of American manufacturers to compete with England in a neutral market. While England every year sends from twenty to thirty million pounds' worth of manufactured goods into the United States, in despite of the heavy tariff, the whole export of American manufactures to all parts of the world seldom exceeds a value of ten millions.

It is as certain as any forecast of the future can be, that so long as America adheres to Protection Great Britain need have no fear of her commercial rivalry; but when America adopts Free Trade the tables will be turned, and England, in all probability, will be beaten out of many neutral markets.

The impossibility, then, of increasing manufacturing industries beyond a certain point, unless the industries are such that they can face the competition of the world, is a consideration which should make Protectionists pause before proposing to hurry the establishment of many industries. The results of interference with commerce are hardly ever calculable, and no one can foresee in any country all the consequences of Protection. We cannot accurately estimate either the demand for manufactured goods or the supply of available labour; we cannot tell beforehand what would be the result of higher prices for manufactures upon the dominating pursuits of the country, and we hardly even know accurately the number or strength of our existing industries. Under such circumstances, the man takes upon himself a heavy responsibility who proposes to interfere by Act of Parliament with the distribution of employment. It may be true that the future is obscure, so that even the clearest-sighted despair at times; but steady faith in man and nature is better than rash play with unknown forces. Things may be bad, and the remedy may not be visible; but it would be the very blindness of unwisdom to attempt to solve the problem without knowing the factors or possessing any test of the result.

§ 12. Nor must it be forgotten that, even if diversity be gained, there is another aspect to the question besides that which is presented by the manufacturers. It is possible to pay too high a price even for the advantage of industrial diversity.

"Development of natural resources," "variety of occupation," and such large phrases, bear a different significance to the man who pays for the development and the variety and to the man who receives the money. The natural-resource theory is admirably comforting to the man who owns the resource; but the man who does not own it sees the theory in another light.

Professor Sumner has thrown the question into an amusing dialogue, which contains none the less of sound sense and good economics than if it were expressed in a more professorial style.

"A man," says Professor Sumner, "discovered iron when there was no duty on imported iron. On the Protectionist doctrine, he won't collect tools and go to work. He goes to Washington, he visits the statesman, and a dialogue takes place:—

"Ironman: Mr. Statesman, I have found an iron deposit on my farm.

"Statesman: Have you, indeed? That is good news. Our country is richer by one new natural resource than we had supposed.

"Ironman: Yes; and I now want to begin mining iron.

"Statesman: Very well; go on. We shall be glad to hear that you are prospering and growing rich.

"Ironman: Yes, of course; but I am now earning my living by tilling the surface of the ground, and I am afraid that I cannot make as much at mining as at farming.

"Statesman: That is indeed another matter. Look into that carefully, and do not leave a better industry for a worse.

"Ironman: But I want to mine that iron. It does not seem right to leave it in the ground when we are importing iron all the time; but I cannot see a profit in it at the present prices for imported iron. I thought perhaps that you would put a tax on imported iron, so that I could sell mine at a profit. Then I could see my way to give up farming, and go in for mining.

"Statesman: You do not think what you ask. That would be to throw on your neighbour the risk of working the mine which you are afraid to take yourself.

"Ironman (aside): I have not talked the right dialect to this man. I must begin all over again. (Aloud.) Mr. Statesman, the natural resources of this continent ought to be developed. American industry must be protected. The American miner must not be forced to compete with the pauper labour of Europe.

"Statesman: Now I understand you. Now you talk business. Why did you not say so before? How much tax do you want?

"The next time that a buyer of pig iron goes to market to get some, he finds that it costs thirty bushels of wheat per ton instead of twenty. 'What has happened to pig iron?' says he. 'Oh! haven't you heard?' is the reply. 'A new mine has been found down in Pennsylvania. We have got a new "natural resource."'

"'I haven't got a new natural resource,' says he. 'It is as bad for me as if the grasshoppers had eaten up one-third of my crop.'"

It would be a good day for the public if the discussion of politics could always be conducted in this simple language. At present, politicians are the only persons, except preachers and art critics, who are thought the more of for talking nonsense! For the picture drawn by Professor Sumner is not in the least exaggerated. The third chapter of Mr. Taussig's most useful work contains numerous illustrations from American experience which are equally grotesque. The most instructive are the duties upon emery, nickel, and copper.

Up to 1864, nickel had been admitted into the States duty-free; but shortly before this date a nickel mine was discovered in Pennsylvania. The opportunity for developing a natural resource was too great, especially as the mine was owned by an influential politician. In 1864 a duty of 15 per cent. was imposed on nickel, and in 1870 the duty was raised to 30 cents per pound, or about 40 per cent. on the value. No other nickel mine has been discovered, and the fortunate proprietor, Mr. Joseph Wharton, is now a millionaire, and joins with Mr. Carnegie in his praises of democracy. It is, perhaps, needless to add that Mr. Wharton is a determined opponent of any reduction of the duty upon nickel. Mr. Wharton is also the founder of the "Wharton School of Finance and Economy" in Philadelphia, and, in the opinion apparently that restrictions, which are so desirable upon the sale of nickel, would be equally applicable to the study of economics, he has expressly enjoined that the professor shall teach Protection; or, in the words of the deed of gift, "how, by suitable tariff legislation, a nation may keep its productive industry alive, cheapen the cost of commodities, and oblige foreigners to sell to it at low prices, while contributing largely towards defraying the expense of its government." It is not mentioned in the deed of gift whether the Whartonian professor is allowed to teach the best means of "cheapening the cost of the commodity," nickel. The present holder of the Chair is the Mr. Patten whose work in defence of Protection has already been referred to.

Copper has fared the same as nickel. Previously to 1869 copper ore was imported from Chili, and was smelted and refined in Boston and Baltimore. But during the years immediately preceding 1869, the great copper mines of Lake Superior had begun to be worked on a considerable scale.

These mines, under ordinary conditions, could have supplied the whole of the United States more cheaply and abundantly than any other country; yet, as Professor Taussig points out, "through the tariff policy these very mines have caused Americans for many years to pay more for their copper than is paid in any other country." The table compiled by Professor Taussig (p. 263), from "The Mineral Resources of the United States," of the prices of copper in London and New York from 1875 to 1886, is conclusive on this point. The process was simple. The duty having shut out foreign copper, a copper trust was formed, which has embraced the new mines one by one as they were opened, and the output of copper was limited so as to keep the price just below that at which copper would have been imported. Needless to add that all the "copper kings" are staunch Protectionists.[1]

But it is unnecessary to multiply examples. American experience is open to all to see. Can Australians hope to escape these evils? No wonder that, with the results before his eyes of the discovery in America of nickel and copper,

[1] The Hon. David A. Wells, on page 23 of his "Practical Economics," has collected some of the more striking examples of American efforts to secure industrial variety. "About 1826 to 1828," he says, "the discovery of the lead mines at Galena, Ill., became generally known, and as the first reports were to the effect that the deposits were of such unparalleled richness, purity, magnitude, and easy accessibility, as to make it only a matter of time when the whole world, from sheer inability to compete, would become wholly dependent for its supplies of lead on this one locality, it was at once considered desirable by many people to establish it, so far as fiscal legislation could do it, on a most extraordinary economic principle, and one which from that day to this has proved popular in all tariff enactments in the United States: and this was to make the discovery or recognition of the existence of any great natural advantages—either in the way of mines, soils, climatic advantages, forests, means of intercommunication, or national characteristics—the immediate occasion for cursing the country by the creation or imposition of some new tax, thereby making dear what was before cheap; endeavouring to work up to a state of abundance through conditions of scarcity artificially created and unnecessarily perpetuated. In this particular instance the principle was exemplified by raising the duty on lead imported in pigs and bars from one cent a pound to three cents."

Pt. IV., Ch. iii., § 13.]

Professor Sumner firmly hopes that tin may not be found. "At the present time," he says, "we have all the tin that we want above ground, because beneficent Nature has refrained from putting any underground in our territory." In the metal schedule, tin is alone free. Should a tin-mine be discovered, the next thing will be a tax on tin of 40 per cent. "The mine-owners say they want to exploit the mine. They do not. They want to make the mine an excuse to exploit the tax-payers." ("Protectionism," p. 53.) Since these words were written, tin has been discovered in the States, and duties on tin-plate have been a prominent feature in the M'Kinley tariff, as many Western canners have already discovered, to their loss.

§ 13. Finally, let the diversity argument have all the strength Protectionists attribute to it: it can never be used as a general defence of a restrictive policy. It rests, as we have seen, on the three assumptions that industry has not, in fact, diversified under Free Trade; that it cannot do so; and that Protection is the best means of causing a diversification.

Now, it is plain that the first two of these assumptions may be true of one industry and not of another; accordingly, whenever the argument is used, it will be necessary to ask for more precision. "What are the new industries which it is desired to establish? and what is to be the rate of duty?" It is most noticeable that Protectionists are always silent upon these questions when they are before constituencies. "The art of taxation," Colbert is reported to have said, "is the art of plucking the goose so as to get the largest possible amount of feathers with the least possible squealing." It would never do, therefore, to let the people know beforehand the nature of the coming taxes. Much better to let everybody think that the tax will fall on his neighbour's back. When gifted legislators meet in caucus, matters can be arranged so much more satisfactorily—to the manufacturers certainly, and possibly to the legislators! Thus the policy of the Protectionist party on the hustings must always be a policy of silence and conceal ment. The strongest argument Free Traders can desire is that no Protectionist leader ever dares to say beforehand either what taxes he requires, or what is to be their amount, or for how long they are to be imposed.

CHAPTER IV.

THE HOME-MARKET ARGUMENT.

§ 1. THE home-market argument is best known in the story of the Irishman who complained that a dollar in New York went no further than a shilling in Dublin. "Then, why did you not stop in Dublin?" was the question of a bystander. "Because there I couldn't get the shilling!" was Pat's reply. This is the platform presentation of the argument. In treatises which pretend to be serious it has three distinct forms or varieties. Sometimes it is used in defence of Protection as a means of rendering a community less dependent upon foreigners in the event of war; at others, as a means of extending or strengthening the market of the local agriculturist in time of peace; while in its more recent developments the necessity of enlarging the home market is insisted upon as the only means of disposing of the surplus from extractive industries.

The economic basis of the argument in all its varieties is that misapprehension of the comparative importance of the home and foreign trade of a community which confused even Adam Smith. The passage is well known. "Capital," he says, "employed in purchasing in one part of the country in order to sell in another part the produce of the industries of that country, generally replaces by such operation two distinct capitals that had both been employed in its agriculture or manufactures, and thus enables them to continue that employment. . . . . The capital employed in purchasing foreign goods for home consumption, when the purchase is made by the produce of domestic industry, replaces, too, by every such operation, two distinct capitals; but one of them only is employed in supporting domestic industry. . . . The other supports foreign industry, and, therefore, foreign trade will give but one-half the encouragement to the industry or productive labour of a country that domestic or internal trade does."

The fallacy of this proposition is in the assumption that the capital which is left unused in consequence of the diversion of the capital, which set it in motion, from the home to the foreign trade will continue to be unused after the diversion has been effected. It is true that trade between England and Scotland will replace both an English and a Scotch capital; and that if the trade be diverted from Scotland to Portugal, it will replace an English and a Portuguese capital. But the Scotch capital is not thereby destroyed, but remains available for new undertakings.

Mr. Henry George ("Protection or Free Trade," p. 117) exposes the fallacy with an admirable lucidity. "If," he says, "we substitute for the terms used by Adam Smith other terms of the same relation, we may obtain, with equal validity, such propositions as this: If Episcopalians trade with Presbyterians, two profits are made by Protestants; whereas, when Presbyterians trade with Catholics, only one profit goes to Protestants. Therefore, trade between Protestants is twice as profitable as trade between Protestants and Catholics.

"In Adam Smith's illustration there are two quantities of British goods — one in Edinburgh and one in London. In the domestic trade which he supposes, these two quantities of British goods are exchanged; but if the Scotch goods be sent to Portugal instead of to England, and Portuguese goods brought back, only one quantity of British goods is exchanged. There will be only one-half the replacement in Great Britain, but there has been only one-half the displacement. The Edinburgh goods which have been sent away have been replaced with Portuguese goods; but the London goods have not been replaced with anything, because they are still there. In the one case twice the amount of British capital is employed as in the other, and consequently, double returns show equal profitableness."

It is astonishing that such a patent fallacy should have misled any one; but Mr. Hoyt, in his eighth chapter, accepts the argument with guileless confidence as a basis of his own view of the theory that the "home market ought to be preserved for home producers:" a maxim which, as Mr. George observes, is in the same category with "*Keep our own appetites for our own cookery*," or "*Keep our own transportation for our own legs!*"

§ 2. Passing now from the supposed economic basis of the home-market argument to its various political props, we shall find that the earliest of these is the dread of an interception of foreign commerce in time of war. This alarm underlies the older mercantile theory of commerce, and pervades the writings of List, Carey, and the earlier Protectionists.

It is, indeed, as Professor Fawcett has observed ("Free Trade and Protection," p. 82), "the only logical basis on which a Protective system can be supported; for if it could be assumed that the normal condition of a country was to be perpetually at war with its neighbours, it would become of the first importance to make it, as far as possible, industrially independent of them. Under such circumstances it might be expedient, at whatever cost, to impose Protective duties with the view of establishing and maintaining various branches of home industry." But can any such assumption be made? Can any conjuncture of circumstances be imagined under which a country with the extensive seaboard of Australia or America, and with their means of commanding supplies from all quarters of the globe, should be unable to import? As

Professor Fawcett points out, even when the facilities of transportation were far inferior to what they are at present—namely, during the wars of the first Napoleon—"there was never a moment even in his unparalleled career of military aggression when all the coasts and all the frontiers of France were so completely blockaded that no foreign product could find its way to her markets."

Assuming, however, that the danger lest any country, in these days of steam and electricity, could be so completely surrounded both by sea and land with foreign foes that it was unable to import any foreign supplies is not wholly imaginary, the question still remains whether the premium for insurance against it is not excessive. The argument then descends into the region of finance, and turns upon the cheapest means of guaranteeing to a particular country the continuous supply of a certain quantity of goods.

Now, it is apparent that since this argument rests on the assumption that the goods in question cannot be produced against foreign competition, the profitable selling price of the home-made article must be higher than that of the imported. In other words, Protection, in this case at any rate, will raise prices.

It becomes, therefore, a simple matter of calculation whether the cost to the community of this increase in prices is not out of proportion to the risk which the expenditure is thought to insure. The salt tax in France, which Professor Fawcett mentions as an illustration of the argument, because it is supported on the ground that without Protection the French might be deprived of this necessity in time of war, has raised the price of salt by a halfpenny a pound. This means a burden of £720,000 a year upon the French consumer.

Seeing that a war such as the alarmist contemplates is not likely to happen more than once in one hundred years, it would be manifestly cheaper to remit the tax and spend

T

£100,000 a year in the purchase of salt, and distribute this from the Government stores when the necessity arose.

It is difficult to deal with such considerations seriously.

§ 3. The second form in which the home-market argument appeared has almost lost its force with the cheapening of transport and the improvement in the means of locomotion. It has, however, played a prominent part in the controversies, and still retains a lingering vitality, so that some examination of it is required.

It is thus stated by List, as usual, in many words (p. 262, Eng. Trans.):—

> "The foreign commerce," he says, "of agricultural nations of the temperate zone, so long as it is limited to provisions and raw materials, cannot attain to importance.
>
> "Firstly, because the exports of the agricultural nation are directed to a few manufacturing nations, which themselves carry on agriculture, and which, indeed, because of their manufactures and their extended commerce, carry it on on a much more perfect system than the mere agricultural nation. This export trade is therefore neither certain nor uniform. The trade in mere products is always a matter of extraordinary speculation, whose benefits fall most to the speculative merchants, but not to the agriculturists or the productive power of the agricultural nation.
>
> "Secondly, because the exchange of agricultural products for foreign manufactured goods is liable to be greatly interrupted by the commercial restrictions of foreign States and by wars.
>
> "Thirdly, because the exports of mere products chiefly benefit countries which are situated near sea-coasts and the banks of navigable rivers, and does not benefit the inland territory, which constitutes the greater part of the territory of the agricultural nation.
>
> "Fourth, and finally, because the foreign manufacturing nation may find it to its interest to procure its means of subsistence and raw materials from other countries and newly formed colonies."

The bare statement of these views is their best refutation.

In truth, commerce follows its natural channels. The foreign trade of a young country is in the surplus of its extractive industries, and that trade is neither more nor less uncertain or varied than trade in manufactured products. The probability, indeed, is that a trade in the necessaries of life is likely to be larger and more steady than one in manufactured articles, which depends to some extent on fashion or caprice, and is liable at any time to be disturbed by changes in the processes of production, or in the pressure of new competitors.

Secondly, a foreign trade in the export of raw materials is far less likely to be interrupted by war than a trade in manufactures, on account of the greater value of such articles to foreign countries. England, for example, would make more strenuous efforts to maintain a continuous supply of raw cotton than of Yankee notions—yet, according to List, trade in the former is more likely "to be interrupted by the commercial restrictions of foreign States and by war."

List's third reason for preferring a home market—"that exports of mere products chiefly benefit countries which are situated near the sea-coasts"—has entirely lost any value which it might have once possessed, in consequence of the improvement in the means of locomotion. The existence and prosperity of the Western States of America and Canada is quite a sufficient answer to the theory that a foreign trade in natural products only benefits a coastal State.

As to List's fourth reason—"that a foreign manufacturing State may stop buying its food or raw materials from abroad"—can any one name any reason why there is not precisely the same danger of an interruption to commerce when the articles exchanged are manufactured goods? Why should a country be less likely to give up the importation of manufactured goods than to give up the importation of food? Surely these professors of Restriction have but little faith in their own theories!

If all countries became their disciples, each would manufacture for itself, and the country which would suffer most from such a change would be that which had been the first to act upon their maxims, and replace the export of food by the export of manufactures.

Again, the appeal must be made to common sense. People abroad buy food and raw materials because they require these things. The country which sells them does so because the sale is profitable. The same rules affect a trade in manufactured goods. Neither is, by its nature, more profitable, more certain, or more steady than the other; that one is likely to possess these attributes in the highest degree which arises out of natural conditions, and is pursued spontaneously by individuals seeking their own advantage.

§ 4. But what shall be said of Mr. Patten—the Whartonian professor? If List preferred a home market because a foreign trade was precarious, the latest oracle—warned, no doubt, by the periodic recurrence of commercial crises, even within the limits of Protected countries—has abandoned this reason, and justifies his preference on the ground that a home market causes the land of a community to be put to new uses. These are the steps of his reasoning:—"There is a foreign demand for one class of crops and not for another; the foreigner takes wheat, and whilst that demand lasts American land is put under wheat, and will always remain under wheat until a home market arises; because until that event happens no one will require any other product of the land. An extension of the home market is required to find new uses for the land." And the proof is that, since Protection corn has been grown in the Western States, "the heavier lands were brought into cultivation, as the home market created a demand for corn instead of wheat".[1]

---

[1] The full text of the argument is subjoined:—" The first settlers, instead of coming upon the best lands, are actually forced to cultivate many of the poorer soils which are easily brought into cultivation, or which are peculiarly adapted to the cultivation of those crops for which there is a foreign demand. For this reason some change in the demand of food must precede the best use of the land of a country. Some new market must be opened up which will

[Pt. IV., Ch. iv., § 5.]

What a blessed consummation of the Whartonian policy, that the Western farmer should change his crop from wheat to maize! But does it really matter to the Western farmer what he grows, provided he gets his price for it? And is the American the only man on earth to whom he could have sold his maize? What, too, of the wheat-growers? What consolation is it to them for the fall in value of the lighter lands which were first used for wheat that the heavier corn lands now command a higher price?

Surely the argument needs no serious answer; and perhaps Mr. Patten—the professor who, by the terms of his appointment, is not allowed to be impartial[1]—is more to be pitied than blamed for having used it.

§ 5. But it is not with arguments like those of Professors List and Patten that the agricultural voter is beguiled, but with others which are more enticing. Put in its most

---

afford a place where the new crops can be sold, thus enabling the producers to use their land in a better manner; with which extension of the home market new uses for the land are found, and at the same time many classes of soil, which were worthless while the few crops demanded by foreigners were produced, now become the more productive part of the land. This fact is clearly illustrated in the changes of value in Western lands which have followed the creation of home markets. The lighter soils were first occupied because better adapted to the cultivation of wheat. These soils commanded a higher price than the heavier lands so long as the main market for the West was in Europe. But when the growth of home markets created a demand for corn instead of wheat, the heavier lands were brought into use, and soon became to be regarded as the better land; and at the present time they command a much higher price than do the lighter lands which were first used for wheat."

[1] It will be remembered that Mr. Wharton, the founder of Mr. Patten's Chair, was the fortunate owner of the only nickel deposit in the United States, and in that capacity developed by means of a tax the natural resource of nickel-mining—"put the land, in fact, to a new use," as Mr. Patten would say —with the result that he became a millionaire, and founded a Chair to teach "how by suitable tariff legislation a nation may keep its productive industry alive, cheapen the cost of commodities, and oblige foreigners to sell to it at low prices." What do foreigners sell to the Western farmer? and how has Protection lowered the price of nickel? These are practical questions for Mr. Patten to answer.

effective form, the home-market argument, as used at election-time in country districts, is something like this :—

> "You are, at present, many miles away from the nearest city, which is your only market. You cannot sell to your neighbours, who are all farmers, but must carry all your produce to the city. The cost of transportation will consume the bulk of your profit; and when you get the goods to market you will find yourself undersold by the man who lives a few miles outside the town. What is the remedy? Why, this: To make your market at your own doors, and keep it when it's made. Agree to pay more than we pay now for woollens, and so make it an object for some one to come here and start a manufactory. Make the same agreement in respect of agricultural machinery, furniture, and all farming and domestic implements, so that you will have a town grow up in your midst, and a market at your very doors. You needn't then depend on wheat, but can grow vegetables and other perishable produce, while your wife will sell eggs, and your children find employment in the factory."[1]

It is done. The mill is built: the town grows up. The New England States become the home of manufacturers. And the farmer—what of him? Strange to say, he sells his homestead for less than cost, and flees to the wilds of Dakota. Where is the mistake? The theory is excellent; why will it not work? It is the agreeing to pay *"just a little more"* that has done all the mischief. If the farmers of *this* locality want a woollen mill, those in *that* locality want a cotton mill, and those in the next county an iron furnace, and so on. The result is that the *farmers everywhere pay "a little more" for everything* they buy, until the cost of their living is increased beyond any possible profit from an extended market.

The success of this argument is a remarkable instance of what can be effected by using big words about simple matters. Suppose that a Protectionist, instead of indulging in large expressions about phrases such as a home market, the development of industry, a concentrated population, and

---

[1] The writer is indebted for the form of this argument to a pamphlet by Mr. Graham M'Adam on "The Protective System: what it costs the American Farmer." (New York Free Trade Club, 1880.)

such-like, were to address a country audience in terms like these :—

> "My friends, I am a poor man, but I am anxious to see you sell all your products at a profit. I want nothing to be wasted because of the cost of taking it to market. I propose to bring a market to you by buying your stuff myself."

These sentiments should be received with cheers; but let the orator proceed :—

> "I propose to build myself a fine mansion on the most eligible site in the country. This will give employment to stonecutters, bricklayers, masons, carpenters, joiners, carters, upholsterers, and many other kinds of tradesmen. I intend that all these men shall do their work within the district. I mean that they shall all live about here whilst they are engaged on my job; and, as I intend my mansion to be very large, I calculate that I shall have five hundred men living here for the next ten years building it and putting the grounds in order; and when it is complete in all its adjuncts, I expect to keep a staff of several hundred servants in the house and about the grounds. Think what this means to you. All these men and their families will want food, which you will supply. No more fruit rotting on your trees, no more vegetables going to seed because you can't afford to carry them to market; you and your wives and children will be busy for the rest of your lives in feeding your own neighbours."

Again applause. The orator proceeds :—

> "But, as I said, I am a poor man. I cannot realise my patriotic dreams without your aid. I am short in my necessary capital by the sum of ten thousand pounds. You can have the privilege of aiding in our national development by giving me this amount. I do not ask for it all at once, but in trifling sums. Let each of you give me a shilling a week for the rest of your lives, and I will get to work at once at building my house and laying out its grounds. None of you will feel the expense, and all of you will share in the advantages."

If Protectionist speeches were made in these plain terms, could any protestations of philanthropy disguise their naked selfishness? And yet, instead of "mansion" read "factory," and by the change of this one word we have a regular Protectionist oration in favour of the home market.

The argument, however it may be disguised, must always resolve itself into an appeal to the farmers to subsidise a number of artisans to settle at the farm gate. "Pay them," says the Protectionist, "for making goods at a loss, and out of their profits they will purchase your abundance." A manufacturer who really believed in this argument would pension an army of tramps to live beside his factory upon condition that they spent their money in the purchase of his goods. The three students of fable who hoped to earn a living by taking in each other's washing were the earliest examples of a delusive faith in a home market. The idea that a farmer, if he pays taxes to bring into existence a factory which would not otherwise exist, will win more than the taxes by selling farm produce to the artisans, is, as Professor Sumner has tersely said, "an arithmetical fallacy. It proposes to get three pints out of a quart. The farmer is out for the tax and the farm produce, and he cannot get back more than the tax, because, if the factory owes its existence to the Protective taxes, it cannot make any profit outside of the taxes. The proposition to the farmer that he shall pay taxes to another man, who will bring part of the tax back to buy produce with it : this is to make the farmer rich. The man who owned stock in a railroad, and who rode on it, paying his own fare, in the hope of swelling his own dividends, was wise compared with the farmer who believes that Protection can be a source of gain to him." ("Protectionism," pp. 125-6.)

§ 6. The latest form of this almost discredited home-market argument is one which had a great vogue during the Presidential campaign of 1888. Its author appears to be Mr. Hoyt, who develops it from an American standpoint with great assiduity.[1] The argument is briefly this :—

"Foreigners can only take a certain amount of American products : *i.e.*, food and raw materials. In return for these, Americans

[1] *See* pp. 193 and 199, and Chapter XI.

receive a certain quantity of foreign manufactures. But the American demand for manufactured goods is far larger than the quantity which is received from abroad in return for American products. Accordingly, unless the export of American products can be increased, which ex-hypothesi is impossible to any appreciable extent, Americans must either go without a certain quantity of manufactured goods or manufacture for themselves. Conclusion—Encouragement of manufactures by Protection is necessary."

The fallacy of this argument—which has been freely used by Mr. Reed and Mr. Blaine—lies in the assumption, first, that the export of American products cannot be appreciably increased; and secondly, that if it cannot, manufactures will not spring up without Protection. The first assumption is probably true, if it is limited to the proposition that foreign trade could not supply all the wants of a country like the United States; but the second has no foundation in fact. Suppose it to be the case that the American demand for manufactured goods is so vast that it cannot be satisfied by exchange, that fact is itself the strongest guarantee that home manufacturing will be profitable; because the greater the necessity for manufactured goods, and the less the opportunity of getting them, the better is the prospect for the manufacturer. Consequently, the very fact on which Protectionists rely to frighten the farmers into accepting Protection—namely, the fear that without Protection they will not be able to satisfy their requirements for manufactured articles—is itself the best assurance that Protection is unnecessary.

The argument, moreover, ignores another aspect of Protection which is being forcibly obtruded upon the notice of American manufacturers—namely, the tendency of Protection to destroy the foreign market by too much cultivation of the home market. At the present time, the most serious problem before the manufacturers of the United States is how to dispose of their manufactured goods. The home market has been over-supplied for some years past, and yet, owing to Protection, there is no outlet for their goods abroad. The last work of Mr. Wells—"Practical Economics"—the Congressional speeches on the Mills tariff, and the collection of facts which was published at the Conference of Free Traders held at Chicago in 1888, contain abundant evidence of the truth of this assertion, which is, indeed, not disputed by Protectionists. It would lie beyond the scope of this work to multiply instances. It is sufficient to refer to the words of Mr. Wells upon this subject, which no one who has any knowledge of current American literature is likely to dispute.

> "No one," says Mr. Wells ("Practical Economics" p. 103), "who has given the subject any attention, has any doubt that the United States has, at present, more active capital, machinery, and labour engaged in the so-called work of manufacturing, than is necessary to supply any present or immediate prospective demand for increased consumption. And as general evidence confirmatory of this position, citation may be made, *first*, of the general and increasing complaint on the part of American manufacturers of *over-production*. . . . *Second*, the interruption of great branches of domestic industry, of which examples are to be found in the recent suspension [written in 1883] of the entire business of cotton manufacture in Philadelphia and vicinity; of the discontinuance in all, or great part, of the India-rubber and gunny-bagging manufacture; of the reduction of the sugar-refining industry to about 60 per cent. of its existing capacity; and the suspension or failure of some of the most important iron-furnaces and rolling-mills of the country. And, *third*, the actual or attempted reduction of wages in almost every department of domestic manufacturing industry. the recent united effort for this end of the representatives of all the iron-works west of the Alleghanies being especially noteworthy."

Mr. Wells might have added that the rapid growth of trusts and combinations is further evidence in the same direction.

In the meantime, while the enormous output of home products is steadily increasing, there is an actual decline even in the small proportion of home-made goods which the tariff allows the Americans to send abroad.

The figures for the year ending June 30th, 1890, show that of the total exports, valued at $845,293,000, only $151,293,000 worth, or 17·88 per cent., were of manufactured goods; while the export of American manufactures in 1889 represented 18·99 per cent. of the whole. Purely agricultural productions gave but 72·87 per cent. of the export values in 1889; whereas they gave 74·51 per cent. of the whole in 1890, and the ratio of all natural productions increased from 81·01 to 82·12 per cent.[1]

§ 7. The home-market argument fails at every turn. It rests on a fallacious economic basis, and its political supports are rotten. The foreign trade is not, from its nature, more precarious than the home trade. The home demand does not necessarily cause the land of a community to be put to more profitable uses than a foreign demand would do. A home market caused by Protection makes farmers pay more than they receive; while every variety of the argument ignores the danger to manufactures of that glut in the home market which is an inevitable consequence of a Protective tariff.

The theory, moreover, is in no instance borne out by facts. Farmers do not, in fact, remain in the Eastern States, where, according to the theory, they should find their market, but emigrate to the West, and sell their products in Europe.

The theory is that the farmer will get a higher price by selling his corn to the hands at a neighbouring factory. The fact is that the farmer sells his produce at the price which rules in Mark Lane; and the neighbouring artisans will not give him a penny more than the market rate for the sake of neighbourliness.

The theory is that the demand of the home market keeps up the prices of agricultural produce. The fact is that men must eat, wherever they live; and that it does not matter to the farmer, who sells food, whether his customers live in America or Europe.

[1] In these calculations leather and lumber are included among manufactured products.

The theory is that the farmer will gain an advantage by being brought into direct relations with consumers, and so save the cost of transportation. The fact is that farmers sell their wheat to millers or produce merchants, and not direct to artisans, whether the latter are neighbours or not.

The theory is that the farmer must be better off if there is a home demand. The fact is, the farmer is best off when he can sell his produce at the highest price, and buy what he wants at the lowest.

The theory is that the American and Victorian farmer ought to be exceptionally prosperous. The truth is that the former is overwhelmed with debt, and the latter is emigrating into New South Wales.[1]

Whatever force the home-market argument has is owing to union with other Protectionist arguments. Even when it is stated by itself, it generally resolves itself, upon analysis, into the statements that Protection causes a diversity of occupation, and attracts population. In this meaning it may appeal to farmers with a certain degree of force—because every increase of population, in whatever part of the world it occurs, may become an advantage to the producers of food. But, although it may be admitted that Australian and American farmers are likely to be benefited by the growth of towns, the questions are still unanswered—" Whether the towns would not grow up as fast without Protection?" and "Whether under Protection the farmers, as a class, will not have to pay more in the form of taxes than they receive back in the form of prices?"

While the price of food all the world over is determined by the ruling price in Mark Lane, the increased demand for food of a few hundred thousand townsmen in Australia or America will not make any appreciable difference in the price

---

[1] An article in *Belford's Magazine*, March, 1889, upon the state and prospects of the American farmer, contains a mass of useful information on this subject. Current American literature is full of the grievances and distress of the farming population, who have to sell at London prices, and buy at American.

of farm produce, unless either of these countries should suddenly cease to export agricultural products.[1] In such a case —if Americans and Australians could only procure their food over a tariff fence—the farmer might, no doubt, raise his prices, as English landlords raised rents in the days of the Corn Laws; but until the artisan and townsman consent to a tax on food, farmers in a Protected country which exports food can expect nothing else but low prices for the articles they sell, and high prices for those they buy. No one will find out sooner than the Protected farmer that the old English proverb, "That the farmer pays for all," has a special significance in a Protected country.

The writer of the paper on the "Decline of the Farmer," which has been already referred to, shows the fate of the farmer in every Protected country[2] when he thus summarises the steps of the American farmer's decline :—

"Captivated," he says, "by the promise of a home market as the result of manufacturing development, which he was led to believe would buy his products at highest price, and sell to him in return at lowest, the American farmer departed from the only true republican principle of strict equality in public privileges and burdens. He consented to be taxed to a limited extent for the encouragement of manufactures—but only upon the understanding that the arrangement was to be temporary : only while the infant industries were struggling for a foothold. The interest thus aided was then so weak and insignificant that

---

[1] Victoria has been a grain-exporting country for many years; while New South Wales, owing to climatic disadvantages in the coastal districts, and the remoteness of other wheat-growing lands, has to import about one-third of her wheat supplies. The price of wheat in Melbourne is, on an average of many years, sixpence a bushel less than the price in Sydney. Protectionists, observing this, tell a Sydney audience that Protection means cheap bread; going into the country, they tell the farmers that Protection means dear wheat. But how cheap bread and dear wheat are to go together they have never explained.

[2] See the English Consular Reports on Farming in France and Italy for any year from 1884-91.

he never dreamt the day might come when it would dispute his supremacy, and, taking him by the throat, demand as a right what he had granted as a favour."

CHAPTER V.

THE PAUPER-LABOUR ARGUMENT.

§ 1. THE pauper-labour argument is the final refuge of all Protectionist disputants, and tends to become relied upon more and more as a justification of the permanent retention of a Protective policy. Although it assumes a variety of forms, its essence is always an assertion that the high rate of wages which is characteristic of young countries cannot be maintained unless both labourers and capitalists are protected against the competition of pauper labour and cheap capital.

"The claim is set up in warrant and justification of a continued high-tariff policy, that the difference of wages in favour of competitive foreign productions constitutes a good and sufficient reason why compensating Protective duties should be levied on their resulting products when imported into this country; and the assertion is further constantly and conjointly made that unless such duties continue to be levied, the American manufacturer will be unable to withstand foreign competition: that our workshops and factories will be closed, and our workmen and their families made dependent on public charities."[1]

Such an argument as this is really the basis of every so-called scientific treatise, such as Professor Patten's, of the Wharton School of Economics, in favour of Protective tariffs; and, from its place in the historic system of Protectionist arguments, may be taken as the last word which the advocates

[1] Hon. David A. Wells, "Practical Economics" (p. 132).

of a restricted commerce are able to advance. It becomes therefore, of the utmost importance to examine this argument fully, both by reference to facts and theory.

First, however, as usual, careful disputants must verify their facts. They must ascertain three things :—

1. What difference in fact exists between the rates of wages paid in the trade, which it is proposed to Protect, by the native and the foreign producers?
2. To what extent does this difference in the wage-rate affect the relative costs of production?
3. What evidence is there that the imposition of a Protective duty will prevent the rates of wages in the two countries in question from assimilating?

These facts, once ascertained—and until they are ascertained no argument is possible—the last question, which has always to be answered in the fiscal controversy, still remains for consideration: viz., Whether Protection may not be too high a price to pay for the preservation of the industries in question? This, however, can only be answered by a consideration of matters which properly belong to a later chapter.

It would be beyond the scope of this work to examine the facts of any country, or any particular trade, in order to see whether the pauper-labour argument can justly be applied to its conditions. All that can be done here is to indicate the line of investigation, and to suggest certain general considerations which must be taken into account. It will not, however, be out of place to refer, in a general way, to the answers which other inquiries in this field have obtained to the questions which have already been suggested, and to mention those which a student of economics would expect to obtain if the working of economic principles were not disturbed by local causes. Let us first, then, examine into the nature of this inquiry as to what difference does in fact exist between the rates of wages paid in a young and an old community.

§ 2. No statistical information is more difficult to obtain than accurate statements of the rates of wages, and no statistics are more misleading or useless than so-called averages of wage-rates.

Even when the sources of information about wages are above suspicion, wage-rates admit of so many qualifications that it is difficult to use them for purposes of comparison. Ten shillings in one country may not go so far as eight shillings in another; while in some mills workmen have advantages in house-rent or allowances which are denied to others.

Any money-rate of daily or weekly wages must therefore of necessity be misleading, unless we know: (1) the number of days worked, (2) the cost of living in the district, (3) whether the workmen have any special allowances in lieu of wages.

And finally, even when all this is known, it is quite useless for controversial purposes to attempt to arrive at any average rate of wages for a given country.

Even in a small country like England, wages in the same industry differ by as much as thirty per cent. in different localities. This is especially the case with agricultural labour; but the same holds true, in a less degree, of the wages in other industries. In the United States the rates vary more or less in every State; and the wages in the West are sometimes double those paid to the same class of workmen in the Eastern States. For these reasons, as Mr. Wright, the chief of the Labour Bureau, has often pointed out, it is idle to speak of an "American rate of wages." There is one rate for New York, and one for Pennsylvania, and a third for California; but to strike an average between all the States would give a rate which no class of workmen ever receive, and which would be useless for any purposes of comparison.

Another reason why averages must be misleading is that in all old countries the "residuum," as Mr. Bright called them—the class, that is, of hereditary paupers and hopeless ne'er-do weels—is much larger than in a young community.

But any average of national wages would have to take into account the starvation rates paid to people of this class, with the result of unfairly lowering the rewards of manufacturing labour.

When, therefore, artisans and manufacturers in a young country ask to be "protected" against the pauper labour of more settled communities, they must, if their request is to receive attention, ignore averages, and confine their comparison to specified industries. This warning will seem superfluous to those who have not lived in the midst of Protectionist controversies nor read Protectionist speeches; but hardly a week passes in Australia or America where the wages of London dockers are not the theme of some Protectionist oration. It ought, however, to be self-evident that a comparison between the wages paid to the lowest class of unskilled labour in London and those paid to skilled Australian artisans is a comparison between two subjects of a different class. Take, for instance, the iron trade. New South Wales Protectionists constantly affirm that the difficulty in the iron trade in that colony is owing to the high rate of wages. This assertion may or may not be true; but it is idle to use as evidence in its support comparisons between the pay of Sydney artisans and London dockers.

Nor is it a sufficient answer to these considerations to reply that the existence of a residuum of low-paid wage-earners reduces the wage of skilled artisans. Within certain limits this statement is true. The reserve army of labour may destroy the success of a strike for higher wages, as was recently the case in Australia; but as a rule, the underpaid starveling has neither the physique nor the intelligence to come into competition with workmen of higher grades. It is thus unfair to argue that the lowest rate of wage in a country is the determinant of its ability to compete with a country of a higher rate. The comparison should be made in every case between the wages paid in the two countries to the workmen of the particular trade for which Protective duties are demanded.

Mr. Edwin Chadwick, in a passage quoted by Mr. Wells in the work already referred to (p. 138), illustrates this view by the following interesting example from his own experience :—

"In Nottingham," he says, "the introduction of more costly and complex machines for the manufacture of lace has, while economising labour, augmented wages to the extent of 100 per cent. I asked a manufacturer of lace whether this large machine could not be worked at the common lower wages by any of the workers of the old machine? 'Yes, it might,' was the answer; 'but the capital invested on the new machinery is very large, and if from drunkenness or misconduct anything happened to the machine, the consequence would be very serious.' Instead of taking any man out of the street, as might be done with the low-priced machine, he (the employer) found it necessary to go abroad and look for one of better condition, and for such a one higher wages must be given."

When industrial activity is highly developed, employers cannot afford to pay low wages.

§ 3. It will be plain, from the foregoing observations, that any statements of comparative wages ought to be received with caution; so that the first duty of a person dealing with an argument which rests upon a difference in the rate of wages in two countries is to verify the facts, and then confine the comparison to the specific trades which are supposed to compete with each other. This method, however, is impossible in the present treatise; and therefore, in order to carry the argument further, we must make the admission that, although the difference between Australian or American wages and those of Great Britain is probably greatly exaggerated by Protectionists, the wages of unskilled labour in a young country are higher than the wages paid to the same class in England.

We may admit, further, that the investigations of Mr. Wright, chief of the Washington Labour Bureau, show almost conclusively that both the nominal and the real rates of wages in the chief manufacturing industries of Massachusetts are higher than those of the same industries in Great Britain.

On the other hand, the wages of miners in Pennsylvania are probably not as high as those of miners in Durham or Northumberland, and are much lower than those paid in New South Wales.

Still, however, it may fairly be assumed, as a basis for discussion of the pauper-labour argument, that wages are higher in a young country than they are in Europe. The difference is greatest on the lowest grade of manual labour, and lessens as the labour rises in the scale. As to skilled labour, personal inquiries from both masters and men have satisfied the writer that the highest grades of this class are less well paid, even in money wages, in Australia than they are in England.

The same is probably true of America,[1] if we may draw an inference from the statistics of immigration, which show that the number of "skilled labourers" who come as immigrants is comparatively small. But the bulk of the labour employed in manufactures is unskilled. The question, therefore, is—Does the higher reward of this class prevent the establishment of manufactures in a young community? The answer to this question will depend upon the number of manufactures which are exposed to foreign competition, and the proportion borne in these by the cost of labour to the price of goods.

---

[1] Mr. Wells, writing in 1868, mentions that artisans imported into America from foreign countries to work in certain employments (e.g., glass-making) were returning to Europe with a view of bettering their condition. ("Practical Economics," p. 140.) See also above, p. 215.

§ 4. It has been estimated by Mr. Wells that of all the manufactures in America not more than twenty per cent., and, perhaps, not more than ten per cent., can ever be exposed to foreign competition. Probably the number of Victorian industries which are able to stand alone bears a less proportion to the whole; but in every country there will be a certain number of industries which, from advantages of climate, means of communication, or acquired industrial skill, are in no danger from foreign competition. These industries can, therefore, be left out of account in the discussion. The real matter of importance is as to the industries which would not be able to withstand foreign competition except by reducing wages. Let us proceed to inquire what kind of industries these are likely to be.

§ 5. The fundamental assumption of those who use the pauper-labour argument is that the price of goods depends upon the rate of wages. It is not too much to say that this theory is wholly incorrect. The price of goods depends not upon the rate of wages, but upon the "cost of labour," which is a very different thing.

Thus, Mr. Donnell, in his pamphlet, contributed to the "Questions of the Day" series (Putnam, 1884), p. 54, says:— "It is a great mistake, though a common one, to suppose that the highest-priced labourer is the dearest. High-priced wages are the cheapest. . . . I am satisfied by personal observation and diligent inquiry that American labour estimated in productiveness—that is, the work accomplished in proportion to wages paid—is the cheapest in the world."

Mr. Edward Atkinson, of Boston, in his work, "The Distribution of Products," after a careful investigation of the cost of production in many industries, has laid it down as a law "that a high rate of wages means a low cost of product, and a low rate of wages means a high cost of product." Mr. Brassey, the famous contractor, said the same thing in another form when he stated that he found it cheaper to employ the high-waged English navvy in preference to any number of low-waged Germans and Asiatics.

The important matter, therefore, in considering whether a particular industry requires Protection on account of the higher rate of local wages, is not so much a knowledge of the difference in money, or even in real wages, between the two countries in question, but to ascertain the difference in labour-cost. And the probability, which is almost a certainty, is that high wages, instead of being evidence of a high cost of production, are, on the contrary, direct evidence of a low cost of production, and therefore, as Mr. Wells says, "in place of being an argument in favour of the necessity of Protection, they are a demonstration that none is needed." It would unduly extend this work even to summarise the evidence on which these statements rest. For further information the reader is referred to Mr. Edward Atkinson's two works, "The Distribution of Products," and "The Industrial Progress of the Nation" (New York and London, 1890).[1]

The question is thus narrowed to a comparison not of the rates of wages in the competing countries, but of the proportion which these bear in each case to the respective costs of production. In other words, we have to deal not with rates of wages, but with labour-cost. We are thus led to two practical conclusions :—

---

[1] Mr. Hirsch, in his pamphlet entitled "Protection in Victoria," which is more fully referred to in the Appendix, makes the following sound observations on this part of the question :— "A comparatively high rate of wages is one of the most important, if not the most important factor in reducing cost of production, not only by forcing into use labour-saving machinery, which at a lower rate of wages could not permit of a saving in wages, but also by the greater intelligence and vigour of the workmen, which high wages produce. Consequently, we find a nation's power in the markets of the world to be somewhat in accordance with the rate of wages to which its workers are accustomed. China, India, Mexico, export no manufactures, Russia least of all European nations, Italy and Spain rank next, Austria stands by itself, Germany and France follow, and Great Britain stands at the apex of industrial power " (p. 9).

1. That Protectionists cannot establish even the appearance of a rightful claim to any duty until they have proved that the labour-cost of producing the article which it is proposed to Protect is so much greater in the young community than it is in other countries that its manufacture in the community cannot be profitably carried on.

2. That when it can be proved that the production of any article is prevented by differences between its labour-cost in a young community and its labour-cost in Europe, then a duty equivalent to the labour-cost, less the cost of importing the article from Europe, might cause the establishment of a manufactory of that article in the young community.

3. Consequently, if the labour-cost of producing any article is lower in Europe than it is in America or Australia, it must be for one of two reasons:—Either (1) the European labourer is more efficient on account of his greater intelligence or on account of the greater assistance he derives from Nature or machinery; or (2) the article is one which is made entirely by either unskilled manual labour, or by manual labour assisted by only cheap and simple mechanical appliances. In either case the difference in labour-cost affords no argument for Protection.

§ 6. The labour-cost of a finished article—by which is meant the proportion which the cost of labour bears to the cost of the whole—depends on two things: namely, (1) the intelligence and ability of the human labourer; (2) the amount of assistance he receives from Nature or machinery.

But the average of education and intelligence is undoubtedly higher both in America and Australia than it is in Great Britain or Europe. In this respect, therefore, the advantage is on the side of the young community. Of the amount of assistance received by either country from natural causes, or from the use of machinery, nothing can be predicate[1]. There is, however, no *à priori* reason why this assistance should be less in a young community than it is in England.

In the first case, as we have seen, the European superiority is very unlikely to be due to the superior intelligence of the workmen or their better tools; and must, therefore, be attributed to the superior natural advantages of climate, soil, or situation by which his labour is assisted. But if Protection is demanded as a compensation for the want of natural advantages, this is a clear admission that Protection is intended to cause a waste of labour by making men in one country do for themselves what Nature has done for them elsewhere.

The competitor whose ravages the tariff is designed to check is not, strictly speaking, "foreign labour," but the natural advantages which foreign labour enjoys, and which, under Free Trade, it would share with the world. Hence follow all those extravagances which Bastiat was fond of turning into ridicule, and which Protectionists always declare to be irrelevant, by the contention that they only desire to Protect industries which can be naturalised in the Protected country.

But it must be remembered that the argument now under consideration is an argument in favour of Protection as a permanent, and not as a temporary policy. If, therefore, any industry demands Protection because its article is produced abroad at a less labour-cost than that at which it would be possible to produce it at home; and if it appear that the difference in labour-cost is due to the possession by foreign labour of superior natural advantages, the case becomes one in which Protection can only be justified by the same arguments which justified Bastiat's petition of the candle-makers against the competition of the sun. If the difference in labour-cost is due to the superiority of the foreign mechanical appliances, the case is obviously equally unfit for permanent Protection, because the same result could be obtained by the adoption in the home country of the same appliances.

There remains the case in which the difference in labour-cost is due to the nature of the product being such that it is the result of unaided manual labour, or of manual labour only slightly aided by mechanical appliances. In such a case it is plain that the labour-cost and the amount of money spent in wages will very closely correspond. Accordingly, if the industry is one which does not admit of a high degree of skill, so that one skilled workman at a high wage could not do the work of several unskilled workmen at a low wage, the rate of wages will be a fair test of the labour-cost of production; and a country of high wages will not be able to compete in this particular line with a country of low wages. To this extent, then, the Pauper-Labour argument may justify Protection in a theoretical discussion.

The next question is, whether the common facts of industrial life give any ground for the belief that this theoretical justification of Protection can have any but the narrowest application? To decide this, we must inquire what the industries are which owe their lower labour-cost to a lower rate of wages. Manifestly, as we have seen, they are handicrafts, such as the making of common pottery, where, as Mr. Wells remarks, "the labourer works almost exactly as did his predecessor 4,000 years ago." In such industries the moral and physical standard of the labourer is necessarily at its lowest. The trades are such as can be learnt by any one; they require neither skill, training, nor continuous effort, and they are carried on for the most part under unhealthy conditions. Is there really any need to establish industries such as these in a young country? The question is purely political. Ought a politician to encourage trades which will inevitably collect the driftwood of society, and render possible in a new country the worst abuses in the industrial history of the old world? Should it not rather be the aim to direct the labour of a young community into channels where intelligence, skill, training, and patience may enable every individual to satisfy the better instincts of his nature? Is it wise to offer to the lazy and unthrifty the chance of making a bare living in a degrading form of occupation? Will not the existence of such a class of workmen tend in time to drag the labourers of other classes down to its own level?

Suppose, however, that the Protectionist politician is obdurate, and passes by these questions without reply, still there remains the consideration: What shall be done with these workmen when they have supplied the home market? Manifestly, their products cannot be exported, because, *ex hypothesi*, they cannot be produced at the same cost in the Protected country as is possible abroad, unless the wages of the former are reduced, which, according to Protectionists, Protection will prevent. The consequence will be that a yearly increasing number of unskilled labourers will join the army of the tramps and unemployed. No other alternative will open to these unfortunate persons, because the very nature of their former employment will have destroyed their industrial aptitude. Well may David Wells ask, "Why, in the name of common sense, America, as a nation, should enter into competition with these low-waged countries?" "What possible reason," he asks, "or inducement is there for wanting to introduce these handicraft industries into this country, and of attempting to keep men alive by means of enormous taxes levied under the tariff upon the whole people, when we can buy all we want of these products with a very small part of the excess of our cotton and grain?"

Finally, it must be remembered that the number of these handicrafts is decreasing every year, as science, the great leveller, elevates wages by increasing the efficiency of the labourer. It follows that the force of the pauper-labour argument, even in the one case where it has a theoretic validity, is constantly diminishing before the application to industry of new mechanical appliances; and it is not a long period to anticipate when the lowest and commonest forms of manual toil will have been rendered entirely unnecessary, and men in all countries and of all classes will have the leisure and the opportunity to train their intelligence and satisfy their instincts in higher forms of industrial activity.

Summing up, then, the results of this discussion, we may say—First, That the pauper-labour argument, although it has a certain theoretic validity, can seldom be applied in practice, because the circumstances on which its assumptions rest seldom co-exist; Secondly, That even in the few cases in which its application might be justified, the result of applying it is both politically and economically harmful to the interests of a young country; Thirdly, That the argument must gradually lose what little force it ever possessed, as science lessens the number of unskilled handicrafts.

§ 7. But we have not yet done with the practical objections to this argument. Any attempt to apply it not only reveals a fatal inconsistency between its assumptions and its promises, but carries the politician along a path of inextricable entanglement.

The theory of the argument, as we recall it, is that manufacturers in a young community are prevented from competing with their European rivals, on account of the high local rates of wages.

Now, if high local wages are really an obstacle to manufactures, that can only be because they cause the prices of the manufactured articles to be too high to find a market in the face of open competition. In other words, the argument is that high wages cause high prices.

But the constant assertion of Protectionists is that Protection will cause lower prices. How, if that be true, can Protection secure higher wages? If wages and prices depend on one another, as Protectionists assert, the same policy cannot at one and the same time make wages high and prices low. So much for an inconsistency in theory; now for a difficulty in practice!

§ 8. If it be true that the ability of manufacturers to compete with one another depends upon the rates of wages which they respectively pay to their workmen, then it is evident that any duties which are levied for the purpose of equalising wages must vary according to the variations in the wages rates of different countries.

If, for example, wages in any industry are 10 per cent. higher in Australia than in England, a duty of 10 per cent. will be more than sufficient to equalise the terms of competition; but if wages in the same industry are 10 per cent. lower in Germany than they are in England, the Protectionists ought to impose two equalising duties—namely, one of 10 per cent. on English goods, and one of 20 per cent. on those which come from Germany. And as the wages of any specified industry differ in nearly all countries, the same article ought to be exposed to many duties. Nor is this all. The duties ought to be constantly revised, so as to adapt them to any changes in the rates of wages which may occur in the foreign competing countries.

It is difficult to see how any person who sincerely believes—and many profess to believe it—that Protective duties are only required to compensate the manufacturer for higher local wages, can deny the force of the above reasoning. Such persons indignantly repudiate any desire to give a manufacturer special favours; but it is obvious that a fixed duty, which is estimated on the wages paid in a particular industry, say in India, will be considerably more than is required to compensate him for the difference between the local rate which he pays and the English rate. He will therefore have the sole benefit of the duty on all English goods up to the amount of the difference between English and Indian wages, and Protection will be a clear privilege to him by that amount.

But this is not the end of the entanglement.

§ 9. The countries whose competition is most dangerous to

a young community are precisely the countries of high wages. Of the total imports into New South Wales from countries beyond the sea for the year 1889, four-fifths were the products of Great Britain and America. It is the same with the United States. Her great commercial rival is not Germany or India, but again Great Britain.

Now, whatever ill-will Protectionists may bear Great Britain —and Protection is openly recommended to the Irish voters in America as a means of damaging British trade—no one is likely to dispute that manufacturing wages are higher in that country than in any other part of Europe. The low-waged countries, which Protectionists term the countries of pauper labour, are not England, Switzerland, Holland, or Norway — these are the countries of industrial freedom, as they are the countries of political and religious freedom—but soldier-ridden and Protected Germany, and harassed and Protected France. How is it possible to admit this fact, and yet maintain that high local wages are an impediment to local manufactures unless foreign competition is forbidden?

But the most disingenuous use of the pauper-labour argument is in New South Wales. In that colony the voters of the cities and centres of population are Free Traders by a large majority. The bulk of the farmers, on the other hand, are Protectionists. The immediate causes of this are agricultural distress and a bitter feeling of resentment against the border duties levied by Victoria. The remoter cause is not improbably the premature settling of the lands by a too-scattered population. But, whatever the cause of this Protectionist feeling among the farmers, they, of all people, could not justify it by the fear that their industry should be exposed to the competition of paupers.

The only competitors of the New South Wales farmers are the farmers of Victoria, South Australia, and New Zealand. For a Protectionist orator to use the pauper-labour argument in such a case, to justify the farmers in their present mistaken view of their own interests, is either a wilful attempt at deceit, or an assertion that the farmers in the Protected colonies are paupers, whose chief products ought not to be admitted into New South Wales, because wages in those Protected lands are at "starvation rates." Protectionists must take their choice of the alternative.

§ 10. We are now in a position to finish off the pauper-labour argument by considering the true causes of those high wages which are declared to be the obstacle to manufacturing growth in a young country. Wages being in their ultimate analysis the labourer's share of the article produced, it is plain that every increase in the efficiency of the labourer tends to increase the quantity of that from which he must receive his share. To ensure that the labourer's share shall be that to which he is fairly entitled is one of the functions of trade-unions; but it is plain that his share cannot be lessened by an increase in the quantity to be divided if everything else remains the same.

Now, the efficiency of labour depends, as we have seen, not only upon human ability to produce, but also upon the amount of assistance received from Nature. Natural advantages of climate, fertility, situation, and such-like, are free gifts to man. The more of these a workman can gain, the less expenditure of effort he requires to produce a given result. Nature does for him what men in less favoured situations have to do for themselves.

But the characteristic of young countries is the possession in exceptional abundance of one or more great natural advantages. Labour is therefore exceedingly productive when it is employed on any of these natural industries. Ten men, for example, can raise more wool in Australia than could be raised by twice that number in Great Britain. Thus, although the wages of station hands are three and four times the wages paid by English sheep-owners to their labourers, Australian wool competes successfully with that of England. Here is a plain case in which higher wages are no bar to successful competition. It is the same in all extractive industries which are followed in a young country. The labourer is able to appropriate a natural instrument of production for his own advantage.

The question is, "How long will this advantage continue?" To this the reply must be, "So long as Nature continues to be bountiful, or so long as man continues by the ingenuity of his hand and brain to make up for deficiency in Nature's gifts." When work becomes less efficient, wages may fall; but while young countries enjoy their peculiar superiority in certain dominating industries, the prevailing rates of wages will continue high. Or, to express the same thing in the words of the market-place : "Men won't take less as artisans than they can get as labourers."

Webster, in a stirring passage, has expressed the same idea. "The chairman," he says, "says it would cost the nation nothing as a nation to make our ore into iron. Now, I think it would cost us precisely that which we can worst afford : that is, great labour. . . . We have been asked . . . in a tone of some pathos, whether we will allow to the serfs of Russia and Sweden the benefit of making our iron for us. Let me inform the gentlemen that those same serfs do not earn more than seven cents a day. . . . And let me ask the gentleman further, whether we have any labour in this country that cannot be better employed than in a business which does not yield the labourer more than seven cents a day? . . . The true reason why it is not our policy to compel our citizens to manufacture our own iron is that they are far better employed. It is an unproductive business, and they are not poor enough to be compelled to follow it. If we had more of poverty, more of misery, and something of servitude ; if we had an ignorant, idle, starving population, we might set up for iron-makers against the world. . . . Multitudes of persons are willing to labour in the production of this article for us at the rate of seven cents a day, while we have no labour which will not command, upon the average, at least five or six times that amount. The question is, then, shall we buy this article of these manufacturers and suffer our own labour to earn its greater reward; or, shall we employ our own labour in a similar manufacture, and make up to it, by a tax on consumers, the loss which it must necessarily sustain?"

§ 11. If the preceding extracts and observations contain a true view of the theory of wages, it is evident that wages will continue to be high in a young country so long as the natural extractive industries continue their exceptional productiveness.

Now, the productiveness of an industry—or, what is the same thing, the efficiency of the labour employed in it—depends to a considerable extent upon the obstacles which labour has to overcome. The fewer these are, the more will be produced by an equal effort.

But the object and effect of Protective duties is to create obstacles where none existed. They are expressly designed to prevent men making use of the free gifts which Nature has bestowed on foreign countries. They thus constitute new and artificial obstacles which labour has to overcome. If these duties affect any of the instruments used in the extractive industries—and it is hard to conceive of any Protective duties which will not affect the farmer and the miner in his tools or wants—they are, clearly, an encumbrance on their natural productiveness, and by that amount they lessen the efficiency of labour.

But by lessening the efficiency of the labour employed in the extractive industries, Protective duties lower the standard of wages for the whole country. The standard of wages is fixed by the profitableness of the dominating industries. These require little skill, and are open to every one of a strong body. Naturally, therefore, a man who has the chance of commanding a certain rate in an industry of this kind will not accept much below it in any other.

It is not meant that every carpenter or joiner, if he cannot get the current wages, will at once turn farmer. That would be a grotesque misrepresentation of the argument. What is contended for is the obvious truism that when, owing to the natural superiority of a country in climate, soil, or mineral wealth, unskilled labour can obtain a high reward, the probability (which over a large number of men becomes a certainty) is that the ruling rate for other kinds of labour will be at least equal to that which prevails in the extractive industries. If this be correct—and it can hardly be denied—the extractive industries set a certain standard of wages, which will not be reduced until these industries become less profitable.

§ 12. The chief charge, therefore, against Protection, from the view of the wage-earner, is that by making the extractive industries less profitable it hastens a decline in wages generally.

Nor is this the only way in which Protection operates injuriously on wages.

High wages depend not only on the efficiency of labour, but on the number of labourers. "When two masters are running after one man, wages rise; when two men are running after one master, wages fall," is a saying attributed to George Stephenson. But, whoever may be the author, the saying expresses a portion of the truth which must not be overlooked.

In most young countries the development of the natural resources is still incomplete, so that every labourer who can turn his hand to one of the extractive industries causes an increase in the national productiveness. He does not displace another workman, but himself adds by his labours to the store from which all workmen are employed. Consequently, there is no fear at present of Australian or American wages being forced down by the competition of immigrants belonging to the classes who will find employment on the soil or in other of the extractive industries. Australia, indeed, is suffering from an insufficiency in the supply of labour for these pursuits. She could employ double the number of men in the extractive industries; and since every man would produce a far greater value than he could consume, the rate of wages would not fall.[1] Competition, where labour is properly organised, only reduces wages when the industry, for employment in which the labourers are competing, has reached the limits of its productiveness. That point is yet far distant in Australia and America. As was observed in the course of the debate on the Mills' tariff proposals in the American House of Representatives in 1888: "Not until the sixty millions of Americans become six hundred millions will men crowd each other in the United States in the fierce struggle for existence and wealth, as they do in Great Britain to-day." When that time comes—unless, as indeed will probably be the case, if we may judge from past experience, the instruments of production should enormously improve in power—wages will have fallen to the European rate. But we may leave the incidents of that far-off time to speculative dreamers.

But although the increase in the number of extractive labourers in a young country is not likely to lower wages, the effect of an increase of manufacturing labourers is entirely different.

The market for manufactured goods in any young community must be smaller than the market for its raw produce. The former is limited by the confines of the colony—the other is the world. Consequently, over-production of manufactured goods will be an early result of a Protective tariff.

---

[1] This is, of course, on the assumption, which ought always to be made in dealing with questions of wages, that trades unions exist in the country. If there were no unions, advantage might be taken of local congestions of labour, or of the ignorance of new-comers, to lower the rates.

Twenty years have been sufficient to supply the market of Victoria, even although for the greater part of that time the markets of the other colonies have been open to Victorian produce. If New South Wales, where Victorians now find a market for their surplus, were to adopt a Protective tariff—and should she take this fatal step, it will in no small degree be owing to a just resentment against the provincial spirit of her Southern neighbour—many Victorian manufactories would run half-time.

The effect of over-production of manufactures upon the general rate of wages is easily understood.

The artisans, unable to find employment in their own trades, flock to the extractive industries. These, being already burdened with the Protective duties, do not respond with elasticity to the new demand. Nor do the labourers themselves generally possess the training or physique which fit them for these pursuits. They do, however, form a large and gradually increasing body of floating unorganised labour, which always presses on the outskirts of trades unionism, and offers to employers an encouragement to resist its just demands.

Nor is this danger to the interests of organised labour always left to its natural growth. The contrary is indeed the case. The experience of America and Victoria shows that Protected manufacturers most frequently import their labour.

The wage-earner is thus oppressed by Protection on every side. The aid of Nature to his efforts has been lessened: the purchasing power of his wages has been diminished: and the number of his competitors has been increased. His old prosperity is destroyed by the very means which he adopted to perpetuate it, until he learns by a bitter experience that Nature is, after all, the best restorer of labour troubles, as of other ills.

CHAPTER VI.

THE COST OF PROTECTION.

§ 1. THE fiscal controversy has now been tracked through all its windings. Starting on the broad and well-worn road of economic demonstration, the argument has wandered into every by-path of expediency and prejudice. None of the appeals to interest, sentiment, or pride, by which Protectionists have tried to cover their defeat in economic argument, has been allowed to pass unnoticed, but each has been considered separately, and has been tested both by experience and by theory. The result is unaltered. The economic demonstration needs no qualification. Both political and economic arguments lead to the same conclusion: namely, that Free Trade—which is voluntary trade—means great trade, and great trade means prosperity.

Nevertheless, where so much is at stake there will never be finality. The theory and experience which seem conclusive to-day will be distinguished to-morrow, if there is only a difference in names to furnish an excuse. Self-interest will never lack a means of working on fanaticism. Protection is hydra-headed, as every Free Trade controversialist must know. It seems useless to expose one fallacy, because the disputant at once ignores what he has said before, and takes his stand upon a fresh position. Prove to a man that Free Trade cannot lower wages, and he will talk about diversity of occupation; quit the argument about wages to discuss diversity, and he is asking for a home market. Quote statistics, the authority is denied. Ask for facts, you are given phrases. Reason logically about the very phrases that are given all reasoning is denounced as "theory."

Fortunately, one resource remains—to disregard the rents and gaps in Protectionist arguments, and treat the question simply as one of expediency. Assume that Protection will do all that its advocates promise, is not the price too dear? May we not buy diversity of occupation at too high a rate, even if we get infant industries and a home market thrown into the bargain? In short, let it be granted that Free Trade is bad, and that Protection remedies its worst defects, and still the question will remain—is the game worth the candle? If it is not, and if Protection prove too high a price to pay for all the promised benefits, a permanent and comprehensive answer is afforded to every form of Protectionist allurement.

Nor can Protectionists complain of this method of controversy, since they themselves implicitly, if not expressly, admit that Protection may be bought too dearly when they protest against being supposed to advocate "extreme" Protection. Bastiat's famous petition of the candle-makers against the competition of the sun, which seems to Free Traders such an unanswerable *reductio ad absurdum* of Protectionist argument, can only be avoided by fixing some limit to the operation of Protective doctrines. Unfortunately, no one knows what that limit is. It can only be guessed at by a series of rough inductions from Protectionist protests.

We know, for instance (to recur to the former illustration), that Protectionists in France and America would not advocate the enclosure of a city in a dome of glass in order to give employment to the makers of glass and the manufacturers of artificial light. However much the light of the sun may prejudice the sale of oils, candles, lamps, and resin, and an infinity of kindred articles, Protectionists will not shut out the competition of that foreign rival. And they will not be moved to alter their decision even by the consideration that if access to natural light were closed in a few of the principal cities, there would be an increase of cattle and sheep to supply tallow, that groves would be planted with resinous trees, that there would be an extended cultivation of vegetable oils, and that the demand for artificial lighting would encourage agriculture in many ways, and at the same time give a home market to the farmer.

We know that Protectionists will not shut out sunlight, because many of them have declared the proposal to be absurd, and have given as their reason that sunlight is a free gift of Nature. The reason is excellent, but it equally applies to iron, coal, and every other natural product which, by reason of the greater liberality of Nature, is cheaper in one place than another.

But the same Protectionists who refuse to exclude cheap light do exclude cheap firing and cheap iron, from which we can only conclude that there are certain limits to the extent to which Protectionists are ready to refuse the gifts of Nature. Sunlight they will accept, because the price of that is always zero; but iron, coal, and corn will be refused, because the price of these articles only approximates to zero. If Nature does the whole work, her gifts will be received; if she does only a part, they will be rejected: or, what comes to the same thing, a tax, equal in amount to the equivalent of Nature's effort, will be imposed upon the import of the completed article.

But even this distinction is not quite exact. Protectionists will accept some gifts of a part from Nature, but not others. For instance, American Protectionists will accept the assistance of Nature in the production of tea, but not of iron. They are ready to recognise that the natural conditions for the production of tea are better in China than in America, but they refuse to recognise the superiority of Australia in producing wool. But the proof of the existence of superior natural conditions for the production of any article must always be the same, viz., a lower price. Although American Protectionists will not encourage the tea industry, it is only a matter of money to grow enough tea under glass in the Southern States to supply the whole Union. Nor would it matter what the tea cost, because even if it cost twenty dollars a pound, the money (according to the Protectionist theory) would not go out of the country; so that instead of America having the tea and China the money, as at present, America would have both the money and the tea! While if there were any surplus production, bounties might be given on its export to China, so as to destroy the foreigner in his own market!

Other instances of a similar character might be quoted to show that Protectionists are not always ready to follow arguments to their logical conclusion. There appears to be some vague and variable limit beyond which Protectionists will not go, for the reason that, if they did, Protection would cost too much.

§ 2. Assuming, then, that Protectionists cannot fairly object to an inquiry into the cost of Protective tariffs, we will proceed in the next and concluding pages to enumerate in order the objections, both economic and political, to this most baneful form of interference with the course of trade.

Protection is indefensible on economic grounds, for the reason that under whatever disguise it may be recommended it is always a device for making work. If the device succeeds, somebody must pay for it. To ignore this truism is to commit the blunder of the alchemists who spent their lives in endeavouring to find a way of making something out of nothing.

But it is said with pride: "See what industries Protection has created!" Granted that they are splendid, whose is the burden of their cost?

If an industry can sell its products at the price of the open market, it needs no Protection. If it cannot sell at market prices, and has to get an Act of Parliament to allow it to charge more, it becomes a parasite upon existing industries, and must be supported out of their profits. The difference between the prices charged by these Protected industries and the price in the open market is a measure of their economic cost to the whole community. The industries themselves may be very fine and large, and a credit to their superintendents, but if they cannot stand alone they owe their support to taxes, and ought to be reckoned in the same category with hospitals, gaols, almshouses, and other kindred institutions.

It must always be difficult to estimate the exact amount of the burden which these parasitic industries cast upon a people. Sometimes, but in rare cases, internal competition so reduces prices that the loss is nil; but in such a case the industry can exist without Protection, and the duty ought to be, but never is, removed. More often the difference between the price charged by the Protected industry and that of the open market is something a little less than the amount of the duty. At times it is equal to the whole of the duty. But whatever the difference between the two prices may be, if the industry requires Protection—and that is the basis of the argument on both sides—it is borne by the community. No consequences of this seem to be too grotesque for a true Protectionist. It has been shown by undeniable figures times out of number that the tariff in many instances takes more from the pockets of the people than would be enough to pension every workman in the Protected industry, and buy up all the capital employed. The kerosene industry in New South Wales has been mentioned as one instance. The tables of Mr. Hayter, the statistician of Victoria, contain many others. Yet no such demonstrations can weaken the enthusiasm of the true believer.

Nor do the figures of the Custom House reveal the whole of the loss. The increased price of the home-made article by reason of the duty must also be added to the account.

There is also a further item of loss, which it is almost impossible to estimate, in the value of the industries which the tariff has destroyed or crippled. These are never mentioned in the boastful calculations of Protectionists; yet it is certain that no tariff was ever passed which did not interfere prejudicially with some industries already in existence, and prevent others from growing up. Why, then, should Protectionists keep silent about this source of destruction and loss except that it is in the nature of all men to "mark when they hit, but not when they miss?"[1]

§ 3. But the cost of a Protective tariff is beyond what can be measured in mere money, because it weakens the fibre of national life, by giving rise to political and social evils, which must be counted as of graver consequence than any economic loss.

From the standpoint of a politician it produces many evils, which differ from each other only in degrees of harmfulness. In the first place, it is a policy of inequality; because it confers special advantages upon certain classes without regard to the value of the services which they render in return. Under Protection every person, who is able to interest a majority of legislators in his favour, can shield his industry from foreign competition, and is allowed, with others in his own trade, to sell certain goods at an artificially high price. In other words, the tariff allows him and his fellows to compel the rest of the community, who are in a large majority, to deal exclusively with them, under penalty of a fine in the shape of a customs duty should they choose to purchase the goods which they desire from some one else. Protectionists sometimes resent this

[1] Previously to the American tariff of 1862, there was a considerable smelting industry carried on in the seaboard States. The duty on pig-iron destroyed it. The decline of the American shipping trade is another familiar instance. The tariff has made iron and steel so dear, and so enhanced the price of other raw materials, that shipbuilding has ceased to be profitable, and the American marine, which once ranked next to that of England, has almost disappeared.

The tariff has produced a similar result in Victoria. The shipbuilders have openly asserted, and proved their assertion to the Government, that they can no longer build ships to compete with those of New South Wales, because of the high price of the raw material occasioned by the Protective tariff.

manner of stating the case, upon the ground (as they say) that the internal competition of producers will reduce the prices of Protected articles below those at which they could be imported. Of course, if this were true, there would be no need of Protection; and the best proof of sincerity which those who make the assertion could give, would be to become Free Traders. But in fact, as so often happens with Protectionist arguments, they are theoretically true under certain assumed conditions, but in practice they have no bearing on the controversy, because the conditions are absent. The internal competition of which we hear so much seldom takes place with sufficient activity to reduce prices. Rings, trusts, combines, pools and every other device of a closed commerce to secure for itself a profitable field of plunder, are resorted to by the Protected manufacturers to prevent a decline in prices through the competition of their own number. A Protected country furnishes new illustrations every year of the old adage that "where combination is possible competition is impossible." It may, indeed, be put as the head and front of Protectionist offending, that it destroys healthy competition in order to create an unhealthy combination. The manufacturing magnates of a Protected country are as truly the privileged class of to-day, as were their prototypes in the Rhine castles, who exacted tolls from every passing trader.

Not only is Protection a policy of inequality, but it is a policy of inequality without system. It is a haphazard policy, which confers its favours and strikes its blows equally at random. This is inevitable from the nature of the object which it sets before itself. The selection of this or that industry for special legislative favour places a power in the hands of Parliament, which, even if it is not exercised corruptly, must be exercised more or less blindly. The woollen duties of the United States are the typical illustration of this feature of Protection. They are so intricate and delicately graduated that even experts in the trade are said to be unable to estimate exactly either their amount or their incidence.[1] What, then, must be the position of the legislator who imposed the duties? No man can be master of the technicalities of every trade; and the most honest legislator cannot fail to be misled by the interested statements of commercial experts. The settlement of a tariff has been described by an American eye-witness as "a game of grab," in which each interest takes what it can, and by combination with others secures the utmost. The iron men support the farmers, if the farmers vote for a duty on steel rails; and the woollen manufacturers form a close alliance with the copper trust in order to prevent the pastoralists from getting too much for wool. How infinitely hard, in such a chaos of no principles, to detect corruption or insure wise judgment! Ignorance attempting to legislate according to the dictates of self-interest! Grant that ignorance acts honestly, yet into what an unseemly scramble for money-aids is politics degraded!

Unfortunately, however, ignorance is not always honest. It would be assuming too much of human nature to look for the continuance of a high standard of public integrity in any Protected country. With whatever high motives men may at first delude themselves into the support of a Protective tariff, they run a constantly increasing risk of being conquered by the temptations with which the policy surrounds them. The virtue of a legislator must indeed be adamant, if, when he sees others plundering all about him, he keeps his own hands pure from bribes. Let the recent experience of Canada, or the revelations of the methods of the contest for the United States Presidency in 1888, be a sufficient warning!

Politically, then, Protection ought to be condemned, because it creates vested interests, the existence of which is dependent upon Acts of Parliament, and which tend inevitably to become monopolies; because it creates these interests without

---

[1] See on this subject the chapter on the Woollen Duties in Professor Taussig's "History of Protection."

due regard to the evil which it inflicts on others, and because it entrusts the power of enriching individuals to legislators, who are all the more exposed to the influence of improper motives, because their want of knowledge must prevent them from acting with complete fairness, even if they had the best intentions.

§ 4. But it is as a social rather than a political evil, that the baleful influence of Protection is the most apparent. As an abuse of the law-making power, it injures respect for law by creating artificial offences against which both self-interest and the sense of justice equally rebel. There is no surer means of accustoming citizens to view with complacency disobedience to the laws, than by awarding heavy punishments for acts (such as smuggling) which are not morally wrong. No one can trace in detail or estimate in bulk how much is lost to a community, if the public once lose faith in its law-makers and respect for its laws; but that the loss is considerable few would attempt to deny. Nor does the evil of Protection rest here. Men are influenced by it also in the more self-regarding relations of their lives; because it tends to weaken the motives of self-reliance and enterprise. After a long course of Protection manufacturers seem to lose the power of facing difficulties like practical and courageous men. In the face of competition they become like silly children, and are scared by it as by a ghost. Instead of calling their men together to devise new processes, or calculating how to cheapen or improve their present ones, they run whining to Parliament for help at the first sign of successful rivalry. Instead of trusting to the old-fashioned virtues of enterprise and self-reliance, they lean entirely on Protective duties. A system is thus initiated which, if it were continued long enough upon a people whose numbers were not constantly recruited by energetic immigrants, could only end in the destruction of national life. The vigour of a people which becomes accustomed to apply to Government in every difficulty, must be gradually sapped. Private energy will put forth no power, when it is without assurance that it will be allowed to reap success, and when a vote of the Assembly may at any moment bring its enterprise to an untimely end. Thus Protection defeats the object of its advocates; and the very policy which is designed to stimulate new qualities and develop the natural powers both of a country and its citizens, becomes a subtle instrument for the destruction of originality, ambition, and enterprise. For Protection is essentially antagonistic to progress.

It runs counter to one of the most elementary and permanent of human instincts, viz., the desire to satisfy wants at the least cost. We spend millions in dredging harbours, in removing sand-bars, and by every means improving the facilities for commercial intercourse. Yet, so soon as we experience the effects of this work in a reduced cost of foreign goods, the Protectionist would have us lay a new tax, like restoring the sand-bars, in order to bring up prices. Well may Professor Sumner say, "To build sand-bars across our harbours would be a far cheaper means of reaching the same end." If the Protectionist theory be correct, all the thought, energy, time and money devoted to improving the means of communication between foreign nations is wasteful and injurious. A great steamship or an international railway only exists to cheapen the cost of transportation; improvements in processes of manufacture are only designed to cheapen the cost of production; improved markets, co-operation, and similar devices, are only resorted to in order to cheapen the cost of distribution. The net result of this manifold exertion of human power is a reduction in prices. Yet, let prices fall in any country save their own, Protectionists at once declare that the result is ruin, not advantage, to their fellow-citizens. The Chinese are the true Protectionists, for they build a wall around their territory and exclude foreigners.

§ 5. Finally, Protection deserves to be condemned as a moral abuse.

It is no doubt unfashionable, at present, to judge political measures by ethical standards; partly because the dominance of reactionary ideas and the rule of force, of which Protection is only one expression, are unfavourable to moral criticism, and partly owing to a just resentment against the egotism, cant and malice with which some prominent political moralists apply the ethical test. Nevertheless, those who believe that the foundations of a national policy must rest upon sound morality will be compelled to give consideration to the ethical basis of a Protective system. Yet it would seem as if Protectionists always shrank from this duty. Their policy has no ethical maxim connected with it. It is, on the contrary, an open outrage on the moral sense of a community, and a defiance of all moral maxims. It rests avowedly on selfishness – "Germany has nothing to do with Russia, nor Russia with Germany," says List, its champion!—and it justifies its action by appeals to national prejudice and class interests. Where Free Trade preaches the brotherhood of man, and urges that, in foreign as in private commerce, a nation should "Do unto others as it wishes to be done by," Protection advocates national isolation, and inculcates the doctrine of doing to others in commercial matters as they do unto us. "Peace on earth, good-will towards men," which is the motto of the Cobden Club, can have no meaning to the ears of men who wage an internecine warfare with every nation by the means of hostile tariffs, which are not the less deadly than murderous weapons because they do not leave their victims mangled on the ground. The "nationalist" who rejoices over the distress which the McKinley tariff has caused in Germany or Wales, and claims every dislocation of foreign commerce and every injury to foreign traders as a sign of a worthy triumph, evidently stands upon a different moral plane from those who hold that each nation finds its own true strength in a joint and peaceful progress with neighbouring countries.

It is characteristic of those who view with satisfaction the injurious effects of their policy on other countries, that they should be indifferent to the liberties of their own people. Yet the moral aspect of Protection is no brighter, if the policy is contemplated only in its home results. Protection is an interference with human liberty, of the same nature, and differing from it only in degree, as human slavery. "If it is criminal," said Cobden, with his usual insight, "to steal a man and make him work for nothing, it is equally criminal to steal from a free man the fair reward of his labour." Every increase of price in a Protected article means an addition to the forced labour of those who desire to buy it. Such an invasion of human freedom may be justified (as negro slavery was justified) by more or less sincere assertions that the interest of the poor requires it; but in its essence it is always, as in practice the facts prove, a device to secure advantages for rich men in which the poor do not share.

It is this consciousness of the deep-lying immorality of a Protective policy that justifies the confident belief among Free Traders in its ultimate destruction. Those who believe that "morality is the nature of things" are not likely to be much disheartened by the passing victories of restrictive policies. Periods of reaction are inevitable; and when the reaction takes the form of military despotism and belief in force, tariffs, which are the accompaniment of militarism and the denial of justice, are necessary incidents of the reaction. Even already, however, there are signs that the nightmare of Protection is lifting; while the causes of discouragement to Free Traders have never been so great as those which darkened the days of the Abolitionists only twenty years before the Civil War.

§ 6. It is no wonder, then, that, in every civilised country, those who try to find the best expression of a nation's moral life in its political system, and who recognise that sense of duty is the safeguard of society, and not self-interest—all, in fact, who are men of ideas, with hardly one exception—are waging an undying battle with the creature Protection. It is no wonder, also, if at times the language of the disputants grows heated. "Protectionism," says Professor Sumner—and his words will find an echo in the heart of every one who has lived in a Protected country, and has seen the desperate shifts to which Protectionists resort, or read the nonsense and the falsehoods of their journalistic champions—"is such an arrant piece of economic quackery, and it masquerades under such an affectation of learning and philosophy, that it ought to be treated as other quackeries are treated—with scorn, contempt, satire, and ridicule." If this method has not been adopted in the present work, it has been out of deference to the feelings of others, and from a real desire to see the matter as they see it, and not from any belief that Protectionist arguments can bear even the sound of plausibility to men who study the course of trade and the growth of industrial life. Students of economics are virtually unanimous in condemning the policy. But voters are not students, and often lack the means of information. Such persons, if they will reflect upon the matter, need no study to become Free Traders. Protectionism is an outrage on the moral sense. "It is a subtle, cruel, and unjust invasion of one man's rights by another. It is done by force of law. It is at the same time a social abuse, an economic blunder, and a political evil." The system saps self-reliance, because it leads men to depend upon the laws of Parliament when they should be studying the laws of nature; it is repugnant to justice, because it introduces artificial inequalities; it is destructive of political purity, because it turns the power of law-making into an engine for enriching individuals. It is at once the offspring and the parent of corruption. It lowers the standard of wages and creates monopolies. It widens the breach between classes by introducing systematic spoliation under the forms of law. No possible advantage which Protection can give can compensate for these tremendous evils. The true policy, therefore, is to trust in freedom, even when the path seems lost, remembering that the confusion and obscurities of industrial life cannot be relieved by efforts to turn back the hands upon the clock of time.

The Free Trade controversy presents anew all the features of the old controversy against ingrained abuses. The struggle, which, in one form or another and under varied names, has divided men into opposing camps, since the first existence of political societies, is now waging round the issue of Free Trade. Religious, political, and industrial freedom are the constituent elements of a stable and prosperous State. Two of these—religious and political freedom—have already been achieved; but the struggle is yet being waged around the third. Yet, of the three, industrial freedom is of most importance to a democratic State; because under the modern conditions of civil life, neither religious nor political freedom is likely to be long enjoyed, if the fabric of liberty is once impaired upon the side of industry. The matter of primary importance in any industrial society is the preservation, against all attacks, of its individual freedom. Those who, in their zeal for socialism, temperance, or other objects, refuse to take their part in the fiscal battle, need to be reminded of Mr. John Morley's advice to another class of earnest reformers, that " They should not let the eternities bulk so big as to shut out this perishable speck, the human race," and to be guided in their practice by Cobden's sage direction that "in politics we must only do one thing at a time." The first thing to be done now throughout the greater part of the English-speaking world is, to destroy Protection. That once accomplished, the path is clear, and other reforms will follow.

APPENDIX I.

TABLES OF WAGES IN THE ENGLISH COTTON, WOOLLEN, WORSTED, AND IRON TRADES.

IN order to illustrate the statements in Chapter IV., Part I., relating to the diffusion of wealth in Great Britain, some tables are subjoined, exhibiting the fluctuations in the wages of the four principal English Industries—the Cotton, Woollen, Worsted, and Iron manufactures—since 1830. The figures are extracted from the Reports issued by the Board of Trade, under the title "Miscellaneous Statistics of the United Kingdom." Unfortunately, these reports contain very little evidence upon which positive conclusions can be based. They contain, it is true, a good deal of miscellaneous information about wages; but they appear at irregular intervals, and their information is exhibited on miscellaneous principles of inconvenience and confusion. In one report an industry is scheduled by itself, which in the next is lost among a mass of details of the state of trade in certain districts. Sometimes wages are estimated by the hour, sometimes by the week, and sometimes by the piece. Upon occasions the employments of workmen are distributed; while upon others an industry is treated as a whole, and its rate of wages is expressed in averages; and, not unfrequently, an important trade, the condition of which has been described for several years with a most useful fulness, drops out entirely from the record, never to appear again.[1]

But, in spite of the impaired value of such ill-arranged statistics, the figures are useful up to a certain point for purposes of comparison; and, in respect of the four great industries already named, they have been presented with some approach to an uniform method. These trades together give employment to about one-half of the working-class, so that the varying rate of wages paid in them during the last thirty years will indicate an approximate answer to the question "Whether wages in England have on the whole risen or decreased?"

A.—WAGES IN THE COTTON INDUSTRY.

The wages paid in the Cotton industry are particularly valuable indications of the rates in other trades, both because for the last

---

[1] These deficiencies have been remedied of late years; but the remarks apply to the years over which these figures have been taken.

forty years that industry has maintained the same position of importance, and because it has also, during that time, been singularly free from any disturbing fluctuation in the number of hands employed.[1] This is mainly owing to the gradual introduction of machinery, by which, in spite of the great increase in the production of cotton goods, the necessity for employing more labour has been avoided.

In examining the fluctuations, it is convenient to adopt a rough division of the Cotton operatives into four classes, according to the degree of skill required in their several occupations.

In the first class would come the overlookers and superior artisans in each department, together with those spinners who, according to the number of spindles each man can manage, would be classed above No. 100 in the technical language of the factory. The bulk of the adult males would fall into the second class, as being spinners and weavers of average skill. Women should be ranked alone as a third class; and, for greater clearness, the wages of children under sixteen should also be considered separately.

The subjoined Tables are an attempt to carry out this principle of division.

TABLE SHOWING THE FLUCTUATIONS IN THE AVERAGE RATE OF WEEKLY WAGES PAID TO PERSONS EMPLOYED IN THE COTTON TRADE DURING THE YEARS 1839-77 IN MANCHESTER AND THE NEIGHBOURHOOD:—

Occupation.	1839.	1849.	1859.	1874.	1877.
	s. d. s. d.	s. d. s. d.	s. d. s. d.	s. s. d.	s. s. d. s. d.
1ST CLASS. Superior Operatives.					
(i.) Overlookers	24 0 to 25 0	28 0	28	30 0 to 45 0	30 0 to 45 0
(ii.) Skilled spinners, above No. 100	40 0 to 45 0	36 0 to 40 0	40 to 45 45	0 to 50 45	0 to 55 0
(iii.) Engineers	24 0	28 0	30	42 0	58 3
2ND CLASS. Unskilled Operatives.					
(i.) Spinners below No. 100	23 0 to 25 0	21 0		23 to 25 42 0	40 0
(ii.) Bleachers	21 0	18 0	15	24 0	28 0
(iii.) Strippers and grinders	11 0 to 13 0	12 0 to 13 0	12 to 13 22	0 to 23 21	0
(iv.) Labourers	15 0	15 0	15	19 6	18 9
3RD CLASS. Women.					
(i.) Carding Department	6 6 to 7 6	6 6 to 8 6	7 to 9 11	0 to 16 15	6 to 18 7
(ii.) Doublers	7 0	7 6	9	10 0 to 13 12	0
(iii.) Weaving	9 0 to 17 0	9 0 to 16 0	10 to 20		12 0 to 24 0
Weekly hours of labour	69	60	60	59	56½

[1] The number of hands employed in all branches of the Cotton trade is given at 420,000 for 1874, and in 1839 it was estimated at 300,000.

It appears from these Tables that in the year 1839 the wages of the highest paid overlooker, in any department, was 25s. for a week of sixty-nine hours, which is twelve hours a day, with nine hours on Saturday for a half-holiday. Ten years later—after Free Trade—his wages had risen to 28s., and his hours of work had been reduced to sixty in the week. Since that date there has been a steady improvement in wages, together with a further reduction in the hours of work. The lowest paid overlooker now gets more for fifty-six and a half hours' work than the best paid overlooker received in 1849 for sixty hours; while the remuneration of the more skilled overlookers has increased more than fifty per cent. in the same period. The increase in the wages of the engineers is even more remarkable. They have more than doubled in the last thirty years. The skilled spinners—after a temporary fall, through the introduction of machinery—are also better off than they were. Those who are the least skilled among them are paid higher for less work, and the rewards open to them for a higher exercise of skill are considerably increased. Even the class of unskilled labourers, whose progress, as already noted in the text,[1] is generally slower, have, in some cases, doubled their wages in the same thirty years; although, with reference to this class, it should not be forgotten that many of its members are constantly pushing forward into better paid employments, and that it is also being constantly recruited from below by those who, in former days, would have lived as paupers or vagabonds.

The figures which show the wages paid to women need no further explanation. They will show, with sufficient clearness, how low is the market value of woman's labour, and how little has been done to raise that value by intelligent and powerful combination. Unlike men, women are not yet paid by reference to any standard of class comfort, but are content with any pittance which may increase the family resources, however insufficient that may be, by itself, to keep one person in a position of health and decency. By such ill-judged economy, they only depress the general labour market, without obtaining for themselves independence or security; so that they tempt men, who are heedless of the impossibility of bringing women back to a state of subjection, to clamour for their exclusion from male employments.

[1] See page 303.

WEEKLY WAGES PAID IN THE WOOLLEN TRADE AT LEEDS AND HUDDERSFIELD. THE FIGURES FROM 1855 TO 1851 ARE OF THE WAGES PAID AT LEEDS, THOSE FROM 1866 TO 1879 OF THOSE PAID AT HUDDERSFIELD.

	1855 to 1856	1850 to 1851	1850-1	1851.	1866.	1867-8.	1874.	1877.
SKILLED LABOUR.								
Wool Sorters	30/- to 35/-	35/- to 36/-	30/- to 36/-	30/- to 36/-	See note.	See note.		
Slubbers, Mule spinners	28/-	28/-	28/-	28/-	18/- to 30/-	16/- to 30/-	28/-	35/-
Woolcombers	19/-	24/-	24/-	24/-	22/- to 32/-	22/- to 32/-	28/-	25/-
LABOURERS &c. GROUP ADULTS.								
Piecers, Scourers	15/9 to 28/-	16/- to 20/-	16/- to 20/-	16/- to 20/-	16/- to 21/-	16/6 to 21/-	21/-	24/-
Dyers		16/- to 18/-	16/- to 18/-	16/- to 18/-	15/- to 22/-	15/- to 22/-	21/-	24/-
Powerloom Weavers	15/-	15/-	15/-	15/-	18/- to 23/6	18/- to 23/6	25/-	26/-

NOTE. The wages of overlookers are not given beyond 1851. The highest skilled labour in the trade after that date is paid between 50s. and 60s.

TABLE OF WEEKLY WAGES PAID AT BRADFORD IN THE WORSTED MANUFACTURE.

Occupation.	1855-7.	1858.	1860.	1861.	1863.	1866.	1867-8.	1874.	1877.
CLASS 1.									
Overlookers	18/- to 27/-	21/- to 27/-	28/- to 40/-	28/- to 40/-	28/- to 40/-	35/-	30/-		29/- to 34/-
Warehousemen	14/- to 27/-	14/- to 27/-	15/- to 35/-	15/- to 35/-	15/- to 35/-				
Heads of Departments of Dye Houses	20/-	20/-	Average 32/-	Average 32/-	Average 32/-	50/- Average 40/-	30/- to 50/-		
Engine Tenters	30/- to 36/-	30/- to 36/-					28/- to 35/-	28/- to 35/-	30/- to 40/-
CLASS 2.									
Weavers	14/- to 24/-		12/- to 16/-	12/- to 16/-	12/- to 16/-	18/-		20/- to 21/-	18/- to 22/-
Dyers	14/- to 21/-	14/- to 24/-	20/-	20/-	20/-	18/-	20/-		18/- to 26/-
W-l Sorters	15/- to 25/-	18/- to 27/-	20/- to 24/3	20/- to 24/3	24/- to 21/3	28/-	28/-		31/-
CLASS 3.									
W-l Washers	11/6 to 18/-	14/- to 18/-	14/2 to 18/-	15/- to 18/-	15/- to 18/-	16/6	17/6	16/- to 18/-	17/- to 19/-

TABLE OF WEEKLY WAGES PAID IN THE IRON TRADE OF SHEFFIELD.

	1840.	1850.	1860.	1861.	1863.	1866.	1868.	1871.	1874.
Table Knives (fine) ...	40/-	40/-	42/-	42/-	42/-				
Scissors (fine) ...	23/-	28/-	24/6	24/6	24/6			32/-	
Edge Tools (best) ...	29/-	32/6	36/-	36/-	36/-	31/- to 36/-	31/- to 36/-		
Table Knives (common) ...	22/-	27/-	18/- to 24/-	Reduced to 30 per cent, in consequence of American War.	Advance of 8 to 10 per cent.	28/-	28/-	35/-	
Scissors (common) ...			22/6 to 25/6			20/- to 30/-	20/- to 30/-	20/-	
STEEL MAKERS.									
Converters ...	36/-	36/-	37/-			28/- to 40/-	28/- to 40/-	30/- to 35/-	
Converters' Labourers ...	18/-	18/-	18/-			18/- to 21/-	18/- to 21/-	19/-	20/-

No figures are given for Sheffield wages beyond 1874.

APPENDIX II.

J. S. MILL AND PROTECTION.

THE idea that the abnormal economic circumstances of a young country justify the imposition of Protective duties is sometimes supposed by Protectionists to have approved itself to no less eminent a thinker than John Stuart Mill. Indeed, much of the Protectionist argument from natural difficulties is professedly adopted from one passage in the writings of this economist. As this passage has been so much misunderstood, it will be well to quote it in full before entering upon any criticism of Mr. Mill's views.

"The only case," says he, "in which, on mere principles of political economy, protecting duties can be defensible, is when they are imposed temporarily (especially in a young and rising nation) in hopes of naturalising a foreign industry in itself perfectly suitable to the circumstances of the country. The superiority of one country over another in a branch of production often arises only from having begun it sooner. There may be no inherent advantage on one part or disadvantage on the other, but only a present superiority of acquired skill and experience. A country which has this skill and experience yet to acquire may, in other respects, be better adapted to the production than those which were earlier in the field; and, besides, it is a just remark that nothing has a greater tendency to promote improvements in any branch of production than its trial under a new set of conditions. But it cannot be expected that individuals, at their own expense, or, rather, at their certain loss, would introduce a new manufacture, and bear the burden of carrying it on until the producers have been educated up to the level of those with whom the processes are traditional. A protecting duty continued for a reasonable time will sometimes be the least inconvenient mode in which the nation can tax itself for the support of such an experiment. But the Protection should be confined to cases in which there is good ground of assurance that the industry which it fosters will, after a time, be able to dispense with it; nor should the domestic producers ever be allowed to expect that it will be continued to them beyond the time necessary for a fair trial of what they are capable of accomplishing."

As this passage has been so often misinterpreted to convey an approval of the Protective policy in America and Australia, it may be well to set out clearly at starting what are the conditions under which Mill thinks Protection might be justifiable. They are four in number :—

(1) Where the tariff is imposed to *start* a new industry.
(2) Where such industry is plainly *suitable* to the country.
(3) Where it is only the *want of experience* on the part of either labourer or capitalist which deters individuals from running the risk of establishing the industry.
(4) Where there is good reason to believe that the fostered industry will soon be able to stand alone.

It is not an excessive admission that in such a case "Protection might be one mode" in which a nation could tax itself in support of an industrial experiment. Mill's error lay in thinking that it could ever be "the least inconvenient mode" of raising such a tax. The error of those that quote Mill lies in not perceiving that his observations only apply to the cases in which the conditions which he requires are present, and that in these cases he only contemplates giving Protection during that short interval in the history of an industry between the first production of an article and the time when the home manufacturer is able to compete with his foreign rival both in quality and quantity. In the whole history of the Protective movement in America and Australia it is, I believe, impossible to cite a single industry, the circumstance of which would have justified Protection according to the canons laid down by Mr. Mill.

Even, however, if it be granted that the condition of things conceived by Mr. Mill is theoretically possible, it cannot be too strongly insisted upon that Protection is the most wasteful, unjust, and inconvenient method of Government assistance.

In the first place, whatever aid it gives comes too late : because it cannot be of service in starting an industry, whatever advantages it may give after the industry is set going. Take, for instance, Mill's imaginary case of an industry which is delayed by want of skilled labour. This labour must either be imported from abroad or created at home by instruction ; and in neither case is the object sought for immediately furthered by Protective duties. It would be better for the Government either to pay the passages of the imported labourers, if immigration were necessary, or to bear the cost of giving the required instruction to a sufficient number of home labourers. Either of these methods of aid would be directed immediately to the object aimed at, and would be free from the grave objection to which Protection is open, of placing difficulties in the way of every industry which requires to make use of the Protected article. In fact, it must be plain that Protective duties can be of no advantage until the producers have begun to make the article; but none the less they lay a heavy burden on the community from the first day on which they are collected; while the benefits which they confer at a later stage in the history of an industry—after it has been started, but before it is able to hold its own—are open to the further objections that they come too late and are scattered indiscriminately upon those who may deserve them and those who certainly do not.

The founder of a new industry in a young country does undoubtedly confer a benefit upon the whole community at his own personal expense and risk; so that it may be sometimes desirable, in the cases which Mr. Mill has put, that Government should encourage men to make experiments in new industrial ventures. But of all modes of giving this encouragement, Protection is the most ill-advised, being at once unjust and unsuccessful. The help which it gives comes after the time of difficulty has gone by, and is given with equal readiness both to the enterprising originator of the industry and every one who rushes into the business upon the strength of his experience. By this competition prices are certain to be reduced, until the originator of the industry may lose the advantages of the monopoly, which was created as his reward If Government aid is really required, either as a stimulus to new experiments or a reward for successful ones, it ought to take a form which will give the benefit with as much discrimination as possible to those who deserve it, and with as little hardship as possible to the mass of the consumers. Either the payment of a money sum by way of bonus for the first production of the required article at home, or the granting of an allowance to the originator of an industry to enable him to sell his goods at market rates during his temporary inability to compete with the foreigner, or the letting of a Government contract at a non-competitive rate would serve the double purpose of reward and encouragement without much inconvenience to the mass of consumers. Any of these methods of aid, moreover, has the advantage that it can be easily withdrawn; while a Protective tariff, once imposed, remains an incubus which can only be removed by serious civil strife. The essential ingredients in any form of Government assistance should be that it was terminable at a fixed period, and that both the persons who receive it and the amount which each receives should be easily ascertainable. Protection does not satisfy either of these requirements.

No form of Government aid, however, is free from objection. Bonuses, bounties, special contracts, or any other form of subsidy, are in the long run demoralising both to the recipients and to the public life of the country, both as being premiums on laziness and occasions for fraud. It is so easy for all concerned to receive and pay money according to the terms of some agreement, that neither can a manufacturer be expected to shorten this period of gratuitous assistance nor a civil servant to watch very closely all the details of a manufacturing process or check the figures of a ledger. In any bargain of this kind with the State the manufacturer is sure to get the best of it.

Fortunately, experience proves that Government assistance is not required to start new industries in a young country. If there is a risk of failure in a young country owing to the inexperience of all concerned, the conditions of the country soften the failure very much. In a small country new industries must be on a small scale; and no large expenditure, whether Government assistance be extended or withheld, would be required to embark upon the experimental stages of a new industry. Consequently, we may watch every demand for State aid with more than ordinary suspicion, without being haunted by any sentimental fear lest in protecting the State purse against the raids of interested persons we are delaying the development of our country. Healthy enterprises and profitable trades are sure to be developed without assistance; while if there be any natural industry which ought to start at once, and is prevented by the want of Government assistance, the question must be still answered whether it is not better to lose the industry than to enter on the perilous path of State aid.

APPENDIX III.

Comparison between the Respective Rates of Progress of New South Wales and Victoria since 1866.

§ 1. The risk of pressing too far any argument, which rests upon a comparison between the condition of different countries, has been already alluded to in these pages, and attention has been called to the passage in which Mr. Giffen points out, with admirable lucidity, the requisites under which alone any such comparison is admissible. These requisites exist more nearly as between New South Wales and Victoria than between any other countries, so that, if the argument from comparison is ever admissible, it will be in their case. Both of them are young countries, and are inhabited by men of the same race, speech, and training : capital and labour oscillate freely between them : both use substantially the same methods and forms of government : while, against the larger territory of New South Wales may be set the superior climate and easier development of its southern neighbour. Whatever may be the balance of the natural advantages, whether of climate or population, is on the side of Victoria, whose compact, fertile, and well-watered territory gained for it, on its first discovery, the well-deserved title of Australia Felix. The striking and ultimate point of difference between the two countries is their fiscal policy. Since 1866 Victoria has lived under a system of gradually increasing Protection, while the policy of New South Wales has been, in the main, one of Free Trade. According to all Protectionist theory Victoria should be prosperous and New South Wales distressed ; there should be variety and growth in the one country, stagnation in the other. At least the progress of Victoria ought to have been more rapid than that of New South Wales, because she has added to the natural advantages which she already enjoyed, the artificial benefits which are claimed for a Protective tariff.

If, in fact, neither of these conclusions is correct, and, while both countries have been phenomenally prosperous, New South Wales has prospered the most, one of two conclusions is inevitable—namely, either that certain special influences have caused the more rapid progress of New South Wales which were not felt in Victoria, or that Protection has retarded instead of assisted the development of Victoria's natural superiority.

§ 2. Writers of all schools admit that activity in certain departments of national life is a fair indication of prosperity and progress. It is, for instance, generally allowed that an increase in population, a development of agricultural and manufacturing industry, a growth of foreign commerce, an increase in shipping, or an improvement in the public revenue, are all signs of health and well-being; and that a concurrence of such symptoms over a lengthened period indicates an increase in material wealth.

Accepting these tests of progress, our comparison proceeds thus: first, we examine the position of the two Colonies as regards population, foreign commerce, shipping, agriculture, manufactures, and revenue, at the time when both of them adhered to Free Trade; from which we find that, according to all these indications of prosperity, Victoria was then very much the better off: In 1866 she outnumbered New South Wales in population by 200,000 souls: her foreign commerce was larger by £8,300,000: she had a greater area of land under cultivation: her manufactures were well established, while those of New South Wales were few and insignificant: she was ahead in shipping, and her revenue was greater by one-third.

Passing next to the years which follow 1866, we observe that New South Wales gradually bettered her position in every province of national activity, and that, as the fetters of Protection became tighter, Victoria receded in the race. She gave way first in the department of foreign commerce, next in population, shipping, and revenue, until, in 1887, she maintained her old superiority in agriculture alone.

From this accumulation of facts—and not from any one of them—we infer that the rate of progress in New South Wales under Free Trade has been greater than that of Victoria under Protection; and we use this fact (without at present claiming the credit of it for Free Trade, or seeking for its explanation as one, which, whatever its explanation may be, is proof by itself that the Protectionist dogma as to the inability of a young country under any circumstances to make rapid progress without Protection is contrary to experience. "Either prosperity in a Free Trade country, or distress in a Protectionist country, is," as

Professor Summer has said, "fatal to the Protectionist theory."

§ 3. Having established our facts, we next seek to explain them; and in doing so have first to consider the various explanations offered by Protectionists. These are three in number. First, they say that the comparison between New South Wales and Victoria ought not to be made, because the conditions of the two countries are not similar; and they specially insist upon the earlier foundation and the larger territory of the Free Trade Colony. This argument we meet by a plea in confession and avoidance, to drop for a moment into the apt language of the lawyer's art; the facts may be admitted, but the use which is made of them must be contested. We shall have to show that whatever advantages the circumstances referred to may give to New South Wales are more than compensated for by other advantages peculiar to Victoria.

The second argument by which Protectionists attempt to depreciate the significance of the New South Wales superiority is by insisting that her growth is due to certain special causes—such as the expenditure of borrowed money, and the sale of public lands—which have no connection with the fiscal dispute. Here, again, the facts will be admitted, and it will be conceded that both these and other causes have contributed most materially to the rapid progress of New South Wales. But it will also be shown that whatever influences besides Free Trade have aided New South Wales, have also aided Victoria with even greater intensity. Thus, the very facts which are advanced as a disparagement will be used as further evidence of the efficacy of a Free Trade policy.

Having thus sketched the outline of the argument which follows, we are in a position to enter upon the details with less risk of confusion.

POPULATION.

The first element of greatness to a young country is population. A new land needs to be developed by strong arms, and everywhere cries aloud for men. It is true that congestions in the labour market occur at times in Australia as elsewhere, but they must not be taken as indications of over-population. Every new country contains a residuum of criminals and ne'er-do-weels who, from one cause or another, are unfit for work; while Australia possesses in addition a class of genuine *lazzaroni*, whose dislike of any steady occupation is encouraged by a genial climate and a reckless system of public and private almsgiving. During the greater part of the year the shelter of a roof at night is neither requisite nor comfortable; while for the inclement season, food and lodging can be had in every capital either gratuitously or for a minimum of work. Besides this voluntary pauperism, there is in every Colony a certain element of casually employed persons, consisting of artisans and clerks, who experience real suffering in times of depression, from inability or unwillingness to leave the cities and seek new kinds of occupation in the country. Still, after making every allowance for temporary dislocations of industry, it is safe to say that the danger of over-population is not within the limits of practical Australian politics; and that, even in times of greatest depression, thousands of able-bodied men could always obtain work in any Colony at good, and even high, wages. The growth of population is thus a crucial test of Australian prosperity, which can be applied without qualification to all the Colonies, because none has any pre-eminence in "unemployed." The class of the "unemployed" contains the same elements in all, and passes freely from one to the other, as political agitation or other causes makes its existence notorious.[1]

In 1866, the year in which Protection was introduced, the

[1] An illustration of this occurred in Sydney towards the close of 1886, when a Protectionist Government gave indiscriminate relief, without any labour test, shortly before a general election. The natural consequence was that the floating population of all the Colonies drifted to Sydney, where 6,000 men were at one time being lodged and fed by the Government. After the elections, during which this body of "unemployed" was freely used as an argument against Free Trade, Sir Henry Parkes, who had succeeded to power, found himself unable to disband so large an army in the streets of Sydney, and adopted the plan of creating employment on Crown lands for all who wished it, while at the same time he stopped the indiscriminate relief in Sydney. It was more than a year before the labour market—which had become quite disorganised by the inducements offered to country labourers to throw up their work, either to enjoy a visit to Sydney, or to earn (as good workmen could) more than their usual wage by piece-work on the Crown lands—resumed its normal condition. An incident occurred during this period which illustrates in an amusing fashion the popular view of the "right to employment" as it finds expression in Australia. In June, 1887, the "unemployed," who were then working at the Field of Mars for 5s. a day, petitioned the Cabinet to be allowed "a day's holiday to celebrate the Jubilee," so completely had they come to regard themselves as a State institution.

population of Victoria amounted to 636,982 human beings, as against 431,412 in New South Wales. In 1881, the relative numbers were 862,346 and 751,468. In 1886 the numbers were estimated in both Colonies at a million. Victoria then gained a little during the Exhibition year in 1888, but in 1889 New South Wales again took the lead with 1,122,200, as against 1,118,077, and has maintained it to the present time. During the period from 1866-89, the increase was only 75 per cent. for the Protected Colony, while it was 140 per cent. for the Free Trade Colony. The increase from 1871 to 1881 was 30·91 per cent. in New South Wales, and only 18 per cent. in Victoria ; and from 1881 to 1888 it was 44·43 per cent. in the former, and only 26·50 per cent. in the latter Colony. While in the former decade the difference in the rate of increase was 12·91 per cent., it was 18·43 per cent. during the latter period, thus proving that the increase of Protective duties is not necessarily accompanied *pari passu* by an increase in population.[1]

Popular prejudice, anxious to minimise as much as possible this rapid growth in the numbers of a Free Trade Colony, where, according to all theory, no man ought to be able to get a living, has attributed it to State-assisted immigration. There were, however, during the period from 1881-87, when the increase in population was most rapid, only 32,744 assisted immigrants ; while the whole number of State-assisted immigrants between 1866 and 1889 only amounted to 59,000, as against a total increase of 690,788 souls. Assisted immigration can accordingly account for only 8·5 per cent. of the whole increase.

The real reasons must be sought elsewhere, and will be found in the greater attractiveness of New South Wales as a place of residence, in its higher marriage rate, and its higher birth rate— three causes which, either separately or together, indicate a higher range of material prosperity. We will treat of each separately.

The most noticeable fact which is disclosed by the Victorian Census of 1871 and 1881, is that, next to the little island of Tasmania, Victoria has the greatest proportion of females to males of any Australian Colony, which is the more remarkable when we recall

---

[1] I am indebted for these calculations, which are taken from the official records, to a pamphlet by W. Max Hirsch, entitled, "Protection in Victoria" (Melbourne : *Echo* Publishing Company, 1891)— see p. 10.

the circumstances of her origin in the gold fever of the early fifties. Victoria in those days had an enormous excess of males. Further, we find that this unhappy disproportion between the sexes is growing rather than diminishing in the Protected Colony. The following table shows the figures as compared with those of New South Wales :—

PERCENTAGE OF FEMALES IN THE TOTAL POPULATION.

Year.	New South Wales.	Victoria.
1881	45·8	47·5
1888	44·3	46·6
1891	46·5	47·8

Pursue the investigation a little further.

The census returns for 1881 showed that Victoria—like the exhausted countries of Europe—was actually not sustaining her own population! During the ten years, 1871 to 1881, the returns show that 53,000 persons emigrated to Victoria, but that 68,000 persons left. In other words, during these ten years of active Protection, adopted professedly in order to "give employment," Victoria not only lost all her immigration, but also 15,000 of her natural increase! The figures of the last census in 1891 will be awaited with much interest.

More significant still is the change in the quality of the Victorian population. The class of citizen which every country wishes most to keep is that of the "soldier's age," from 20 to 40. Yet in 1881, in spite of her much larger population, Victoria was found to possess about 18,000 fewer men at this desirable range of age than New South Wales. On this point, Mr. Hayter, who certainly cannot be accused of giving undue prominence to any fact which tells against Victoria, makes the following remarks in his "General Report" on the Census :—"It will be noticed that the contingent available from Victoria is smaller by 18,000 than that from New South Wales, and a simple calculation will show that relatively to the total population, males at the soldier's age are fewer in Victoria than in any of the other Australasian Colonies. In fact, it may be stated that the deficiency of males, at this important period of life, is the weakest point in the Victorian population." Upon this passage Mr. Edward Pulsford, who was the first to investigate the bearing of the Victorian population returns upon the fiscal controversy, remarks as follows: "The cream of the 'effective' population of a country may be said to be the males between 25 and 45. The changes in this portion of the people in the two Colonies during the decade were simply extraordinary. New South Wales showed a gain of 32,716, whilst Victoria showed a positive loss of 35,916. In 1871, Victoria was 52,138 ahead; in 1881, she was 16,494 behind—a change against Victoria in the relative position of no less than 68,632."

The following two tables will bring out more clearly still the greater attraction which New South Wales exercises on men in the prime of life, and the loss which Victoria sustains through the emigration of this economically most valuable section of its population:—

MALES IN 1881.

	Victoria.		New South Wales.	
Up to 25 years old	257,069 = 56·86 per cent.	...	229,342 = 55·78 per cent.	
From 25 to 45 years old	99,497 = 22 ,, ,,	...	115,991 = 28·22 ,, ,,	
45 years old and over	95,579 = 21·14 ,, ,,	...	65,816 = 16 ,, ,,	
	452,143	...	411,149	

MALES BETWEEN THE AGES OF 25 AND 45 YEARS.

	Victoria.		New South Wales.
1871	135,413 = 18·1 per cent.	...	83,275 = 10·7 per cent.
1881	99,497 = 11·5 ,, ,,	...	115,991 = 15·4 ,, ,,
Loss	35,916	... Gain .	32,716

Mr. Hirsch makes the following remarks upon these figures:—
" In the first of these tables the percentages are those of the male population; in the latter, the percentage of the males in their prime to the total population is given. The first table shows the result, viz., the greater percentage of men in the prime of life in New South Wales; the latter table shows that the shifting took place in the years during which Victoria *enjoyed* Protection; that on account or in spite of Protection young men are avoiding and leaving the Protected Colony in which, if Protectionists are right, they ought to find it easiest to make a living—are flocking into the Colony in which they ought to find it most difficult to make a living. In estimating the significance of these figures, it must not be forgotten that, according to the general increase of population, we ought to have had [in Victoria] in 1881 20,987 more males of from twenty-five to forty-five years than in 1871, making our total

loss of men in the prime of life 56,903—surely a most disastrous retrogression in one decade. There is, however, nothing new in these tables ; they are merely a confirmation of what has long been generally known. Every traveller remarks upon the number of Victorians engaged in trade and agriculture in New South Wales and other Colonies, and the paucity of natives or former inhabitants of New South Wales similarly engaged in Victoria. A more significant fact by which to measure the result of Protection can scarcely be asked for, for if the Protective policy had added to the natural advantages of Victoria, then surely Victoria would have powerfully attracted the workers in the prime of life from every Colony, and even from over-sea. But the opposite is the case ; the strong, the hopeful, the energetic, leave the Protected Colony, and flock into the Free Trade Colony instead, proving conclusively that there it is easiest for them to gain a comfortable livelihood."

But gain by immigration is not the only cause of the more rapid increase of population in New South Wales, which is due also to a higher marriage rate and a higher birth rate.

Now, as Mr. Hirsch points out, " it is one of the most firmly established facts in the science of statistics that under present social and economic conditions the numbers of marriages and births rise and fall with any fall in the nation's prosperity : that steady employment at decent wages especially has the invariable result of increasing the number of marriages and births. And it must be held as similarly true that in two nations of similar origin, the members of which are constantly intermingling, the social and political institutions of which are the same, the more prosperous nation, the one in which employment is more constant and effective, wages higher, will show the greater number of marriages and births." Tried by this unerring test, New South Wales again holds her superiority over her Protected neighbour.

The mean annual marriage rate per 1,000 during the years 1866-1889 was, for Victoria, 6·90 ; for New South Wales, 8·00. While the annual birth rate for the same period was, for Victoria, 34·54, and for New South Wales 38·90.

The excess of births over deaths tells the same tale : its mean per 1,000 of the population for the ten years from 1878-87 being 112 for Victoria, and 148 for New South Wales.

Indeed, from whatever standpoint the movements of population and the vital statistics of the two Colonies are considered, it is clear that under Free Trade New South Wales has gained upon

Victoria, not only by immigration, but by a more rapid increase in the number of her native-born—a significant commentary indeed upon the theory that "Protection gives employment." Why did it not give employment to those thousands of young men, within the soldier's age, who emigrated from her borders into New South Wales? Is it that New South Wales is the more attractive because she has a larger territory? But had she not just the same extent of territory in 1866, when Victoria, under Free Trade, was able to feed her own sons? Or is Victoria, with its 87,884 square miles of territory, not able to find employment for more than a million people? When Victoria is over-populated it will be time enough to raise the cry that New South Wales is drawing young Victorians to her territory because their own land does not give them so good an opportunity of earning a livelihood. It is "Protection" that was to have given the employment! It has done so! It has made every one who stayed in Victoria work longer for what he wants, and has driven the cream of Victorian youth out of the Colony to earn honest livings in a Free Trade country! But was that the kind of employment which was so fraudulently promised?

The truth is manifest to all who will not refuse to see it—that the labour-market has been better in New South Wales than in Victoria, and that the Free Trade Colony has offered the most employment. One would as soon expect water to run uphill as labour to leave a country of good wages and steady work for one of inferior attractiveness from either point of view. Accordingly, if New South Wales has gained upon Victoria in population, both by voluntary immigration and by natural increase, since the latter adopted Protection, the reason must be that the Free Trade Colony has been more prosperous, and better able to offer work at good wages; and further evidence in support of the fact should be superfluous. It may, however, be useful to pile up testimony upon this crucial point, and to show by other tests that Victorians have gone to New South Wales for one very good reason—that they were better off there than they would have been at home.

First, as to the respective rates of wages in the two countries. So far as any comparison can be made between these—and the difficulty of such a comparison has been already pointed out[1]—it is

[1] See above, p. 337.

in favour of New South Wales. Mr. Hirsch has compiled a table from the Victorian Year-Book, showing the fluctuations in the nominal wages of 121 trades, as returned by the Government statist. This table shows that between 1878 and 1888, during which period new duties were imposed to the annual amount of £180,000, no change in wages had taken place in 58 of these 121 industries. The alteration in the rates of wages for the remaining 63 employments classify themselves as follows :—

	Increase.	Decrease.
Protected trades	13	26
Unprotected trades	16	9

showing that, while there has been, on the whole, a decline rather than a rise in wages during the decade, the fall has taken place more in the protected than in the unprotected trades. The rise in wages has occurred chiefly in the farm pursuits, owing to the scarcity of this kind of labour. It should also be remembered that the official wage rates make no disclosure of the condition of the large number of home-workers, who, as recent revelations have shown, are working in Melbourne dens for 1s. 6d. and 2s. a day under conditions which the *Age*, the leading Protectionist journal, has described as being "as bad as anything to be found in London."

It is true that wages have also fallen in New South Wales from the highest point which they reached since 1866 ; but the Free Traders have never claimed to be possessors of a patent system for keeping wages high. Besides, so far as comparisons are possible, they are higher in New South Wales than in Victoria. There is a special difficulty in the way of making any such comparison in this case, owing to the different methods of collecting the returns in the two Colonies, and the different designations of many trades. Still, Mr. Hirsch has collected twenty-nine trades—all which it was possible to collect—and found that in 1888 wages in four of these were equal in the two Colonies, were higher in Victoria in ten, and lower in Victoria in fifteen instances. As he properly remarks, "If the assertion that Protection increases wages were well founded, no such result of even a partial comparison would be possible." But perhaps the best guide to the average wage rate of the two Colonies is furnished by the wages paid by the Governments of each. In each Colony the Government owns the railways, post-office, telegraphs, roads, forests, and carries on a great quantity of public works. In all the Government departments the wages are from sixpence to a shilling a day higher in New South Wales than in Victoria. It is impossible to believe that the highly organised trades in Victoria would allow railway servants, for example, to receive a shilling a day less than the same class of labour was receiving in New South Wales, unless they were conscious that the lower rate fairly represented the average wage rate of the Colony. In addition to these sources of information must be added private experience. It is matter of common observation that the wages paid to miners are higher in New South Wales than in Victoria, and the writer verified the same fact by personal inquiry in regard to the building trades for the year 1889–90.

All other possible sources of information point to the same conclusion.

The consumption of working-class luxuries, such as tea, coffee, sugar, currants, raisins, beer, spirits, and tobacco, is larger per head in the Free Trade country, showing the obvious truth that men who receive more have more to spend.

The following are the figures for the year 1884–5, which is taken as a normal year, being before the boom in Victoria and after that in New South Wales:—

CONSUMPTION OF LUXURIES IN 1884-5 PER HEAD.

	New South Wales.	Victoria.
Tea	127 ozs.	110 ozs.
Coffee	11 ,,	16 ,,
Sugar	102 lbs.	92¼ lbs.
Currants, raisins, etc.	111 ozs.	98½ ozs.
Spirits	20¾ gills.	18⅜ gills.
Beer	16½ gals.	16 gals.
Tobacco	46 ozs.	35½ ozs.

Pointing, again, in the same direction are the figures which show the quantity of postal and telegraphic communication in the two Colonies.

In 1866 Victoria received and despatched nearly two million more letters than New South Wales, the figures being 8,631,133 as against 6,678,371. In 1885 the positions were reversed, and New South Wales received and despatched three million more letters than Victoria, the figures being : New South Wales, 39,351,200, or 40 per head of the population ; and 36,061,880, or 36 per head, for Victoria.

The number of telegrams sent in Victoria in 1866 was 277,788, as against 143,523 in New South Wales. In 1885, New South Wales sent 2,625,992, against 1,634,666.

In fact, to whatever test of progress we look, we arrive at the same conclusion—namely, that since Victoria adopted Protection, New South Wales has been steadily gaining upon her. But some of the tests are of sufficient importance to demand a detailed consideration. Chief among them is the progress in either Colony of the manufacturing industry.

MANUFACTURES.

No young country can pass from the agricultural or pastoral to the manufacturing stage of its existence until it has obtained a sufficient density of population to enable production to be carried on with that effective cheapness which comes from the subdivision of employments and the establishment of subsidiary industries for using up bye-products. In 1866 the population of Victoria was already concentrated in the mining centres; while that of New South Wales was scattered over a wide area, through which the means of communication were few and primitive. As a natural consequence Victoria became a manufacturing Colony earlier than New South Wales. It is true that New South Wales has better facilities for manufactures in her rich deposits of coal and iron; but the advantage of these may be easily overestimated, unless it is remembered that the coal goes to both capitals by sea, and that the cost of 500 miles longer sea carriage is not a serious item in these days of fuel economy. It is accordingly not surprising to find that, while there were 869 manufactories and works in Victoria in 1866, exclusive of 114 flour mills, the manufactories and works of New South Wales were at that date too insignificant to be counted.

Since 1866 the whole energy of Victorian legislation has been directed to the development of manufactures; while, except as to a few industries, such as the kerosene and candle, which have benefited by duties originally imposed for revenue purposes, the development of manufactures in New South Wales has taken a natural growth. The figures speak for themselves.

In twenty-five years of Free Trade the pastoral Colony of New South Wales had made so good an entrance into the manufacturing stage of its existence that in 1890 it employed 46,135 hands, or more than one-tenth of its adult population, in one or other of the 120 distinct varieties of manufacturing industries, in which the plant and machinery was valued at £4,526,821, and worked to a horse-power of 24,662. Surely this would not be a bad record, either of growth or diversity, even for a Protected country!

The record of Victoria is also good, but certainly not better than, if, indeed, it is equal to, that of New South Wales. It is difficult, however, to decide this question, because the method of classification, and the dates of making the returns of manufacturing statistics, do not correspond in the two Colonies. The subjoined table, however, will show the respective rates of progress of each.

YEAR.	1880.		1885.		1889.		1890.	
	Victoria.	N. S. W.	Victoria.	N. S. W.	Victoria.	N. S. W.	Victoria.	N. S. W.
Number of hands employed	33,247	28,259	49,066	41,669	59,163[†]	46,135	58,175[†]	46,525[†]
Value of machinery, plant, and land (*Thousands omitted*)	6,711	—[*]	10,166	—[*]	15,612	11,603	—[*]	—[*]
Number of establishments[¶]	2,239	—[*]	2,841	—[*]	3,137	2,926	—[*]	2,183
Horse power	—	—	—	—	—	—	—	—

[*] Where blank spaces are left the figures are either untrustworthy or at present unattainable. The method of collecting New South Wales figures was radically altered after 1886, when the present statistician, Mr. Coghlan, was first appointed.

[†] These figures are from an estimate made by Mr. Hayter, the statistician of the Victorian Government, as published in the *Argus* of December 30th, 1891.

[¶] Many of these employ very few hands. Thus over three hundred of the works included in the Victorian returns employ less than six hands, and more than one thousand employ less than ten.

The above table puts the case of the Victorian manufactories in the most favourable light. Not only are some 2,300 hands included in the Victorian returns which are excluded from those of New South Wales,[1] but these also include between four and five thousand more females, whom the harder conditions of life in the Protected Colony have driven from the home to the factory.[2] Further, the later Victorian figures are for a time of high prosperity consequent upon the lavish expenditure of imported and borrowed capital, while during the same period New South Wales was experiencing the pangs of a period of economy, and was also

[1] Namely, employees in chaff-cutting and corn-crushing establishments, in flour mills, in cheese factories, and the Royal Mint.

[2] There were 662 females included in the New South Wales returns for 1890.

recovering from the most severe drought known in her history. The figures for 1891 would show an increase for New South Wales and a decrease for Victoria. Let us, however, pass by all these considerations, and grant a superiority (and, if it be desired, even a substantial superiority) to Victoria in manufactures : two questions will still remain to be answered—first, Whether this superiority is as great now as it was in 1866, having regard to the increase of population? and, secondly, Whether, if it be so, such a superiority has been worth the expenditure required to obtain it? Let no deductions be made on any score, and even count it a good thing that women should be forced to leave their homes to seek employment in a factory ; let us, in short, admit that Victoria has an excess over New South Wales of fully 12,000 manufacturing hands ; yet at what cost has this excess been gained? The Customs duties levied on Protected articles have by themselves amounted during the last twenty-five years to twenty millions of pounds, without taking into account the increase in the price of the home-made article, which is consequent upon the tariff. May not Free Traders fairly ask whether, if it was really necessary to Victorian prosperity that she should confine 12,000 of her population (of whom one-third are females) within the four walls of factories in order to be by that number superior to New South Wales in the tale of manufacturing employees, twenty millions of pounds sterling is not a high price to have paid for this questionable advantage? Twenty millions of pounds would have pensioned those 12,000 working hands, men, women, and children (and children, too, are being driven with their mothers to enter the Protected factories, so hard is the stress of life becoming in this Victorian paradise !), many times over, at more than the rate which they are now receiving in wages from the afflicted consumer ! If only the recipients of Protective charity could be compelled to receive their alms, as honest beggars, in a public manner !

Nor is an inside view of the condition of Victorian manufactures any more encouraging. On the contrary, while the number of employees is declining, and women and boys are taking the place of men, the exports of manufactured produce show a steady annual decline, and the imports of foreign goods a steady increase. The limit of consumption within the Colony has long ago been reached, and although an outlet was afforded for several years into the neighbouring Colonies by means of an elaborate system of fraud, under which the drawbacks were manipulated in such a way as to become a bonus upon exports,[1] the productiveness of the Protected industries is steadily decreasing. Year by year, Mr. Hayter, who certainly cannot be accused of giving undue prominence to facts which tell against Victoria, has pointed out the ominous decrease in the value of Victorian exports, and the equally ominous increase in Victorian indebtedness. The figures from 1880 are subjoined.

EXPORTS OF ARTICLES MANUFACTURED OR PRODUCED IN VICTORIA FROM 1880-90.

Year.	Total Value, omitting Thousands.	Value per Head of the Population.		
	£	£	s.	d.
1880	11,220,000	13	3	11
1881	12,480,000	14	7	3
1882	12,570,000	14	2	5
1883	13,292,000	14	11	9
1884	13,155,000	14	1	8
1885	12,452,000	12	19	10
1886	9,054,000	9	3	6
1887	8,502,000	8	6	9
1888	10,356,000	9	15	0
1889	9,776,000	8	17	1
1890				
1891				

In this table the exports of manufactured articles and of home produce are lumped together. If the former were dealt with separately, the decline would be still more apparent. On p. 131 of vol. ii. of the "Victorian Year-Book" for 1889-90, Mr. Hayter gives a list of thirty-five lines of Victorian articles of export. The majority of these are raw materials, which are not affected by duties. More than half of the value in the list is provided by the two articles of wool and gold, although more than one-half of the wool exported as Victorian produce is grown in New South Wales and shipped from Melbourne—either because of its proximity, or because "Port Phillip" wool commands a traditionally high price. Taking out from this list all articles which may, with a

[1] Public attention was first called to this system of fraud in 1886 by Mr. Edward Pulsford, Secretary of the Free Trade Association of New South Wales, and Honorary Member of the Cobden Club. His assertions were at first denied and ridiculed; but ultimately, after an official investigation, his charges were verified. Many of the first firms in Melbourne were found to be implicated, but no prosecutions followed. There could hardly be a better illustration of the demoralisation which a tariff causes.

stretch of the term, be classified as manufactured products, we get at the following result :—

EXPORTS OF ARTICLES THE MANUFACTURE OF VICTORIA SINCE 1883.

Articles.	1883.	1884.	1885.	1886.	1887.	1888.	1889.	Increase +; Decrease —
	£	£	£	£	£	£	£	£
Stationery	23,300	22,100	17,900	14,300	13,200	15,400	16,000	— 7,300
Agricultural Implements	14,100	10,300	11,000	11,700	15,600	15,600	22,000	+ 7,900
Machinery	138,000	98,000	73,000	48,000	90,000	56,000	62,000	— 76,000
Saddlery, Harness	22,000	14,000	13,000	9,800	7,100	10,000	6,800	— 15,200
Furniture and Upholstery	46,800	43,700	39,000	24,000	20,000	22,000	17,600	— 29,300
Drugs, Chemicals	15,000	12,000	17,000	13,000	10,600	7,000	4,700	— 10,300
Woollen Piece Goods	12,000	10,600	4,100	2,700	1,800	9,000	2,600	— 9,400
Apparel & Slops	246,000	257,000	242,000	155,000	117,000	121,800	98,000	— 148,000
Boots and Shoes	40,000	37,000	25,000	21,000	23,000	21,000	16,000	— 24,000
Cordage	27,600	29,000	20,600	9,000	5,000	4,000	4,600	— 23,000
Preserved Meats	76,000	116,000	99,800	58,000	41,000	16,000	16,000	— 60,000
Confectionery	15,700	13,000	11,000	6,700	3,700	2,800	2,700	— 13,000
Biscuits	27,600	40,000	45,000	37,600	26,800	20,000	20,600	— 7,000
Bone dust	8,900	11,300	14,400	9,600	5,200	11,300	11,000	+ 1,100
Candles	300	3,600	7,000	5,000	1,650	500	300	
Glue Pieces	600	1,000	1,000	1,700	1,700	1,500	900	+ 300
Leather	359,000	338,000	342,000	254,000	207,000	181,000	190,000	— 289,000
Soap	12,700	15,500	18,000	13,000	10,000	10,000	9,000	— 3,700
Stearine	13,000	6,000	—	5	96	500	85	— 12,900
Tallow	232,000	256,000	155,000	121,000	85,000	157,000	49,000	
Oil	8,000	9,000	7,000	7,000	3,600	2,000	1,800	— 6,200
Hardware	28,000	24,000	19,000	20,800	16,000	15,800	15,000	— 13,000
Oilmen's Stores	13,000	15,000	14,000	11,800	13,600	11,000	9,000	— 4,000
All other Articles	410,700	439,000	375,000	324,000	265,000	222,000	234,000	— 177,000
Total	1,792,300	1,824,100	1,570,000	1,207,705	983,576	934,100	819,685	— 1,110,300 — 2,300

The same conclusion as to the decline of Victorian manufactures is given by another table in Mr. Hayter's book (p. 133), in which the total increase or decrease of exports of all articles of home produce, as between 1889 and 1888, is given in detail, with the result of showing a nett decrease on the year of £579,963. It is noticeable, however, that this nett decrease is kept down to this comparatively low figure by reason of an increase of £1,438,593 in the value of wool exported, and of £129,498 in the value of the export of gold bullion. Deducting these two items, the nett decrease in the year would be £2,148,054; while if the nett decrease on manufactured products only were considered, it would amount to the large sum of £2,256,395.

These figures have a double significance. First they show that the export of Victorian manufactures has not been anything to boast of during the last eight years, and that, in spite of every effort to force manufactures, eleven-twelfths of the exports from Victoria consist of food-stuffs and raw materials. They also show, in the plainest manner, the withering influence of Protection upon the aggregate of national industry. The export trade of a country is a generally accepted test of the vigour of its national productiveness. Consequently, a fall in eight years from £14 11s. 9d. per head to £8 17s. 1d. in the total export trade—which is equivalent to a fall of 39·303 per cent.—and a fall of 32·925 per cent. during the same period in the exports of manufactured produce, ought to shake the confidence of the most infatuated believer in the infallibility of the Protectionist dogma! Further, when this decline in exports —which are the only means by which a borrowing country is able to discharge its indebtedness and pay its interest on loans—is accompanied by a rapidly increasing excess of imports, no one who remembers that the excess of imports over exports represents in a young country—which does not receive much from foreign investments, or for shipping, or other services rendered by its citizens in other countries, or by immigration—the amount of new capital which it has borrowed—can view the present condition of Victorian commerce without alarm. Unless the tariff is altered in such a way as to give the natural industries of Victoria a better opportunity of growth, or unless the irrigation experiments, which are being pushed with so much vigour, falsify the predictions of many experts and provide new articles of exports in the shape of fruit and wine, it is certain that the task of dealing with the finances of Victoria will tax the capacity and ingenuity of her rulers for many years to come.[1] The combination of Protection and borrowing must result in a serious crisis.

[1] The following figures show the excess of imports over exports since 1881, omitting figures below five hundred :—

£

Year			£	
1881	...	...	456,000	
1882	...	...	2,254,000	
1883	...	...	1,341,000	Of this sum, £11,219,000 represented an increase in the public indebtedness, not taking into account redemption loans, amounting to £5,800,000.
1884	...	...	3,151,000	
1885	...	...	2,402,800	
1886	...	...	6,735,000	
1887	...	...	7,671,000	
1888	...	...	10,118,000	
1889	...	...	11,668,000	
Total	...	...	46,200,700	

Since 1873 the exports have only once exceeded the imports—namely, in 1880. Bearing in mind that between three and four million pounds' worth of wool which is the product of New South Wales is shipped annually from

AGRICULTURE.

The boast of Victorians is, rightly enough, in their agriculture; and in this great department of national activity their country has maintained her lead over New South Wales, although she has not succeeded in increasing it. Even this partial success cannot be attributed to Protection, because Victoria was an exporter of foodstuffs even in her Free Trade days, but is owing partly to the fact that in the variable climate of New South Wales the land that is good for crops is not near the markets, and the land that is near the markets is not good for crops, and partly to the early alienation of the best agricultural lands to large proprietors, who have not yet shown themselves inclined to use it for any but pastoral purposes. Even in this direction, however, there are already signs of decline,[1] and while the area of cultivation is increasing in New South Wales it is declining in Victoria. Fortunately, the farmers have at last realised their position, and during the years 1890-91 every " Farmers' Protection Association " has omitted the word Protection

---

Port Phillip, and therefore included among the exports of Victorian produce, it will be seen that the nett annual value of Victorian exports is between eight and nine millions, as against an importation of nearly twenty-four millions for the year 1889. Of the imports a certain sum—which cannot, on the most liberal estimate, exceed £500,000—must be allowed for freight due to Victorian shipowners; an allowance must also be made for interest on Victorian capital invested abroad. It is difficult to ascertain how much this should be; it is, however, a rough but perhaps a fair estimate to take the value of New South Wales wool shipped from Melbourne as equivalent to the value of the returns to Victorian capital invested abroad. Most of the wool which comes to Melbourne from the other Colonies is sent there because the stations are owned by Victorians. The wool which is sent to Melbourne by New South Wales station owners, may be set off against the proceeds of Victorian investments in Queensland properties. But, after all these allowances are made, the fact remains that during recent years the indebtedness of Victoria has increased more rapidly than its exports. This increase has continued through 1890 and 1891, although the official returns are not yet available at the time of writing.[2] It is this enormous expenditure of borrowed money, both by the Government and by private persons, which has maintained the rate of wages in Victoria, and successfully disguised from the multitude the evil influences of Protection.

[1] The official figures for 1890-91 are not yet published, but unofficial returns show a decline of more than 50,000 acres in the area of cultivation during the last two years.

[2]
	Exports. £	Imports. £	
1890	13,256,000	22,653,000	The increase in exports in 1890 and 1891 will probably be found due to an increase in the shipments from Melbourne of New South Wales wool.
1891	15,679,000	21,622,000	

from its title, and declared in favour of Free Trade. It is one of the most amazing instances of the power of words over unthinking men that the farmers in any country should ever advocate Protection. The maxim that "the farmer pays for all" can never be more plainly illustrated than by farmers who hope to get rich by paying customers to buy their crops. If a young country exports food, Protection can be of no use to the farmers, who have to buy everything they want at Protective prices, and sell everything they produce at Free Trade prices. If, on the other hand, a young country requires to import food, the farmers have already the best market they can desire, viz., one which is short supplied. For example, the average price of wheat in Sydney has been for many years 6d. a bushel more than in Melbourne. The following are the figures relating to agriculture :—

AREA OF LAND IN CULTIVATION IN ACRES.

	1866.	1870.	1880.	1885.	1888.	1889.	1890.
Victoria	592,915	909,015	1,997,943	2,405,157	2,564,742	2,627,252	—
New South Wales	451,223	426,976	710,337	868,093	999,298	1,164,475	1,241,419

COMMERCE.

The figures which follow as to commerce, revenue, and shipping, require no comment. They all point the same moral—that Victoria has not only failed to hold her superiority over New South Wales, but has fallen far behind :—

IMPORTS AND EXPORTS OF NEW SOUTH WALES AND VICTORIA.

Colony.	Year.	Imports.		Exports.	
		Total Value.	Value per Head.	Total Value.	Value per Head.
		£	£ s. d.	£	£ s. d.
Victoria.	1866	14,771,000	23 9 7	12,889,000	20 9 9
	1880	14,556,000	17 2 4	15,954,000	18 15 3
	1885	18,044,000	18 16 0	15,551,000	16 4 6
	1888	23,972,000	22 11 5	13,853,000	13 0 11
	1889	24,402,000	22 2 0	12,734,000	11 10 8
	1890	22,953,000		13,239,000	
	1891	21,622,000 (estimated)		15,679,000 (estimated)	
New South Wales.	1866	9,403,000		9,613,000	
	1880	13,950,000	19 4 6	15,525,000	21 7 11
	1885	23,305,000	25 2 0	16,541,000	17 15 4
	1888	20,885,000	19 12 6	20,859,000	19 12 0
	1889	22,863,000	20 14 2	23,294,000	21 2 0
	1890				
	1891				

SHIPPING.

Colony.	Year.	INWARDS.		OUTWARDS.	
		No. of Vessels.	Tonnage.	No. of Vessels.	Tonnage.
New South Wales...	1866	2,099	730,354	2,259	784,381
Victoria	1866	2,078	649,979	2,203	675,741
New South Wales...	1889*	3,254	2,632,081	3,229	2,689,098
Victoria	1889	2,855	2,270,827	2,886	2,328,351

* The year 1889 was one of great depression in New South Wales. Later years would show a wider difference between the two Colonies.

REVENUE.*

Colony.	1866.	1889.	1891.
	£	£	£
New South Wales ...	2,012,079	9,003,397	10,079,000
Victoria	3,079,160	8,675,990	(estimated)

* The excess of revenue in New South Wales is due to the elasticity of her returns and not to the weight of taxation. The charge of taxation per head in 1889 in the two Colonies was as follows:—Victoria, £3 9s. 1d.; New South Wales, £2 8s. 6d. Thus, although every citizen of Victoria pays £1 0s. 7d. more in taxes than his Free Trade neighbour, the revenue of Victoria is about two millions less than that of New South Wales.

The figures which have been set out in the preceding pages have been treated by Protectionists in various ways at different times. For a long period they were ignored; then, after Mr. Edward Pulsford, of Sydney, brought them into public notice, their accuracy was denied, and the Statistical Office of New South Wales was assailed with scurrilous abuse. Finally, after Mr. Hayter, the Victorian official statist, had verified their substantial correctness, every effort was made to depreciate their significance. It was alleged that the greater success of New South Wales was owing to special causes—such as her larger territory, her greater expenditure of borrowed money, and her larger land revenue—which had not operated in Victoria to the same extent. Here, again, however, the Protectionists were foiled. Mr. Pulsford—and this is not among the least of the services which he has rendered to the cause of Free Trade—undertook an elaborate series of investigations into the statistical returns of the two colonies, and demonstrated even to the satisfaction of Protectionists that the "special causes" of prosperity, so far from being peculiar to New South Wales, had operated with even greater intensity in Victoria during the period under review. It is chiefly due to Mr. Pulsford's untiring industry and clearness of exposition that the example of Victoria is never cited now in the neighbouring colonies as an instance of the benefits of a Protective policy. As, however, the energy of Victorian *réclame* has not exhausted itself in other fields, it may be well to indicate very briefly the heads of the answer to Protectionist disparagements of the progress of New South Wales.

First, it is said that New South Wales owes her success to her earlier foundation. It is a sufficient reply to this that, in spite of her earlier foundation, she was far behind Victoria in 1866, when both colonies were Free Trade. The development of the Colony was so slow in the transportation days, which ended in 1856, that Victoria, in 1866, had gained from her active population of gold diggers more of the advantages of roads, bridges, and other incidents of civilisation, in ten years than New South Wales had by two generations of convict labour.

Next it is said that New South Wales owes her more rapid progress to her larger territory. To a certain extent this is true; but it is the merit and object of Free Trade to make use of natural advantages. A large territory, however, is not altogether an advantage to a young country. There is a power in concentration, and a weakness in scattered forces. "Wealth," as Mr. Pulsford has well remarked, "grows richer by population than by square mile, and, as a rule, it will be found that the most important and wealthy countries are of limited area. A larger area is often a great weakness." Certainly this has proved to be the case in New South Wales, whose rural population is badly served in all local requirements, and grievously handicapped by the difficulty of providing for the wants of so vast a territory. The greater advantages which a settler enjoys in the compact territory of Victoria become immediately apparent to any one who looks upon a railway map of the two Colonies. In New South Wales the railways stretch in three long lines, each to a distance of about 500 miles from the city to the sea-board. In Victoria the railways divide the country into small rectangles and unite every little township with the capital; and where railways fail the Southern settler, rivers play their part and give him that assurance of a return to his annual labour which the resident in the more variable climate of New South Wales is never able to anticipate.

Indeed, in physical and climatic advantages, Victoria is vastly the superior of New South Wales. Not only does its compactness make the former cheap to govern and easy to develop, but its fertile and well-watered lands lie close to the markets. In New South Wales, on the contrary, except a narrow strip upon the coast of Ilawarra, the good land lies beyond the coastal ranges at a distance of at least 200 miles from Sydney and the sea-board. There are, moreover, in New South Wales no large mining townships (except that of Broken Hill, which is, for practical purposes, part of South Australia) where the farmers are able to find a market. Moreover, even the best lands in New South Wales are subject alternately to droughts and floods. Further, while the lands of New South Wales are heavily timbered, so that the expense of preparing them for the plough is very great, most of the arable land in Victoria was naturally clear. In fact, it is difficult to exaggerate the natural advantages which are enjoyed by the fertile, extensive, open, well-watered lands of Victoria, over those of its larger, but more variable, neighbour. Nor does this complete the catalogue of the natural superiorities of the favoured province. Victoria has a distinct advantage in the character of its early settlers. The renown of her gold-fields attracted the very pick of the world, for energy, enterprise, and power. Through their aid she gained a start in wealth and population, which, but for the folly of her rulers, she would not have lost for many generations. The richness of her alluvial gold-fields, and the character of her early population, caused the easy establishment and rapid growth of great cities, whose position rendered her singularly fitted to be the seat of manufactures; while the extent of fertile land, which was immediately available, made her from the outset rich in the more durable elements of natural prosperity.

What wonder that in such a country progress has been rapid? The matter rather for remark is, that it has so soon ended. Of all the lessons which Australia has given to the world in politics, not the least instructive is to be drawn from the rise and decline of the Colony of Victoria! The "might-have-beens" of history are notoriously unprofitable matters of speculation; but no one can read the history of Victoria, with impartial mind, without being moved to wonder what her fate might have been, if she had been left to expand to her natural growth unhindered by the cruel restrictions of a cramping tariff.

Another strangely perverted argument is that New South Wales owes her more rapid progress to her greater production of coal and wool, which, it is said, are two raw materials, the production of which could not be affected by any fiscal policy. Supposing this were so, it is in the eyes of a Free Trader precisely a reason why the Colony of New South Wales should make as much profit as it can out of its natural industries instead of diverting its capital and labour into less productive channels. As the facts stand, however, Victoria has produced a larger quantity of raw materials than New South Wales during the period under review. The aggregate production of wool and gold in Victoria from 1866 to 1885 [1] was £27,410,950 more than in New South Wales. The following are the figures:—

GOLD AND WOOL.—TOTAL PRODUCTION 1866-1885.

	Victoria. £	New South Wales. £
Gold raised ...	85,819,216	15,763,365
Wool produced *	67,891,880	110,536,781
Total	153,711,096	126,300,146

* The figures representing wool are the aggregate of the exports after deducting the imports.

The total value of the coal raised in New South Wales from the foundation of the colony does not equal the excess of Victoria in her production of the two articles of wool and coal during the twenty years, 1866-1885, being only £23,891,629. The production of coal during that period amounted to £11,282,325.

The Protectionist theorist, driven to explain the, to him, astounding fact that New South Wales has prospered more under Free Trade than Victoria under Protection, finds his last refuge in the assertion that New South Wales owes her more rapid

---

[1] The year 1885 is taken to avoid errors on either side on account of the disturbing influence either of the New South Wales good seasons or the Melbourne "boom."

Y

progress to a more lavish expenditure of borrowed money. "A spurious prosperity," says the *Age*, in 1886, "or the appearance of prosperity, has been kept up for some eight or ten years past by a monstrously lavish expenditure of public money, which has either been borrowed or obtained from the sale of land." Upon this passage Mr. Pulsford ("Freedom in New South Wales *v.* Oppression in Victoria," p. 49) makes the following observations:—

"Believing that, perhaps, after all, New South Wales might not be so black as she is painted, I have carefully investigated the subject of the money obtained by sales of land, and by public borrowing in the two colonies. The result of my investigations will, I venture to say, be a surprise to all. I find that, for many years, Victoria led the way in both sales of land and public borrowings. That, in point of fact, Victoria for many years borrowed more rapidly than New South Wales, and also sold land much more rapidly. I confess I was very much surprised myself to find that, up to the year 1883, the aggregate of the moneys obtained by loans and land sales in New South Wales had always been exceeded in Victoria. It is perfectly obvious that the colony that obtained the lead in the construction of useful public works had a great advantage. I find that in the year when Victoria entered upon her policy of Protection, she had received twenty-one million pounds from the sources named, against only eleven millions in New South Wales. The early expenditure of so much money in Victoria represented a great advantage over this colony. It was not till 1875—that is, nine years later—that New South Wales reached this sum of twenty-one millions, and then the Victorian total had risen to thirty-one millions, or still the ten millions ahead. In 1880 Victoria was six millions ahead. In 1885 the tables were turned, so that New South Wales was eight millions in advance of Victoria.

"When I come to take the totals of these twenty years—1866-1885—I find that Victoria has had the use of capital equivalent to *thirty-four* millions for the whole period, against only *twenty-eight* millions on the part of New South Wales. I claim, therefore, that Victoria, and not New South Wales, is the colony that has received the greatest impetus towards prosperity from the expenditure of moneys obtained by loans and land sales." A full table of these moneys is subjoined.

Appendix III.

New South Wales.

Year.	Loans. £	Land Sales. £	Total. £
1860 to 1865 Average	5,212,771	4,061,732	9,274,503
1866	6,418,030	4,781,653	11,199,683
1867	6,917,630	5,046,313	11,963,943
1868	8,564,830	5,311,563	13,876,393
1869	9,546,030	5,631,176	15,177,206
1870	9,681,130	5,882,019	15,563,149
1871	10,614,330	6,143,420	16,757,750
1872	10,773,230	6,575,793	17,349,023
1873	10,842,415	7,421,203	18,263,618
1874	10,516,371	8,532,244	19,048,615
1875	11,470,637	10,292,814	21,763,451
1876	11,759,519	12,806,218	24,565,737
1877	11,724,419	15,774,075	27,498,494
1878	11,688,119	17,850,086	29,538,205
1879	14,937,419	19,236,773	34,174,192
1880	14,903,919	20,618,799	35,522,718
1881	16,924,019	23,102,137	40,026,156
1882	16,721,219	25,557,178	42,278,397
1883	21,632,459	26,826,657	48,459,116
1884	24,601,959	28,190,150	52,792,109
1885	30,064,259	29,414,372	59,478,631
Average 1866 to 1886	13,515,097	14,249,732	27,764,829

We are now in a position to appreciate the whole significance of the tale which the preceding figures have disclosed.

Every Protectionist argument, either expressedly or impliedly, assumes that no country can develop under natural conditions, but that a home market, a diversity of industries, a high rate of wages, and all other ingredients of prosperity, can only be secured by means of a Protective tariff. It is not that Protectionists claim a mere superiority for their policy over the policy of Free Trade as an instrument of national development, but they insist that Free Trade is a positive evil that prevents development. Consequently when we find that a country, which is also one of those young countries in whose case Protection is declared to be most plainly demanded, has, while faithfully adhering to Free Trade, developed its resources, diversified its industries, maintained a high rate of wages, given its farmers a profitable market for their produce, and steadily advanced in prosperity in every path of progress, we are entitled to question the truth of the assumptions which Protectionists invariably take for granted. If we can go further, and show that another country which has enjoyed greater natural advantages, and where the other influences which make for national welfare have operated with greater intensity, has advanced much more slowly under Protection than our first example has under Free Trade, the conclusion is irresistible that Protection, not Free Trade, is the clog upon national progress. At the same time, no sensible Free Trader would rest his case upon the records of any country during the short period of twenty-five years. The example of New South Wales is of importance in a Free Trade argument, not so much on account of the support which it gives to Free Trade, as because it pushes the rude thrust of fact into the cobweb of a Protectionist theory. It has also this more limited value—that it makes it impossible for restrictionists to make use of the undoubted progress of Victoria since 1866 as an illustration in their favour, without also attributing the still greater progress of New South Wales to the opposite policy of Free Trade.

THE END.

A SELECTED LIST

OF

CASSELL & COMPANY'S

PUBLICATIONS.

G G 9.91.

Selections from Cassell & Company's Publications.

Illustrated, Fine Art, and other Volumes.

Abbeys and Churches of England and Wales, The: Descriptive, Historical, Pictorial. Series I. and II. 21s. each.
Adventure, The World of. Fully Illustrated. Complete in Three Vols. 9s. each.
Anglomaniacs, The : a Story of New York Life of To-day. By Mrs. BURTON HARRISON. 3s. 6d.
Animal Painting in Water Colours. With Eighteen Coloured Plates by FREDERICK TAYLER. 5s.
Arabian Nights Entertainments (Cassell's). With about 400 Illustrations. 10s. 6d.
Architectural Drawing. By R. PHENÉ SPIERS. Illustrated. 10s. 6d.
Art, The Magazine of. Yearly Volume. With several hundred Engravings, and Twelve Etchings, Photogravures, &c. 16s.
Artistic Anatomy. By Prof. M. DUVAL. Translated by F. E. FENTON. 5s.
Bashkirtseff, Marie, The Journal of. Translated from the French by MATHILDE BLIND. With Portraits and an Autograph Letter. *Cheap Edition*, 7s. 6d.
Bashkirtseff, Marie, The Letters of. Translated by MARY J. SERRANO. 7s. 6d.
Birds' Nests, Eggs, and Egg-Collecting. By R. KEARTON. Illustrated with 16 Coloured Plates of Eggs. 5s.
Black America. A Story of the ex-Slave and his late Master. By W. LAIRD CLOWES. Cloth, 6s.
Black Arrow, The. A Tale of the Two Roses. By R. L. STEVENSON. Illustrated, 3s. 6d.
Blue Pavilions, The. By Q, Author of "Dead Man's Rock," &c. 5s.
British Ballads. 275 Original Illustrations. Two Vols. Cloth, 15s.
British Battles on Land and Sea. By JAMES GRANT. With about 600 Illustrations. Three Vols., 4to, £1 7s. ; *Library Edition*, £1 10s.
British Battles, Recent. Illustrated. 4to, 9s. *Library Edition*, 10s.
Browning, An Introduction to the Study of. By ARTHUR SYMONS. 2s. 6d.
Butterflies and Moths, European. By W. F. KIRBY. With 61 Coloured Plates. Demy 4to, 35s.
Canaries and Cage-Birds, The Illustrated Book of. By W. A. BLAKSTON, W. SWAYSLAND, and A. F. WIENER. With 56 Fac-simile Coloured Plates, 35s.
Cassell's Family Magazine. Yearly Volume. Illustrated. 9s.
Cathedrals, Abbeys, and Churches of England and Wales. Descriptive, Historical, Pictorial. Edited by Prof. T. G. BONNEY, D.Sc., LL.D., F.R.S. With nearly 500 Original Illustrations. *Popular Edition*. Two Vols. 25s.
Celebrities of the Century. Being a Dictionary of the Men and Women of the Nineteenth Century. *Cheap Edition*, 10s. 6d.
Chess Problem, The. With Illustrations by C. PLANCK and others. 7s. 6d.
China Painting. By FLORENCE LEWIS. With Sixteen Coloured Plates, and a selection of Wood Engravings. With full Instructions. 5s.
Choice Dishes at Small Cost. By A. G. PAYNE. *Cheap Edition*, 1s.
Christianity and Socialism, Lectures on. By BISHOP BARRY. 3s. 6d.
Cities of the World. Four Vols. Illustrated. 7s. 6d. each.
Civil Service, Guide to Employment in the. *New and Enlarged Edition*, 3s. 6d.
Civil Service—Guide to Female Employment in Government Offices. Cloth, 1s.
Climate and Health Resorts. By Dr. BURNEY YEO. 7s. 6d.
Clinical Manuals for Practitioners and Students of Medicine. (*A List of Volumes forwarded post free on application to the Publishers.*)
Clothing, The Influence of, on Health. By FREDERICK TREVES, F.R.C.S. 2s.
Cobden Club, Works published for the. (*A Complete List on application.*)
Colonist's Medical Handbook, The. By E. ALFRED BARTON, M.R.C.S. 2s. 6d.
Colour. By Prof. A. H. CHURCH. *New and Enlarged Edition*. 3s. 6d.
Commerce, The Year-Book of. Edited by KENRIC B. MURRAY. 5s.
Commercial Botany of the Nineteenth Century. By J. R. JACKSON, A.L.S. Cloth gilt, 3s. 6d.

Selections from Cassell & Company's Publications.

Conning Tower, In a. By H. O. ARNOLD-FORSTER, Author of "The Citizen Reader," &c. With Original Illustrations by W. H. OVEREND. 1s.
Conquests of the Cross. Edited by EDWIN HODDER. With numerous Original Illustrations. Complete in Three Vols. 9s. each.
Cookery, A Year's. By PHYLLIS BROWNE. *New and Enlarged Edition.* Cloth gilt, 3s. 6d.
Cookery, Cassell's Dictionary of. Containing about Nine Thousand Recipes. 7s. 6d.; roxburgh, 10s. 6d.
Cookery, Cassell's Shilling. 80*th Thousand.* 1s.
Cookery, Cassell's Popular. With Four Coloured Plates. Cloth gilt, 2s.
Cookery, Vegetarian. A Manual of Cheap and Wholesome Diet. By A. G. PAYNE. 1s. 6d.
Cooking by Gas, The Art of. By MARIE J. SUGG. Illustrated. Cloth, 3s. 6d.
Copyright, The Law of Musical and Dramatic. By EDWARD CUTLER, THOMAS EUSTACE SMITH, and FREDERIC E. WEATHERLY. 3s. 6d.
Countries of the World, The. By ROBERT BROWN, M.A., Ph.D., &c. Complete in Six Vols., with about 750 Illustrations. 4to, 7s. 6d. each.
Cremation and Urn-Burial; or, The Cemeteries of the Future. By W. ROBINSON. With Plates and Illustrations. 1s.
Cromwell, Oliver: The Man and His Mission. By J. ALLANSON PICTON, M.P. *Cheap Edition.* With Steel Portrait. 5s.
Culmshire Folk. By the Author of "John Orlebar," &c. 3s. 6d.
Cyclopædia, Cassell's Concise. Brought down to the latest date. With about 600 Illustrations. *New and Cheap Edition,* 7s. 6d.
Cyclopædia, Cassell's Miniature. Containing 30,000 Subjects. Cloth, 3s. 6d.; half roxburgh, 4s. 6d.
Dairy Farming. By Prof. J. P. SHELDON. With 25 Fac-simile Coloured Plates, and numerous Wood Engravings. Demy 4to, 21s.
David Todd: The Romance of his Life and Loving. By DAVID MACLURE. 5s.
Dickens, Character Sketches from. FIRST, SECOND, and THIRD SERIES. With Six Original Drawings in each, by FREDERICK BARNARD. In Portfolio, 21s. each.
Dictionaries. (For description see alphabetical letter.) Religion, Bible, Celebrities, Encyclopædic, Mechanical, Phrase and Fable, English, English History, English Literature, Domestic, Cookery. (French, German, and Latin, see with *Educational Works.*)
Disraeli, Benjamin, Personal Reminiscences of. By HENRY LAKE. 3s. 6d.
Disraeli in Outline. By F. CARROLL BREWSTER, LL.D. 7s. 6d.
Dog, Illustrated Book of the. By VERO SHAW, B.A. With 28 Coloured Plates. Cloth bevelled, 35s.; half-morocco, 45s.
Dog, The. By IDSTONE. Illustrated. 2s. 6d.
Domestic Dictionary, The. An Encyclopædia for the Household. Cloth, 7s. 6d.
Doré Gallery, The. With 250 Illustrations by GUSTAVE DORÉ. 4to, 42s.
Doré's Dante's Inferno. Illustrated by GUSTAVE DORÉ. *Popular Edition,* 21s.
Doré's Milton's Paradise Lost. Illustrated by GUSTAVE DORÉ. 4to, 21s.
Dr. Dumány's Wife. A Novel. By MAURUS JÓKAI. Translated from the Hungarian by F. STEINITZ. 7s. 6d. net.
Earth, Our, and its Story. Edited by Dr. ROBERT BROWN, F.L.S. With 36 Coloured Plates and 740 Wood Engravings. Complete in Three Vols. 9s. each.
Edinburgh, Old and New, Cassell's. With 600 Illustrations. Three Vols. 9s. each; library binding, £1 10s. the set.
Egypt: Descriptive, Historical, and Picturesque. By Prof. G. EBERS. Translated by CLARA BELL, with Notes by SAMUEL BIRCH, LL.D., &c. Two Vols. 42s.
"89." A Novel. By EDGAR HENRY. Cloth, 3s. 6d.
Electricity, Age of, from Amber Soul to Telephone. By PARK BENJAMIN, Ph.D. 7s. 6d.
Electricity, Practical. By Prof. W. E. AYRTON. Illustrated. 7s. 6d.
Electricity in the Service of Man. A Popular and Practical Treatise. With nearly 850 Illustrations. *Cheap Edition,* 9s.
Employment for Boys on Leaving School, Guide to. By W. S. BEARD, F.R.G.S. 1s. 6d.
Encyclopædic Dictionary, The. Complete in Fourteen Divisional Vols., 10s. 6d. each; or Seven Vols., half-morocco, 21s. each; half-russia, 25s. each.
England, Cassell's Illustrated History of. With 2,000 Illustrations. Ten Vols., 4to, 9s. each. *New and Revised Edition.* Vols. I., II., III., and IV., 9s. each.

Selections from Cassell & Company's Publications.

English Dictionary, Cassell's. Containing Definitions of upwards of 100,000 Words and Phrases. Demy 8vo, 1,100 pages, cloth gilt, 7s. 6d.
English History, The Dictionary of. *Cheap Edition*, 10s. 6d.; roxburgh, 15s.
English Literature, Library of. By Prof. HENRY MORLEY. Complete in Five Vols. 7s. 6d. each.
VOL. I.—SHORTER ENGLISH POEMS.
VOL. II.—ILLUSTRATIONS OF ENGLISH RELIGION.
VOL. III.—ENGLISH PLAYS.
VOL. IV.—SHORTER WORKS IN ENGLISH PROSE.
VOL. V.—SKETCHES OF LONGER WORKS IN ENGLISH VERSE AND PROSE.
English Literature, Morley's First Sketch of. *Revised Edition*, 7s. 6d.
English Literature, The Dictionary of. By W. DAVENPORT ADAMS. *Cheap Edition*, 7s. 6d.; roxburgh, 10s. 6d.
English Literature, The Story of. By ANNA BUCKLAND. 3s. 6d.
English Writers. By HENRY MORLEY. Vols. I. to VIII. 5s. each.
Æsop's Fables. Illustrated by ERNEST GRISET. *Cheap Edition*. Cloth, 3s. 6d.; bevelled boards, gilt edges, 5s.
Etiquette of Good Society. 1s.; cloth, 1s. 6d.
Eye, Ear, and Throat, The Management of the. 3s. 6d.
Faith Doctor, The. A Novel. By EDWARD EGGLESTON. 7s. 6d. net.
Family Physician. By Eminent PHYSICIANS and SURGEONS. *New and Revised Edition.* Cloth, 21s.; roxburgh, 25s.
Father Mathew: His Life and Times. By FRANK J. MATHEW. 2s. 6d.
Father Stafford. By ANTHONY HOPE, Author of "A Man of Mark." 6s.
Fenn, G. Manville, Works by. Boards, 2s. each; or cloth, 2s. 6d.
Dutch the Diver; or, a Man's Mistake. In boards only.
My Patients.
The Parson o' Dumford. In boards only.
Poverty Corner.
The Vicar's People. In Cloth only.
Field Naturalist's Handbook, The. By Rev. J. G. WOOD & THEODORE WOOD. 5s.
Figuier's Popular Scientific Works. With Several Hundred Illustrations in each. 3s. 6d. each.
The Human Race. | Mammalia. | Ocean World.
The World before the Deluge. Revised Edition.
Figure Painting in Water Colours. With 16 Coloured Plates by BLANCHE MACARTHUR and JENNIE MOORE. With full Instructions. 7s. 6d.
Flora's Feast. A Masque of Flowers. Penned and Pictured by WALTER CRANE. With 40 pages in Colours. 5s.
Flower de Hundred. The Story of a Virginia Plantation. By Mrs. BURTON HARRISON, Author of "The Anglomaniacs," &c. 3s. 6d.
Flower Painting, Elementary. With Eight Coloured Plates. 3s.
Flower Painting in Water Colours. With Coloured Plates. First and Second Series. 5s. each.
Flower Painting in Water Colours. With Coloured Plates. First and Second Series. 5s. each.
Flowers, and How to Paint Them. By MAUD NAFTEL. With Coloured Plates. 5s.
Fossil Reptiles, A History of British. By Sir RICHARD OWEN, K.C.B., F.R.S., &c. With 268 Plates. In Four Vols. £12 12s.
Four Years in Parliament with Hard Labour. By C. W. RADCLIFFE COOKE, M.P. *Third Edition*. 1s.
France as It Is. By ANDRÉ LEBON and PAUL PELET. With Maps. 7s. 6d.
Garden Flowers, Familiar. By SHIRLEY HIBBERD. With Coloured Plates by F. E. HULME, F.L.S. Complete in Five Series. Cloth gilt, 12s. 6d. each.
Gardening, Cassell's Popular. Illustrated. Complete in Four Vols. 5s. each.
Geometrical Drawing for Army Candidates. By H. T. LILLEY, M.A. 2s.
Geometry, First Elements of Experimental. By PAUL BERT. 1s. 6d.
Geometry, Practical Solid. By Major ROSS. 2s.
Gilbert, Elizabeth, and her Work for the Blind. By FRANCES MARTIN. 2s. 6d.
Gleanings from Popular Authors. Two Vols. With Original Illustrations. 4to, 9s. each. Two Vols. in One, 15s.
Great Eastern Railway, The Official Illustrated Guide to the. 1s.; cloth, 2s.
Great Northern Railway, The Official Illustrated Guide to the. 1s.; cloth, 2s.
Great Western Railway, The Official Illustrated Guide to the. *New and Revised Edition*. 1s.; cloth, 2s.
Gulliver's Travels. With 88 Engravings. Cloth, 3s. 6d.; cloth gilt, 5s.

Selections from Cassell & Company's Publications.

Gun and its Development, The. By W. W. GREENER. Illustrated. 10s. 6d.
Guns, Modern Shot. By W. W. GREENER. Illustrated. 5s.
Health at School. By CLEMENT DUKES, M.D., B.S. 7s. 6d.
Health, The Book of. By Eminent Physicians and Surgeons. Cloth, 21s.
Health, The Influence of Clothing on. By F. TREVES, F.R.C.S. 2s.
Heavens, The Story of the. By Sir ROBERT STAWELL BALL, LL.D., F.R.S. With Coloured Plates and Wood Engravings. *Popular Edition*, 12s. 6d.
Heroes of Britain in Peace and War. With 300 Original Illustrations. *Cheap Edition*. Vol. I. 3s. 6d.
Holiday Studies of Wordsworth. By F. A. MALLESON, M.A. 5s.
Horse, The Book of the. By SAMUEL SIDNEY. With 28 Fac-simile Coloured Plates. Demy 4to, 35s.; half-morocco, £2 5s.
Houghton, Lord: The Life, Letters, and Friendships of Richard Monckton Milnes, First Lord Houghton. By T. WEMYSS REID. Two Vols., with Portraits, 32s.
Household, Cassell's Book of the. Illustrated. Complete in Four Vols. 5s. each.
How Women may Earn a Living. By MERCY GROGAN. *Cheap Edition*, 6d.
Hygiene and Public Health. By B. ARTHUR WHITELEGGE, M.D. 7s. 6d.
India, Cassell's History of. By JAMES GRANT. With 400 Illustrations. 15s.
In-door Amusements, Card Games, and Fireside Fun, Cassell's Book of. With numerous Illustrations. *Cheap Edition*. Cloth, 2s.
Irish Leagues, The Work of the. The Speech of the Right Hon. Sir HENRY JAMES, Q.C., M.P., Replying in the Parnell Commission Inquiry. 6s.
Irish Parliament, A Miniature History of the. By J. C. HASLAM. 3d.
Irish Union, The: Before and After. By A. K. CONNELL, M.A. 2s. 6d.
Italy from the Fall of Napoleon I. in 1815 to 1890. By J. W. PROBYN. *New and Cheaper Edition*. 3s. 6d.
"Japanese" Library, Cassell's. Consisting of 12 Popular Works bound in Japanese style. Covers in water-colour pictures. 1s. 3d. each, net. Handy Andy. Oliver Twist. Ivanhoe. Ingoldsby Legends. The Last of the Mohicans. The Last Days of Pompeii. The Yellowplush Papers. The Last Days of Palmyra. Jack Hinton the Guardsman. Selections from the Works of Thomas Hood. American Humour. Tower of London.
John Orlebar, Clk. By the Author of "Culmshire Folk." 2s.
John Parmelee's Curse. By JULIAN HAWTHORNE. 2s. 6d.
Karmel the Scout. A Novel. By SYLVANUS COBB, Junr. Cloth, 3s. 6d.
Kennel Guide, Practical. By Dr. GORDON STABLES. Illustrated. *Cheap Edition*, 1s.
Khiva, A Ride to. By Col. FRED BURNABY. 1s. 6d.
Kidnapped. By R. L. STEVENSON. Illustrated. 3s. 6d.
King Solomon's Mines. By H. RIDER HAGGARD. Illustrated. 3s. 6d.
Ladies' Physician, The. By a London Physician. 6s.
Lake Dwellings of Europe. By ROBERT MUNRO, M.D., M.A. Cloth, 31s. 6d.
Law, How to Avoid. By A. J. WILLIAMS, M.P. *Cheap Edition*, 1s.
Legends for Lionel. With Coloured Plates by WALTER CRANE. 5s.
Letts's Diaries and other Time-saving Publications are now published exclusively by CASSELL & COMPANY. (*A List sent post free on application.*)
Little Minister, The. By J. M. BARRIE. Three Vols. 31s. 6d.
Loans Manual. By CHARLES P. COTTON. 5s.
Local Option in Norway. By THOMAS M. WILSON, C.E. 1s.
Locomotive Engine, The Biography of a. By HENRY FRITH. 5s.
London and North Western Railway, Official Illustrated Guide. 1s.
London and South Western Railway, Official Illustrated Guide. 1s.
London, Brighton and South Coast Railway, Official Illustrated Guide. 1s.
London, Greater. By EDWARD WALFORD. Two Vols. With about 400 Illustrations. 9s. each. *Library Edition*. Two Vols. £1 the set.
London, Old and New. By WALTER THORNBURY and EDWARD WALFORD. Six Vols., with about 1,200 Illustrations. Cloth, 9s. each. *Library Edition*, £3.
London Street Arabs. By MRS. H. M. STANLEY (DOROTHY TENNANT). With Pictures printed on a Tint. 5s.
Master of Ballantrae, The. By ROBERT LOUIS STEVENSON. Illustrated. 3s. 6d.
Mechanics, The Practical Dictionary of. Containing 15,000 Drawings. Four Vols. 21s. each.

Selections from Cassell & Company's Publications.

Medical Handbook of Life Assurance. By JAMES EDWARD POLLOCK, M.D., F.R.C.P., and JAMES CHISHOLM, Fellow of the Institute of Actuaries, London. 7s. 6d.
Medicine, Manuals for Students of. (*A List forwarded post free on application.*)
Metropolitan Year-Book, The, for 1892. Paper, 1s.; cloth, 2s.
Metzerott. Shoemaker. A Socialistic Novel. 5s.
Midland Railway, The Official Illustrated Guide to the. Cloth, 2s.
Modern Europe, A History of. By C. A. FYFFE, M.A. Three Vols. 12s. each.
Music, Illustrated History of. By EMIL NAUMANN. Edited by the Rev. Sir F. A. GORE OUSELEY, Bart. Illustrated. Two Vols. 31s. 6d.
National Library, Cassell's. In Volumes. Paper Covers, 3d.; cloth, 6d. (*A Complete List of the Volumes post free on application.*)
Natural History, Cassell's Concise. By E. PERCEVAL WRIGHT, M.A., M.D., F.L.S. With several Hundred Illustrations. 7s. 6d.; roxburgh, 10s. 6d.
Natural History, Cassell's New. Edited by Prof. P. MARTIN DUNCAN, M.B., F.R.S., F.G.S. Complete in Six Vols. With about 2,000 Illustrations. Cloth, 9s. each.
Nature's Wonder Workers. By KATE R. LOVELL. Illustrated. 5s.
Naval War, The Last Great. By A. NELSON SEAFORTH. With Maps. 2s.
Navy, Royal, All About the. By W. LAIRD CLOWES. Illustrated. 1s.
Nelson, The Life of. By ROBERT SOUTHEY. Illustrated with Eight Plates. 3s. 6d.
Nursing for the Home and for the Hospital, A Handbook of. By CATHERINE J. WOOD. *Cheap Edition*, 1s. 6d.; cloth, 2s.
Nursing of Sick Children, A Handbook for the. By CATHERINE J. WOOD. 2s. 6d.
Orations and After-Dinner Speeches. By the Hon. C. M. DEPEW. 7s. 6d.
Our Own Country. Six Vols. With 1,200 Illustrations. Cloth, 7s. 6d. each.
Pactolus Prime. A Novel. By ALBION W. TOURGÉE. 5s.
Painting, The English School of. By ERNEST CHESNEAU. Translated by L. N. ETHERINGTON. With an Introduction by Professor RUSKIN. 5s.
Paxton's Flower Garden. With 100 Coloured Plates. (*Price on application.*)
People I've Smiled With. Recollections of a Merry Little Life. By MARSHALL P. WILDER. 2s.
Peoples of the World, The. By Dr. ROBERT BROWN. Complete in Six Volumes. With Illustrations. 7s. 6d. each.
Phantom City, The. By W. WESTALL. 5s.
Phillips, Watts. Artist and Playwright. By Miss E. WATTS PHILLIPS. With 32 Plates. 10s. 6d.
Photography for Amateurs. By T. C. HEPWORTH. Illustrated, 1s.; or cloth, 1s. 6d.
Phrase and Fable, Dictionary of. By the Rev. Dr. BREWER. *Cheap Edition, Enlarged*, cloth, 3s. 6d.; or with leather back, 4s. 6d.
Picturesque America. Complete in Four Vols., with 48 Exquisite Steel Plates, and about 800 Original Wood Engravings. £2 2s. each.
Picturesque Australasia, Cassell's. With upwards of 1,000 Illustrations. Complete in Four Vols. 7s. 6d. each.
Picturesque Canada. With about 600 Original Illustrations. Two Vols. £3 3s. each.
Picturesque Europe. Complete in Five Vols. Each containing 13 Exquisite Steel Plates, from Original Drawings, and nearly 200 Original Illustrations. £21; half-morocco, £31 10s.; morocco gilt, £52 10s. *Popular Edition*. In Five Vols. 18s. each.
Picturesque Mediterranean, The. With a Series of Magnificent Illustrations from Original Designs by leading Artists of the day. Two Vols. Cloth, £2 2s. each.
Pigeon Keeper, The Practical. By LEWIS WRIGHT. Illustrated. 3s. 6d.
Pigeons, The Book of. By ROBERT FULTON. Edited by LEWIS WRIGHT. With 50 Coloured Plates and numerous Wood Engravings. 31s. 6d.; half-morocco, £2 2s.
Poems, Aubrey de Vere's. A Selection. Edited by JOHN DENNIS. 3s. 6d.
Poets, Cassell's Miniature Library of the :—

Burns. Two Vols. Cloth, 1s. each; or cloth, gilt edges, 2s. 6d. the set.
Byron. Two Vols. Cloth, 1s. each; or cloth, gilt edges, 2s. 6d. the set.
Hood. Two Vols. Cloth, 1s. each; or cloth, gilt edges, 2s. 6d. the set.
Longfellow. Two Vols. Cloth, 1s. each; or cloth, gilt edges, 2s. 6d. the set.

Milton. Two Vols. Cloth, 1s. each; or cloth, gilt edges, 2s. 6d. the set.
Scott. Two Vols. Cloth, 1s. each; or cloth, gilt edges, 2s. 6d. the set.
Sheridan and Goldsmith. 2 Vols. Cloth, 1s. each; or cloth, gilt edges, 2s. 6d. the set.
Wordsworth. Two Vols. Cloth, 1s. each; or cloth, gilt edges, 2s. 6d. the set.

Shakespeare. Twelve Vols., half cloth, in box, 12s.

Political Questions of the Day, A Manual of. By SYDNEY BUXTON, M.P. *New and Enlarged Edition*. Paper Covers, 1s.; or cloth, 1s. 6d.

Selections from Cassell & Company's Publications.

Polytechnic Series, The. Practical Illustrated Manuals specially prepared for Students of the Polytechnic Institute, and suitable for the Use of all Students.
    Forty Lessons in Carpentry Workshop Practice. 1s.
    Practical Plane and Solid Geometry, including Graphic Arithmetic. Vol. I. ELEMENTARY STAGE. 3s.
    Forty Lessons in Engineering Workshop Practice. 1s. 6d.
    Technical Scales. Set of Ten in cloth case, 1s. Also on celluloid (in case), 10s. 6d. the set.
    Elementary Chemistry for Science Schools and Classes. 1s. 6d.
    Building Construction Plates. A Series of 40 Drawings, Royal Folio size, 1½d. each.
Portrait Gallery, The Cabinet. *First and Second Series*, each containing 36 Cabinet Photographs of Eminent Men and Women of the day. With Biographical Sketches. 15s. each.
Poultry Keeper, The Practical. By LEWIS WRIGHT. Illustrated. 3s. 6d.
Poultry, The Book of. By LEWIS WRIGHT. *Popular Edition.* Illustrated. 10s. 6d.
Poultry, The Illustrated Book of. By LEWIS WRIGHT. With Fifty Exquisite Coloured Plates, and numerous Wood Engravings. *Revised Edition.* Cloth, 31s. 6d.
Public Libraries, Free. *New and Enlarged Edition.* By THOMAS GREENWOOD, Author of "Museums and Art Galleries." Illustrated. 2s. 6d.
Queen Summer; or, The Tourney of the Lily and the Rose. Penned and Portrayed by WALTER CRANE. With 40 pages in Colours. 6s. *Large Paper Edition*, 21s., *net*.
Queen Victoria, The Life and Times of. By ROBERT WILSON. Complete in 2 Vols. With numerous Illustrations. 9s. each.
Rabbit-Keeper, The Practical. By CUNICULUS. Illustrated. 3s. 6d.
Railway Library, Cassell's. Crown 8vo, boards, 2s. each.

    The Astonishing History of Troy Town. By Q.
    The Admirable Lady Biddy Fane. By Frank Barrett.
    Commodore Junk. By G. Manville Fenn.
    St. Cuthbert's Tower. By Florence Warden.
    The Man with a Thumb. By W. C. Hudson (Barclay North).
    By Right Not Law. By R. Sherard.
    Within Sound of the Weir. By Thomas St. E. Hake.
    Under a Strange Mask. By Frank Barrett.
    The Coombsberrow Mystery. By J. Colwall.
    Dead Man's Rock. By Q.
    A Queer Race. By W. Westall.
    Captain Trafalgar. By Westall and Laurie.
    The Phantom City. By W. Westall.
    Jack Gordon, Knight Errant. By W. C. Hudson (Barclay North).
    The Diamond Button: Whose Was It? By W. C. Hudson (Barclay North).
    Another's Crime. By Julian Hawthorne.
    The Yoke of the Thorah. By Sidney Luska.
    Who is John Noman? By C. Henry Beckett.
    The Tragedy of Brinkwater. By Martha L. Moodey.
    An American Penman. By Julian Hawthorne.
    Section 558; or, The Fatal Letter. By Julian Hawthorne.
    The Brown Stone Boy. By W. H. Bishop.
    A Tragic Mystery. By Julian Hawthorne.
    The Great Bank Robbery. By Julian Hawthorne.

Redgrave, Richard, C.B., R.A. Memoir. By F. M. REDGRAVE. 10s. 6d.
Richard, Henry, M.P. A Biography. By CHARLES MIALL. With Portrait. 7s. 6d.
Rivers of Great Britain: Descriptive, Historical, Pictorial. RIVERS OF THE EAST COAST. Royal 4to. 42s.
Rivers of Great Britain: THE ROYAL RIVER; THE THAMES, FROM SOURCE TO SEA. With Descriptive Text and a Series of beautiful Engravings. *Original Edition*, £2 2s. *Popular Edition*, 16s.
Robinson Crusoe. *Cassell's New Fine-Art Edition.* With upwards of 100 Original Illustrations. 7s. 6d.
Rossetti, Dante Gabriel, as Designer and Writer. Notes by WILLIAM MICHAEL ROSSETTI. 7s. 6d.
Russia, Through, on a Mustang. By THOMAS STEVENS. 7s. 6d.
Russo-Turkish War, Cassell's History of. With about 500 Illustrations. Two Vols., 9s. each; library binding, One Vol., 15s.
Sanitary Institutions, English. By Sir JOHN SIMON, K.C.B., F.R.S. 18s.
Saturday Journal, Cassell's. Illustrated throughout. Yearly Volume, 7s. 6d.
Science for All. Edited by Dr. ROBERT BROWN, M.A., F.L.S., &c. *Revised Edition.* With 1,500 Illustrations. Five Vols. 9s. each.
Sea, The: Its Stirring Story of Adventure, Peril, and Heroism. By F. WHYMPER. With 400 Illustrations. Four Vols. 7s. 6d. each.
Secret of the Lamas, The. A Tale of Thibet. Crown 8vo, 5s.
Sent Back by the Angels; and other Ballads of Home and Homely Life. By FREDERICK LANGBRIDGE, M.A. *Popular Edition*, 1s.
Shaftesbury, The Seventh Earl of, K.G., The Life and Work of. By EDWIN HODDER. With Portraits. Three Vols., 36s. *Popular Edition*, in One Vol., 7s. 6d.
Shakespeare, Cassell's Quarto Edition. Edited by CHARLES and MARY COWDEN CLARKE, and containing about 600 Illustrations by H. C. SELOUS. Complete in Three Vols., cloth gilt, £3 3s.—Also published in Three separate Volumes, in cloth, viz.:—The COMEDIES, 21s.; The HISTORICAL PLAYS, 18s. 6d.; The TRAGEDIES, 25s.

Selections from Cassell & Company's Publications.

Shakespeare, Miniature. Illustrated. In Twelve Vols., in box, 12s.; or in Red Paste Grain (box to match), with spring catch, lettered in gold, 21s.
Shakespeare, The Plays of. Edited by Prof. HENRY MORLEY. Complete in Thirteen Vols. Cloth, in box, 21s.; half-morocco, cloth sides, 42s.
Shakespeare, The England of. By E. GOADBY. Illustrated. *New Edition.* 2s. 6d.
Shakspere, The International. *Édition de luxe.*
  "Othello." Illustrated by FRANK DICKSEE, R.A. £3 10s.
  "King Henry IV." Illustrated by Herr EDUARD GRÜTZNER. £3 10s.
  "As You Like It." Illustrated by Mons. ÉMILE BAYARD. £3 10s.
  "Romeo and Juliet." Illustrated by FRANK DICKSEE, R.A. Is now out of print.
Shakspere, The Leopold. With 400 Illustrations, and an Introduction by F. J. FURNIVALL. *Cheap Edition,* 3s. 6d. Cloth gilt, gilt edges, 5s.; roxburgh, 7s. 6d.
Shakspere, The Royal. With Exquisite Steel Plates and Wood Engravings. Three Vols. 15s. each.
Skin and Hair, The Management of the. By MALCOLM MORRIS, F.R.C.S. 2s.
Social Welfare, Subjects of. By the Rt. Hon. SIR LYON PLAYFAIR, M.P. 7s. 6d.
South Eastern Railway, The Official Illustrated Guide to the. 1s.; cloth, 2s.
Spectacles, How to Select. By CHARLES BELL TAYLOR, F.R.C.S. 1s.
Splendid Spur, The. By Q, Author of "Dead Man's Rock," &c. Illustrated. 3s. 6d.
Sports and Pastimes, Cassell's Complete Book of. With more than 900 Illustrations. *Cheap Edition.* 3s. 6d.
Standard Library, Cassell's. Stiff covers, 1s. each; cloth, 2s. each.

Coningsby.
Mary Barton.
The Antiquary.
Nicholas Nickleby. Two Vols.
Jane Eyre.
Wuthering Heights.
The Prairie.
Dombey and Son. Two Vols.
Night and Morning.
Kenilworth.
The Ingoldsby Legends.
Tower of London.
The Pioneers.
Charles O'Malley.
Barnaby Rudge.
Cakes and Ale.
The King's Own.
People I have Met.
The Pathfinder.
Evelina.
Scott's Poems.
Last of the Barons.
Adventures of Mr. Ledbury.
Ivanhoe.
Oliver Twist.
Selections from Hood's Works.
Longfellow's Prose Works.
Sense and Sensibility.
Lytton's Plays.
Tales, Poems, and Sketches (Bret Harte).
The Prince of the House of David.
Sheridan's Plays.
Uncle Tom's Cabin.
Deerslayer.
Eugene Aram.
Jack Hinton, the Guardsman.
Rome and the Early Christians.
The Trials of Margaret Lyndsay.
Edgar Allan Poe. Prose and Poetry, Selections from.
Old Mortality.
The Hour and the Man.
Washington Irving's Sketch-Book.
Last Days of Palmyra.
Tales of the Borders.
Pride and Prejudice.
Last of the Mohicans.
Heart of Midlothian.
Last Days of Pompeii.
Yellowplush Papers.
Handy Andy.
Selected Plays.
American Humour.
Sketches by Boz.
Macaulay's Lays and Selected Essays.
Harry Lorrequer.
Old Curiosity Shop.
Rienzi.
The Talisman.
Pickwick. Two Vols.
Scarlet Letter.
Martin Chuzzlewit. Two Vols.

Stanley in East Africa, Scouting for. Being a Record of the Adventures of THOMAS STEVENS in search of H. M. STANLEY. With 14 Illustrations. Cloth, 7s. 6d.
Star-Land. By Sir ROBERT STAWELL BALL, LL.D., &c. Illustrated. 6s.
Storehouse of General Information, Cassell's. Fully Illustrated with High-Class Wood Engravings, and with Maps and Coloured Plates. In Vols. 5s. each.
Story of Francis Cludde, The. A Novel. By STANLEY J. WEYMAN. 7s. 6d. net.
Strange Doings in Strange Places. Complete Sensational Stories by Popular Authors. 5s.
Teaching in Three Continents. Personal Notes on the Educational Systems of the World. By W. C. GRASBY. 6s.
Thackeray, Character Sketches from. Six New and Original Drawings by FREDERICK BARNARD, reproduced in Photogravure. 21s.
The Short Story Library.
  Noughts and Crosses. By Q. 5s.
  Otto the Knight, &c. By OCTAVE THANET. 5s.
  Fourteen to One, &c. By ELIZABETH STUART PHELPS. 6s.
  Eleven Possible Cases. By various Authors. 5s.
  A Singer's Wife. By Miss FANNY MURFREE. 5s.
  The Poet's Audience, and Delilah. By CLARA SAVILE CLARKE. 5s.

Selections from Cassell & Company's Publications.

Tot Book for all Public Examinations. By W. S. THOMSON, M.A. 1s.
Treasure Island. By R. L. STEVENSON. Illustrated. 3s. 6d.
Treatment, The Year-Book of. A Critical Review for Practitioners of Medicine and Surgery. Greatly Enlarged. 500 pages. 7s. 6d.
Tree Painting in Water Colours. By W. H. J. BOOT. With Eighteen Coloured Plates, and valuable instructions by the Artist. 5s.
Trees, Familiar. By Prof. G. S. BOULGER, F.L.S., F.G.S. Two Series. With Forty full-page Coloured Plates by W. H. J. BOOT. 12s. 6d. each.
"Unicode": The Universal Telegraphic Phrase Book. Pocket and Desk Editions. 2s. 6d. each.
United States, Cassell's History of the. By the late EDMUND OLLIER. With 600 Illustrations. Three Vols. 9s. each.
Universal History, Cassell's Illustrated. With nearly ONE THOUSAND ILLUSTRATIONS. Vol. I. Early and Greek History.—Vol. II. The Roman Period.—Vol. III. The Middle Ages.—Vol. IV. Modern History. 9s. each.
Vaccination Vindicated. By JOHN C. MCVAIL, M.D., D.P.H. Camb. 5s.
Verdict, The. A Tract on the Political Significance of the Report of the Parnell Commission. By A. V. DICEY, Q.C. 2s. 6d.
Verses Grave and Gay. By Miss E. T. FOWLER. 3s. 6d.
Vicar of Wakefield and other Works, by OLIVER GOLDSMITH. Illustrated. 3s. 6d.; cloth, gilt edges, 5s.
Vision of Saints, A. By LEWIS MORRIS. *Edition de luxe.* With 20 Full-Page Illustrations. 21s.
Water-Colour Painting, A Course of. With Twenty-four Coloured Plates by R. P. LEITCH, and full Instructions to the Pupil. 5s.
Waterloo Letters. Edited by MAJOR-GENERAL H. T. SIBORNE, Late Colonel R.E. With Numerous Plans of the Battlefield. 21s.
Web of Gold, A. By KATHARINE PEARSON WOODS. 6s.
What Girls Can Do. By PHYLLIS BROWNE. 2s. 6d.
Wild Birds, Familiar. By W. SWAYSLAND. Four Series. With 40 Coloured Plates in each. 12s. 6d. each.
Wild Flowers, Familiar. By F. E. HULME, F.L.S., F.S.A. Five Series. With 40 Coloured Plates in each. 12s. 6d. each.
Wood, The Life of the Rev. J. G. By his Son, the Rev. THEODORE WOOD. With Portrait. Extra crown 8vo, cloth. *Cheap Edition.* 5s.
Work. An Illustrated Magazine of Practice and Theory for all Workmen, Professional and Amateur. Yearly Volume, cloth, 7s. 6d.
World of Wit and Humour, The. With 400 Illustrations. Cloth, 7s. 6d.
World of Wonders, The. With 400 Illustrations. Two Vols. 7s. 6d. each.
World's Lumber Room, The. By SELINA GAYE. Illustrated. 2s. 6d.
Yule Tide. CASSELL'S CHRISTMAS ANNUAL. 1s.

ILLUSTRATED MAGAZINES.

The Quiver, for Sunday and General Reading. Monthly, 6d.
Cassell's Family Magazine. Monthly, 7d.
"Little Folks" Magazine. Monthly, 6d.
The Magazine of Art. Monthly, 1s.
Cassell's Saturday Journal. Weekly, 1d.; Monthly, 6d.
Work. An Illustrated Magazine of Practice and Theory for all Workmen, Professional and Amateur. Weekly, 1d.; Monthly, 6d.

*** *Full particulars of* CASSELL & COMPANY'S **Monthly Serial Publications** *will be found in* CASSELL & COMPANY'S COMPLETE CATALOGUE.

Catalogues of CASSELL & COMPANY'S PUBLICATIONS, which may be had at all Booksellers', or will be sent post free on application to the Publishers:—

CASSELL'S COMPLETE CATALOGUE, containing particulars of upwards of One Thousand Volumes.
CASSELL'S CLASSIFIED CATALOGUE, in which their Works are arranged according to price, from *Threepence to Fifty Guineas.*
CASSELL'S EDUCATIONAL CATALOGUE, containing particulars of CASSELL & COMPANY'S Educational Works and Students' Manuals.

CASSELL & COMPANY, LIMITED, *Ludgate Hill, London.*

Bibles and Religious Works.

Bible, Cassell's Illustrated Family. With 900 Illustrations. Leather, gilt edges, £2 10s.; full morocco, £3 10s.

Bible Dictionary, Cassell's. With nearly 600 Illustrations. 7s. 6d.; roxburgh, 10s. 6d.

Bible Educator, The. Edited by E. H. PLUMPTRE, D.D. With Illustrations, Maps, &c. Four Vols., cloth, 6s. each.

Bible Student in the British Museum, The. By the Rev. J. G. KITCHIN, M.A. 1s.

Biblewomen and Nurses. Yearly Volume, 3s.

Bunyan's Pilgrim's Progress, and the Holy War, Cassell's Illustrated Edition of. With 200 Original Illustrations. Demy 4to, cloth, 16s.

Bunyan's Pilgrim's Progress (Cassell's Illustrated). 4to. 7s. 6d.

Bunyan's Pilgrim's Progress. With Illustrations. *Cheap Edition*, 2s. 6d.

Child's Bible, The. With 200 Illustrations. Demy 4to, 830 pp. 150th Thousand. *Cheap Edition*, 7s. 6d. *Superior Edition*, with 6 Coloured Plates, gilt edges, 10s. 6d.

Child's Life of Christ, The. Complete in One Handsome Volume, with about 200 Original Illustrations. *Cheap Edition*, cloth, 7s. 6d.; or with 6 Coloured Plates, cloth, gilt edges, 10s. 6d. Demy 4to, gilt edges, 21s.

"Come, ye Children." By the Rev. BENJAMIN WAUGH. Illustrated. 5s.

Commentary, The New Testament, for English Readers. Edited by the Rt. Rev. C. J. ELLICOTT, D.D., Lord Bishop of Gloucester and Bristol. In Three Volumes. 21s. each.
    Vol. I.—The Four Gospels.
    Vol. II.—The Acts, Romans, Corinthians, Galatians.
    Vol. III.—The remaining Books of the New Testament.

Commentary, The Old Testament, for English Readers. Edited by the Rt. Rev. C. J. ELLICOTT, D.D., Lord Bishop of Gloucester and Bristol. Complete in 5 Vols. 21s. each.
    Vol. I.—Genesis to Numbers. | Vol. III.—Kings I. to Esther.
    Vol. II.—Deuteronomy to Samuel II. | Vol. IV.—Job to Isaiah.
    Vol. V.—Jeremiah to Malachi.

Commentary, The New Testament. Edited by Bishop ELLICOTT. Handy Volume Edition. Suitable for School and general use.

St. Matthew. 3s. 6d.	Romans. 2s. 6d.	Titus, Philemon, Hebrews, and James. 3s.
St. Mark. 3s.	Corinthians I. and II. 3s.	Peter, Jude, and John. 3s.
St. Luke. 3s. 6d.	Galatians, Ephesians, and Philippians. 3s.	The Revelation. 3s.
St. John. 3s. 6d.	Colossians, Thessalonians, and Timothy. 3s.	An Introduction to the New Testament. 2s. 6d.
The Acts of the Apostles. 3s. 6d.		

Commentary, The Old Testament. Edited by Bishop ELLICOTT. Handy Volume Edition. Suitable for School and general use.

Genesis. 3s. 6d.	Leviticus. 3s.	Deuteronomy. 2s. 6d.
Exodus. 3s.	Numbers. 2s. 6d.	

Dictionary of Religion, The. An Encyclopædia of Christian and other Religious Doctrines, Denominations, Sects, Heresies, Ecclesiastical Terms, History, Biography, &c. &c. By the Rev. WILLIAM BENHAM, B.D. *Cheap Edition*. 10s. 6d.

Doré Bible. With 230 Illustrations by GUSTAVE DORÉ. *Original Edition.* Two Vols., best morocco, gilt edges, £15.

Early Days of Christianity, The. By the Ven. Archdeacon FARRAR, D.D., F.R.S.
    LIBRARY EDITION. Two Vols., 24s.; morocco, £2 2s.
    POPULAR EDITION. Complete in One Volume, cloth, 6s.; cloth, gilt edges, 7s. 6d.; Persian morocco, 10s. 6d.; tree-calf, 15s.

Family Prayer-Book, The. Edited by the Rev. Canon GARBETT, M.A., and the Rev. S. MARTIN. Extra crown 4to, cloth, 5s.; morocco, 18s.

Gleanings after Harvest. Studies and Sketches. By the Rev. JOHN R. VERNON, M.A. Illustrated. 6s.

Gospel of Grace, The. By a LINDESIE. Cloth, 2s. 6d.

"Graven in the Rock." By the Rev. Dr. SAMUEL KINNS, F.R.A.S., &c. &c. Illustrated. 12s. 6d.

Selections from Cassell & Company's Publications.

"Heart Chords." A Series of Works by Eminent Divines. Bound in cloth, red edges, 1s. each.

My Father. By the Right Rev. Ashton Oxenden, late Bishop of Montreal.
My Bible. By the Rt. Rev. W. Boyd Carpenter, Bishop of Ripon.
My Work for God. By the Right Rev. Bishop Cotterill.
My Object in Life. By the Ven. Archdeacon Farrar, D.D.
My Aspirations. By the Rev. G. Matheson, D.D.
My Emotional Life. By the Rev. Preb. Chadwick, D.D.
My Body. By the Rev. Prof. W. G. Blaikie, D.D.
My Soul. By the Rev. P. B. Power, M.A.
My Growth in Divine Life. By the Rev. Prebendary Reynolds, M.A.
My Hereafter. By the Very Rev. Dean Bickersteth.
My Walk with God. By the Very Rev. Dean Montgomery.
My Aids to the Divine Life. By the Very Rev. Dean Boyle.
My Sources of Strength. By the Rev. E. E. Jenkins, M.A., Secretary of the Wesleyan Missionary Society.

Helps to Belief. A Series of Helpful Manuals on the Religious Difficulties of the Day. Edited by the Rev. TEIGNMOUTH SHORE, M.A., Canon of Worcester, and Chaplain-in-Ordinary to the Queen. Cloth, 1s. each.

CREATION. By the Lord Bishop of Carlisle.
MIRACLES. By the Rev. Brownlow Maitland, M.A.
PRAYER. By the Rev. T. Teignmouth Shore, M.A.
THE MORALITY OF THE OLD TESTAMENT. By the Rev. Newman Smyth, D.D.
THE DIVINITY OF OUR LORD. By the Lord Bishop of Derry.
THE ATONEMENT. By William Connor Magee, D.D., Late Archbishop of York.

Hid Treasure. By RICHARD HARRIS HILL. 1s.

Holy Land and the Bible, The. A Book of Scripture Illustrations gathered in Palestine. By the Rev. CUNNINGHAM GEIKIE, D.D. With Map. Two Vols. 24s. *Illustrated Edition.* One Vol. 21s.

Life of Christ, The. By the Ven. Archdeacon FARRAR, D.D., F.R.S., Chaplain-in-Ordinary to the Queen.
ILLUSTRATED EDITION, with about 300 Original Illustrations. Extra crown 4to, morocco antique, 42s. *Cheap Illustrated Edition.* Large 4to, cloth, 7s. 6d. Cloth, full gilt, gilt edges, 10s. 6d.
LIBRARY EDITION. Two Vols. Cloth, 24s.; morocco, 42s.
POPULAR EDITION, in One Vol. 8vo, cloth, 6s.; cloth, gilt edges, 7s. 6d.; Persian morocco, gilt edges, 10s. 6d.; tree-calf, 15s.

Marriage Ring, The. By WILLIAM LANDELS, D.D. Bound in white leatherette. *New and Cheaper Edition*, 3s. 6d.

Moses and Geology; or, the Harmony of the Bible with Science. By the Rev. SAMUEL KINNS, Ph.D., F.R.A.S. Illustrated. *Cheap Edition*, 6s.

My Comfort in Sorrow. By HUGH MACMILLAN, D.D., LL.D., &c., Author of "Bible Teachings in Nature," &c. Cloth, 1s.

Protestantism, The History of. By the Rev. J. A. WYLIE, LL.D. Containing upwards of 600 Original Illustrations. Three Vols., 27s.; *Library Edition*, 30s.

"Quiver" Yearly Volume, The. With about 600 Original Illustrations and Coloured Frontispiece. 7s. 6d. Also Monthly, 6d.

St. George for England; and other Sermons preached to Children. *Fifth Edition.* By the Rev. T. TEIGNMOUTH SHORE, M.A., Canon of Worcester. 5s.

St. Paul, The Life and Work of. By the Ven. Archdeacon FARRAR, D.D., F.R.S., Chaplain-in-Ordinary to the Queen.
LIBRARY EDITION. Two Vols., cloth, 24s.; calf, 42s.
ILLUSTRATED EDITION, complete in One Volume, with about 300 Illustrations, £1 1s.; morocco, £2 2s.
POPULAR EDITION. One Volume, 8vo, cloth, 6s.; cloth, gilt edges, 7s. 6d.; Persian morocco, 10s. 6d.; tree-calf, 15s.

Shall We Know One Another in Heaven? By the Rt. Rev. J. C. RYLE, D.D., Bishop of Liverpool. *New and Enlarged Edition.* Paper Covers, 6d.

Shortened Church Services and Hymns, suitable for use at Children's Services. Compiled by the Rev. T. TEIGNMOUTH SHORE, M.A., Canon of Worcester. *Enlarged Edition.* 1s.

Signa Christi: Evidences of Christianity set forth in the Person and Work of Christ. By the Rev. JAMES AITCHISON. 5s.

"Sunday:" Its Origin, History, and Present Obligation. By the Ven. Archdeacon HESSEY, D.C.L. *Fifth Edition*, 7s. 6d.

Twilight of Life, The: Words of Counsel and Comfort for the Aged. By JOHN ELLERTON, M.A. 1s. 6d.

Selections from Cassell & Company's Publications.

Educational Works and Students' Manuals.

Agriculture Series, Cassell's. Edited by JOHN WRIGHTSON, Prof. of Agriculture.
Soils and Manures. By J. M. H. Munro, D.Sc. (London), F.I.C., F.C.S. 2s. 6d.
Crops. By Professor Wrightson. 2s. 6d.
Alphabet, Cassell's Pictorial. Size, 35 inches by 42½ inches. Mounted on Linen, with rollers. 3s. 6d.
Arithmetic:—Howard's Anglo-American Art of Reckoning. The Standard Teacher and Referee of Shorthand Business Arithmetic. By C. F. HOWARD. Paper, 1s.; cloth, 2s. *New Enlarged Edition*, 5s.
Arithmetics, The Modern School. By GEORGE RICKS, B.Sc. Lond. With Test Cards. (*List on application*.)
Atlas, Cassell's Popular. Containing 24 Coloured Maps, 3s. 6d.
Book-Keeping. By THEODORE JONES. FOR SCHOOLS, 2s.; or cloth, 3s. FOR THE MILLION, 2s.; or cloth, 3s. Books for Jones's System, Ruled Sets of, 2s.
Chemistry, The Public School. By J. H. ANDERSON, M.A. 2s. 6d.
Classical Texts for Schools, Cassell's. (*A list sent post free on application*.)
Cookery for Schools. By LIZZIE HERITAGE. 6d.
Copy-Books, Cassell's Graduated. Complete in 18 Books. 2d. each.
Copy-Books, The Modern School. Complete in 12 Books. 2d. each.
Drawing Copies, Cassell's "New Standard." Complete in 14 Books. 2d., 3d., and 4d. each.
Drawing Copies, Cassell's Modern School Freehand. First Grade, 1s. Second Grade, 2s.
Electricity, Practical. By Prof. W. E. AYRTON. 7s. 6d.
Energy and Motion: A Text-Book of Elementary Mechanics. By WILLIAM PAICE, M.A. Illustrated. 1s. 6d.
English Literature, A First Sketch of, from the Earliest Period to the Present Time. By Prof. HENRY MORLEY. 7s. 6d.
Euclid, Cassell's. Edited by Prof. WALLACE, M.A. 1s.
Euclid, The First Four Books of. *New Edition.* In paper, 6d.; cloth, 9d.
French, Cassell's Lessons in. *New and Revised Edition.* Parts I. and II., each 2s. 6d.; complete, 4s. 6d. Key, 1s. 6d.
French-English and English-French Dictionary. *Entirely New and Enlarged Edition.* 1,150 pages, 8vo, cloth, 3s. 6d.
French Reader, Cassell's Public School. By GUILLAUME S. CONRAD. 2s. 6d.
Galbraith and Haughton's Scientific Manuals.
Plane Trigonometry. 2s. 6d. Euclid. Books I., II., III. 2s. 6d. Books IV., V., VI. 2s. 6d. Mathematical Tables. 3s. 6d. Mechanics. 3s. 6d. Natural Philosophy. 3s. 6d. Optics. 2s. 6d. Hydrostatics. 3s. 6d. Astronomy. 5s. Steam Engine. 3s. 6d. Algebra. Part I., cloth, 2s. 6d. Complete, 7s. 6d. Tides and Tidal Currents, with Tidal Cards, 3s.
Gaudeamus. Songs for Colleges and Schools. Edited by JOHN FARMER. 5s. Words only, paper, 6d.; cloth, 9d.
Geometry, First Elements of Experimental. By PAUL BERT. Illustrated. 1s. 6d.
Geometry, Practical Solid. By Major ROSS, R.E. 2s.
German Dictionary, Cassell's New. German-English, English-German. *Cheap Edition*, cloth, 3s. 6d.
German of To-Day. By Dr. HEINEMANN. 1s. 6d.
German Reading, First Lessons in. By A. JÄGST. Illustrated. 1s.
Hand-and Eye Training. By G. RICKS, B.Sc. Two Vols., with 16 Coloured Plates in each Vol. Crown 4to, 6s. each.
"Hand-and-Eye Training" Cards for Class Work. Five sets in case. 1s. each.
Handbook of New Code of Regulations. By JOHN F. MOSS. *New and Revised Edition.* 1s.; cloth, 2s.
Historical Cartoons, Cassell's Coloured. Size 45 in. × 35 in. 2s. each. Mounted on canvas and varnished, with rollers, 5s. each. (Descriptive pamphlet, 16 pp., 1d.)
Historical Course for Schools, Cassell's. Illustrated throughout. I.—Stories from English History, 1s. II.—The Simple Outline of English History, 1s. 3d. III.—The Class History of England, 2s. 6d.
Latin-English Dictionary, Cassell's. Thoroughly revised and corrected, and in part re-written by J. R. V. MARCHANT, M.A. 3s. 6d.
Latin Primer, The New. By Prof. J. P. POSTGATE. 2s. 6d.
Latin Primer, The First. By Prof. POSTGATE. 1s.
Latin Prose for Lower Forms. By M. A. BAYFIELD, M.A. 2s. 6d.
Laundry Work (How to Teach It). By Mrs. E. LORD. 6d.

Selections from Cassell & Company's Publications.

Laws of Every-Day Life. For the Use of Schools. By H. O. ARNOLD-FORSTER. 1s. 6d.
Little Folks' History of England. By ISA CRAIG-KNOX. Illustrated. 1s. 6d.
Making of the Home, The. By Mrs. SAMUEL A. BARNETT. 1s. 6d.
Map-Building Series, Cassell's. Outline Maps prepared by H. O. ARNOLD-FORSTER. Per set of 12, 1s.
Marlborough Books:—Arithmetic Examples. 3s. Arithmetic Rules. 1s. 6d. French Exercises. 3s. 6d. French Grammar. 2s. 6d. German Grammar. 3s. 6d.
Mechanics For Young Beginners, A First Book of. By the Rev. J. G. EASTON, M.A. 4s. 6d.
Mechanics and Machine Design, Numerical Examples in Practical. By R. G. BLAINE, M.E. With Diagrams. Cloth, 2s. 6d.
"Model Joint" Wall Sheets, for Instruction in Manual Training. By S. BARTER. Eight Sheets, 2s. 6d. each.
Natural History Coloured Wall Sheets, Cassell's New. Consisting of 18 subjects. Size, 39 by 31 in. Mounted on rollers and varnished. 3s. each.
Object Lessons from Nature. By Prof. L. C. MIALL, F.L.S., F.G.S. Fully Illustrated. 2s. 6d.
Physiology for Schools. By ALFRED T. SCHOFIELD, M.D., M.R.C.S., &c. With Wood Engravings and Coloured Plates. 1s. 9d. Three Parts, paper covers, 5d. each; or cloth limp, 6d. each.
Poetry Readers, Cassell's New. Illustrated. 12 Books. 1d. each. Cloth, 1s. 6d.
Popular Educator, Cassell's New. With Revised Text, New Maps, New Coloured Plates, New Type, &c. To be completed in Eight Vols. 5s. each.
Reader, The Citizen. By H. O. ARNOLD-FORSTER. 1s. 6d.
Reader, The Empire. By G. R. PARKIN. 1s. 6d.
Reader, The Temperance. By Rev. J. DENNIS HIRD. Crown 8vo, 1s. 6d.
Readers, Cassell's "Higher Class." (*List on application.*)
Readers, Cassell's Historical. Illustrated. (*List on application.*)
Readers, Cassell's Readable. Illustrated. (*List on application.*)
Readers for Infant Schools, Coloured. Three Books. 4d. each.
Readers, The Modern Geographical. Illustrated throughout. (*List on application.*)
Readers, The Modern School. Illustrated. (*List on application.*)
Reading and Spelling Book, Cassell's Illustrated. 1s.
Round World, The. By H. O. ARNOLD-FORSTER. 3s. 6d.
School Bank Manual, A. By AGNES LAMBERT. 6d.
School Certificates, Cassell's. Three Colours, $6\frac{1}{4} \times 4\frac{3}{4}$ in., 1d.; Five Colours, $11\frac{1}{4} \times 9\frac{1}{2}$ in., 3d.; Seven Colours and Gold, $9\frac{1}{2} \times 6\frac{7}{8}$ in., 3d.
Science Applied to Work. By J. A. BOWER. Illustrated. 1s.
Science of Every-Day Life. By J. A. BOWER. Illustrated. 1s.
Sculpture, A Primer of. By E. ROSCOE MULLINS. Illustrated. 2s. 6d.
Shade from Models, Common Objects, and Casts of Ornament, How to. By W. E. SPARKES. With 25 Plates by the Author. 3s.
Shakspere Reading Book, The. By H. COURTHOPE BOWEN, M.A. Illustrated. 3s. 6d. Also issued in Three Books, 1s. each.
Shakspere's Plays for School Use. Illustrated. 5 Books. 6d. each.
Spelling, A Complete Manual of. By J. D. MORELL, LL.D. 1s.
Technical Educator, Cassell's. Illustrated throughout. *New and Revised Edition.* Four Vols. 5s. each.
Technical Manuals, Cassell's. Illustrated throughout. 16 Vols., from 2s. to 4s. 6d. (*List free on application.*)
Technology, Manuals of. Edited by Prof. AYRTON, F.R.S., and RICHARD WORMELL, D.Sc., M.A. Illustrated throughout.

The Dyeing of Textile Fabrics. By Prof. Hummel. 5s.
Watch and Clock Making. By D. Glasgow, Vice-President of the British Horological Institute. 4s. 6d.
Steel and Iron. By Prof. W. H. Greenwood, F.C.S., M.I.C.E., &c. 5s.
Design in Textile Fabrics. By T. R. Ashenhurst. 4s. 6d.
Spinning Woollen and Worsted. By W. S. McLaren, M.P. 4s. 6d.
Practical Mechanics. By Prof. Perry, M.E. 3s. 6d.
Cutting Tools Worked by Hand and Machine. By Prof. Smith. 3s. 6d.

Test Cards, Cassell's Combination. In sets, 1s. each.
Test Cards, Cassell's Modern School. In sets, 1s. each.

Selections from Cassell & Company's Publications.

Books for Young People.

"**Little Folks**" **Half-Yearly Volume.** Containing 432 pages of Letterpress, with Pictures on nearly every page, together with Two Full-page Plates printed in Colours and Four Tinted Plates. Coloured boards, 3s. 6d.; or cloth gilt, gilt edges, 5s.

Bo-Peep. A Book for the Little Ones. With Original Stories and Verses. Illustrated with beautiful Pictures on nearly every page, and Coloured Frontispiece. Yearly Volume. Elegant picture boards, 2s. 6d.; cloth, 3s. 6d.

Story Poems for Young and Old. By Miss E. DAVENPORT ADAMS. 6s.

Pleasant Work for Busy Fingers. By MAGGIE BROWNE. Illustrated. 5s.

The Marvellous Budget: being 65,536 Stories of Jack and Jill. By the Rev. F. BENNETT. Illustrated. Cloth gilt, 2s. 6d.

Magic at Home. By Prof. HOFFMAN. Fully Illustrated. A Series of easy and startling Conjuring Tricks for Beginners. Cloth gilt, 5s.

Schoolroom and Home Theatricals. By ARTHUR WAUGH. With Illustrations by H. A. J. MILES. Cloth, 2s. 6d.

Little Mother Bunch. By Mrs. MOLESWORTH. Illustrated. Cloth, 3s. 6d.

Heroes of Every-Day Life. By LAURA LANE. With about 20 Full-page Illustrations. 256 pages, crown 8vo, cloth, 2s. 6d.

Ships, Sailors, and the Sea. By R. J. CORNEWALL-JONES. Illustrated throughout, and containing a Coloured Plate of Naval Flags. *Cheap Edition*, 2s. 6d.

Famous Sailors of Former Times, History of the Sea Fathers. By CLEMENTS MARKHAM. Illustrated. 2s. 6d.

The Tales of the Sixty Mandarins. By P. V. RAMASWAMI RAJU. 5s.

Gift Books for Young People. By Popular Authors. With Four Original Illustrations in each. Cloth gilt, 1s. 6d. each.

The Boy Hunters of Kentucky. By Edward S. Ellis.
Red Feather: a Tale of the American Frontier. By Edward S. Ellis.
Fritters; or, "It's a Long Lane that has no Turning."
Trixy; or, "Those who Live in Glass Houses shouldn't throw Stones."
The Two Hardcastles.
Seeking a City.
Rhoda's Reward.
Jack Marston's Anchor.
Frank's Life-Battle.
Major Monk's Motto; or, "Look Before you Leap."
Tim Thomson's Trial; or, "All is not Gold that Glitters."
Ursula's Stumbling-Block.
Ruth's Life-Work; or, "No Pains, no Gains."
Rags and Rainbows.
Uncle William's Charge.
Pretty Pink's Purpose.

"**Golden Mottoes**" **Series, The.** Each Book containing 208 pages, with Four full-page Original Illustrations. Crown 8vo, cloth gilt, 2s. each.

"Nil Desperandum." By the Rev. F. Langbridge, M.A.
"Bear and Forbear." By Sarah Pitt.
"Foremost if I Can." By Helen Atteridge.
"Honour is my Guide." By Jeanie Hering (Mrs. Adams-Acton).
"Aim at a Sure End." By Emily Searchfield.
"He Conquers who Endures." By the Author of "May Cunningham's Trial," &c.

"**Cross and Crown**" **Series, The.** With Four Illustrations in each Book. Crown 8vo, 256 pages, 2s. 6d. each.

Heroes of the Indian Empire; or, Stories of Valour and Victory. By Ernest Foster.
Through Trial to Triumph; or, "The Royal Way." By Madeline Bonavia Hunt.
In Letters of Flame; A Story of the Waldenses. By C. L. Matéaux.
Strong to Suffer; A Story of the Jews. By E. Wynne.
By Fire and Sword; a Story of the Huguenots. By Thomas Archer.
Adam Hepburn's Vow; A Tale of Kirk and Covenant. By Annie S. Swan.
No. XIII.; or, the Story of the Lost Vestal. A Tale of Early Christian Days. By Emma Marshall.
Freedom's Sword; A Story of the Days of Wallace and Bruce. By Annie S. Swan.

Five Shilling Books for Young People. With Original Illustrations. Cloth gilt, 5s. each.

Under Bayard's Banner. By Henry Frith.
The Champion of Odin; or, Viking Life in the Days of Old. By J. Fred. Hodgetts.
Bound by a Spell; or, the Hunted Witch of the Forest. By the Hon. Mrs. Greene.
The Romance of Invention. By Jas. Burnley.

Albums for Children. Price 3s. 6d. each.

The Chit-Chat Album. Illustrated.
The Album for Home, School, and Play. Set in bold type, and illustrated throughout.
My Own Album of Animals. Illustrated.
Picture Album of All Sorts. Illustrated.

"**Wanted—a King**" **Series.** Illustrated. 3s. 6d. each.

Robin's Ride. By Miss E. Davenport Adams.
Great-Grandmamma and Else. By Georgina M. Synge.
Wanted—a King; or, How Merle set the Nursery Rhymes to Rights. By Maggie Browne.

Selections from Cassell & Company's Publications.

Crown 8vo Library. *Cheap Editions.* 2s. 6d. each.

Rambles Round London. By C. L. Matéaux. Illustrated.
Around and About Old England. By C. L. Matéaux. Illustrated.
Paws and Claws. By one of the Authors of "Poems Written for a Child." Illustrated.
Decisive Events in History. By Thomas Archer. With Original Illustrations.
The True Robinson Crusoes. Cloth gilt.
Peeps Abroad for Folks at Home. Illustrated throughout.
Wild Adventures in Wild Places. By Dr. Gordon Stables, R.N. Illustrated.
Modern Explorers. By Thomas Frost. Illustrated. *New and cheaper Edition.*
Early Explorers. By Thomas Frost.
Home Chat with our Young Folks. Illustrated throughout.
Jungle, Peak, and Plain. Illustrated throughout.
The England of Shakespeare. By E. Goadby. With Full-page Illustrations.

Three and Sixpenny Books for Young People. With Original Illustrations. Cloth gilt, 3s. 6d. each.

The King's Command. A Story for Girls. By Maggie Symington.
A Sweet Girl Graduate. By L. T. Meade.
The White House at Inch Gow. By Mrs. Pitt.
Lost in Samoa. A Tale of Adventure in the Navigator Islands. By E. S, Ellis.
Tad; or, "Getting Even" with Him. By E. S. Ellis.
Polly. By L. T. Meade.
The Palace Beautiful. By L. T. Meade.
"Follow my Leader."
For Fortune and Glory.
The Cost of a Mistake. By Sarah Pitt.
On Board the "Esmeralda."
Lost among White Africans.
In Quest of Gold.
A World of Girls. By L. T. Meade.

Books by Edward S. Ellis. Illustrated. Cloth, 2s. 6d. each.

The Hunters of the Ozark.
The Camp in the Mountains.
Ned in the Woods. A Tale of Early Days in the West.
Down the Mississippi.
The Last War Trail.
Ned on the River. A Tale of Indian River Warfare.
Footprints in the Forest.
Up the Tapajos.
Ned in the Block House. A Story of Pioneer Life in Kentucky.
The Lost Trail.
Camp-Fire and Wigwam.
Lost in the Wilds.

Sixpenny Story Books. By well-known Writers. All Illustrated.

The Smuggler's Cave.
Little Lizzie.
The Boat Club.
Luke Barnicott.
Little Bird.
Little Pickles.
The Elchester College Boys.
My First Cruise.
The Little Peacemaker.
The Delft Jug.

Cassell's Picture Story Books. Each containing 60 pages. 6d. each.

Little Talks.
Bright Stars.
Nursery Joys.
Pet's Posy.
Tiny Tales.
Daisy's Story Book.
Dot's Story Book.
A Nest of Stories.
Good Night Stories.
Chats for Small Chatterers.
Auntie's Stories.
Birdie's Story Book.
Little Chimes.
A Sheaf of Tales.
Dewdrop Stories.

Illustrated Books for the Little Ones. Containing interesting Stories. All Illustrated. 1s. each; or cloth gilt, 1s. 6d.

Scrambles and Scrapes.
Tittle Tattle Tales.
Wandering Ways.
Dumb Friends.
Indoors and Out.
Some Farm Friends.
Those Golden Sands.
Little Mothers and their Children.
Our Pretty Pets.
Our Schoolday Hours.
Creatures Tame.
Creatures Wild.
Up and Down the Garden.
All Sorts of Adventures.
Our Sunday Stories.
Our Holiday Hours.

Shilling Story Books. All Illustrated, and containing Interesting Stories.

Seventeen Cats.
Bunty and the Boys.
The Heir of Elmdale.
The Mystery at Shoncliff School.
Claimed at Last, and Roy's Reward.
Thorns and Tangles.
The Cuckoo in the Robin's Nest.
John's Mistake.
Diamonds in the Sand.
Surly Bob.
The History of Five Little Pitchers.
The Giant's Cradle.
Shag and Doll.
Aunt Lucia's Locket.
The Magic Mirror.
The Cost of Revenge.
Clever Frank.
Among the Redskins.
The Ferryman of Brill.
Harry Maxwell.
A Banished Monarch

"Little Folks" Painting Books. With Text, and Outline Illustrations for Water-Colour Painting. 1s. each.

Fruits and Blossoms for "Little Folks" to Paint.
The "Little Folks" Proverb Painting Book. Cloth only, 2s.
The "Little Folks" Illuminating Book.

Eighteenpenny Story Books. All Illustrated throughout.

Wee Willie Winkie.
Ups and Downs of a Donkey's Life.
Three Wee Ulster Lassies.
Up the Ladder.
Dick's Hero; & other Stories.
The Chip Boy.
Raggles, Baggles, and the Emperor.
Roses from Thorns.
Faith's Father.
By Land and Sea.
The Young Berringtons.
Jeff and Leff.
Tom Morris's Error.
Worth more than Gold.
"Through Flood—Through Fire."
The Girl with the Golden Locks.
Stories of the Olden Time.

Selections from Cassell & Company's Publications.

The "World in Pictures" Series. Illustrated throughout. 2s. 6d. each.

- A Ramble Round France.
- All the Russias.
- Chats about Germany.
- The Land of the Pyramids (Egypt).
- Peeps into China.
- The Eastern Wonderland (Japan).
- Glimpses of South America.
- Round Africa.
- The Land of Temples (India).
- The Isles of the Pacific.

Cheap Editions of Popular Volumes for Young People. Illustrated. 2s. 6d. each.

- Esther West.
- Three Homes.
- For Queen and King.
- Working to Win.
- Perils Afloat and Brigands Ashore.

Two-Shilling Story Books. All Illustrated.

- Stories of the Tower.
- Mr. Burke's Nieces.
- May Cunningham's Trial.
- The Top of the Ladder: How to Reach it.
- Little Flotsam.
- Madge and her Friends.
- The Children of the Court.
- A Moonbeam Tangle.
- Maid Marjory.
- The Four Cats of the Tippertons.
- Marion's Two Homes.
- Little Folks' Sunday Book.
- School Girls.
- Two Fourpenny Bits.
- Poor Nelly.
- Tom Heriot.
- Aunt Tabitha's Waifs.
- In Mischief Again.
- Through Peril to Fortune.
- Peggy, and other Tales.

Half-Crown Story Books.

- Little Hinges.
- Margaret's Enemy.
- Pen's Perplexities.
- Notable Shipwrecks.
- Golden Days.
- Wonders of Common Things.
- At the South Pole.
- Truth will Out.
- Pictures of School Life and Boyhood.
- The Young Man in the Battle of Life. By the Rev. Dr. Landels.
- The True Glory of Woman. By the Rev. Dr. Landels.
- Soldier and Patriot (George Washington).

Three-and-Sixpenny Library. Illustrated. Cloth gilt, gilt edges.

- The Family Honour.
- The Half-Sisters.
- Peggy Oglivie's Inheritance.
- Krilof and his Fables.
- Fairy Tales. By Prof. Henry Morley.

Cassell's Pictorial Scrap Book. In Six Sectional Volumes. Paper boards, cloth back, 3s. 6d. per Vol.

- Our Scrap Book.
- The Seaside Scrap Book.
- The Little Folks' Scrap Book.
- The Magpie Scrap Book.
- The Lion Scrap Book.
- The Elephant Scrap Book.

Library of Wonders. Illustrated Gift-books for Boys. Paper, 1s.; cloth, 1s. 6d.

- Wonderful Adventures.
- Wonders of Animal Instinct.
- Wonderful Balloon Ascents.
- Wonders of Bodily Strength and Skill.
- Wonderful Escapes.

Books for the Little Ones. Fully Illustrated.

- Rhymes for the Young Folk. By William Allingham. Beautifully Illustrated. 3s. 6d.
- The Sunday Scrap Book. With One Thousand Pictures. Boards, 5s.; cloth, 7s. 6d.
- The History Scrap Book. With nearly 1,000 Engravings. 5s.; cloth, 7s. 6d.
- Cassell's Robinson Crusoe. With 100 Illustrations. Cloth, 3s. 6d.; gilt edges, 5s.
- The Old Fairy Tales. With Original Illustrations. Boards, 1s.; cloth, 1s. 6d.
- My Diary. With Twelve Coloured Plates and 366 Woodcuts. 1s.
- The Pilgrim's Progress. With Coloured Illustrations. 2s. 6d.
- Cassell's Swiss Family Robinson. Illustrated. Cloth, 3s. 6d.; gilt edges, 5s.

The World's Workers. A Series of New and Original Volumes by Popular Authors. With Portraits printed on a tint as Frontispiece. 1s. each.

- Dr. Arnold of Rugby. By Rose E. Selfe.
- The Earl of Shaftesbury.
- Sarah Robinson, Agnes Weston, and Mrs. Meredith.
- Thomas A. Edison and Samuel F. B. Morse.
- Mrs. Somerville and Mary Carpenter.
- General Gordon.
- Charles Dickens.
- Sir Titus Salt and George Moore.
- Florence Nightingale, Catherine Marsh, Frances Ridley Havergal, Mrs. Ranyard ("L. N. R.").
- Dr. Guthrie, Father Mathew, Elihu Burritt, Joseph Livesey.
- Sir Henry Havelock and Colin Campbell Lord Clyde.
- Abraham Lincoln.
- David Livingstone.
- George Muller and Andrew Reed.
- Richard Cobden.
- Benjamin Franklin.
- Handel.
- Turner the Artist.
- George and Robert Stephenson.

*** *The above Works (excluding Richard Cobden) can also be had Three in One Vol., cloth, gilt edges, 3s.*

CASSELL & COMPANY, Limited, Ludgate Hill, London;
Paris & Melbourne.

www.ingramcontent.com/pod-product-compliance
Lightning Source LLC
Chambersburg PA
CBHW030551300426
44111CB00009B/943